The Catholic Answer BOOK 4

The Catholic Answer BOOK 4

REVEREND
PETER M. J.
STRAVINSKAS

Our Sunday Visitor Publishing Division
Our Sunday Visitor, Inc.
Huntington, Indiana 46750

Our Sunday Visitor Publishing Division
Our Sunday Visitor, Inc.
200 Noll Plaza
Huntington, IN 46750

ISBN: 1-931709-81-5 (Inventory No. T46)
LCCN: 2003105355

Cover design by Monica Haneline
Interior design by Sherri L. Hoffman

PRINTED IN THE UNITED STATES OF AMERICA

Contents

Introduction to
The Catholic Answer Book IV

໙

It seems like only yesterday that we began publication of *The Catholic Answer* magazine; in reality, it was more than sixteen years ago. Catholic publishing was a shaky business in those days, giving us ample reason to fear that our new effort would go the way of hundreds of other periodicals in the postconciliar period. We had confidence, however, that this would not happen for two reasons: First, we intended to reflect faithfully the teachings of the Church; second, we believed that faithful Catholics would appreciate that approach and respond accordingly. Having gone from strength to strength, we find ourselves serving as a kind of periodical of record, having credibility with the average Catholic in the pew, as well as with Church authorities, both at home and in Rome.

Very soon into the life of *The Catholic Answer* magazine, readers began to ask for a compilation of the question-and-answer section, arranged in user-friendly form, so that they could have a file of reliable information on the whole range of Catholic truth: Scripture, doctrine, morality, liturgy, and Catholic practices. We obliged with *The Catholic Answer Book* in 1990. It was so popular that we have put out new volumes every three or four years, and we are happy to provide you with *The Catholic Answer Book IV* at this time.

I write this introduction as the Church honors the memory of St. Catherine of Siena, the great mystic, doctor of the Church, and reformer. Her capacity to unite faith, reason, spirituality, and courageous action have always inspired me; may they do the same for you — and for the whole Church as she moves forward toward her Lord in this new millennium.

Rev. Peter M. J. Stravinskas, Ph.D., S.T.D.
Editor

Catholic Practices

Papal claims

Q. Recently, a Baptist acquaintance and I were discussing human frailties and their impact on religious traditions and beliefs — how, because of man's imperfections, our beliefs and faith are oftentimes shaken by the improprieties committed by religious leaders. He pointed out that the papacy committed many improprieties, including the fact that there were three individuals serving as Pope at the same time. I was taken aback by this comment and decided to research the issue. I discovered that this indeed was the case between 1431 and 1455. I also noted other periods between 159 and 1455 where there appeared to be more than one Pope, due in every case to the inclusion of men labeled "anti-popes." Can you please explain the discrepancies, and define the term "anti-pope"?

A. As you suggest, since about the third century, the Church has been harassed by pretenders to the papal throne. The term "anti-pope," however, did not gain currency until the twelfth century. Approximately thirty-seven men have made illegitimate claims on the papal office; most of them were little more than cranks, but some did indeed garner significant support from civil authorities. With more stringent rules for the election of a Pope, the existence of anti-popes became a practical impossibility since the fifteenth century.

Absurd statement

Q. I recently heard the allegation that "the Pope has the largest collection of pornography in the world." How does one respond to this?

A. How absurd! I, too, have heard the statement made, and they are referring to the works of art in the Vatican Museum and the Sistine Chapel. If they don't know the difference between pornography and serious art, nothing you or I say will be of much help. Pray for their enlightenment.

Jewish Christians

Q. During Christ's time on earth, He performed many miracles for and with the Jewish people. Being filled with the Holy Spirit, St. Peter raised up his voice to the Jewish visitors from all parts of the world and converted some three thousand souls. It would seem to me that there should be many Jewish Christians today, if only from the trickle-down theory. I never hear anything about Jewish converts today. Why is this?

A. Mahatma Gandhi once said, "I love Christ, I do not love Christians." That may be applied to the present topic at various points in our history. Initially, Jewish conversions were quite normal; then tensions set in between the Church (especially Jewish converts) and Jewish religious authorities. When Christianity ceased to be persecuted by civil authorities and actually ended up becoming the religion of the Roman Empire, it was not uncommon for public officials to force Christianity down people's throats — not necessarily for religious purposes but for civic unity, resulting in resentment among the proselytized. And the situation deteriorated from that time on.

There are, however, a number of Jews who are Catholic — some of them most famous: St. Edith Stein, a martyr at the hands of the Nazis; Msgr. John Oesterreicher, the late founder of Seton Hall's Judaeo-Christian Institute; Cardinal Jean-Marie Lustiger, the present archbishop of Paris. There is even an association of Hebrew Catholics — that is, people of Jewish heritage who are (or have become part of) the Catholic Church.

Papal appointees

Q. How can the man-made rules of the Church ever change when our existing Pope (who is conservative) keeps nominating conservative cardinals and bishops to succeed him? This is not the answer of a free democracy.

A. First of all, the Church is not, never was and never will be a democracy. The Church is hierarchical in nature, which means governance by a holy order. It seems to me that many people want democracy in the Church only when they think democracy will push forward their vision of what the Church ought to be. Ironically, we discover that folks who wanted the laity consulted about Church affairs in the 1970s don't speak too much about that today, when they suspect the votes might not go so clearly in their direction.

At a very human level, does it not make sense for the Pope to appoint men who are like him? If the Holy Father is convinced that he is right, then shouldn't he make appointments that reflect that orientation? If he doesn't think he's right, but continues to act in that way, then we are all in trouble.

Dialogue notes

Q. The installation of the new Greek Orthodox metropolitan in New York — not to mention the documents of last year on the Eastern Church — has made me think about the status of the current dialogue with the Orthodox Church. Is there any good resource to examine the dialogue?

A. *The Quest for Unity: Orthodox and Catholics in Dialogue: Documents of the Joint International Commission and Official Dialogues in the United States, 1965-1995,* has been produced by the United States Catholic Conference and St. Vladimir's Seminary. This compendium presents the history and current state of the dialogue between the Catholic and Orthodox Churches. It includes two forewords, one by the former archbishop of Milwaukee, Rembert Weakland, O.S.B., and the other by the Greek Orthodox Bishop

Maximos, of Pittsburgh, the co-chairmen of the U.S. Orthodox-Catholic Theological Consultation. The documentation takes up two hundred sixty-two pages; the cost is $11.95.

Priests for Life

Q. Lately, I have been hearing about an organization called Priests for Life. Is this a reputable operation?

A. Yes, it most certainly is. Priests for Life is a national pro-life organization headed by Father Frank A. Pavone. Since 1991, Priests for Life has been an officially recognized private association in the Catholic Church, maintaining close contact with the bishops' pro-life office, as well as diocesan respect-life coordinators.

The purpose of Priests for Life is to unite and encourage all priests and deacons to give special emphasis to the life issues in their ministry. It also seeks to help them take a more vocal and active role in the pro-life movement, with predominant emphasis on the issues of abortion and euthanasia.

The question is often asked: "Isn't every priest 'for' life?" The answer is, "Yes." In fact, every person is called to stand up for life. But just as there is a Society of Jesus, even though every priest is "for" Jesus, so too is there a group — Priests for Life — to serve as a reminder that being "for" life is essential to the life of every priest.

And Priests for Life is not just for priests. It is for everyone — clergy and laity alike. Serving as a nationwide network for all pro-lifers, Priests for Life encourages cooperation among individuals and groups from all religious denominations on the life issues.

For more information, please contact: Priests for Life, P.O. Box 141172, Staten Island, NY 10314; phone: 914-937-8243; fax: 914-937-9207; e-mail: pfl@ix.netcom.com.

Topsy-turvy

Q. Our parish just celebrated an outdoor Mass for our sesquicentennial. The program for the Mass had a large upside-down cross on it. When I first saw it, it reminded me of something used in the occult — not holy or sacred. I am troubled by its use for such an occasion. Our parish priest told us that it symbolized the death of St. Peter, but he seems to lean toward a humanistic understanding of most things. Could you help me to understand the use of this symbol and explain where the notion came from?

A. Freud was right: Sometimes a cigar is just a cigar.

The upside-down cross was used for your parish Mass program because he is your parish patron — and Peter was crucified upside down.

Faithful adorers

Q. I know you have given some advice regarding solid communities of women Religious before. Unfortunately, I have never seen anything written about the community I am interested in. Do you have any information on the Sisters of the Precious Blood?

A. Founded in 1861 in Canada, the Sister Adorers of the Precious Blood are a cloistered, contemplative religious order. They have a few houses outside of Canada; in the United States they are in Manchester, N.H. They are completely faithful to the magisterium, to their religious identity and to prayer (both in adoration and reparation). For more information on the community, write to the Directress of Vocations, Monastery of the Precious Blood, 700 Bridge Street, Manchester, NH 03104.

Sisterhood

Q. Any more suggestions for good communities of women Religious?

A. Yes, I am happy to suggest two more contemplative communities.

The first are the Visitation nuns in Toledo, whom I have had the joy of assisting with conferences for two consecutive years.

They are faithful, joyful, and growing. They can be reached at: Monastery of the Visitation, 1745 Parkside Avenue, Toledo, OH 43607.

The second group just came to my attention recently. The Hermits of Jesus the Eternal Priest are a community of nuns devoted to prayer and penance for priests and for vocations to the priesthood, under the auspices of the Maronite rite. For further information, write to: Box 216, North Brookfield, MA 01535.

Pray from the heart

Q. What is the difference between a nine-day and a fifty-four-day Rosary Novena? Let's face it: It is easier to say the Rosary nine days in a row versus fifty-four straight days, so why wouldn't I pick the shorter one?

A. I'm not comfortable with playing a kind of numbers game. Jesus warned us in the Gospel that we do not win a hearing by the mere multiplication of words. There is a distinction between praying and saying prayers, and if our heart is not in the project, there is generally very little praying going on. Hence the entire exercise has been reduced to empty formalism, and even superstition in some instances. I don't want to come off as harsh or judgmental, but I just don't think we ask the right questions all too often. My simplest answer would be: Pray as long, as fervently and as devoutly as you can — whether that is nine hours, days, weeks, months or years — but be sure that the underlying attitude is proper, for that is what the Lord sees and responds to.

Seeks baptism

Q. I have been given confusing information by a priest regarding the baptism of my children. My husband is Baptist, but has agreed to raise our children Catholic. On the telephone I explained that my husband had been married before, but this was my first marriage. The priest said I could have the children baptized, but we should also see about the possibility of getting my husband's first marriage annulled. When we went to see him, his attitude changed, and he told us that the children cannot be baptized unless we are married in the Catholic Church. I hesitate to say that what changed his mind upon meeting us was the fact that we are an interracial couple, but it is the only logical explanation I can find. He has been backed up by some other priests in the area with whom we have spoken. Is it true that my children cannot be baptized in this present situation? Does the Church teach anything against interracial marriage? Can I still receive Communion? I'm trying to hang on, but need some straight answers.

A. Many complex matters surface here. Let's try to untangle as much as possible.

Working from the back up, it is important to say straightaway that the Church has no difficulties at all with interracial marriages — and never has in her history. Whether or not they are good for children, or even the spouses themselves (given the social and cultural climate), is a determination the couple themselves must make.

Did the priest change his mind once he discovered you were an interracial couple? I hope not, and there is no way of ever discovering that. If he was kind to you and pastorally helpful, I would tend to discount that explanation. One more palatable notion does suggest itself, and that is that in between his phone conversation with you and your arrival, he checked with some other priests for their input.

No priest can make a child's baptism contingent on the marriage of his parents for several reasons, not the least being that such a marriage bond's validity could be called into question, because the couple could subsequently say that they did not really want a sacramental union, but merely did it for the sake of the children's baptism. That having been said, a priest should certainly do everything in his power to convince a couple in an invalid marriage to get their situation rectified; beyond that, he has every right to expect the couple (or at least one parent) to be practicing the Catholic Faith in every way possible — for example, attending

Sunday Mass, even if unable to receive Holy Communion because of the irregular marital relationship.

So, at the moment, I would offer the following advice: Prevail upon your partner to submit his first union to an ecclesiastical tribunal for a possible decree of nullity; fulfill your Sunday Mass obligation; refrain from receiving Holy Communion since you are in an objectively adulterous union due to the presence of a previous marriage bond; establish and then maintain contact with your parish priest, so that he is aware of the steps you are taking; and then ask him to reconsider his decision about the postponement of your children's baptism. If you follow the plan I have outlined and still obtain a negative judgment, you should either seek out another priest or contact the diocesan chancery for a review of the situation.

Pastor's priorities

Q. We have a pastor who has been assigned here for three-and-a-half years. During that time, a large number of our parishioners have started attending other Catholic churches in the neighborhood because all he ever talks about is money, and every penny is used to support the school. I understand that the school runs in the red and needs parish support, but I don't think other parish needs should be put aside for lack of funds. For example, most parishioners are in favor of saving for an all-purpose building; the pastor is opposed. Instead, he wants to use the money to build onto the school (an extension to the library and offices). Those items could be included in a building from which the entire parish could benefit. While our pastor is a good financial administrator, he is not in any way compassionate or caring. He never visits the sick or families of the deceased. He won't even allow us to continue a tradition of mentioning during Mass the person for whom the Mass is being offered — even at the general intercessions. The only fundraisers he supports are for the school. Our charity fund is growing because he is very selfish when it comes to helping the poor and needy in the community. I work in close contact with him as a member of the parish council and a catechist, and would classify him as a cold and distant individual. Since I am active in the church, deserting the place like so many others does not seem an option. He has been approached, but takes offense at any criticism or suggestion. I have called the chancery and been told that he's here for at least three more years. Would you please offer some advice?

A. You're talking to the wrong man if you want me to speak against a priest who is pro-school. One of the biggest problems of parochial schools in the past thirty years has been a dearth of pastors who are even remotely sympathetic toward Catholic education. Frankly, I cannot think of any wiser investment for a parish than its school; short of the Mass itself, I would place no priority higher in spending than the school. Indeed, I would say that the sky should be the limit. In terms of his school commitment, I would simply say, "May his tribe increase!"

Regarding other matters you cite, allow me to react briefly. First, I have often heard that priests talk too much about money, but, in all honesty, I have never worked in parish where a single homily was ever preached on that topic. Announcement time is often used for it, but not the homily. Truth be told, Catholic giving patterns are embarrassingly niggardly, and I maintain that our clergy have not sufficiently challenged our people to generosity, let alone the concept of sacrificial giving.

Second, there is no need to mention anyone's name during the Mass, either at the beginning, the prayer of the faithful or the commemoration of the dead. The bulletin can provide that information rather adequately. However, there is no reason *not* to mention the names, either, which is to say it is often a matter of taste.

Third, I find it difficult to believe that he never visits the sick, etc. If that is the case, he needs correction from diocesan officials.

Fourth, his personality. Perhaps he is lacking in social skills or human warmth — or perhaps he has been so much under siege from negative parishioners that he has retreated into a cocoon. I'm not making excuses for poor clerical behavior; if it is truly as you describe, there's something wrong, but most stories do have two sides to them.

Good information

Q. So many groups seem to be competing for the attention of those who truly desire to know what the Church teaches, that I hope you can provide me with some information on the Catholic Information League. Their tracts are different, done in cartoon-style. Would you recommend them for use?

A. The material I have seen is thoroughly orthodox and attractively presented, as well as inexpensive and user-friendly. This seems to be one more sign of the coming of the renewal envisioned by the Second Vatican Council. The Catholic Information League can be reached at: Box 5162, Warren, MI 48090; phone: 810-545-0485.

To grow in holiness

Q. I don't understand why someone enters the religious life. Is it better or deeper than the life of a lay person? If there is a hunger or thirst that is special to Religious, how does one express this without sounding proud and, therefore, being offensive to lay people? How does one justify a completely contemplative life? Isn't this wasteful when there is such a need for teachers, nurses, etc.? It seems to me that the contemplative neglects the corporal works of mercy.

A. You raise several good and important questions.

Within the one Body of Christ, which is His holy Church, there exists a variety of gifts and offices. All can be means of sanctification for the individual (first of all) and for the rest of the world touched by that person's Christian commitment lived through that particular vocation. The goal of the entire Christian life is holiness, and for that to be achieved, the believer must ascertain God's holy Will for him or her. In other words, becoming a Religious when one has really been called by God to be a spouse and parent will not bring holiness or happiness. This, of course, underscores the central place of spiritual direction before and during the process of vocational discernment.

One does not choose the religious life because the lay state is bad or inferior. It is not a matter of choosing between a good and an evil, but between two goods — one of which is, objectively speaking, higher. Now, let's take note of some carefully chosen words here. The basic Christian vocation is the lay state; it is the Sacrament of Baptism that grants us access to the life of grace. By Christ's wise plan, ninety-nine percent of the people in the Church remain laity: to witness to Him in the secular city by their lives and professions; to raise up domestic churches through Christian family living; to perform the corporal and spiritual works of mercy. Within the unity of the Church, some people perceive a call from the Lord and His Church to live their baptismal commitment with greater intensity as a way of challenging the rest of us (clergy and laity alike) to live up to our unique vocations. By consecrating themselves through the vows of poverty, chastity, and obedience, Religious stand forth as dramatic examples of Gospel living in the world today.

Their voluntary living of evangelical poverty reminds us all that happiness is not found in material possessions; their free decision to forego the joys of Christian marriage points all of us to the need to have our love ultimately focused on Almighty God, and stresses the fact that all human love (even one so good and holy as that lived in the Sacrament of Matrimony) is a temporary state; their obedience highlights the necessity of having Christ as the first and last Word in our lives. For all these reasons, the Church regards religious life as a higher way of life, but, you will remember, I qualified it with the expression, "objectively speaking." In other words, Religious *ought* to be holier because of the public profession they have made, because of the responsibility they have freely undertaken for the sake of the Church, and because of the graces available to them to be faithful to their promises. If, however, a Religious fails to live up to his vocation, the objectively higher state of life stands as a condemnation of him, not as his glory.

No one should be offensive about a vocation for the simple reason that every vocation in the Church is a gift from God, and each vocation is sustained by God's grace — given according to each person's need. No competition should ever exist in the Church, smacking of drives for political power or personal aggrandizement; the only contest should be to grow in holiness and in fidelity to the Lord's Will.

As far as contemplative life goes, never forget the tremendous insight of Alfred, Lord Tennyson: "More things are wrought by prayer than this world dreams of." Also, remember Jesus' admonition that Martha's posture of waiting upon the Lord to hear His word was evidence of her having chosen "the good portion" (Lk 10:42). For my part, I must admit that I find myself constantly calling cloistered nuns to ask for their prayers for various needs of mine and my personal apostolates. Therefore, one can say that they are, in fact, intimately involved in the advancement of the works of mercy. I should also note that for more than a decade, I have been privileged to teach a monthly theology class to the Dominican nuns in Newark, N.J., and I can say with all candor that I gain far more out of those sessions than the sisters do; being with them is a joy and an inspiration.

Private revelations

Q. What are we to think of private revelations? Are we to infer that prophecy (private revelation) ended with the apostolic period? Don't we regard authentic prophecy to be a gift of the Holy Spirit? What about the fact that the prophecies given at Fátima have already largely come true? It's true that the great majority of purported private revelations are hoaxes or aberrations, but are we to throw the baby out with the bath water? I am particularly impressed with Maria Valtorta's *Poem of the Man-God*. While private revelation is not essential to achieving salvation, it can surely help, and God must have a good reason for doing it.

A. Private revelations are phenomena that carry no formal weight in the Church — even if endorsed — which means that Catholics always remain totally free in their regard, even if one Pope or ten Popes should be inclined to accept one or all of them. In this regard, I would refer you to the *Catechism of the Catholic Church* (nos. 65-67).

Surely, prophecy can be a manifestation of the Holy Spirit, but it should not be sought out. St. Paul gives the clearest criteria for appreciating charisms in the Church in the twelfth chapter of 1 Corinthians. You will note that he says the most important gifts are faith, hope, and charity, and that charity holds pre-eminence, even within that triad.

As far as Maria Valtorta is concerned, the Church has, in fact, reacted to her work and given a negative judgment. Therefore, Catholics are not free to be instructed by her ideas.

Tough situation

Q. My husband, who is not Catholic, was married before. He and his first wife were married in a civil ceremony, and his first wife was never baptized. My husband refuses to go through an annulment of his first marriage because he does not feel it is the Church's business. We were married in a civil ceremony. In 1992, I went to see my parish priest about having my marriage blessed so that I could receive Communion again. I told him the situation with my husband. He told me he would talk to someone at the diocese in our area about getting me special permission to receive the sacraments again. He called me the next day and informed me that I did get that special permission. He said that because my husband refused to get an annulment, I shouldn't be denied the sacraments. Am I committing a mortal sin by receiving Communion, even though I was given permission by the diocese? I live in a really liberal diocese. I really hate the thought of not being able to receive Jesus — I have had such peace and happiness since I could receive Him again. What do I do now? Please help me!

A. From the information you have shared, it appears that your husband was validly married; therefore, short of submitting that union to a marriage tribunal to test the validity, there is no way that your present union can be blessed by the Church — and without that, you cannot receive Holy Communion. My heart goes out to you since you come across as a very sincere believer. Refrain from receiving the sacraments, and offer up that pain and suffering in the hope that it will move your husband to go through the process that could enable you to resume a sacramental life. If he does truly love you, he should not allow his own idiosyncrasies to get in the way of your temporal happiness, let alone eternal salvation — a point I would suggest you make to him. I am confident the Lord will reward your fidelity with a much deeper experience of His life and love — far deeper than an arrangement that you know, in your heart of hearts, is just wrong.

New invocation

Q. Is it true that the Church has added some new invocations to the Litany of Loreto, specifically, "Mother of the Church" and "Queen of Families"?

A. Yes. "Mother of the Church" has been there for some time, while "Queen of Families" was added last year.

Patience is a virtue

Q. I love *The Catholic Answer* magazine, but wonder if you would consider giving references for your answers. It would be helpful in discussions with those who disagree. Is it better to believe in so-called popular visionaries even when they haven't been sanctioned by the Church, or should we wait?

A. I think I am pretty conscientious about providing support for positions that could be misconstrued or debated. When I don't, I presume I am merely explaining data that is broadly available to anyone who has (or has access to) some basic Catholic reference tools (for example, the *Catechism of the Catholic Church*, *Code of Canon Law*, *General Instruction of the Roman Missal*, *Bible*), or else just putting into a coherent form loose arguments or bits of information.

As far as apparitions are concerned, Catholics are free to hold various positions on the legitimacy or illegitimacy of them until an official declaration comes, either from the diocesan bishop or the Holy See. If approval is given, that means one is free to accept the phenomenon, but is not required to do so; if it is not, one is not free to support the apparition, the visionary or the site in question. In the waiting period, one should never speak of the event as a fact, only as a putative supernatural occurrence, thus allowing the authorities in the Church the opportunity to make an appropriate declaration.

Abstinence info

Q. My husband and I are young Catholics trying to learn orthodox teachings so we can pass them on to our children (whom we chose to home school). For the past two years, we have not eaten meat on Fridays. Is it permissible to use meat broths when preparing meals on Fridays or not?

A. In the past, the answer would have been in the negative, and that would still be the response if one were observing Friday abstinence as law rather than personal discipline or mortification.

Proper Spirit

Q. Is it proper for a priest, in the spirit of ecumenism, to give the blessing at a new Protestant church?

A. I see no difficulty with the act; ecclesiastical norms permit it and even recommend it. I think we are beyond the time when we thought our very presence at a non-Catholic event gave tacit approval to heresy, schism, or religious indifferentism. Pope John Paul II could not be any clearer on the absolute necessity of maintaining and propagating the Catholic Faith in its entirety, yet he has also led the way in extending acts of kindness and Christian brotherhood.

Last moments

Q. In the matter of a mixed marriage, one partner had a heart attack and had a little time before death. The wife said that her husband did not interfere with her practice of the Faith, but never joined the Church. Should the Catholic spouse baptize the dying partner in such a case?

A. Did the non-Catholic give any evidence during his life or in his dying moments that he desired entrance into the Church? If not, baptism would be inappropriate.

Inquire the groups

Q. I have received solicitations to support several pro-life and/or Catholic organizations, which all seemed to be legitimate and serving good causes. Some such organizations, however, serve only to enrich their organizers. I would appreciate your advice regarding the following: Catholic League for Religious and Civil Rights; American Life League, Inc.; Human Life International for Family Life; America Needs Fátima, and The Foundation for a Christian Civilization.

A. I don't want to endorse or condemn individual organizations, but all of them would, I am sure, be happy to provide you with the required information regarding the amount of money taken in annually, and the percentage of it used for overhead, administration, etc.

Watching the dogs

Q. Mothers Watch is a small group of mothers who act as watchdogs on sex education in Catholic schools. In its fall 1996 newsletter, the group published a severe attack on *New Corinthians*. On the other hand, you have endorsed the program. What of its critique? It seems too risky a business to suggest any type of sex-ed program.

A. In the past month, I have received nearly a hundred letters to this effect, leading me to conclude that something was orchestrated in the response tunnel. Be that as it may, allow me to note the following. First, I have read the Mothers Watch critique in great detail and find no merit in it whatsoever. Second, when it comes to conflicting evaluations from Mothers Watch and a Vatican dicastery, I (and any other Catholic, I hope) would trust the judgment of the Holy See. Third, the authors of the program in question have responded to this critique in a point-by-point fashion, available from the publisher (Couple to Couple League, Box 111184, Cincinnati, OH 45211). The shorter version is available gratis, while a $3 donation is requested for the seventeen-page edition. Finally, one thing comes across loud and clear in the Mothers Watch reaction: They are opposed to *any* form of classroom education in sexuality, pure and simple, and hence would — in principle — stand against any program, no matter how perfect. And that position of theirs (no matter how well-intentioned) is not the official position of the Church.

Crossing the line

Q. A friend of mine went to confession, and at the end of her confession the priest looked her straight in the eyes and said, "I forgive you." That was all; no words of absolution or Sign of the Cross (the usual way). Was this confession valid?

A. If all that the priest said was what you have recounted, I do not believe a valid absolution was conferred. Why? Because no priest can forgive sins; he does so only by the authority of Christ, hence, "I absolve you *in the name of the Father, and of the Son, and of the Holy Spirit.*" To suggest otherwise is both arrogant and blasphemous, as well as useless. What should it matter to a penitent that I forgive him? Who am I? By what right do I say such a thing? Did the penitent offend me, that I presume to forgive him?

The Church is extremely hesitant to question the validity of sacraments, and sets rather minimal standards so as to keep the consciences of the faithful at ease, but in this instance it appears that a clear line was crossed.

Working from within

Q. I am concerned that there are many priests (subtly) leading people away from the truths and teachings of the Catholic Faith. Why is this being allowed to happen? Why would Catholic organizations — especially Catholic media — participate in this undermining of the authority of the Church?

A. There is such a thing as de facto schism and another called de jure schism. In the latter, we find people who, because they do not accept ecclesiastical authority in general or one voice of it in particular, separate themselves from ecclesial communion. The former brand of schism, however, is much different, in that people who disagree with magisterial positions remain within the fold, giving the semblance of communion, all the while undermining the very fabric of Church unity. This is both insidious and reprehensible. Basic human honesty would demand a fish-or-cut-bait approach, but many of these folks know that they have everything to lose and nothing to gain by leaving visible communion with the Church. After all, how would they do their damage if they lost their credit cards and other perks? And, furthermore, who would be interested in inviting them to lecture if they were outside the Church? They get their audience precisely by being dissenters who work against "the institution" by remaining within it.

Tough situation

Q. My son went through Catholic grade school and Catholic high school. Until he went to college, he always went to church every Sunday and holy day with us. For years he was an altar boy and enjoyed being one. While on a six-month internship, he met his future wife, who comes from a Greek Orthodox family. When my son informed us that he wanted to marry her, I spoke with our pastor and was told that their wedding in the Greek Orthodox Church would be sanctioned by the Catholic Church. Our local pastor was at the wedding and told us that our son could continue to receive all the sacraments. Now my daughter-in-law has become overly religious in her Church and insists that my son go with her to church on Sundays, etc. She is pregnant and does not want the child baptized in the Catholic Church, but in the Greek Orthodox Church. I have a big problem with this! I see my son drifting away from the Catholic Church by giving in to his wife's demands. I do not want to not accept our future grandchild because of this and thus negatively influence my son's marriage. He loves us very much and knows that he will be hurting us, and it definitely hurts him. He is agreeing with his wife just to save the marriage. I need your advice and help.

A. These situations are always very difficult to deal with.

First of all, I hope that you accept your grandchild because he is your flesh and blood, and not simply so as not to affect your son's marriage adversely.

Second, your son was supposed to have promised to do everything in his power to raise any children in the Catholic Faith, and his wife should have been informed of that obligation. Did she agree to that then and now reneges?

Third, your son needs to be a faithful witness to his own faith commitment, even as he supports his wife in her own. Dialogue and understanding are important; compromise is devastating. He should attend Sunday Mass, but there would certainly be no problem with his attending her church on a regular basis, too. As you undoubtedly know, the theology of the Orthodox Church is very close to ours; differences need to be acknowledged, but not blown out of proportion, by either side. This impasse should be able to be confronted by two rational people of faith who, equally importantly, love each other and their child.

Peace attitudes

Q. When and how did it come about that the attitudes of the very early Christians changed from a pacifist inclination, which was strictly abiding by the teachings of Jesus, to a more militaristic one, which accepted violence and war under certain conditions? At the Last Supper, in instituting the Sacrament of the Holy Eucharist, wasn't Jesus making use of a ceremony called the Kiddush, which was already practiced by the Jews for thousands of years on the Sabbath and at Passover? Since all who believe in the Divinity of Jesus are called Christians (and for the most part are Gentiles), why is there not more emphasis made of our Jewish heritage?

A. Taking the second question first, I would encourage you to obtain a copy of *Salvation Outside of the Church?*, which I wrote and in part deals with Jewish-Catholic relations. It is published by Our Sunday Visitor (phone: 800-348-2440).

Regarding pacifism, we must be careful not to make too stark a distinction between earlier and later positions of the Church on war and peace. The first point to recall is that for four centuries, the Church was persecuted at worst and tolerated at best by political powers. This did not give the Church the opportunity to come up with a very finely honed political philosophy. Furthermore, soldiering in the Roman Empire required participation in pagan worship. With the legalization of Christianity and its eventual attainment to the state religion, the Church had to come to grips with how to relate to new situations and new questions.

St. Augustine's development of the just-war theory was one such attempt, and one that faithfully combines biblical theology and sound philosophical principles. It is significant that this teaching has been broadly accepted in the political community for nearly fifteen centuries, whether the nations have been Catholic or not, and even non-Christian.

Popess fable

Q. Recently, I have read about the reported existence of a Pope Joan sometime in the ninth century. Could you please advise me if such a person did exist, and if so, what was her position in the Church? Was she really a Pope?

A. For a detailed account of this story, I would recommend the entry in Our Sunday Visitor's *Encyclopedia of Catholic History*. For our purposes, suffice it to say that Pope Joan is an entirely fictional character. According to the story, a woman succeeded in disguising herself sufficiently that she got elected Pope, only to be discovered a woman when she became pregnant. Now, if you believe that, I've got a great land deal for you in the Mojave Desert.

Take a breather

Q. Church teaching instructs us to avoid servile work on Sundays. We do not allow our four teenagers to work at their part-time jobs on Sundays. However, since they work at eating establishments, they are pressured to work on Sundays like the rest of the employees. They are told that the restaurants are providing a service to others, so that they do not have to cook at home. They are also told that if they don't work at the restaurant on Sundays, they shouldn't go out to eat, either. Should we as a family not go out to eat, or go bowling, etc., on Sundays, so that others won't have to work? Should our teens be allowed to work on Sundays so that others will be able to rest from home cooking? Your help on these questions will be greatly appreciated.

A. The problem you raise is not easily resolvable, particularly for those committed to living according to the spirit of the law more than its letter.

Yes, we are commanded to abstain from all unnecessary work on the Lord's Day. However, as you note, certain very enjoyable activities (for us) can be a source of labor for others. Of course, that would be equally true if, for example, we stayed home for dinner rather than go out — wouldn't someone still have to prepare the meal and do the clean-up?

I would offer the following pastoral advice. First, all should endeavor to avoid servile work. Second, be sensitive to not causing such labor for others. Third, do not encourage businesses (such as department stores) to operate on Sundays, and do not use them on Sundays if they are open. Fourth, as a form of training and discipline, try to keep your teenagers from working on the Lord's Day.

We don't want to be so rigorous on this score that we end up like some of the scribes and Pharisees whose behavior was condemned by Christ, but, at the same time, all too many Catholics have lapsed into an extremely lax notion of what is required and forbidden by the Third Commandment nowadays.

Good news

Q. I have come across a newsletter called *For the Love of God!* Its stated goal is to help individuals: (1) To learn a bit more about being a Catholic; (2) Hopefully to keep some people from straying from the Catholic Faith; and (3) To plant a seed in people who may be "just" thinking of becoming a Christian, and Catholic in particular. The letter is free and has the blessing of the bishop of Sacramento. Would you please comment?

A. I have seen a couple of issues of this periodical and think it is very helpful. Just as an aside, I would observe that any project that has the endorsement of Bishop William Weigand of Sacramento can be trusted completely.

A work of fiction

Q. St. Thomas More is known outside the English-speaking world principally because of his book *Utopia*. Is this an orthodox book? It seems that free love is practiced in the ideal society that More depicts in that writing.

A. *Utopia* is essentially a novel, and every detail should not be taken as a precise prescription for human flourishing. If one wants a complete understanding of what an author considers right and just, one should consult his overtly theological writings, not his fictional creations.

Spiritual union

Q. Why do nuns wear wedding rings? They cannot all be married to Christ because we believe in one husband and wife at a time. When did this tradition start?

A. This is a very ancient tradition, but not one universally employed by all communities of women Religious, past or present. A similar practice was the use of a bridal costume for religious profession — to make the same point, that sisters are indeed brides of Christ. But they are so in a spiritual or mystical sense, just as Mary's motherhood of the Church is not a physical maternity, but a spiritual one.

Untenable changes

Q. I am the director of religious education for a large parish. Both of our priests are liberal. Masses are changed (including the wording), teachings are turned upside down, and documents of the Church are just plain bypassed. What should a person do when these things are done? Do I have a moral duty to correct these errors on account of my students?

A. To the extent that you can teach the truth without compromise and without causing even graver scandal than is already occurring, you should do so. If the situation is as bad as you claim, it appears you are in a completely untenable situation, from which you ought to extricate yourself. One question does come to mind, however: If the parish clergy are as off-base as they sound, why do they retain your services?

Proper home

Q. In a retreat house where my son was making a retreat, the priest-in-charge left the Sacred Host in his room all night, so that he could meditate better. Is this allowed? How is it possible for two people who were not married in the Catholic Church to receive Communion?

A. The Blessed Sacrament should never be reserved in a place other than a tabernacle. If the priest wanted to meditate better, he should have made the sacrifice to go to the chapel for prayer before the Eucharistic Lord's proper home.

On the second front, my initial reaction would be to say that the couple in question cannot do so. However, there is one possibility to the contrary: Were they married in a civil or non-Catholic ceremony, but with ecclesiastical permission? This can be done for substantive reasons. In that situation, their marriage would have lacked standard canonical form, but would nonetheless be regarded by the Church as a valid, sacramental union.

Dating woes

Q. I am a divorced Catholic, and also have received a decree of nullity. I have a question about dating. I am reluctant to date non-Catholic divorced men to avoid the situation of falling in love and not being able to be married in the Catholic Church. I have dated a few divorced Catholic men. When the subject of annulments comes up, they say they would never get one because it would make their children illegitimate. Telling them this is not the case and encouraging them to see their parish priests has fallen on deaf ears. I've been surprised to find this attitude even in a Catholic singles group. Finding a Catholic man my age is an uphill battle. Is dating a divorced man stepping into that gray area? What about dating non-Catholic divorced men? My friends said I should "lighten up" and have a good time.

A. You deal with several concerns at once. Let's try to unravel some of them.

As has been pointed out repeatedly, but apparently to little avail, a decree of nullity does not de-legitimize children because they are viewed, canonically and civilly, as products of putative marriages — that is, unions entered into in good faith.

Whether a man is Catholic or not — but divorced — makes no difference in general because a non-Catholic married to another non-Catholic in a civil or non-Catholic religious ceremony is still validly married in the eyes of the Church.

On a practical level, dating divorcés is often just looking for trouble, particularly where no decree of nullity already exists, because it often leads to temptations to enter into a civil union while waiting for a Church tribunal to examine the previous union. And what happens if the ecclesiastical decision is not favorable?

As far as the advice of your friends to "lighten up" is concerned, I would remind them that that was not the Lord's counsel; He tells us to get burdened by carrying our crosses. That, however, is done in union with Him, which makes the burden light, ultimately.

Canon 914

Q. At my parish, children go through the formal program for First Confession in the fourth grade. Although second- and third-graders are allowed to participate (with parental discretion), the fact is that they are not invited. The controversy seems to center around the understanding of Canon 914. Of course, no one can force a child to go to confession before First Communion, but with the program being geared to fourth-graders, it seems that the parish treats Canon 914 as nothing more than a recommendation. Could you please give me an interpretation of Canon 914?

A. The Church has consistently given an authoritative interpretation to Canon 914, and that is that children are to be catechized for reception of first Penance before First Holy Communion — and are to make their confession before their first reception of the Eucharist as well. The canon in question gives no leeway for alternative interpretations; pastoral practices to the contrary violate both the letter and the spirit of the law.

Improper function

Q. May a bishop employ a laicized priest for a public position in the Church — for example, as chancellor or another diocesan position? What if the priest, after laicization, was married and then divorced? Is there not potential scandal to the faithful involved? My understanding of canon law suggests that a laicized priest is to have very limited public functions in ecclesial matters, especially if he is known. Am I wrong?

A. Your evaluation is totally correct. This situation would be thoroughly improper. In point of fact, a laicized priest cannot even function as a lector at Mass, let alone in the positions of trust and authority you outline.

Prayers for the dead

Q. What is the best way to pray for the dead, especially for those who have committed a great evil? It may be that some of these people are impenitent at their death and cannot be forgiven by God. Would I be offending God by praying for someone who cannot reach heaven through his own fault? I am sure that the Lord is greatly saddened by the loss of such souls, and I would not want to remind Him by praying for a permanently lost soul. How can we know who has been lost, or who can benefit by our prayers after death? The answer seems easier when we pray for a loved one who has died, because we are almost certain that he can be helped by our prayers.

A. We should always pray for the dead — all the dead, even those who may have given the appearance of final impenitence, since we are commanded to hope for the salvation of all. After all, God can move the heart of someone to repentance with little more than a second of consciousness left — and that is all that would be required.

The Church's attitude toward judgment and the afterlife is like her Lord's — very merciful. I like to make the point that while the Church feels very comfortable in declaring — infallibly, no less —

who is in heaven (that is what canonization is), she has never attempted to name a single human being who is in hell. This is the case for two reasons: First, we have no way of knowing such a fact; and second, we are always to hope and pray for the salvation of all.

Truly sorry

Q. Can a priest really deny absolution? If so, when and why? I thought even if a person had committed a grievous sin, such as murder, that he could be absolved if truly sorry. Is that not correct? I have also read a little about people being automatically excommunicated, although I am not sure how that happens and for what offenses. What if an excommunicated person confesses and is truly sorry? Isn't he forgiven? Isn't God the only one Who knows if we are really sorry? And doesn't forgiveness actually come from God, not the priest?

A. Most of your points are clearly and correctly stated, except for the lack of one basic principle. Yes, all sins can be forgiven; only God can read men's hearts; it is God Who forgives and not the priest. However, God in Christ willed to make His forgiveness available through the Church's sacramental system. Therefore, on Easter night, He conferred on His apostles and their successors the power to forgive sins in His name (see Jn 20:19-23).

The forgiveness we receive, then, is a mediated forgiveness, mediated through the Church which, as custodian of the sacraments, sets norms and standards for all sacramental encounters with the Lord Jesus. One of the most fundamental requirements for a valid reception of the Sacrament of Penance is that the penitent be truly sorry, that the sorrow be conveyed to the confessor, and that the penitent exhibit also a firm purpose of amendment. If someone comes into the confessional, confessing murder, and does so in a cavalier manner, the priest has a serious obligation to determine if the person is truly sorry for the sin. If that statement is not made, the priest may not proceed with the sacrament. Similarly, the priest must ascertain if the individual intends to avoid the sin in question in the future; if the penitent is unwilling to make such a declaration, the priest cannot go on. Why? Logic and honesty make the reason obvious: The rite would be reduced to a sham celebration, in which a person would claim to be sorry (in the Act of Contrition, for example), while everything else would point in the opposite direction. God would be asked to forgive a sin the penitent (who really would not be a penitent since he would not be truly repentant) did not fully intend to avoid henceforth.

One aspect of this question needs to be touched upon, however, and that relates to the "firm purpose of amendment." A confessor should never badger a penitent or seek to extract a promise such as, "I pledge never again to commit this sin," which would be beyond the power of anyone to make. The purpose of amendment is much more within the grasp of anyone — namely, a positive intention to make a sincere effort to avoid this particular sin in the future. No one can make a total or absolute declaration that this will never happen again, but the intention needs to be firm, springing from an awareness of the evil done, gratitude to Almighty God for His gracious mercy, and a hope nevermore to offend so loving a Father.

As far as excommunication goes, it is important to state upfront that its purpose is not punitive but medicinal, which means that the Church does not see it as a tool to punish her children, but to warn them in advance of the seriousness of particular acts and, should they be committed, to make an incredibly strong statement about how grievous they are and what needs to be done to return to the communion of the Church. Under the 1983 *Code of Canon Law*, the number of automatic excommunications has been reduced to a handful — for example, violation of the seal of confession; profanation of the Eucharistic Species; procuring for oneself or assisting another in procuring an abortion. One can be excommunicated for other actions, but they are not necessarily automatic — unless, for instance, the diocesan bishop has issued a decree outlining such actions and noting the penalty of excommunication in the decree.

In all of this, however, it is crucial to underscore that the Church operates in this manner not to lord it over the members of the Church, but to provide them with the means that will ensure their safest and surest way home to the Father.

Superstitious claim

Q. I have enclosed a prayer card containing a prayer to St. Joseph. I find the prayer beautiful, and I continue to say it regularly. The two paragraphs following the prayer, however, have troubled me since I first saw them. The first difficulty is the purported age of the prayer. It was "found" only about twenty years after the resurrection of the Lord. How long was it "lost"? Is it really older than the Gospels? Furthermore, if this prayer is so powerful, why doesn't someone spend nine mornings praying for an end to hunger, war, sin, etc. The assertions about the prayer reek of superstition. Your thoughts, please?

A. I agree with you completely. Approaches to the devotional life such as this give all legitimate devotions a bad name, and I think the right word for it all is indeed superstition, which is a sin and condemned as such in the *Catechism of the Catholic Church* (see no. 2111).

Papal election

Q. Where might I find information on the election of a Pope? What makes the smoke white instead of black when a Pope has been elected? Any information that you could provide would be most appreciated.

A. The stove that contains the discarded ballots has straw inside as well. To obtain black smoke, signifying no election, the straw is dampened.

For further information on the process, consult Our Sunday Visitor's *Catholic Encyclopedia*. Avoid, at all costs, sensationalized versions such as those of Andrew Greeley and Malachi Martin.

Prudent and charitable

Q. Please help me to understand what my attitude ought to be toward Protestant friends (divorced or single) who wish to marry other divorced Protestants. I don't wish to judge them, but neither do I wish to condone behavior that is unacceptable to the Church. Though these people are not members of the Catholic Church, surely the words of the Lord (see Mk 10:11-12) are meant for them as well. These friends are dear to me, therefore, I want to be a real friend to them. Please help me to know how I can best help them.

A. Most Protestants do not read the scriptural evidence as we do, leading them to practice divorce and remarriage. They will be judged by their own lights. That does not mean that we say nothing about divergent teachings (on a host of issues, really; not just divorce and remarriage), but we do so prudently and charitably — and when circumstances naturally dictate. On this particular topic, it is interesting to note that many evangelical Protestants are now coming to the Catholic position on divorce and remarriage, even as many are also coming to accept Catholic teaching on the immorality of artificial contraception.

FOCUS

Q. Despite the large number of Catholics entering universities these days, almost every family can tell stories of how their well-educated, well-informed sons and daughters are no longer practicing the Faith. The triple threat of secularism (as it is presented in the classroom), hedonism (as it is presented on the campus) and Protestantism (as it is zealously presented by our evangelical brothers and sisters) has proven to be a gauntlet through which few college-aged Catholics have been capable of passing. This has to end. The Fellowship of Catholic University Students (FOCUS) is a new Catholic apostolate designed to reclaim society for Christ and His Church by forming effective Catholic leaders on college campuses. Founded earlier this year by Executive Director Curtis A. Martin and Scott Hahn, FOCUS provides a positive, proactive solution to the "crisis of faith" found on many college campuses. Would you be kind enough to apprise your readers of our association? To find out more about this apostolate, call 1-800-693-2484, or write to FOCUS, c/o Catholics United for the Faith, Inc., 827 N. Fourth St., Steubenville, OH 43952.

A. Happy to provide the above information. Know that your efforts have the support of my prayers.

Mission statement

Q. My suburban parish recently hosted a four-evening mission. I am confused as to what place missions have in Church practice. Could you please answer some questions about them? (1) Why are they considered of importance? (2) What criteria does a parish use to decide if it wants to host a mission? (3) Where do they get the speakers? (4) Are the people putting on the mission paid from parish funds or some other source? (5) Officially, does the Church encourage or discourage missions, or is this purely a parish decision?

A. Missions were once extremely popular, attracting as much as ninety percent of parishioners in large cities, with many of them running for two consecutive weeks. In some ways, missions were a Catholic response to Protestant revival meetings, intended to reignite the spark of faith in believers. Many religious congregations specialized (and still do) in conducting such exercises — for example, the Passionists, Dominicans, and Paulists.

The questions you ask have no uniform answer because so much depends on the local pastoral scene. Inasmuch as the Church encourages all kinds of renewal movements that bring people to a deeper level of faith and commitment, she encourages missions.

Kitty heaven?

Q. This letter may seem rather bizarre, however, a dear lady in my church — a convert of many years — cannot seem to accept that her cat, which died recently, is really and thoroughly dead. She says she believes she read where the Catholic Church teaches a limbo for souls of beloved pets, and that she will see her pet again in the next life. The matter is not specifically addressed in the *Catechism of the Catholic Church*. Can you shed some light on the question, please?

A. This question keeps coming up, so it might be worthwhile to attempt an answer. To begin with, we have to say that the Church has no official teaching on the matter, however, we can come to some tentative conclusions.

On the one hand, we can say that living beings below man have no immortal soul. Hence, that would seem to suggest that no future life would be possible for dogs, cats, etc. And that would surely seem to be the common theological judgment through the centuries. On the other hand, several of the Pauline epistles speak of the "recapitulation" of all things in Christ at the end of the world (see Eph 1:10; Phil 3:21; Col 1:20). This theme was picked up by many Fathers of the Church, especially Irenaeus. In other words, the original harmony and unity of creation will be restored; Eden will return, with all alienation between man and God and among human beings obliterated, but also the alienation between man and nature, which began with the sin of our first parents. With such a viewpoint, I suspect it is feasible to look toward a heaven with animals. The *Catechism* also gives some fine reflections on the notion of recapitulation in nos. 1042-1050.

Confession confusion

Q. I am writing because I am confused about the new method of confession, which our priest is promoting. Enclosed is a copy of the handout he gave us. This just doesn't sound like confession to me. He said that we no longer confess our sins and seek absolution. Instead, we follow four steps: (1) We tell the priest the virtue that Christ wants us to develop in our life; (2) Then we tell the success we have had; (3) After that we tell how we have failed in this area; and (4) We tell the priest the penance we intend to practice. Is this a real confession? Are all Catholic churches doing this? I know it's possible that I am wrong, but I'm definitely confused and need direction.

A. What you outline has a great deal of merit as a form of spiritual direction and also as part of one's confession (particularly since it tries to put a more positive spin on the process), but the Sacrament of Penance is primarily concerned with the confession of sin, and that seems to be somewhat lacking here.

It is fair to say that the Lord wants us to develop all the virtues (not just one) and, to the extent that we don't, we have matter for confession. Admittedly, we may want to focus on one virtue at a time (and probably should operate that way), but that does not mean that we are thereby blameless for failing to attend to the entire moral life.

As unpleasant as sin is to discuss, we must admit that it is indeed a part of the human equation since the days of Adam, as the third chapter of Genesis so painfully records it all. Refusing to deal with the facts of life is what psychologists call "denial," and that is most unhealthy, both spiritually and psychologically, and we do no one any favors by handling life in that way. Granted, we may want to be more positive in our approach to penance, but we cannot be ready to hear the good news of forgiveness if we are unwilling or unable to deal with the bad news of the human condition as we share in it.

Eucharistic fast

Q. A priest told me that anyone over the age of sixty-five is required to fast for no more than fifteen minutes prior to receiving the Holy Eucharist if that person is taking medication, as is usually the case in retirement homes and hospitals. I am given to understand that everyone is bound to fast for at least one hour — even if sick and, presumably, taking medication. Could you please clarify the present laws for the eucharistic fast and any exceptions?

A. Age has nothing to do with the eucharistic fast. People taking medication are not held to the one-hour rule, but I don't think that exception ought to be taken to the extreme. In other words, I don't think the vast majority of senior citizens are taking medication around the clock — at least I hope not. Church law is not meant to be odious, but the element of sacrifice should be present for all, according to their abilities. And senior citizens are not exempt from the divine precept to do penance and to be properly disposed to receive our Eucharistic Lord.

Healing touch?

Q. I have seen on television certain Protestant televangelists who touch people during their crusades, and these people fall back as if they were touched by the Holy Spirit. At the same time, many claim to have been healed either by being present at the crusade or simply by being touched by one of these televangelists. Does the Catholic Church accept these healings as acts from God? Are these televangelists deceivers, or are they some of the many instruments of God? If they are deceivers and what they do is wrong, why isn't the Catholic Church challenging such people and warning them about their many evils? If they are not deceivers, why is there not an equal number of priests appearing on television and doing the exact same thing?

A. St. John's Gospel teaches us, "The wind blows where it wills" (3:8), referring to the Holy Spirit. In the Old Testament, Moses exhorted his listeners to delight in the work of God, regardless of who was accomplishing it (see Nm 11:29), a point also made by Our Lord (see Mk 9:38-41). So, we have to have an open mind as we approach questions of this nature. But having an open mind is not the same thing as being so open-minded that one's brain falls out.

P.T. Barnum gave some cynical but realistic counsel when he warned that "There's a sucker born every minute." And because that is true, there are charlatans born every minute, too. Many of these alleged healings are nothing more than fraud, with supposed cures being experienced by folks who could probably enjoy the services of a psychiatrist more than those of a would-be evangelist. The Catholic Church is not the police force of the United States; I don't know why we should get involved in pronouncing on affairs that really have nothing to do with us (it would accomplish little and perhaps even exacerbate the situation).

Niceties won't do

Q. There seems to be a new book out on American sisters that is causing quite a commotion. Everyone appears to have chosen up sides, with nobody in the middle. What's your take on this?

A. The book to which the writer is referring is Ann Carey's blockbuster, *Sisters in Crisis: The Tragic Unraveling of Women's Religious Communities*, published by Our Sunday Visitor. You are correct in asserting that there is no middle ground reacting to this book. What amuses me about responses from certain quarters is that the most some can say is that the author hasn't been "nice." Well, I'm sorry. When literally tens of thousands of women have had their lives destroyed by an unfortunate experiment and when they, in turn, have exerted a negative influence on the rest of the Church, niceties won't do.

Ann Carey tells the truth, the whole truth and nothing but the truth. Dozens of my sister-friends have said that the only problem with the work is that it is two decades too late to save their communities. The fact that the book's detractors have not engaged in a substantive, point-by-point rebuttal of alleged misstatements of fact is proof positive that they have no honest response. I strongly recommend this book to anyone who has ever expressed amazement, disappointment, shock or anger about the demise of female Religious in our country. This well-documented study will explain it all for you. The importance of all this, however, is not simply to become involved in an "I-told-you-so" approach to life; taking to heart the lessons can preserve other communities from going over the precipice with their predecessors.

By the way, it might be good to make a Christmas gift of this book for every sister you know.

The good sisters

Q. I think your review of Ann Carey's book on women Religious was disgraceful. Her *Sisters in Crisis* was bad, but your editorial comments were even worse. As a committed Religious, I am offended at the unsubstantiated swipes taken at us by theological Neanderthals who have never taken the Second Vatican Council seriously. What makes me even angrier is that I bet you were educated by "the good sisters," and this is how you repay us! Why not promote something that shows women Religious in a positive light?

A. I have been alternately amused and annoyed by the way Ann Carey has been treated. If her book is so full of inaccuracies, why has no one produced an article to point them out? Furthermore, why have literally hundreds of sisters contacted her to say that she has completely captured both the spirit of the revolution and the gory details? Beyond that, if women's congregations had taken the Second Vatican Council seriously, most communities would not presently be on their way to extinction. The sad facts, however, are that everything that caused the demise (moving out of convents; abandonment of a community apostolate; forswearing religious garb; loss of communal prayer; angry and irrational feminism) had no connection to the renewal called for by the Council and, in reality, were in direct contradiction to the law of the Church.

As far as having been educated by sisters, you'd better believe it. I have never tired of declaring at every opportunity that ninety-five percent of what I am is what the sisters made me. They were wonderful Religious, committed and competent educators, and real ladies. The substantial loss of their breed is what makes me very sad because young people are denied the benefit of such a glorious witness. Thankfully, there are some communities that have remained faithful, and there are dozens of new congregations springing up that have a clear understanding of religious life, as the Church has always understood and continues to understand it.

Now, if you want me to recommend a book that shows sisters in a positive light, I have a great suggestion: *Behold the Women*, by Daniel Paulos. It is subtitled, *A Tribute to Sisters and Nuns of the Catholic Church in the United States and other Countries*, and that it is. Given your attitude, though, I doubt you will appreciate this pictorial survey of happy women in beautiful habits ministering to God's people in a host of ways, with reflections written by folks whose lives they touched and changed forever for the good. This is a moving and inspiring work; my prayer is that it will inspire many young women to take up the mantle from these legendary women. If the author's name is familiar, it should be, as he is the man who has continued the lovely and delicate paper-cutting art-work of the late Sister Jean Dorcy, O.P.

Conversion surge

Q. Is it my imagination, or is there a kind of surge in conversions to the Catholic Church over the past few years? Is there any documentary evidence to that effect?

A. Yes, indeed, there is a glut of conversions, if we can speak thus. What is fascinating about most of these folks is that they are buying the whole Catholic package, unlike many cradle Catholics who have become cafeteria Catholics, picking and choosing what is pleasing to them and rejecting the rest. I have been involved with hundreds of these converts, especially among the clergy, and am most impressed by their intelligence, their conviction, and their realism — that is, they don't think they're entering a Church of perfect souls. To a person, they have a deep devotion to the Holy Eucharist, a love for Our Lady and a fierce fidelity to the Holy Father.

Some literature you might find interesting would include the following: A biography of one of the great converts in history — *Wisdom and Innocence: A Life of G.K. Chesterton*, written by Joseph Pearce; from Erich Przywara, S.J., *The Heart of Newman* (a synthesis of Cardinal John Henry Newman's thoughts on the whole range of theological topics); from Thomas Howard, *On Being Catholic* (written ten years after his conversion); and from

Stephen K. Ray, *Crossing the Tiber: Evangelical Protestants Discover the Historic Church* (a rare combination of autobiography and theology). All of the above come to us courtesy of Ignatius Press. In addition, *By What Authority?: An Evangelical Discovers Catholic Tradition*, by Mark P. Shea, who has written for *The Catholic Answer* on occasion, is available from Our Sunday Visitor (800-348-2440).

Complexities

Q. I am a member of the U.S. military and, as such, must submit a blood and skin-cell sample for use as a DNA sample kept in a secure file for the purpose of identifying remains in the event that the manner of death would make other types of identification impossible. Without submitting to this procedure, it is not possible to continue in the military. It might well be that there is more to this procedure than we are being told — scientific experiments with DNA and the like. By submitting a sample, am I violating my Faith in any way — turning away from God to do an evil just to keep my job?

A. The complexity of life and society today is such that often we do not have full knowledge of what is being done with many facets of our existence. For example, when I invest in mutual funds, do I have absolute assurance that my money will not be used for immoral purposes? Probably not. My moral obligation is to determine, as far as possible, that nothing untoward will happen. Once that has occurred, there is little more I can do at any level. If my conscience is satisfied at that point, I can proceed with moral impunity.

Just a bit of pastoral advice: Although things can get somewhat murky today, we need not look under every rock for a snake.

Apostolic origins

Q. I have always been interested in the Gospel passage of Jesus curing Simon Peter's mother-in-law. Obviously, we know from this reading that Peter was married or had been married. The Church uses as one of its arguments for not allowing women priests, and even married priests, that Christ, in picking the Twelve Apostles, established a tradition for the Church today. Wouldn't it then follow that, to be Pope, the man would have to be married or (at least) widowed, since this seems to be the case with Peter? Are the Gospels to be believed or not?

A. The Church has always maintained that there are certain things she is bound to in Holy Scripture, and others to which she is not. The Church's position on the ordination of women is rooted in her conviction that the express Will of Christ was *not* to ordain women, and that the Church throughout the ages has felt bound to abide by His sovereign Will. Clerical celibacy is not so much a matter of what is or is not in the Gospels — although they are formative of the practice — but in the evolution of the ordained ministry in the early Church.

While the early Church, both East and West, most definitely had married priests, it is also historically sure that married priests freely gave up their marital rights. In fact, part of the ordination rite consisted in the bishop's asking the wife of the future priest if she agreed to this new arrangement. We see a remnant of that in the contemporary ordination ceremony for a permanent deacon who is married (although the meaning of that element has changed). The Churches of the East and West then embarked on divergent but parallel paths in handling the matter of clerical celibacy: The West decided that if marital intimacy would not be permitted, it would be better for only celibates to be called to the priesthood; the East mitigated the apostolic practice by requiring abstinence from sexual relations only the night before the priest would offer the Eucharist. In this century, the East eventually dropped even that requirement.

The finest discussion of this very complex and fascinating question comes from the pen of Father Christian Cochini, S.J., published under the title of *The Apostolic Origins of Priestly Celibacy*, by Ignatius Press. A scaled-down version of this monumental study was written by Cardinal Alfons Stickler, *The Case for Clerical Celibacy* (it, too, is available from Ignatius).

Bishop elections

Q. Recently, our parish bulletin sported an article that described St. Ambrose as being "elected the bishop of Milan by the people." There is a certain amount of historical truth to what is said; I suspect there is also a personal bias on the part of the author, who wants to push for the election of bishops in the contemporary Church. The *Catechism of the Catholic Church* (no. 861) and *Lumen Gentium* (Dogmatic Constitution on the Church, no. 20) discuss how bishops are chosen as successors to the apostles. Popular election is not part of the Church's ordinary method of succession for bishops. Was the situation regarding Ambrose an isolated incident?

A. Bishops in the early Church were appointed in a variety of ways. The clergy of Rome, for example, elected their bishop, who, of course, by that very fact was also the Pope. In some places, all the faithful elected the bishop. As time went on, the process became more standardized throughout the universal Church for many reasons, not the least being the importance of controlling political machinations. In the Latin Church today, potential episcopal candidates usually have their names forwarded to the Holy See by the apostolic nuncio (the Pope's representative to a particular country or region), then the Congregation for Bishops reviews the candidates and makes its recommendations to the Holy Father. In most of the Eastern churches, local synods of bishops elect bishops. Such men are then presented to the Pope for his ratification, which is most often automatically granted.

Confusion ensues

Q. When the Sacrament of Anointing of the Sick is given in a group setting, is it proper for those attending the service to follow after the priest and lay hands on the sick person(s)? The practice was begun several years ago by a former pastor in the presence of one of the religious-education classes, I believe, to teach them about the sacrament. Each time such a service has occurred, there is a considerable amount of giddiness and disrespectful behavior. My criticism has made it back to the pastor, who defends the practice. I would be grateful for your opinion.

A. No involvement of those who are not priests, including deacons, is permissible in the anointing of the sick. It seems to me that proper pedagogy would call for a simulation of the sacrament, not the celebration of a real rite. Once more, confusion can only ensue from the procedure you relate.

Making a statement

Q. We have been involved in the fund-raising efforts of the local pregnancy-care center (pro-life) for several years now. This past spring, the center decided to make such efforts official by giving us and others the title of "Ambassador." Along with this title, we are supposed to be in agreement with the Statement of Faith (of which I enclose a copy). We were not asked to sign it. We understand the advantages of having a statement of faith in this ministry; however, we do not want to go along with something if it is anti-Catholic. We are concerned particularly with the first item, which states that "the Bible [is] inspired, the only infallible authoritative Word of God." Does that item or any of the others contradict our Catholic beliefs? What should our response be? Should we decline the title if the statement of faith is problematic for us as Catholics? Or are we being too picky?

A. The statement is completely unacceptable from a Catholic theological stance, but more than that, it is completely out of place in the context of attempting to save the lives of unborn babies. Whether or not you are required to sign it, it is offensive. If I were you, I would bring this up to the organization's board of directors and ask them to remove either the problematic language or the entire document. In order to be effective pro-life agents, we need not have total theological agreement — or any at all, for that matter. After all, there are theists, atheists and agnostics united in their opposition to the monstrosity of abortion. Indeed, our very argument is that abortion is not a religious issue but one grounded in the natural law, to which all men of good will have access, independent of Divine Revelation. This type of narrow sectarianism is exactly what helps destroy the effectiveness of the right-to-life cause in our society.

If the organization's leadership refuses to change, I would follow the infallible Word of God's advice by "shaking the dust" from my feet (see Mt 10:14) and find another venue in which to work for the unborn.

A bad movie

Q. I have just seen the film "Priest." My two friends — good Catholics — thought it was great, and it convinced them that priests should marry. It seemed to me that there was a lot of erroneous teaching coming from the older priest. Could you please spell out these false teachings for me and others who might have overlooked them?

A. What could have brought your friends to suppose that a married clergy was desirable after seeing that film? Most people I know came to the exact opposite conclusion. Would a married priesthood eliminate homosexual behavior? No, because I know many Protestant clergy who are married and are practicing homosexuals. Would a married priesthood ensure marital fidelity? No, because the statistics sadly show that there is a very high rate of adultery among married clergy. Neither marriage nor celibacy can guarantee goodness.

The older priest's behavior is reprehensible in many ways: He is living a lie by having a concubine; his liturgical style is cavalier; his preaching and teaching are heterodox; his moral theology, in particular, is heavily tainted by moral relativism; and he never appears in clerical garb. Perhaps most obnoxious of all, however, is how he seeks to make the young priest "feel good" about himself. Why? So that the young fellow won't judge the older man's lifestyle too harshly. The end result, of course, is that he makes the young priest worse, not better.

On the first anniversary of the film's debut, I reviewed it for the National Catholic Register. One of the points that I made was that, bottom line, the film was soupy sentimentality at its lowest.

Validity

Q. Under the heading "Tough Situation" in *The Catholic Answer* magazine, you gave an answer that I would like you to take a second look at. The questioner was anxious to be able to receive the sacraments, and the problem keeping her from it was her husband's refusal to have his first marriage annulled. You stated that "it appears your husband was validly married, since the Church accepts the validity of a marriage between two non-Catholics." If I recall correctly from my Catholic education, there is an important word missing here, and the word is "baptized." The husband's first wife was never baptized, and to have a valid marriage, the marriage would have to have been between two baptized non-Catholics. Am I correct?

A. Not quite. To have a sacramental marriage, one must have two baptized Christians; one can have a valid marriage without a baptized person. For example, a Jewish man and a Catholic woman contract a valid union, albeit a non-sacramental one.

Trusteeship

Q. I understand that a trustee of a parish holds a civil position. What are the duties of the trustee when the priest dies and the bishop does not appoint another administrator? Who can dismiss a trustee?

A. A parish trustee does indeed hold a civil position. Because some states require them and others do not, and since the laws of the various states differ, I shall only be able to give a generic answer to your question.

In most places, the parish corporation is part of the diocesan structure, formally known as a corporation sole — that is, each institution within the diocese belongs to the entire diocese, with the bishop as the president of the whole corporation and some other diocesan official (often the vicar general) as the vice-president; the treasurer (and secretary, usually) is the parish priest; two laymen are nominated by the parish priest as trustees, with their appointments being ratified by the other officers of the corporation.

When a priest is transferred, it is normal for another to be appointed at least temporary administrator. If that does not happen immediately, however, such responsibilities as need to be fulfilled are handled by a diocesan official — for example, the chancellor or another designee of the bishop. Therefore, the situation you describe is almost impossible. If it were the case, the trustee would have no authority apart from the bishop as president of the civil corporation of that parish.

We are sinners

Q. A prayer group that I attend is in need of your spiritual advice. A woman in our group subscribes to *Signs and Wonders of Our Times*. Recently, it carried an article on a visionary called Louisa Picarrita, who writes that "passions will lose their power to lead them into sin. (Those who pray and receive His divine Will.)" In other words, while here on earth, we will not commit a sin, just as Adam and Eve before the Fall, or as our Blessed Mother. I find this hard to believe. The Bible and the *Catechism of the Catholic Church* tell us that we are sinners as long as we are in the flesh. Since the magazine that carried the article has an imprimatur, I am confused about what I should believe. Should we believe her writings even though they go against our teachings?

A. It would be necessary to see the complete text for a complete analysis, however, as our readers know, I am a strong skeptic when it comes to visions and private revelations, and this is, in my considered judgment, the Catholic way.

For the theological point under discussion, we must realize that, since the sin of Adam, any human being touched by that sin (and so, the Blessed Mother is a case apart) suffers the effects of that sin — even after we have been made right with God through baptism. Some of that scar tissue we call concupiscence, which is the basis for the disordered desires we experience deep within our person. It is the phenomenon to which St. Paul referred when he explained: "I do not understand my own actions. For I do not do what I want, but I do the very thing I hate" (Rom 7:15-16).

Through leading a holy life, through the practice of virtue, through the proper use of the sacraments (especially Penance and Holy Communion), this disordered nature of ours can be held at bay, but never totally eliminated. Virtue (because it is a habit, like vice) can replace vice as our normal reaction to courses of action presented for our judgment, but life here below always involves temptation and struggle, which is why St. Paul warned: "Therefore let any one who thinks that he stands take heed lest he fall" (1 Cor 10:12). The worst thing the devil can convince us of is that we are beyond the pale of falling victim to his allurements.

Faith fact-sheets

Q. I am writing in regard to a question about Luisa Piccarreta. Catholics United for the Faith (CUF) has an excellent faith fact-sheet on her and the devotion known as the *Kingdom of the Divine Will*. A copy of the fact-sheet will help tremendously in clearing up her confusion and questions. CUF has many other fact-sheets, not to mention their phone line for answering questions regarding the Catholic Faith.

A. Yes, I enthusiastically recommend CUF's faith fact-sheet series (1-800-MY-FAITH). And, yes, the one on Luisa Piccarreta is especially helpful. There we find the following information: "She claims that all we have to do is abandon our own will to the Divine Will, which can be found everywhere. There is an emphasis on complete passivity of the soul in Luisa's writings . . . condemned by the Church in the seventeenth century. Luisa's writings openly promote the idea that she has received a new revelation. The faithful must accept this revelation to achieve the new way of holiness, which equates the sanctity of Luisa Piccarreta with the sanctity of the Mother of God. According to Luisa, once a person receives this 'new sacrament' of the Divine Will, the human will, in effect, acts in such a way that the action is purely divine. This basic error was taught in the early centuries of Christianity and became a cardinal principle of the absolute predestination of such founders of Protestantism as John Calvin."

I hope this is helpful.

Deathbed baptism

Q. You told a person writing to ask about the baptism of a non-Catholic spouse on his deathbed that the baptism was inappropriate. How in the world can any baptism be inappropriate? Especially on a deathbed! Didn't Our Lord make careful plans for the salvation of all men? Doesn't the Church even allow for non-Catholics to be baptized in danger of death? I ask because I was in a similar situation. My father was not Catholic and not baptized. Since experiencing loss in his youth, he was angry with God, yet he had a heart of pure gold. In later years, he often went to Mass with my mother. Once, he jokingly told her, "Well, if I'm going to church, I might as well be Catholic." However, he never asked for baptism in so many words. Near the end of his life, Dad was in a hospital fifty miles away from me. Day by day, I watched him change: moving from fear in his eyes, to understanding, to peace — as if he and God were striking a bargain. He died at 3:20 one morning while I struggled to get there. At 3:40, I arrived and did what I begged God for all my life. I baptized my dad. How could obeying His command to "baptize all nations" ever be inappropriate?

A. I don't think you read my original response too carefully. I said that it would be inappropriate to baptize someone who had either expressed disapproval of such a possibility or never mentioned it, or given any indication of interest in Christianity. Your father surely did not fit those categories. The reason baptism would be inappropriate in the situations I cited is because it involves an act of one's free will. No one can be forced to act contrary to his conscience, and if he is, the act has no validity — hence, no merit. However, in your specific situation, it was not possible to baptize your father because he was already deceased.

Sacraments of initiation

Q. I am on the religious-education committee in our parish. We have been sent a great deal of material from our diocesan office, which is designed to return us to the practice of combining the Sacraments of Baptism, Confirmation, and Eucharist, all at one time. Is this something the Pope and the magisterium have advocated? Have you ever heard of the Tempus program?

A. I am not aware of the Tempus program. As to your more fundamental question, let me offer the following.

In the early Church, it is clear that the "sacraments of initiation" — that is, the Sacraments of Baptism, Confirmation/Chrismation, Holy Eucharist — were received together as part of a unified rite of Christian initiation, generally at the Easter Vigil liturgy. For a variety of reasons, especially in the West, the sacraments got separated from one another. Beyond that, in the West, their order became inverted when Pope St. Pius X gave permission for the reception of Holy Communion at the age of reason, rather than later. Now, since Confirmation was not made to move with First Holy Communion, it meant a different sequence of sacraments.

The *Catechism of the Catholic Church* explains all this in great detail, and it is worth reading for both historical and theological insights (see nos. 1286-1292). I don't think Catholics need to be slaves to so-called primitive ways of doing things; after all, simply because something was done in the early Church does not necessarily mean that such a practice was right, good, or beneficial. The age of an idea is not a guarantee of its value.

That having been said, I think we need to remedy the anomaly of at least the inverted order of the sacraments of initiation, if not return to the reception of them all at once — as is the case in the Eastern Churches (both those in union with the Holy See and those not in communion with us). Minimally, then, I would see great usefulness in having children confirmed at the age of reason, with the reception of their First Holy Communion at the very same Mass. Optimally, my preference would be to return the Church of the West to the original practice of baptizing, confirming, and communicating infants in the same ceremony. This approach gives strong testimony to the sovereignty of divine election and the power of God's grace — a healthy and necessary antidote to much of the Pelagianism we find afloat today.

I know that some pastors and religious educators argue that if we operate in such a manner, we will never get the kids into CCD classes, to which I have two responses: First, sacraments should not be used as carrots to ensure attendance; second, much more effort ought to be expended to make Catholic school attendance the norm — that is, building more schools and making them more affordable — so that CCD becomes obsolete.

Validating a marriage

Q. I have divorced and remarried. My former spouse and my wife's former spouse are both deceased. Can I rightly receive Holy Communion?

A. From what you say, it appears that both you and your partner are now free to marry in the Church — that is, to have your marriage validated. And that is what needs to be done. It should be a very simple, low-key procedure. Once you have received the Sacrament of Penance and had your union blessed, you will then be free to return to Holy Communion. God bless your full reintegration into the bosom of Mother Church.

The cardinals' duty

Q. Are there other ways for a man to become Pope other than being elected by the cardinals? Can a reigning Pope appoint his successor? If he can, has any Pope ever done so?

A. The process of obtaining a Pope has undergone many changes, due to the vicissitudes of history. At the outset, some were elected by popular acclamation of the faithful of Rome; some were elected by the clergy of Rome. As time went on, in order to gain a more universal appeal, the College of Cardinals was deputed to perform the task. In this century (with particular impetus coming from Pope Paul VI), the composition of the College of Cardinals has been thoroughly internationalized, truly representative of a universal Church. The norms for a papal election were revised by Pope John Paul II, and appointment is not a valid method. To the best of my knowledge, only one Pope (Felix III, c. 492) in history ever appointed his own successor.

Sin against unity

Q. I have recently received a brochure from a group, CITI (Celibacy is the Issue), advertising "Rent A Priest." It is a "FREE Married Priest referral service for Roman Catholic individuals and parish communities lacking adequate sacramental and pastoral care. Married priests are also providing nonjudgmental ministry to Catholics who have been turned away by the institutional Church, but still want to take part in their Catholic faith. Jesus never turned anyone away, especially from receiving Communion, and married Catholic priests follow that tradition in their ministry." The brochure goes on to suggest that "through the canons, we have the power to call upon married priests," citing that in the early Church it was the community "who recruited the elders to preside over the Eucharist." They cite canons from the present *Code of Canon Law*, but surely their reading is incorrect. Could you comment on this group and the validity of their claims?

A. This is, pure and simple, an advocacy group of former clerics, perpetual malcontents, contaminated by a severe case of sour grapes. Their reading of Church history, like their reading of canon law, is jaundiced — selective to the point of dishonesty. Therefore, several points need to be stressed in reply.

First, every little boy knows that if he wants to be a priest in the Latin Church he will have to make a commitment to clerical celibacy. The possession of that charism is tested through a period of priestly formation. The promise of celibacy at one's diaconal ordination is freely made, by a man who must be at least twenty-three years of age — presumably mature enough to know what he is getting into, and equally mature enough to be a man of his word.

Second, while we know that once a man is ordained a priest he is a priest forever, we also know that the Church that conferred sacred ordination on him and gave him the faculties to function, likewise has the authority from Christ to revoke those faculties when the man has ceased to live according to the Church's norms, and/or when the common good demands. In other words, the priesthood is not a personal hobby horse of the individual; it exists for the good of the Church. When a man reneges on his promise of celibacy, his priestly faculties are suspended. If he requests it, or if the Church judges it opportune, his faculties can be permanently revoked, allowing him to perform priestly duties only when someone in danger of death does not have access to a priest in good standing.

Third, it is clear, therefore, that what "Rent A Priest" proposes has no grounding in the law of the Church. Anyone cooperating with their agenda sins against the unity of the Church, especially because the Eucharist (sign and cause of ecclesial unity) is being used as a tool to advance a political agenda that is totally at odds with Catholic teaching and practice.

Fourth, as far as their propaganda goes regarding the shortage of priests being related to mandatory celibacy, we should note that only North America and Western Europe have such shortages. Do young men on the other continents have less forceful libidos? Or, is it that the Faith has been so corrupted in these environments that the situation drowns out the voice of God calling men to serve Him and His people? Finally, Eastern Orthodoxy (which has had a married priesthood for centuries) has a massive shortage of priests. What is the solution for their difficulty, we might ask "Rent A Priest"?

Spiritual diary

Q. Can you comment, please, on the book authored by Catherine de Hueck Doherty, *O Jesus*?

A. This new book of prayers, taken from the spiritual diaries of Catherine de Hueck Doherty, is perhaps the most intimate look to date at this remarkable woman's personal relationship with Jesus. Its pages pour out her struggles and deepest yearnings, her most unguarded thoughts, and her most frank conversations with Jesus, her beloved Lord.

The book covers a period from 1931 to 1938, while she was working with the poor, first in Toronto and then in New York City, where she began an interracial apostolate. She later founded Madonna House, a community based in Combermere, Ontario, which continues to serve the physical and spiritual needs of the world's poor. She was also a wife and, later, a single mother who faced many of the personal tragedies that confront people today.

Cultural marks

Q. Our Lord said to spread His Gospel in every nation. In our age of modern communication, this would seem like an easy thing to do. It seems that there should be roughly the same percentage of Catholics in each nation. Are some cultures more inclined to accept the Gospel than others? How do you explain the unequal distribution of Catholics around the world: France versus Japan, Ireland versus Saudi Arabia, Brazil versus Nepal, etc.?

A. Every culture is different, and every culture needs to be evangelized. And, yes, some cultures are more naturally attuned to certain Gospel values than are others. For example, my own visits to African countries have persuaded me that there is among those peoples a innate sense of the sacred, which makes appreciation of the transcendence of the one true God much easier, while the historical and cultural experiences related to polygamy in those places cause tremendous difficulties. No person and no nation, however, can come to Christ apart from the offer of grace and the willingness to accept that grace. In that sense, then, all comparisons are odious.

Misplaced mania

Q. I have been browsing the Internet and came across the following article on Satanism in the Vatican. The third "Fátima 2000 International Congress on World Peace" was held in Rome, November 1996. It was there that Archbishop Emmanuel Milingo chose to make public formal allegations that satanic activity is taking place inside the Vatican in a speech entitled "God and Evil Toward the Year 2000." This archbishop works in the Vatican as a special delegate to the Pontifical Council for Pastoral Care of Migrants and Itinerant Peoples. He is also an official exorcist and has written several books. Would you please comment on the article that I enclosed?

A. Archbishop Milingo is "a loose cannon on deck," having been removed by the Holy Father from his diocese in Africa because of all the difficulties he caused with his self-appointed ministry of healing and exorcism. The purpose of bringing him to Rome was not to promote him but to rein him in — an unachieved goal, apparently.

The Fátima conference to which you refer was organized by Father Nicholas Gruner, a priest who works without faculties and ecclesiastical approval. The primary thrust of his efforts seems to be to convince people that the Pope has disobeyed Our Lady in regard to the consecration of Russia to her Immaculate Heart.

Much of the mania surrounding the allegations of Satanism in the Vatican is fostered by Malachi Martin, an ex-Jesuit who also has no priestly faculties since his departure from the Society of Jesus. Martin's usual method of operation in terms of such accusations is to insert them into his novels, so that the bad effect can be attained, yet he could never be held legally liable for the charges since he can always say the work was fictional.

We know that the devil is real, and that the children of the Church are not exempt from his clutches. We also know that one of the clearest signs of diabolical presence is the existence of confusion; indeed, the devil's name in Greek comes from two words that mean "to throw into confusion." To the extent that people (clergy, in particular) lead Christ's faithful into confusion, they are agents of the diabolical.

Still effective

Q. Are the effects of prayer diminished if you pray for more than one person? For example, if one hundred people had a deadly disease, would each receive one-one-hundredth of the grace that one person would receive if you had prayed for him alone instead of all of them?

A. God is both omniscient and omnipotent, hence, what are normal limitations for us in terms of time, space, etc., do not apply to Him. Furthermore, a prayer is effective in terms of its intention, which is to say that the intercessor's desire to affect the salvation or earthly welfare of an entire group is surely possible. In fact, in every offering of the Eucharistic Sacrifice, we pray for the whole Church and the whole world, just as Jesus died for all men.

Differences abound

Q. My wife attends an Episcopal church. I attend a Catholic church. On occasion we go to both churches on Sundays when the schedule allows it. From all outward appearances, the liturgies and beliefs are identical. The external elements are supposed to reflect the internal meaning of the sacraments and our Creed. How can we talk of differences between these denominations when they appear to be identical at this point — after all, many Catholics are calling for women priests, validating homosexual unions, etc.? I know there is a difference, but what arguments might I use to convince my wife to convert to the Catholic Faith?

A. A couple of aphorisms remind us: "All that glitters is not gold." "Appearances can be deceiving." The truth of the matter is that the spiritual and theological nakedness of the Episcopal Church is now apparent for all to behold — and it is not a pleasant sight. I find this kind of statement very difficult to make because, as a young seminarian, I often found spiritual comfort and liturgical guidance by attending Anglican churches — in a time when my own seminary was a spiritual wasteland and a three-ring circus as far as divine worship went. But history shows us that the Anglican Church was spawned in rebellion and increased through successive compromises, so that one could believe everything and nearly nothing and find an easy and pleasant home therein.

The hemorrhaging of Episcopal laity has been massive, beginning in 1976 with their so-called ordination of priestesses and continuing right up to the present; hundreds of their clergy have left, more often than not, coming into the Catholic Church. Now, some of their defenders are fond of pointing out that the road is a two-way street, with traffic moving in both directions: out of Canterbury into Rome, yes, but also out of Rome into Canterbury. There is some truth there, of course, but there is no traffic jam at the doors of the Canterbury Cathedral caused by ex-Catholics and, much more importantly, the best and brightest of Episcopalians have come into full communion with the Church of Rome — and at a great price economically, socially, and personally. Most Catholics who have gone over to Anglicanism have done so because they want an easier road to travel, with few demands; the vast majority of our clergy who have moved into the Episcopal Church had serious problems with Catholic doctrine and, often enough, Catholic morality.

This should in no way be seen as an attack on many fine Christians who, for whatever reason, continue on in the Anglican Communion. We need to pray for their spiritual consolation because many of them suffer terribly within that ecclesial community. Without a doubt, however, it is no longer possible for Anglicanism to continue the charade and pretense of being part of "the Church Catholic," as they have sought to do for the past five centuries. Interestingly enough, a great mind like Cardinal John Henry Newman saw through it all a full century ago, which emboldened him to abandon the Anglican ship at that time, again suffering horribly for his commitment to the truth and for acting in accord with an informed conscience.

Wounded Anglicans

Q. Although an Anglican fed up with much of the nonsense in my faith, I think you were rather harsh in your judgment on us. After all, many of us believe everything the Catholic Church does, but we just find it difficult to make the move. And you really must admit that Anglicanism is a lot closer to the Roman Church than any other non-Catholic community.

A. I think I really hit a raw nerve because your letter was but one of dozens I received from hurt Anglicans. Frankly, I am surprised that so many Anglicans are subscribers to *The Catholic Answer* magazine! First of all, as I attempted to say in my response, I had no intention to be polemical or uncharitable; all I wanted was to make it eminently clear that Anglicanism had theological and historical problems from the very beginning, and that the situation has just worsened with the passage of time. If anyone doubts this assessment, allow me to recommend a new book by Paul F.M. Zahl, an Episcopal priest in Alabama. Proudly, the author entitles his work, The Protestant Face of Anglicanism (Eerdmans Publishing, Grand Rapids, Mich).

Two other clarifications: (1) To refer to the Catholic Church as the "Roman" Church is generally an Anglican effort to make the Catholic Church less "catholic" and more idiosyncratic, and to justify the so-called branch theory, which holds that Orthodoxy, Anglicanism, and "Romanism" are all valid "branches" of the one tree of the Catholic Church. (2) Theologically, Orthodoxy is and always has been "closer" to Catholicism than is, or was, Anglicanism.

New orders growing

Q. I will soon be a high school freshman and am considering becoming a sister. However, some of my family members tell me that sisters in America are ceasing to exist and, that by the time I finish high school, they will be completely gone. Is this true?

A. The vast majority of communities of women Religious in the United States (and most of Western Europe as well) are well-nigh extinct, due to the nonsense of the past thirty years. In other words, the experiments have largely been abysmal failures; that is not to say, however, that true religious life has failed— and the proof of such an assertion is that new, faithful communities are sprouting up all over the ecclesial landscape.

In keeping with a fairly regular practice of mine now, let me offer the names of some communities that have come to my attention most recently: Sisters Adorers of the Precious Blood (contemplative), 400 Pratt Street, Watertown, NY 13601; Dominican Nuns of the Perpetual Rosary (contemplative), 335 Doat Street, Buffalo, NY 14211; School Sisters of Christ the King (active), Villa Regina Motherhouse, 4100 S.W., 56th Street, Lincoln, NE 68522; Discalced Carmelite Monastery of St. Teresa of the Child Jesus, 75 Carmel Road, Buffalo, NY 14214.

Age not an excuse

Q. In a recent issue of *The Catholic Answer* magazine, you said that age has nothing to do with the eucharistic fast, yet canon 919 would appear to excuse people from fasting who are advanced in age.

A. I still do not read that canon to suggest that. It seems to me that the intent of the law is to enable the sick — or those burdened by age (and thus, frail) — to receive our Eucharistic Lord without grave inconvenience. That surely does not apply to those who are able to get around with facility.

As a parish priest, I was always amused at senior citizens who expected to be dispensed from Friday abstinence, the eucharistic fast and the Sunday Mass obligation — all because "we are senior citizens." Yet these same folks took weekly bus trips to gamble in Atlantic City, went to bingo three and four nights a week, and never missed a Friday visit to the hairdresser. As we say, "Something does not compute." I hope everyone can see my point.

Guadalupe phenomenon

Q. What's the scoop on Guadalupe? I hear that the priest who headed the shrine declared that nothing ever really happened there!

A. The priest in question was summarily dismissed from his post after his bizarre statements; some say he had some personal difficulties. My own reading of the Guadalupe phenomenon makes me regard it as one of the best documented apparitions in history, and with the most astonishing effects — namely, the conversion of an entire nation to Christianity! I have also had the privilege of visiting the site on several occasions and have always been impressed by the spirit of prayer and the devotion of the faithful, especially the Mexicans.

A new work has appeared, *A Handbook on Guadalupe*, covering the historical, sociological, theological, and scientific aspects of it all (224 pages). The preface is written by Archbishop Sean O'Malley, O.F.M.Cap., of Boston.

Annulment book

Q. With all the talk about the Kennedy annulment and his ex-wife's book, what is one to make of the whole situation — annulments in general, and the Kennedy debacle in particular?

A. As I have said repeatedly, I am not at all surprised by the large number of annulments granted in this country. Indeed, I am amazed that there are not more, especially when one considers three decades of inadequate catechesis and four decades of a climate encouraging a mentality hostile to permanent commitment.

Remember the basic principle of theology: Grace builds on nature. In other words, when the human person has improper preparation — personally, psychologically, theologically — obstacles are put in the way of God's grace. And without divine assistance, a permanent, stable union is well-nigh impossible.

An excellent book has just appeared on this topic, written by Dr. Edward Peters, who is no stranger to readers of *The Catholic Answer* magazine. It is called *100 Answers on Annulments*; and is insightful, pastoral, and completely faithful to Church teaching and proper ecclesiastical jurisprudence. I cannot recommend this book more enthusiastically for all concerned with this very difficult question, either personally or pastorally.

Burial protocol

Q. I recently had a cousin who committed suicide at the age of thirty-three. He was not a Catholic, but was raised in a somewhat Christian home. However, he seemed to be a lost soul since his teenage years. When discussing his death with my sister-in-law, who is also a Catholic, questions were raised regarding Catholic teaching on suicide. If he had been Catholic, is suicide considered a mortal sin? If so, would he have been permitted to have a funeral Mass? What are the things that can prevent someone from having a funeral Mass? The family honored my cousin's wish by having his body donated to science; anything not used for scientific purposes was cremated. Is there any teaching in regard to cremation?

A. Suicide isn't a sin just for Catholics, just as murder, rape, and robbery are not esoteric actions prohibited to us but permissible for those with weaker moral constitutions. These offenses are sins against the natural law and are objectively evil. Now, of course, moral culpability is not determined *solely* on the basis of the presence of an objective evil. You will recall that full knowledge and full consent are likewise required for a mortal sin. It is in the realm of full consent that most theologians and priests would say that many (if not all) people who commit suicide fail to complete the trilogy — that is, that their mental state is usually so defective that they cannot truly give full consent.

Since psychology has helped us understand the human person and the complexity of various contending emotions and forces, the Church has modified her posture in relation to suicide. In other words, whereas suicide was considered an automatic disqualifier for Christian burial decades ago, that is no longer the case, precisely because of the assumption (quite legitimate) that such persons generally do not act in total freedom. The *Catechism of the Catholic Church* deals with this topic with clarity and sensitivity in nos. 2280-2283.

On the matter of cremation, the Church permits this practice — so long as no attempt is thereby made to call into question the doctrine of the resurrection of the body. Again, see the *Catechism* (no. 2301), which also approves of organ donation for scientific and/or humanitarian reasons.

Cremation

Q. Is the Church still completely opposed to cremation? If so, why? People die in fires everyday; it is doubtful that that condemns them.

A. The Church has a predisposition against cremation because it makes more difficult the apprehension that the body is indeed raised on the last day. To equate dying in a fire with deliberate burning after death is ludicrous. The Church took an adamant stand against cremation during the era of the Enlightenment precisely because it was being used by many rationalists as a means to deny and/or mock the notion of the resurrection of the dead. Now that that phenomenon has practically ceased, the Church allows for cremation — so long as the motive is not one of denying this fundamental doctrine of the Christian faith. Finally, the Church never said that someone who is cremated is "condemned"; under earlier law, that individual was denied Christian burial — no more, no less.

Double standard?

Q. In 1994 I lost a son. Abiding by his request, we proceeded to cremate him. Although it is contrary to my belief, I spoke to a priest from the church I attend, and he agreed to it. The ashes were not permitted to be present inside the church during the funeral Mass. He explicitly directed that the ashes be buried. I understood that these are the requirements of the Catholic Church when cremation is requested. My question is this: If these are the rules of the Catholic Church to all her members, how is it the ashes of John F. Kennedy Jr., were scattered in the ocean, and in the presence of a Catholic priest? Do these rules pertain to Catholics worldwide, or do they differ from state to state here in the United States, or are these rules flexible according to the prestige and position you have?

A. You are one of many inquirers on this topic! Once again, a raw nerve has been hit. Cremation for Catholics is a complicated issue, in general, let alone when particular personalities get involved. Let me try to unravel some of the concerns for you.

First of all, the Church is not at all enthusiastic about the idea of cremation and, as you probably know, forbade it until recently because its use for centuries was an implicit way of denying the resurrection of the body. Since few people have that idea today, the doctrinal concern is not so pressing, but there are other matters to be considered. Furthermore, the Church's discipline on cremation has evolved over the past two decades. I suspect that when your son's body was cremated, the rule was indeed that the body had to be brought to the church for the funeral Mass, with cremation occurring later. Therefore, that was not your priest's personal whim.

But, also to show that what I am saying is not my personal whim, I am going to reproduce here verbatim the clarification issued by the Bishops' Committee on the Liturgy in Washington at the time of the Kennedy funeral; I should note that they rely heavily on the 1998 statement of the committee's *Reflections on the Body, Cremation and Catholic Funeral Rites*. Therein, we find the following:

> "The Church's belief in the sacredness of the human
> body and the resurrection of the dead has traditionally

found expression in the care taken to prepare the bodies of the deceased for burial.

"This is the body once washed in baptism, anointed with the oil of salvation, and fed with the Bread of Life. This is the body whose hands clothed the poor and embraced the sorrowing. Indeed, the human body is so inextricably associated with the human person that it is hard to think of a human person apart from his or her body. Thus the Church's reverence and care for the body grows out of a reverence and concern for the person whom the Church now commends to the care of God.

"Thus, while cremation is now permitted, it does not enjoy the same value as burial of the body. . . . The Church clearly prefers and urges that the body of the deceased be present for the funeral rites, since the presence of the human body better expresses the values which the Church affirms in its rites. However, when extraordinary circumstances make the cremation of a body the only feasible choice, pastoral sensitivity must be exercised by all who minister to the family of the deceased.

"The rites of burial for the cremated remains of a body may be found in the appendix to the Order of Christian Funerals. This appendix recommends that when cremation is chosen, the body be cremated after the funeral, thus allowing for the presence of the body at the funeral Mass. When pastoral circumstances require it, however, cremation and committal may take place even before the funeral liturgy.

"Any catechesis on the subject of cremation should emphasize that the cremated remains of a body should be treated with the same respect given to the corporeal remains of a human body. This includes the use of a worthy vessel to contain the ashes, the manner in which they are carried, the care and attention to appropriate placement and transport, and the final disposition.

"While cremated remains may be buried in a grave, entombed in a mausoleum or columbarium or even buried at sea, the practice of scattering cremated remains on the sea, from the air or on the ground, or keeping cremated remains in the home of a relative or friend of the deceased are not the reverent disposition that the Church requires. The cremated remains of the body may be properly buried at sea in the urn, coffin or other container in which they have been carried to the place of committal."

It should be clear, then, exactly what the Church expects from all her sons and daughters. The scattering of the ashes, which apparently occurred, was in violation of these norms. Now, that having been said, did the priest who presided know in advance that that would happen? I have no way of knowing. If he did, he was wrong to tolerate it and surely to be present for it. If he did not, the people who performed the action were in the wrong. At any rate, a great amount of catechetical damage was done by this very high-profile act. I am particularly sympathetic toward parish priests who will be explaining this situation for a long time to come and, even more importantly, trying to enforce proper procedures within their parishes — without looking as though, either, that they are hard-liners or that the Church has a double standard.

Mass benefits

Q. Is one Memorial Mass for a departed soul more advantageous than to be remembered in ten thousand Masses? Can you gain more grace from a Mass said for you while you are still alive?

A. To start with, I don't know what distinction you are trying to make between a memorial Mass and some other kind of Mass. All Masses offered for the dead are the same, and every single Mass is of infinite value.

We could argue that a Mass offered for someone while still alive could be of greater value for the simple reason that presumably the person could receive the graces necessary to lead a holy, blameless life, thus entering directly into heaven; which, of course, is everyone's hope, even if that is not generally the reality.

Stations' changes

Q. Earlier this year, while in Salt Lake City, a cousin of mine visited the renovated cathedral and noticed that the Stations of the Cross were not the same scenes as described in Father Hardon's *Catholic Dictionary*. A month or so later, he and a friend stopped to visit another church and noticed that those stations were different from the traditional ones, as well as those he had seen in Salt Lake City. Where can I find what changes were authorized, including when and why the changes were made?

A. As a devotion, the Stations of the Cross are not subject to the same scrutiny or control as the Sacred Liturgy. Therefore, an element of personal creativity is possible. We have seen, for example, that the Holy Father has invited various individuals over the past several years to compose Stations of the Cross for the Good Friday observance in Rome. Many scenes from the Gospels could be used in addition to the traditional fourteen, to which we have been accustomed. However, I do not think that any other than those fourteen carry the same indulgences — at least not at present.

Breathing orthodoxy

Q. I have an undergraduate degree in philosophy and theology and want to continue on with my education, but I can't seem to find a Catholic graduate program that offers what I want — that is, wholly orthodox teaching rooted in Scripture (as interpreted by the Church), which explores the fullness of the Catholic Faith from the Fathers to contemporary theologians, East and West. I want to breathe with "both lungs of the Church," and I want to read original texts, not just the comments of some twentieth-century theologians who seem to have fallen away from the Faith. Is this an impossible dream, or does such a place exist?

A. Such a place does exist: The International Theological Institute for Studies on Marriage and the Family (ITI) in Gaming, Austria. It is represented in the United States by the Heart of the Church Foundation. Anyone interested in more information should contact: Heart of the Church Foundation, St. Joseph Center, Franciscan University, Steubenville, OH 43952.

Role of the laity

Q. Our present parish situation is really difficult; we have no resident priest or lay parish director. Since we have a number of visiting priests, much of the normal schedule has been kept intact. But is it really the future of the Church to have a parish entirely run by the laity? If a priest cannot be present to celebrate Mass, might a parish director lead a service? If so, then how? What other duties may a layperson have that traditionally have been reserved to the priest? Finally, what is my responsibility in this situation as a parishioner: to question what's going on or just accept it as best?

A. The offering of Communion services should not be regarded as normal or normative; indeed, the recent document from the Holy See on the collaboration of the non-ordained in the priestly ministry makes this eminently clear. It seems to me that a wrong turn was taken a few years back, allowing such an option. It is at least mildly ironic that fifty years ago and more (with transportation being much less than it is today), folks traveled miles and miles on a weekend to get to the closest Catholic church for Mass and, yet, today, with people willingly going to malls twenty-five to thirty miles away for shopping, we don't expect them to do half as much to fulfill their Sunday obligation.

I am unalterably opposed to this phenomenon for many reasons. Such services do the following: separate sacrament and sacrifice; drive a wedge between the confector of the Blessed Sacrament and the distributor; ultimately make people comfortable with a liturgical and theological aberration, eventually having harmful effects on Catholic sacramental theology and on potential vocations to the priesthood (which would obviously make unnecessary such services), and; often have a not-so-subtle agenda of getting people used to seeing a woman preside at a liturgical or quasi-liturgical service. For all these reasons, I think that when a Mass is not possible, the lay faithful ought to gather for a Liturgy of the Word, followed by the recitation of the Rosary — offered for the specific intention of an increase in priestly vocations.

Spotlighted

Q. I recently attended a Marian hour of prayer in our church during which all fifteen decades of the Rosary were prayed. While the experience was spiritually moving, I'm wondering about one thing: a large picture of the Blessed Virgin, highlighted by a spotlight and flowers, was on the altar. Was this proper?

A. I don't think anything ought to be put on the altar, except what is needed for the celebration of the Mass, or the Blessed Sacrament, for purposes of adoration. Surely, some other spot — prominent and dignified — could have been found. In fact, by doing just that, an important truth of faith would have been subtly taught — namely, that no one and nothing ever takes center stage from Jesus Christ, Who is our sole Mediator. This would not have insulted Our Lady, who would never even appear to displace her Son; after all, it was she who directed the stewards at Cana's feast: "Do whatever he tells you" (Jn 2:5).

Eucharist to babies

Q. The *Catechism of the Catholic Church* states: "In the Eastern rites the Christian initiation of infants . . . begins with Baptism followed immediately by Confirmation and the Eucharist" (no. 1233). Do Eastern-rite priests continue to give the Eucharist to babies after this initial ceremony?

A. Practices vary among the various ritual churches, but both the *Catechism* (as you point out) and the *Instruction* from the Holy See two years ago for Eastern Churches make clear that the practice of communicating infants is to continue or be restored; besides that, infants and children are to receive Holy Communion regularly thereafter.

As I have noted here on several occasions, the proper order for the reception of the sacraments of initiation — historically and theologically — is that followed by the Eastern Churches: Baptism, Confirmation (chrismation), and Holy Communion. And, surely, if one has already received Holy Communion, there is no good reason to discontinue it until the age of reason approaches. Granted, the methods and psychology of catechesis will have to be dramatically revised if this catches on in the Latin rite.

Enneagrams

Q. Enclosed is an article from our diocesan paper, co-authored by our bishop, dealing with the enneagram. Isn't this practice a problem? Is there an official Catholic position on this?

A. The article in question refers to the fact that "throughout the ages the Church has borrowed what is good and true from the secular sciences, and even from pagan customs." This is unquestionably so. The difficulty with the enneagram, however, is that it is of no scientific value. Perhaps the best analysis of the enneagram comes from the pen of Father Mitch Pacwa, who was a devotee of the method and became disenchanted with it, first of all, because of its shoddy psychological pedigree, and later due to the spiritual problems associated with it. No, there is no official Catholic position on this, just as there is not on a host of other practices within counseling and spiritual direction.

Marriage rules

Q. Last June, there was an article that appeared in the newspaper entitled "Catholic Church revamps cohabitation rules." The article goes on to mention several dioceses that are revising marriage policies so that cohabitation does not affect the preparation process for marriage in the Church. Chastity before marriage is described as a moral ideal, with the only rationale being that Catholics who abstain from sex before marriage are more likely to be faithful in marriage. What happened to obeying the commandments? This policy seems to encourage not taking the Church's teaching on sexuality seriously. Would you please comment on this?

A. Cohabitation is becoming more and more of a problem. When I was a young seminarian and conducted prenuptial interviews, those who were cohabitating had enough moral sense to lie about their relationship (which does not mean that I approve of lying, but it demonstrated an awareness that something was wrong at least). Today, most priests will tell you that the boldness and amoral sensibilities of even a majority of would-be couples is such that they see nothing wrong with the situation and expect priests to find nothing objectionable, either. It seems to me that the United States Conference of Catholic Bishops is going to have to come up with some policies (for the sake of uniformity of pastoral practice), but, in the interim, diocesan and even parochial policies would be helpful. Let me offer a few suggestions and approaches.

First, it is true that, canonically speaking, a couple cannot be denied a Church wedding simply because they are cohabitating. But that is not as black-and-white as it might appear. We must distinguish it in a variety of ways. Are both partners free to marry? Has their current relationship produced any children? In other words, is there anything keeping them from committing themselves to a permanent, stable, sacramental union at this point? If they are not prepared to separate before the wedding, is there a reason? For example, are there children involved?

If they cannot separate or will not (for whatever reason), I would insist that any Church wedding be little more than what we normally do for a convalidation — that is, for those who are in a civil union they want blessed by the Church. Practically speaking, I would not permit a Mass and no more than the civilly and canonically required witnesses. Why? Because such folks tell us they consider themselves already married; therefore, we ought not to treat them as newlyweds. Furthermore, their attitude reveals they do not think Church teaching to be very important, so why should the Church accommodate herself to their desires for big weddings that have little to do with faith and much to do with secular and social standards. Truth be told, their own refusal to live by Catholic moral principles is a strong indicator that their exchange of vows might well be defective, which is why I suspect the Church will have to come to grips with a more restrictive policy.

Finally, I should note that I believe we need to make it more difficult for people to marry in the Church, precisely to eliminate problematic marriages from the outset and future petitions for decrees of nullity. And this goes beyond matters of cohabitation: if people don't go to Mass; if they are promiscuous; if they dissent from the teaching of *Humanæ Vitae* (Of Human Life) can we seriously expect them to live up to Catholic marital norms and live out their commitment? I don't think so — and the accumulated and accumulating evidence of the past three decades clearly supports my grasp and intuition.

Catholic Internet sites?

Q. There is so much religious information available from on-line sources. Is there a guide to good Catholic sites?

A. With more than two thousand mainstream Catholic sites, there is no doubt that the Internet is being used as a tool for bringing Catholics together and for evangelizing the world. "Information on the Internet that claims to be for Catholics may in whole or in part deviate from authentic Church teaching," writes Brother John Raymond, also known as "The Cyber Monk," who has just authored *Catholics on the Internet*. In his book, he excluded questionable sites and information while still listing thousands of sites that allow people to: visit the Vatican's own home-page; engage in lively discussions in Catholic chat rooms; check out Catholic schools, colleges and universities; bring Catholic resources into the home, and; explore Catholic communities worldwide. *Catholics on the Internet* is a tool that will guide people on a pilgrimage through the abundant source of Catholic information on-line.

Missing Mass

Q. My husband, a convert, is an avid Civil War re-enactor. Many times he ends up in places where there is no Catholic church for miles around and no priest to celebrate Sunday Mass. As his sponsor, I felt duty-bound to tell him that if he knows of a particular place where he knows there will be no chance to attend Mass, he probably should not go. He asked two priests about this and they both said it was OK to miss Mass to attend these Civil War events.

I just wonder if they really understood the question. Somehow, I just can't believe that one can dismiss his Sunday obligation so easily.

A. The old law of the Church made provision for missing Mass when on vacation and the like, should a church be unavailable; the current law would have the same thrust, but the impossibility of finding or getting to a church today is hardly like that of 1917.

What I mean is that Civil War sites are not tucked away in the middle of deserts, as far as I know, and transportation today is almost never a problem. The combination, therefore, strikes me as most unlikely to qualify for a valid missing of Sunday Mass. In the extreme situation that it is not morally possible to attend and your husband does attend regularly under normal circumstances, I would agree with your two priests that the extraordinary circumstances would excuse him.

Not in communion

Q. During Holy Week, my husband and I were traveling out West and on Holy Thursday looked in the Yellow Pages for a

Catholic church. This is a listing I copied word for word: "Our Lady Queen of Angels, The Liberal Catholic Church, traditional Catholic worship with freedom of conscience and open communion offered to all." How can a church like that be a Catholic church, and how can it be allowed? It seems to me that the priests at the church should be silenced or excommunicated.

A. Truth be told, the priests at that church are not in communion with either the local bishop or the Bishop of Rome, which is to say that they are guilty of schism at best and are heretics at worst. They are using Catholic nomenclature to fool the gullible. Their deceitful advertising is reprehensible, but in a free and pluralistic society, there is nothing to stop them from presenting themselves fraudulently.

Find the substance

Q. My third-grade son attends a parochial school, and his next field trip is to see a play that is about a little girl who travels to Africa to be reunited with the father she barely remembers and to meet his new wife and children. Am I being a reactionary when I think that a Catholic school should not have students view plays that tolerate divorce and remarriage in an attempt to redefine the family?

A. Whether or not there is a conscious decision to tolerate a redefinition of the traditional family (which I doubt), I think it a waste of time to view material that has no genuine cultural or historical value. There is so much of substance in our patrimony, and it is readily available today thanks to videos and the like, that it is a crime to waste our time and other resources on materials of doubtful value, either culturally or theologically.

Feeling lost

Q. Why has all been removed from modern Catholic churches that lifted our hearts to God in the tabernacle? I miss the statues of Mary, Joseph, and the Sacred Heart; and the kneeling benches are gone, forcing me to stand during the consecration. Why is Jesus in the tabernacle off in an enclosed room? As an eighty-eight-year-old woman, I really feel lost because God's presence is not there, since I can't see the tabernacle, a saint, or a crucifix.

A. I empathize with you totally. Although your expressions are not precise, your instincts are thoroughly Catholic. Getting rid of statues and marginalizing the Blessed Sacrament has no grounding in the Second Vatican Council or any other official document of the Church, likewise for your being forced to stand. Pray for the faith and enlightenment of those who have perpetrated these abuses, and pray for all your fellow sufferers. May the time of this nonsense soon end.

Recommended

Q. A friend of mine recently received the book *The Authority of Women in the Catholic Church* as a gift. The title seemed to have all the current jargon included, so I counseled caution when reading it. Have you seen this book, and would you recommend it?

A. Yes, I would. Crisis Books has published this fine work by Monica Migliorino Miller. The author offers a detailed analysis of key concepts such as authority, womanhood, and ecclesial life. The book concludes with a chapter on "Mothers of the Church," which is extremely worthwhile.

Intercommunion

Q. Recently, in the interest of ecumenism, our priest invited an Orthodox Catholic priest to celebrate Mass for our teenage youth group, during which everyone (including the priests that were present) received Holy Communion. Is this practice permissible?

A. Your terminology is confused, therefore, I have difficulty giving a straight answer to your question. You speak of "an Orthodox Catholic priest." This is an oxymoron. Either he was a priest of the Orthodox Church or of the Catholic Church. Perhaps you meant a Catholic priest of one of the Eastern rites in communion with the Holy Father. If that was it, then there was no problem whatsoever. On the other hand, if he was Orthodox, there would not have been any obstacle to the scenario you offer from the Catholic side, however, he would have been in violation of the law of the Orthodox Church, which has an even stricter discipline on intercommunion than we do.

Mercy shown

Q. In a previous answer, you indicated what functions a laicized priest could perform in the Church today. Your response was very legalistic and expressed a punitive, vindictive side of the Catholic Church. What doctrinal foundation is there for such Church discipline? Are we talking about our merciful Savior's actions in this temporal period? When sinners are converted, are they to be accepted only partially into the life of the Church? When Christ gave us the great command of evangelization, did He give it with strictures for certain baptized and converted Catholics?

A. Your last few questions have me rather befuddled. I really don't know what you're getting at. So, to return to the original point: The Church believes it is wrong, bad, and unhealthy for men to leave the active ministry, and that it is scandalous. Therefore, the Church seeks to minimize the harm done by the infidelity by restricting the public actions of such an individual, lest people in the Church get the idea that what he has done is acceptable. Frankly, the mercy of the Church has already been shown the man in that she has given him a rescript of laicization, with dispensations from both celibacy and the recitation of the Divine Office. For the most part, prior to Pope Paul VI, the Church granted laicizations on the condition that the priest agreed to live as a celibate and to fulfill his obligation to the Divine Office.

Proper procedures

Q. I am familiar with individuals entering the priesthood in their late fifties. This is only after the spouse was deceased and the marriage annulled and special diocesan dispensation granted. However, I know of a case where a person in his late fifties was granted a marriage annulment by the diocese, while the wife and the children were still living, and was ordained a priest in the Roman rite. After ordination, he was assigned to a parish for a very short time and then transferred to another diocese as an administrator and conducts all priestly duties. Is this a special concession of priest recruitment sanctioned by the magisterium of the Church, or is this a special case of who knows who?

A. Let's clear up some confusion at the outset.

If a man is widowed and then wishes to enter the priesthood, there is no annulment or special dispensation involved. His previous union was dissolved by death, therefore, he is free to enter another marriage or to embark on studies for the priesthood. If, after a civil divorce, a man then presents his case to a diocesan tribunal which, in turn, grants a decree of nullity, he is then free to enter another union or to seek a bishop who might accept him for priesthood studies. You will notice that I said he could seek out a bishop who "might" accept him. That is because many bishops will not take as candidates men whose previous marriages failed.

So, with the man in question, it appears that everything was done according to proper procedures.

Back in the fold

Q. I returned to the Catholic Faith shortly after my wife's death over two years ago after having been away for forty years. I had no idea of the changes that had taken place, and they sicken me. Am I being disobedient if I refuse to hold anyone's hand during the Lord's Prayer and refuse to make the sign of peace with others, which I think is overbearing and disruptive? I now kneel during the Our Father and put my face in my hands during the sign of peace. Am I committing a sin by doing what I do?

A. My heart always goes out to people like you, especially since someone once suggested to me the image of Rip Van Winkle to understand your experience. Unfortunately, there is often more truth than poetry to that metaphor.

No one is supposed to hold hands during the Our Father, so don't feel that you're doing something wrong on that score. As far as exchanging the sign of peace is concerned, if you don't want to shake hands or make some other tactile gesture, a respectful bow or friendly smile would suffice, but I would discourage your being discourteous to others who have no idea of why you would be behaving in that way. That would be counterproductive and offensive to Christian charity. As far as adopting your own posture during the Lord's Prayer, please do not forget that the Church mandates certain positions for the various parts of the Sacred Liturgy. The mandated posture for that point is standing. If you refuse to do what the Church wants there, how can you complain when others, for instance, insist on standing during the eucharistic prayer, even though the Church says they must kneel?

Liturgy is communal worship, which means all must be possessed of a common mentality and exhibit common behavior patterns to ensure an external unity indicative of an internal unity of mind and heart. That is why priests or liturgists who violate rubrics do such violence to individuals and to the community as a whole. Don't fall prey to that, please.

Christian burial

Q. A recent newspaper article indicated that Sonny Bono had been married four times. How was it possible for him to receive Christian burial within the celebration of Mass from the Catholic Church?

A. Divorce and remarriage never constituted an automatic excommunication in the universal Church. It did, however, in the United States until the 1970s, when the American hierarchy brought its approach to the issue into conformity with the rest of the Church. Therefore, in and of itself, a divorced/remarried person cannot be denied Christian burial. It is also important to remember that

Christian burial does not imply sinlessness of life; it merely indicates that the deceased never formally left the communion of the Catholic Church and that the Church now prays for the repose of his soul. Only notorious public sinners can be denied the final suffrages of the Church. I don't think Sonny Bono fell into that category.

What I did have a problem with in his funeral, however, was the eulogy of Cher which, if press reports can be believed, was an in-your-face assault on basic Christian principles of morality. Of course, it is for that very reason that I am adamantly opposed to allowing eulogies to be offered within the context of the Mass of Christian Burial. Such talks can be given at the funeral home or at the graveside once the priest leaves, but to interject them into the liturgy gives people a platform to say all kinds of inappropriate things, to engage in rambling discourses and to undo much of the spiritual and psychological work of the Church's rite. Any priest who has endured some of these talks can witness to the inanity of most of them, as well as the theologically confused and confusing material served up to the congregation. To me, that was the biggest disaster of the Bono funeral.

Abbess role

Q. The enclosed is an extract from our weekly parish paper. This is the third time in the past three years that our pastoral associate has published the portion that says: "In the Middle Ages, women became heads of monastic communities and had some powers that bishops possess, such as giving 'faculties' to hear confession, and making assignments of priests to parishes." Do you know of any authentic teaching or credible source for the above seemingly preposterous statement?

A. There is some substance to what is said, however, what is *not* said is also important, which is to say that we are gazing at half-truths.

Yes, in the Middle Ages abbesses had considerable authority, including the faculties to hear the "confessions" of their sisters, but such "confessions" were limited to violations of the community rule and thus did not concern sins against the Ten Commandments, etc. As far as assigning priests goes, yes, abbesses certainly had the authority to determine whether or not a priest would serve as chaplain for her community — which authority any Religious superior effectively has today as well. These powers were symbolized by the abbess' reception of the miter and crosier, just like an abbot, leading one author some years ago to write a book entitled, *The Lady Was a Bishop*.

Some female communities continue to have what are called "mitered abbesses." In fact, such abbesses do not wear the miter (since it could not fit over their veils), but have it carried before them in solemn procession — although they do carry the crosier. To the best of my knowledge, only two Benedictine abbeys in the United States have mitered abbesses: St. Walburga Abbey in the Archdiocese of Denver and Regina Laudis in Bethlehem, Conn. Historically, however, it is important to observe that neither abbesses nor abbots ever performed strictly episcopal functions — unless, of course, the abbot also happened to have been consecrated a bishop.

The existence of mitered abbesses, both historically and to the present, points to the Church's constant affirmation of the fundamental equality of women and men in the Church, but can never be used to demonstrate that women once had certain faculties related to sacramental ordination, which were subsequently taken away under the drive of a patriarchal and chauvinistic institution. Interestingly enough, many of the honorifics held by women Religious in the Middle Ages ended up destroyed not by the Catholic Church but in the heady collaboration of Protestantism and the modern secular state.

Yet another fascinating aspect to this is that readers my age or older can recall that women Religious, in formal settings, were always referred to as "Reverend Mother" and "Reverend Sister," which titles women Religious demanded be dropped in the 1960s and 1970s. As the proverb asserts, "Damned if you, and damned if you don't!"

Jesus' ethnicity

Q. Two parishes where I have attended Mass have a "black Jesus" behind the altar. The face and hair are the features of an African. I was taught that Jesus was a Jew from Galilee. What will be next, a female Jesus?

A. Inculturation is the attempt to "incarnate" the Gospel in a particular cultural setting; it is an important task, but one fraught with difficulties. Making black Catholics feel comfortable in the Church is a much-needed thing, but Christianity is a historical religion, taking history seriously. Therefore, while we know that God the Father has neither gender nor ethnicity, we are equally certain that His Son, when He came among us, was a Jewish male. Presenting Him otherwise is, in my opinion, an unwise effort at inculturation because it does not correspond to reality and, in some fashion, seems to suggest that were Jesus not portrayed as black (or Indian or Oriental), either He could not relate to such people or they could not relate to Him. This is, obviously, false. Indeed, the essential point to make is that in spite of the particularities of the Incarnation, the God-Man by His Incarnation has united Himself to every human being. The intelligent incorporation of ethnic customs and music and respect for the culture is the route to go, not a denial or falsification of history.

Readiness clarification

Q. Could you clarify a few questions that I have? First, regarding sacramental readiness, about reception of the Sacrament of Reconciliation prior to reception of First Communion: In our diocese, the guidelines for sacramental preparation of children for first Eucharist, as I understand them, have been that children are to receive preparation for the Sacrament of Reconciliation prior to preparation for First Communion, though actual reception of that sacrament is left to the discretion of the parents, since generally the age of reason and formation of conscience, though posited as around seven years of age, is only a generalization and widely dependent on the maturity of the child. If a fathoming of the human reality of sin and the divine reality of forgiveness is necessary for a child to be in the proper disposition to receive First Holy Communion, what is an understandable rationale for reception of this sacrament in infancy? I imagine the rationale will involve a look at different approaches in the Eastern and Western Churches. Also, regarding *The People's Companion to the Breviary*, and use of inclusive language, would you explain your position on this? Is the particular publication one you object to?

A. Regarding your first question, the *Code of Canon Law* mandates sacramental confession *before* First Holy Communion. I would add the following item, however, given your mention of parents as the primary educators of their children: That they are, but parents are not the custodians of the sacraments; the Church is. As such, it is up to the Church to set standards and norms for receiving the sacraments. If a parent argues that his child is not ready for auricular confession, that parent is certainly free to withhold his child from the experience; in choosing to do so, however, he automatically has chosen to postpone the child's First Holy Communion.

You are correct in intuiting that a different psychology and theology are operative in the Eastern scheme of things, and to anticipate some responses: Just because something is done in one rite of the Church does not immediately justify its incorporation into all the others, or any others.

The volume in question has no ecclesiastical approval and, as such, cannot be used in any liturgical setting. To set the record straight, I am unalterably opposed to linguistic engineering masquerading as inclusivity and sensitivity. This ploy is used to undermine the foundations of Christian doctrine in general and of Church teaching on sexuality in particular.

Staying for stations

Q. On Fridays, after morning Mass and the Rosary, those of us who wish to, stay and say an abbreviated form of the Stations of the Cross. At Christmas last year, someone told me it was not appropriate to say the Stations of the Cross so close to Christmas. Are not the stations appropriate any season, since they are a reminder of the reasons for Christ's coming in the first place?

A. I suspect one can make an intelligent argument for either position. In our Western mode of linear thinking, however, most people would probably find the juxtaposition somewhat jarring. The question does remind me, however, of how differently the Eastern Churches often do things: Some years ago, Good Friday fell on March 25 (the feast of the Annunciation), and those communities actually celebrated both events in the liturgy.

Genuflecting

Q. I have sciatica in my left lower back and leg. I cannot walk up steps, except one at a time, and I cannot genuflect on my right knee. I can, however, go down on my left knee with no problem, which I have been doing. It disturbs me that so many people no longer genuflect, and I thought genuflecting on the wrong side would be better than not genuflecting. Should I continue doing this, or should I not genuflect and just bow?

A. Your effort to genuflect, given your difficulties, is meritorious. I would encourage you to do what you are doing.

By the way, few people know why we genuflect to the Blessed Sacrament on the right knee rather than the left. In the Byzantine imperial court, subjects made their obeisance by bending their left knee to the emperor. When that courtly gesture was taken into the Church's liturgical life, it was adapted to show the difference between the two acts of homage. To this day, genuflection on the left knee may be used as a sign of reverence for prelates, especially the Pope, while genuflection on the right knee is reserved for the Holy Eucharist, except in cases such as brought up in this question.

Ring bearer

Q. My husband was a Mason before we married. He was later baptized a Catholic. Since he still wears his Masonic ring, he was told by a priest that he could not receive Communion. Is that true?

A. The question is whether or not he is still a Mason. If he is, he cannot receive Holy Communion. If he is not, then why is he wearing the ring? Fond memories? To make a statement? An attractive piece of jewelry? Those are the questions that need to be answered to determine if he can indeed receive.

Validly received

Q. My friend and I were both confirmed while in the state of grave sin. We knew the Church's teaching on the matter, yet we went through with confirmation nonetheless. We have both confessed our grave sins, including the reception of confirmation in a state of mortal sin. After receiving the Sacrament of Reconciliation, did the confirmation become valid, or are we not yet confirmed?

A. The sacrament was always valid; your reception of it in the state of grave sin constituted an obstacle to your reception of the grace of the sacrament. Once that obstacle was removed through sacramental confession, the fruitfulness became available to you.

Forgiveness of sin

Q. If someone commits a venial sin and then receives the Eucharist, is it theologically sound to confess the sin after reception of this most holy sacrament, since by receiving the Eucharist, one's venial sins are wiped away (*Catechism of the Catholic Church*, nos. 1393-1394)?

A. Forgiveness of sin is not the only reason for submitting one's sins to a priest in the Sacrament of Penance — the possibility of receiving advice on avoiding sin and practicing virtue is also important. Having a regular confessor enhances such a possibility because he knows you intimately, even small faults and venial sins, and thus can guide you in developing a more wholesome personal spirituality.

Promises, promises

Q. What happens if a person fails to keep his side of a sacrificial promise? Last year I promised to fast each Friday as a sacrifice for the abortion holocaust. Sadly, about half of the days I forgot. Intellectually, I know that the Blessed Mother will not hurt my children or others to make me suffer, but what is the penalty? I cannot believe I will get off scot-free.

A. The best thing to do is to take a memory improvement course.

Promises are not vows. While one should not make any promises lightly, failure to keep them is not usually sinful. Nonetheless, one should also look closely into why he has failed to keep a promise if it is as poorly as fifty percent of the time. Was the promise made too hastily? Is strength of will lacking? These are rather fundamental aspects of the question you ask — and they need to be addressed before getting into the sinful dimensions.

Daily privilege

Q. Does a priest have to say Mass every day?

A. I once knew a father of five teenage boys who was regularly asked, "Do we have to go to Mass?" His answer was always the same: "You mean, 'Do I get to go to Mass?'" In other words, participation in the Mass is not something that we do grudgingly, but willingly and lovingly.

To answer your specific question, however, no, it is not required, but it is highly recommended. Thus in the *Code of Canon Law* we read: "Priests are therefore earnestly invited to offer the sacrifice of the Eucharist daily" (276.2).

Extremists

Q. After Mass, someone gave me an informational flyer that disturbed me. The author, apparently a priest-theologian, said that the Second Vatican Council contradicted earlier Church teaching. How can this be? His argument seemed quite convincing.

A. Extremists on the "left" and on the "right" have a few things in common: (1) They refuse to accept legitimate ecclesiastical authority; (2) they misinterpret documents to suit themselves; (3) they engage in wishful thinking. That comes out no more clearly than in the topic you raise.

Devotees of Hans Kueng and of Archbishop Marcel Lefebvre both claim that the Second Vatican Council created a new Church, interestingly enough, for opposite reasons.

The first group wants to justify their own bizarre theological positions and essentially Protestant practices; the second needs to make this type of assertion to justify their adamancy in rejecting the reformed liturgy and other lawfully enacted changes in the postconciliar Church.

Council documents — as they were voted on and approved — are the starting points for what is technically known as "conciliar reception." What does that mean? It is of no use to argue that Bishop X said Y during the Council debates; the reference point is the final document. Interpretation and integration of such documents, furthermore, is not the responsibility of theologians or would-be reformers.

A conciliar document means what the Church's magisterium says it means — no more, no less. In the thirty-five years since the Second Vatican Council, the Popes have been careful to offer a very well-thought-out analysis of the Second Vatican Council, and have always insisted that it is to be viewed in light of Catholic Tradition. Before his final schismatic acts, even Archbishop Lefebvre signed a protocol declaring that he accepted the conciliar documents — in light of Catholic Tradition.

Pray for them

Q. My godchildren live in another state. I have learned recently that what I have long suspected is true — that is, since their baptism they have received no religious instruction or any other sacraments. The nineteen-year-old boy is severely hyperactive and has the mentality of a five-year-old. The sixteen-year-old is a normal, healthy teenager. What can I do when we live in different states?

A. Given the circumstances, it would seem that your influence is limited to moral suasion and prayer. Try heavy doses of both.

Pray for us

Q. I've heard it stated that we "hope for the salvation of all." Wouldn't this kind of hope be opposed to Our Lord's teaching that only few enter through the narrow gate to salvation, but that many follow the wide, downhill road to perdition? Isn't Jesus hinting that, in spite of God's sincere desire, the majority of humanity will not be saved?

A. The Church teaches and believes in what theologians have termed God's "universal salvific will," which refers to the fact that God "desires all men to be saved and to come to the knowledge of the truth" (1 Tm 2:4). Hence, whether or not many, few, or all will be saved is beside the essential point — namely, that God desires the salvation of all. What God desires, we should desire — and pray for.

One a day

Q. Years ago, there was a charitable practice loosely called *Toties Quoties* ("As many times as"). On All Souls Day, we made visits to the Blessed Sacrament and said seven Our Fathers, Hail Marys and Glory Bes for the intentions of the Pope. As I recall, this would gain a plenary indulgence for some poor soul in purgatory, and we could gain as many of these indulgences as many times as we made a visit, etc. Is the indulgence still valid? Is confession and Communion also a necessity?

A. Current legislation permits a plenary indulgence only once within a twenty-four-hour period — whether for oneself or for another.

Christ's calendar

Q. What do the A.D. and B.C. abbreviations mean in Latin and English?

A. B.C. is an English abbreviation, meaning "before Christ," while A.D. is a Latin abbreviation for *anno Domini*, for "in the year of Our Lord." In other words, Jesus Christ is the center point of all human history. Many forces within secular society are working mightily to change these designations to B.C.E. for "before the common era" and C.E. for "the common era." At a commonsensical level, the invented expressions are silly. What is the "common era" common to? Of course, it is Christ, Who makes a unity of human history. Christians need to stay the course on this one, lest world history be used for political purposes to deny what everyone knows to be true — namely, that Christ's coming did in fact make the most significant difference in human affairs.

Interestingly enough, even the Orient now uses the Christian calendar for all international reasons; for us to capitulate to a revisionist view of history would be a great treason to Christ and to the truth at the same time.

Privately addressed

Q. If a known public sinner — for example, someone publicly living with a woman who is not his Catholic wife — for reasons of his own, approaches a priest distributing Holy Communion, should the priest, if he knows or has been made aware of the circumstances of the case, refuse the person on the spot, or allow the person to receive the Lord and then take up the issue privately with the person afterward?

A. Much of this depends on precise circumstances. However, I would play it this way: If it were not common knowledge that the couple is living in an invalid union, I would never take public action. If it were known, I still doubt that I would precipitate an episode at the altar, preferring to deal with it later privately. At the time of Holy Communion, however, I would say quietly, "Kindly see me after Mass." In that context, I would remind the party that receiving the Eucharist in that state is not possible and is, in fact, sacrilegious, requiring me to refrain from communicating that person in the future. I would go on to invite the person to meet with me to discuss possible solutions to the dilemma and encourage him to continue to attend Mass, even if incapable of communicating.

For the Kingdom

Q. A Jesuit school-trained friend says the reason priests are not permitted to marry dates back to the early days when priests were itinerant and churches far apart. Requiring long absences from home, they would have been unable to care properly for wives and families. Is there any truth to this?

A. The story of clerical celibacy is not easy to unravel, with some aspects highly theological and others of a more pragmatic nature.

Your Jesuit-trained friend was given a somewhat simplistic explanation for celibacy. I would start with the Scriptures themselves, wherein we find both Our Lord and St. Paul exhorting Christians to celibacy for the sake of the Kingdom (see 1 Cor 7, especially starting at verse 25). Some recent books on the topic include: *The Case for Clerical Celibacy: Its Historical and Theological Foundations*, by Cardinal Alphons Stickler (Ignatius Press); *Theology of Priestly Celibacy*, by Father Stanley Jaki (Christendom Press); and, for the serious and determined student, works by Roman Cholij and Christian Cochini.

A great comment of Pope Paul VI in his encyclical *Caelibatus Sacerdotalis* (on the celibacy of the priest) was his dubbing celibacy "the finest jewel in the crown of the priesthood."

Time to relax

Q. My question is about servile work on Sundays. Cardinal Pietro Palazzini of Italy said that the distinction between liberal, mixed, and servile works is considered obsolete. This distinction was rooted in a past economic system on which society was based, divided into a world of slaves and freemen, with different general conceptions of work. The *Code of Canon Law* makes no mention of this distinction. It simply says: "They are also to abstain from those labors and business concerns which impede the worship to be rendered to God, the joy which is proper to the Lord's Day, or the proper relaxation of mind or body" (Canon 1247). Apart from the excusing cause of grave necessity, there can also be reasons of rendering public service (police, fire, restaurants, shopping, transportation).

A. I would agree with Cardinal Palazzini, but I think abstinence from work means something different today, not that the restriction does not apply. For instance, if a man sits at a desk all week long, the most relaxing thing in the world for him might well be to mow the lawn on Sunday. What must be avoided at all costs is treating Sunday as a general catch-up day, so that it becomes a huge dumping ground for laundry, shopping, etc. Pope John Paul II's apostolic letter *Dies Domini* ("The Day of the Lord") handles the matter in a straightforward manner, with sensitivity to modern conditions, and in a way that is respectful of the constant Tradition of Judaism and Christianity alike in terms of the proper observance of the Lord's Day.

Priestly function

Q. Are sisters permitted to "lay on hands" for the administration of the Sacrament of Anointing of the Sick? Can the laity use other oils, such as oil from the Holy Land, St. Philomena Oil and other oils that come from weeping statues of our Blessed Mother, to bless and anoint sick people? I have attended many prayer groups where we pray for a sick or injured person, laying hands on them and making the Sign of the Cross on their foreheads or wrists. None of us ever thought this was wrong. Please help us to clarify what to do in these situations. Also, if we are not to do this any longer, what should we do with the bottles of oil that we have in our homes? I have asked other priests about this, and they, too,

were not sure, but seemed to think oils that were not specifically
blessed by the bishop for the anointing of the sick were all right
to use.

A. Only a priest may administer the Sacrament of Anointing of
the Sick, and no one else involved in visiting the sick is permitted
to engage in any activities that simulate the sacrament. The 1998
document on the collaboration of the laity in the ministry of
priests underscored this point. Therein we read: "In using sacramentals, the non-ordained faithful should ensure that these are in
no way regarded as sacraments whose administration is proper and
exclusive to the bishop and to the priest" (article 9).

To the end of time

Q. When we recite the Glory Be, we conclude with the phrase
"world without end. Amen." What does this mean? As Catholics,
don't we believe in a new heaven and a new earth, which God will
bring about at the end of time? I came across the Latin version and
a line-by-line translation once, which (if I recall correctly) read
"forever and ever" in reference to that glory which belongs to the
Trinity. If that translation is more faithful to the Latin, then why
isn't it used?

A. The Latin for the line in question is: "*per omnia sæcula sæculo-
rum.*" Literally, that means "through all ages of ages." That can be
rendered in any number of ways in English: "forever and ever," as
well as "world without end." In reality, we do believe in a new
heaven and a new earth, but usually understood as beginning in
time and reaching consummation in eternity — that is, a pro-
gression (rather than a total destruction or interruption) from one
mode of existence to another.

Reverence needed

Q. Recently, the lady who cleans the altar on Sunday afternoons
found a large Host on the floor resting against the back of the
altar. The size was like the one placed in the monstrance. The

priests were not around on this Sunday afternoon. My friend and I had no way of knowing if the Host was consecrated. This not knowing weighed heavily on our minds, so we felt we should consume it, which we did. My friend has found, on two other occasions, small Hosts on the floor around the altar. Did we do the right thing according to the Church's teachings? Within the last six months, I have personally taken the key from the tabernacle (left there carelessly) on Sunday afternoons and given the key to the nuns. I am not a eucharistic minister, but I am terribly upset over this oversight, which has happened too often.

A. It sounds as though the priests in your parish need a refresher course in the custody of the Blessed Sacrament. You should bring these concerns to their attention; absent an improvement in conditions, the dean or vicar of the area should be apprised. Should he accomplish nothing, the bishop himself should be contacted. What you describe is scandalous and sacrilegious. Your own action was correct, for if one is not sure about the status of a Host, it is better to err on the side of devotion and reverence than the other way around.

Apparition guidelines

Q. I am very skeptical about the authenticity of the apparitions at Medjugorje, as well as apparitions that are allegedly occurring all over the world. But the mind-set of those who "preach" these apparitions seems to coincide with a quote that was allegedly made by Pope Urban VII: "In cases which concern private revelation, it is better to believe, for if you believe and it was proven true, you will be happy that you have believed because our Holy Mother Church asked it. If you believe and it should be proven false, you will receive all the blessings as if it had proven true, because you believed it to be true." Three things seem wrong with this statement: (1) My understanding is that the Church does not prove an apparition to be true. (2) The Church permits us to have a devotion to an approved apparition, but does not ask us to believe in it. (3) If one were to believe every private revelation, there would be a danger of believing errors, as some apparitions are false, and the blessings would be dubious. Did Pope Urban VII actually make this statement, and, if so, was he right?

A. I have never seen this supposed quotation from Pope Urban, but it does not ring true because the arguments you set forth are precisely an accurate summary of the Church's attitude toward all alleged apparitions. And even if it were a correct quote, that would be no more than a particular Pope's private and pious opinion.

To summarize, I would say that the Church always operates from what we might call a "hermeneutic of suspicion" in regard to any and all would-be private revelations.

Therefore, the burden of proof is on the person claiming an authentic religious experience and, even should the evidence be convincing, the Church never asks us to believe, but merely allows us to do so.

Monitoring Medjugorje

Q. Could you please tell me what the Catholic Church has determined thus far about the apparitions in Medjugorje? I have seen a book about the situation by Michael Davies, and I understand there is another one by E. Michael Jones. What's the story here?

A. I am unfamiliar with the Davies work, but I have been reading very carefully the one by E. Michael Jones, *The Medjugorje Deception: Queen of Peace, Ethnic Cleansing, Ruined Lives* (Fidelity Press, South Bend, Ind.). It is only fair to point out at the outset that Jones is no neutral party in the Medjugorje fray; he has been an outspoken opponent from the start. That having been said, I cannot help but be impressed by the data he has garnered, which is uniformly negative — extremely damning evidence about the visionaries, about the Franciscan friars and their involvement, about the ongoing negativity of the diocesan bishops, about the bizarre cultic kind of attraction the phenomenon holds for thousands and how it has even been responsible for the break-ups of families and the like. While the relentless presentation of data is most impressive, the book is flawed by horrific and multitudinous errors in spelling, grammar, and punctuation. There is also just too much of a "bite" to it all. Nevertheless, I would recommend this work as a worthwhile source to balance out so much of the starry-eyed evaluations that appear with such regularity and with so little open and honest critique.

The Church, through the local officials in Croatia, have voiced concern, to say the least. That ought to give anyone pause before loading too many eggs into that basket. I say this, by the way, as one who once was quite taken by the alleged apparitions.

Medjugorje details

Q. Your near-blasphemous attack on Medjugorje needs to be retracted — unless you can provide clear, authoritative documentation for your position. Both justice and charity demand it.

A. You and a dozen others have stepped forward to defend the alleged apparitions. Allow me to present, verbatim, an item taken from the newsletter of the International Marian Research Library in Dayton:

"In reply to a letter of the French bishop, Msgr. Gilbert Aubry of St. Denis de la Réunion, concerning the status of the apparitions in Medjugorje, [Archbishop] Tarcisio Bertone of the Congregation for the Doctrine of the Faith replied, 'It is not the custom of the Holy See to pass the first judgment on alleged supernatural phenomena. This dicastery follows the decision established by the bishops of [what was formerly] Yugoslavia in the Declaration of Zadar, April 10, 1991: ". . . On the basis of the investigations conducted, it is not possible to affirm whether there is evidence of a supernatural occurrence." After the division of Yugoslavia into independent countries, it is the prerogative of the members of the episcopal conference of Bosnia-Herzegovina to study the situation and to issue any new judgments on the matter.'

"In a letter to *Famille Chrétienne*, the bishop of Mostar-Duvno, Msgr. Ratko Peric, stated, 'my conviction and position is that the apparitions or revelations of Medjugorje not only *non constat de supernaturalitate* but that also *constat de non supernaturalitate.*'"

Simply put, this all translates thus: (a) The Holy See does not usurp the role of the diocesan bishop in assessing such situations or that of the episcopal conference. (b) The first bishop of Mostar was categorically opposed to these phenomena, and it was handed off to the episcopal conference. Their judgment is rendered above. (c) The new bishop is even more adamantly opposed to the entire situation than his predecessor, as can be seen from his evaluation, which is given in very technical terms. The terminology open to him involved three possibilities; the first was a positive assessment — *constat de supernaturalitate* (it consists of something supernatural); the second he gives means that it does not consist of the supernatural; the third is even more devastating — it consists of the nonsupernatural. I think the responses could not be clearer to anyone who wants to hear what the Church has said.

Misguided recognition

Q. Being a black person, I was a great admirer of Martin Luther King Jr. in his struggle for civil rights and the suffering he had to endure, and I'm all for the celebration of his birthday. I attend Mass daily, and on the week we celebrated Dr. King's birthday, there was a banner across the front of the altar with his name and picture that remained the whole week, which was very distracting to me. He was not a Catholic, and I have read that he was a womanizer. I cannot ever recall anyone else granted this honor, even our most beloved saints. What do you think?

A. I agree wholeheartedly with your reaction. Regardless of what one thinks of the man's personal morality (which was surely subject to much questioning), it is inappropriate to decorate a sanctuary with images of those who have not been accorded the status of either a "blessed" or a saint. While we might want to use King's birthday as an opportunity to recommit ourselves to some of the ideals for which he stood, it is a mistaken approach to "canonize" him, just as it would be for us to do with other historical figures, such as George Washington or Abraham Lincoln.

Civilly divorced

Q. Is it proper, in the eyes of the Church, for me to allow my husband to live in the house after he insisted on a divorce? As far as I am concerned, the only marriage that is valid is the one blessed by a priest, so even though the marriage is null in the eyes of the land, we are still married in the eyes of the Church. I granted him his wish for a divorce after much pressure, but now he has no place to live. We still care for each other, and always have, but he wants to be free, although he does not date other women at all. Because of our four children, who dearly love their father and are concerned for his welfare, I want him to return home. What should I do?

A. You are correct in noting that the civil divorce has no effect in the eyes of God or His Church, therefore, it would be entirely your judgment call as to whether or not you wanted to allow your husband to return to your home to live. Who knows, your kindness and understanding could be the very catalysts needed to bring him to a spirit of reconciliation that would result in a total mending of fences. Of course, this is the reason why the Church allows separation, but not divorce and remarriage — because with a separation, there is always hope for repentance and reconciliation — the ultimate goals in any situation of estrangement.

Blind spot

Q. Our parish church is laid out in such a way that a Blessed Sacrament Chapel is located behind the altar, separated by a decorative iron screen. The tabernacle is situated in the middle of this room and it is surrounded by chairs and kneelers, except for an access. The screen provides a degree of closure, but everything behind it is clearly visible. The General Instruction of the Roman Missal indicates that "if there is a tabernacle with the Blessed Sacrament in the sanctuary, a genuflection is made . . . whenever anyone passes in front of the Blessed Sacrament" (no. 233). My question is: While it is obvious that I would genuflect to the tabernacle when I am behind the screen in the chapel, do I genuflect to the tabernacle behind the screen or do I bow to the altar when I pass by it in the sanctuary? Does the screen effectively take the tabernacle out of the sanctuary?

A. I would say that the screen has the effect of taking the tabernacle out of view. This would even be true if the tabernacle were actually in the sanctuary but covered over by a grille during the celebration of Mass — as is done is some places.

Brokered baptism?

Q. Recently, I returned to the Church (I was one of those misinformed Catholics who believed that because she was divorced she was excommunicated). I am very grateful to a priest that spoke to me honestly and with compassion. I know I have been away awhile, but I can't believe things have changed this much. My son wanted to have his children baptized. So, he set up an appointment to see the person in the Church that handles the scheduling of baptisms. My son is not married to his girlfriend; he is a baptized Catholic, but not practicing. She isn't Catholic, but has a strong interest in our Faith. This person from the church said she had been thinking of this situation all day and her answer was no to having the children baptized. Then she changed her mind when her assistant told her that her parents weren't practicing Catholics, but did drop her off at Mass every Sunday. Then her answer changed to "we will see." She also made the statement that baptism has changed — that is, it isn't to get into heaven any longer, but to bring you into the family (the Church). My question is: What gives her the right to make this decision? I got out my *Catechism of the Catholic Church* and looked up baptism. I found many things that I think contradict her positions. Who's right?

A. Your instinct to check out the *Catechism* was, of course, quite correct. There, I am sure, you found that while baptism incorporates a person into the Church, first of all, it removes original sin from the individual, which then — and only then — makes possible one's membership in the Church. Baptism introduces someone to the divine life of grace, which is, obviously, the necessary precursor to entrance into heaven.

It is not clear to me just who this woman is/was. Is she the RCIA director? Some kind of pastoral associate? Liturgical coordinator? Whoever she is, she appears to have an awful lot of power. Where is the priest in the situation? Not knowing all the details, I am not in a position to give my own definitive judgment on how everything might have been handled. I would say, however, that your son's living arrangement holds out little promise that he would raise a child as a practicing Catholic. Decisions of this kind, however, are very complex, requiring a knowledge of theology, canon law, and pastoral psychology; therefore, I am not comfortable with the idea of delegating such judgments to the non-ordained.

Suggest to your son that he contact the parish priest to involve him; if he refuses, your son certainly has a right to appeal to the bishop. That having been said, I would make sure that your son understands what he is asking of the Church, and that he be prepared to bring his personal life into alignment with those desires.

Deeper problems

Q. During instructions for getting married some forty-five years ago, we were told that refusal to your mate for the marriage act was a serious sin. I took this probably too seriously and never said no for any reason for twenty-five years. Then one night I told him I was too tired. Now, that has been twenty-some years ago, and my husband has never asked for sex since. I can truly say I have not missed this part of married life. I have not asked him, either. My question is: How much sin is involved here? What are the teachings of the Church on this? Where do I stand with God? It is a constant worry, and I have mentioned this in confession many times, but things don't change. We are in our upper sixties, and it's a subject I wish I could find answers to. Some reasons for this might be my bad feeling toward him, especially around my middle forties, his drinking, job-related problems, five children to raise, etc. Please help! Sometimes I feel like he is just being stubborn or maybe punishing me. But to me, it seems his actions are a little strange. We are not a close couple; mostly we just tolerate each other. Neither of us has been involved with anyone else.

A. While life in the bedroom is the not the be-all and end-all of married life, it is usually a decent barometer for the overall picture. Your description of everything would lead one to believe that, from the outset, your marriage was on shaky ground. When spouses merely accede to marital relations, something is off. Your headache two decades into the union probably just gave your husband the excuse he needed or wanted not to have intercourse, either. "Toleration" is a very sad, minimalistic concept to be applied to the Sacrament of Matrimony, particularly for folks in the twilight of their lives. I don't suppose counseling would be very helpful at this stage of the game, but you should probably try. I wouldn't talk about the sin involved in terms of the sexual abstinence, but rather in relation to the blasé attitude, the noncommunication, etc.; the lack of sexual desire is simply a symptom of far deeper problems.

Wedding bells

Q. Please help me with some Catholic answers regarding my grandson's wedding. He is twenty years old, baptized and reared Catholic. His fiancée is nondenominational and nineteen years old (we don't know if she has been baptized). My grandson believes the prenuptial training offered by the Catholic Church is nonsense, therefore, he will not attend. He and his fiancée are getting married in a nondenominational church. My question is: If he marries under these circumstances, will he still be eligible to receive the sacraments, or is he excommunicated?

A. If you are willing to believe that your grandson's only objection to a Catholic wedding is the so-called nonsensical prenuptial program, I have some land to sell you in a Florida swamp. No one will forego a sacramental union just because of three or four classes; much more must be lying below the surface. As to your specific query: A Catholic who marries outside the Church is living in the objective state of mortal sin and, on that score, is ineligible to receive the Sacraments of Penance [unless he is repentant and prepared to rectify the situation] and Holy Eucharist.

Priest bound?

Q. My ultrasound showed that I was pregnant with a boy. I have heard so many comments from other parents that they would never want their son to be a priest, but I would be absolutely delighted. In fact, I have told God I would gladly have as many as He blesses us with, and they all could become priests. What can I do as a mother to encourage vocations in my children? We attend church, we plan on sending our children to our Catholic school, and we truly attempt to live our Catholic Faith. What nudged you along toward the priesthood? How did your family and friends help you with your calling? How can I encourage without being pushy?

A. I think you have laid out the best plan, not only for your son to be open to a priestly vocation, but simply to turn into a fine Christian gentleman.

In regard to the priesthood, two points. First, a negative: Don't push, because you don't want your son to be a priest to make you happy, but because it is God's Will, which, if followed, will make everyone happy.

Second, a positive: Make sure you follow through on the Catholic-school education. Why? The latest surveys — in keeping with consistent data from the past three decades — tell us that the most powerful indicator for a priestly vocation is attendance at a Catholic elementary and secondary school.

Your support for a priestly vocation is most commendable because all too many parents today are neither supportive — nor even neutral — but often are rather downright negative and hostile to such a prospect. And then we express amazement over a shortage of vocations!

I was extremely fortunate that both my parents enthusiastically supported a priestly vocation for their only child.

Real retreats?

Q. My daughter, in her late teens, wanted to make a retreat. After checking into one close by, I found out the director was a woman in her early sixties, living in a remote area on a lake. The retreat house was a modern cabin; the woman wore the older nun's habit and seemed to be self-supporting. I called the bishop's office but found them to be of no help. The young man I talked with told me anyone could set up and give retreats. I wanted to know if the nun was sanctioned by the Church, but could not get a clear answer. Can nuns live on their own? How do I know if I am paying for a qualified counselor in a safe retreat situation — in a one-on-one setting, rather than in a convent setting? This concerned me. I was assured they would attend Mass every day, be fed well and be safe. One main concern was the crucifix in the bed/chapel area — the body of Jesus was extremely bloodied and seemed to have more bruises, over the entire body, than I ever saw on any other crucifix. It was extremely sadistic-looking. I wondered if she hadn't added to the look of pain Jesus had suffered. I was informed the nun is an artist. We found this retreat place in a Catholic-magazine advertisement. Does someone check out these places that are advertised in our Catholic-information sources?

A. Your concerns are surely valid. Unfortunately, there are nuns who choose to live where and however they please and, even more unfortunately, many of them get away with it. It is hardly possible for local bishops to keep track of such individuals. The best way to ensure that you are involved with a legitimate Religious and a legitimate retreat house is to determine if the community and the facility are listed in the Official Catholic Directory. If they are not, chances are that you have surfaced a problem situation. If they are, and something "kooky" goes on, at least you know that you can contact the diocesan bishop to have him investigate.

Prayer and study

Q. Having been away from the Church for twenty-seven years as a strong anti-Catholic fundamentalist, I returned three years ago. However, I feel pulled in two opposite directions and find myself agreeing with both sides. I find Marian devotions totally unacceptable. Often, I have been in the chapel and see people light candles and kneel before statues of saints and pray there, while gazing at the statue. This seems wrong to me. While I believe in the living presence, I find it hard to accept Eucharistic Adoration when the Host is placed in a golden sunburst and worshiped. Purgatory seems absolutely unbelievable. Yet, I cannot leave the Church — it seems I can't live with it or without it. On one hand, I feel I will offend God if I leave; on the other hand, do I offend God by being a Catholic? In fact, will I lose my salvation by being a Catholic? It is very disturbing to me. I do believe in the Eucharist and enjoy Mass, but wonder about the Mass being a sacrifice and a sacrament. An article in *The Catholic Answer* magazine ("Are You Saved?") gave me some comfort. Somehow I still am hanging in there. Do you have any ideas or suggestions that may help?

A. Old habits and deeply ingrained prejudices die hard, especially those we learn at an intellectual level, which is, I think, your situation.

My first bit of counsel would be to pray to the Holy Spirit for the gift of enlightenment. As what we now term a "revert," your situation is not all that different from many "converts," particularly as you are pulled in conflicting directions by both theological and cultural issues. I would suggest that you become acquainted with the works of Cardinal John Henry Newman: his autobiography, his work on the development of doctrine, etc. He had many of your concerns, but especially the conflicted emotions.

On the Marian front, allow me to direct you to two of my books: *The Catholic Response* and *Mary and the Fundamentalist Challenge*, both published by Our Sunday Visitor (call 800-348-2440). Many former fundamentalists have told me they have found these works to be very helpful in allaying their fears and in actually launching them on a healthy and biblically based Mariology.

Posture particulars

Q. We have a choir director at our church who invites the choir, followed by the congregation, to rise for the Great Amen. I have sung in our choir(s) and/or cantored for twenty-three years, and have always waited until after singing the Great Amen to invite the congregation to rise. It didn't feel right, even though I followed her invitation initially; then I checked the missalette and found that I was right. It dictates that we stand after the Great Amen to recite the Lord's Prayer. Something moved me to check with our parish priest. He informed me that there are no rubrics for the people at Mass. With the reforms that have begun to be implemented, I understand there will be some rubrics for the people. There must be a specific way we universally stand, kneel and sit for our celebration of the liturgy.

A. There are most certainly rubrics for the people. There were no rubrics for the lay faithful in the Tridentine Mass, but that has never been the case in the postconciliar rites. All you need do is consult the missal, which sits on the altar, both in the body of the Ordinary of the Mass and in the General Instruction at the front, and you will find ample directives on posture for the congregation.

As far as the choir goes, however, I think a director might have a bit of leeway since many of them believe that anytime the choir is singing, they should be standing — to improve the projection, etc. So, two exceptions come to mind for standing and not kneeling for the choir: the memorial acclamation and the Great Amen. However, since those ought always to be congregational responses, it does not seem to me it is very urgent to have the choir create distraction by standing for parts during which the congregation will have a different posture.

The Risen Christ

Q. I trust you can clarify a request a devout and orthodox member of my congregation has put to me. How do you answer the accusation that we Catholics practice cannibalism? Since this was never a difficulty for me, I felt inadequate and put on the spot, but promised to get more information. After having read just about every commentary on the Real Presence at my disposal, including the *New Catholic Encyclopedia*, the *Catechism of the Catholic Church* and other respectable texts, I realized that this issue simply is not addressed or is not taken seriously. In your own *Catholic Answer Book 2*, we are told to avoid "grossly physical or bizarre notions," and to "do our best to explain the Lord's presence in the Blessed Sacrament," which, I think, is precisely the point of the cannibalism question. Sure, my faith is not affected here, but my practical sense in looking for an adequate and concise answer seems to have left me.

A. The charge of cannibalism is first documented in pagan Roman literature, recorded by the historian Tacitus. This charge works in two directions. First, it shows certain groups of contemporary Christians that the doctrine of the Real Presence was clearly in place within the Church from the very beginning — and was not a medieval invention. Second, it shows that this doctrine was not well-understood by those outside the Church, having only a superficial familiarity with the true teaching.

Catholic teaching holds that the Christ we receive in Holy Communion is the Risen Christ; hence what we receive is His physical Body (since the Risen Christ on earth and now in heaven had/has a physical Body; obviously, by definition, a body must be physical), but that Body is also glorified, mystical, and sacramental. That explains my caution about avoiding a gross physicality in doctrinal explanations. Pope Paul VI makes the same point in his wonderful encyclical *Mysterium Fidei* (on the Holy Eucharist), which I would most heartily recommend for your personal reading and reflection.

Sedevacantist

Q. Sporadically, throughout the last couple of years, I have heard or read the term "sedevacantist." Could you please elaborate on this term and the beliefs of those labeled as such? If one calls himself this or simply adheres to such a belief, is he schismatic? Is there a relationship here to the Pope St. Pius X Society?

A. *Sede vacante*, in Latin, literally means "with the seat/chair being vacant." It refers to the chair of a bishop and, in this specific case, the Chair of Peter. In other words, people who hold to this position maintain that the man who currently occupies the Chair of Peter does so illicitly and is thus not a real Pope. This movement has come and gone over the centuries, and experiences revivals when doctrine or discipline is found wanting by certain individuals. It came to life again after the Second Vatican Council when some disagreed with either conciliar documents or the implementation of those documents.

As a way of evading the charge of disobedience, the mechanism of "sedevacantism" was brought into play, thus asserting that the disobedient ones were not — in reality — being disobedient since there was, in fact, no one to obey because the Pope was not really the Pope since he had fallen away from the true Faith to which they, the dissenters, were being faithful.

Close examination reveals this is just warmed-over Lutheranism, dressed up in cassocks and spouting forth Latin phrases. These folks seem to forget that if the Bishop of Rome has lapsed into heresy, then the promise of Christ has failed, and the whole Church is finished. Thus they cannot be a remnant of anything, for it has all dissolved!

Archbishop Marcel Lefebvre was by no means a sedevacantist, nor is his Society of St. Pius X — at least not officially. The splinter from them (St. Pius V), however, is in that camp.

Keep the context

Q. Your response to an inquiry concerning Genesis included a defense of myths: "For 'myth' is a very profound sociological, literary, and theological category, indicating a reality that is bigger — not smaller — than words." An extension of this logic leads me to ask if it is then correct, even desirable, to refer to the New Testament as resurrection mythology and to call transubstantiation a eucharistic myth? Are you comfortable with these terms?

A. I do not believe — and have never advocated — using mythological terminology in a catechetical, homiletic or liturgical context. In discussions involving the sociology or psychology of religion, I would be so disposed, but that is a unique setting for a unique community of scholars, for whom the language has that very specific meaning. That does not apply where cases of average Catholics are involved.

Gambling bug

Q. I have recently discovered a sad pastime for some clergy and Religious: gambling. I know a member of a religious community who plays the horses several times a week. I've spoken to him about this, and he insists that it is not a violation of his vow of poverty. Likewise, I know diocesan priests who like to spend their time at casinos and regularly vacation in Las Vegas. Is this really a "priestly" hobby? Perhaps I am being too old-fashioned about this issue.

A. Gambling, in and of itself, is not sinful — a point made in the *Catechism of the Catholic Church* (see no. 2413). For a Religious with a vow of poverty, an entirely different question is raised. My trouble in answering you is that the vow of poverty is interpreted so differently in different communities. For example, if a Religious receives a monthly allowance of $25 to use as he pleases, would it be wrong for him to go to a movie? I don't think anyone would deem it so. And so, if that same allowance were used at the horse races, why should we feel otherwise? On the other hand, if he belongs to a community that takes poverty in a more traditional vein, then I think he is violating his vow. For a secular (or diocesan) priest, obviously there is no vow that comes into play. For either a Religious or a priest, some sensitivity would demand a concern about what people would think seeing a person in consecrated life at the track — that is, is there potential for scandal? If the person in question goes incognito, he is violating Church law, which calls for clergy and Religious to be identifiable at all times.

Overscrupulous

Q. A while ago, I had some sins on my soul that I thought were mortal. I confessed them as such to the priest. He didn't ask any questions and quickly gave me absolution; there were a lot of people in line behind me. Later, I went to another priest and, just to double check, told him those sins and asked if he thought they were mortal. I told him all the details, and he said that they were not mortal sins. What can I do to relieve my conscience about confessing the wrong type of sin to the first priest? Have I made an abuse of the sacrament?

A. It sounds as though you have at least the beginnings of a problem with scrupulosity. You should seek out an experienced and prudent priest to help you nip it in the bud. Laxity is no good, but its opposite extreme is just as harmful, both spiritually and psychologically.

Unworthy?

Q. I am a young woman who was just baptized into the Catholic Church this past Easter. My problem is that I feel unworthy to receive the Eucharist. I felt better and enjoyed Mass more when I had to stay in my pew. I think it's because a part of me still believes that Catholics are bad people, and now I'm a bad person, too. Perhaps that's even why I joined the Catholic Church instead of a

Protestant Church in the first place. I felt as though the Catholic Church would accept me (with all my faults), whereas a Protestant Church would not. I think I still feel guilty about things that happened before my baptism. I know I don't need to confess those things because my baptism washed those sins away. However, I'm still affected by my past. My question is: Should I receive the Eucharist even though I feel funny about it? Will I grow out of this? Should I stop going to Mass until I feel better about it? Sometimes, I think I should have joined the Protestant church of my grandparents. Please don't tell me I'm being overly scrupulous, and don't tell me to talk to a priest about it! I have another problem. During RCIA (Rite of Christian Initiation of Adults) I developed an attraction to one of the priests. He was so very nice to me. I think I may have behaved improperly around him. (I paid too much attention to him by staring), and I fear that this may have hurt him by means of temptation. I now go to a different parish, partly because of this. I feel like I should go back there and fix it somehow, but I haven't been back since my baptism.

A. Given the combination of the two issues you cite, I would respectfully suggest that you seek some serious counseling, from a priest or otherwise. It sounds as though you have many unresolved personal problems lurking around, and religion often becomes a convenient dumping ground for such difficulties. My comments are not made to hurt you, but to help you understand that psychological deficiencies can masquerade as spiritual ones. Take a look at the natural concerns first; my guess is that the supernatural matters will fall into line more readily.

Dispensation matters

Q. Is it permissible for a Catholic to attend the wedding of another Catholic in a non-Catholic ceremony whether or not the Catholic getting married is divorced or has never been married before? If the ceremony itself cannot be attended, is it permissible to attend the reception and/or give a gift given?

A. If the Catholic party has not obtained from his bishop what is called a "dispensation from form" — that is, permission to marry without the benefit of a Catholic service or minister — then that union is invalid in God's eyes. Our assessment of it, then, is that — depending on precise circumstances — the relationship would be deemed one of ongoing fornication or adultery. Obviously, no committed Catholic can give the appearance of countenancing such immoral behavior. Attending the reception after refusing to participate in the ceremony makes no sense, since the very purpose of the reception is to continue in a social way what the ceremony purportedly began.

Parish changes

Q. What is canon law pertaining to moving and changing the name of a parish from one community to another? In this case, there is a separation distance of twelve miles. This was done in our church more than one year ago, and as of the writing of this letter, no official statement or other official documents from the bishop have been received by the parishioners of our parish. No one asked, told or answered questions why this took place.

A. Suppression or merging of parishes is a very volatile issue because emotions play heavily into the equation. We need to remember a few facts at the outset: (1) Parishes are erected to serve the spiritual needs of a particular community. (2) Demographics play an important role in the decision to open a parish, therefore, we ought not be surprised that they play an equally important role in the decision to close or merge a parish. When a specific ethnic group, for which the parish was created, no longer lives in the area and — often enough — no longer even has the cohesiveness necessary to maintain regular contact with the parish, the parish priest and the diocesan bishop are faced with the sad and unenviable duty of coming to grips with the new pastoral situation. This is also the situation for parishes in which major population shifts have occurred.

Some questions that require attention: Is the parish viable? Could another community take over the buildings? Could the addition of some other ethnic group or movement aid the original community in maintaining the historical entity? Could some pastoral services be rendered on the original site, even if the parish was not fully functional? If the parish was to be suppressed, how far would people have to go to attend Sunday Mass? Would it be possible to have one priest serve several small communities, enabling those several parishes to continue in existence? Clearly, these are difficult questions to raise, and sometimes they will produce answers that some people don't want to hear.

Having had the pastoral care of two small ethnic parishes for a combined period of a decade, I know the painful nature of this topic. What I always found somewhat strange and rather annoying was the phenomenon of folks who never came near the parish — even for the "high holy days" — but who expressed outrage when these questions surfaced. They wanted a historical reality to last, but they did not see it as their responsibility to be personally involved.

Another piece of objective data that needs to find its way into the hopper is that distances today are not what they were fifty years ago when, ironically enough, Catholics in rural areas traveled twenty or thirty miles to Mass. Today, not a few people are willing to drive twenty-five miles to a mall or a cinema, but not five miles to a church.

Pastoral planning is essential, and a diocese needs to involve the parishioners that will be affected as soon as possible, so that they can express their legitimate concerns and perhaps even offer alternative solutions. As far as changing the name of a parish, Canon 1218 specifically forbids a name change once a church has been dedicated. Thus if three parishes were merged, each church building would have to retain its original title, while the newly created parish could be designated by all three names.

Moral support

Q. I know your eyes and ears get weary from reading all of the tomfoolery that goes on in the name of the Second Vatican Council. Perhaps our parish has been spared over the years. But can I comment to our pastor that he should rethink why he is a priest, and what a priest is and does; what the definition of "ministry" is; and that the Second Vatican Council meant to reaffirm Church Tradition and not turn it one hundred eighty degrees? I would like to do this in a nonconfrontational manner and not hurt his feelings, for he is truly a compassionate and caring man, but he lets the wackos ride over him without putting up a fight. I'm ready to vote with my hip pocket.

A. Your letter has me somewhat puzzled because you begin by stating that your parish has been "spared" much of the "tomfoolery" of the past couple of decades, but then you go on to talk about "wackos" running things in your parish. Which is it?

If your pastor is a good priest but easily swayed, perhaps he needs some moral support to take more courageous stands against those who manipulate him to do things that are either incorrect or go against his natural Catholic instincts.

Not infrequently, traditionally oriented Catholics think that all priests ought simply to do what is right, and don't see that doing what is right is not easy for anyone today, including priests. And so, it is good and valuable to praise and encourage priests who take unpopular stands because they are going to get heat from their positions — and it is very helpful for them to know that there are at least some parishioners out there who appreciate what they're doing. By the way, the same goes for bishops.

Superstition

Q. What is the Church's position on moneymaking chain letters? Is this ethical and acceptable for a Catholic to participate in?

A. Chain letters are not appropriate to become associated with, independent of whether or not money is involved. They are rooted in superstition and are unacceptable on that count alone.

Unity sought

Q. I am a baptized, practicing Catholic. I am engaged to be married to a baptized Lutheran. He was educated in Catholic schools and attends Mass (without participating) with me every week. He eventually wishes to convert. The problem is that my parish priest will not allow his Lutheran family to receive the Eucharist. I understand the reasons, and this is not the first I have heard of such a rule. However, how come Greek Orthodox can receive at a Catholic Mass? Lutherans believe that the Eucharist is the Body of Christ, and not just a symbol. (I do understand, but I need a logical reason to explain to my future in-laws, who are practicing, devout Lutherans.)

A. First of all, I think we should make your opening comment a bit more precise when you say that your fiancé attends Mass "without participating." I suspect you mean that he attends without receiving Holy Communion.

Anyone (Catholics included) can participate in the Mass without receiving — and if we are in irregular situations or not in the state of grace, we are forbidden to receive. Reception of Our Lord in Holy Communion is the fullest way of participating — but not the only way.

Explain to your future in-laws that the Catholic Church requires not only the same Eucharistic Faith of recipients (and not all Lutherans believe what we do regarding the Eucharist), but also substantial unity.

A sufficient degree of ecclesial unity exists between us and the Orthodox that eucharistic sharing can be seen as appropriate in certain cases. I should point out, however, that the Orthodox are opposed to such intercommunion, except in danger of death or other similar emergency situations.

The public eye

Q. Mother Angelica has endorsed Medjugorje and other questionable and unapproved apparitions on EWTN many times. Yet, good Catholic magazines insist upon endorsing EWTN as if nothing is wrong. I've skimmed through some of these organizations that were invited by Mother Angelica on the Internet, and they even include condemned Maria Valtorta as a valid seer. If you look at enough of these things, you can see that a cult is developing with the Virgin Mary as the new head of the Church because, they imply, we can no longer rely upon the magisterium. I think this is serious business. Instead of mentioning Mother Angelica's weakness, many of our good apostolates are treating her as a saint. I wrote to her and received a reply from someone else stating that it is permissible to promote these things as long as people are praying. Since when does the Church approve this type of reasoning? Isn't it a sin to promote obviously false apparitions that are an insult to the Blessed Virgin Mary and Jesus Christ?

A. I have never heard Mother Angelica or anyone else on the network publicly endorse any unapproved apparitions — although I think there is a general tenor among several hosts in that direction. While I have been a supporter of EWTN because it does indeed provide much worthwhile programming, I do not believe in treating Mother Angelica or anyone else in her position "as a saint." In other words, if you're going to be in the public eye, you must be willing to hear and accept criticism — both positive and negative.

Beyond that, when you engage in a very high-profile apostolate such as a television network (or a publication like *The Catholic Answer* magazine) and claim to represent the Church, you must be extremely attentive to all input, which alerts you to deficiencies or to potential improvement. Folks such as Mother Angelica and I have a heavy responsibility to ensure that those who follow us are hearing precisely what the Church wants them to hear. And when we offer our private opinions (to which we are certainly entitled when they do not conflict with Church teaching), we need to make clear that this is just what we are doing. Finally, we can't afford to be too thin-skinned. As amazing as it may seem to loyal readers of *The Catholic Answer* magazine, there are some people who don't like what I say or what this periodical represents. I feel obliged to listen to their comments and make suitable judgments based on the validity of their claims and how they stack up against official positions of the Church.

Politics as usual?

Q. I have just read Father Thomas Reese's book *Inside the Vatican*. He makes a lot of allegations about Vatican politics. Is this all accurate?

A. That there are politics involved in Vatican life should come as a surprise to no one; after all, inasmuch as the Church is as human as she is divine, politics will be operative. I have read the book in question and find it to be rather snide and disrespectful of Church authorities (especially those with whom the author disagrees) and highly infected with an ideological agenda hostile to more mainstream postconciliar positions.

At times, the ideology seriously affects accuracy. For example, to "prove" that the prefects of the Congregation for Divine Worship and the Discipline of the Sacraments are incompetent (presumably because they are not liberal enough), the author asserts that we have never had a professional liturgist in that post since the Second Vatican Council; this is patently false: Cardinal Augustin Mayer held that position with great distinction and, for years before and during the Second Vatican Council, served as the rector of the Anselmo — the pontifical liturgical institute in Rome. *Caveat emptor!*

Mixed marriage

Q. My daughter recently became engaged to a man who is a member of the United Methodist Church. He will remain Methodist, and she will remain Catholic. The wedding will take place in the Catholic Church. When they went to visit our pastor to make plans, he informed them that our daughter is to remain Catholic and she must see to it that any children born of this union must be baptized and raised Catholic. Our pastor also said that the bishop strongly recommended no Mass be celebrated during the ceremony because it would make the groom's family feel uncomfortable. Needless to say, our future son-in-law seems to be relieved that now his relatives won't be sitting while the Catholics are kneeling and praying during Mass. When our relatives heard this, we were all shocked because Mass is the center of our religion. Are we Catholics supposed to refrain from making the Sign of the Cross or genuflecting, etc., in the presence of non-Catholics inside our church, so as not to make them feel uncomfortable? We feel damaged by the bishop's recommendation.

A. Rest assured that all the advice you have received is completely in accord with the best canonical practice.

Some readers are old enough to remember that, in the old days, the Church expressed her strong reservations about a mixed marriage — that is, a union between a Catholic and a non-Catholic — by permitting the exchange of vows in a simple ceremony celebrated only in the rectory. Then the ceremony was permitted in the church building but outside the sanctuary; then, in the sanctuary, but still with no Mass. Under the impulse of ecumenical considerations, Mass was allowed to be celebrated for a mixed marriage, with the understanding that the non-Catholic party (and all other non-Catholics in attendance) could not receive Holy Communion.

With at least two decades of this permission under our belts, we are in a decent position to evaluate its pastoral utility, and I think the overwhelming conclusion is negative. And so, you will find most clergy actively discouraging a Mass in such circumstances. This decision has nothing to do with downplaying our Catholic identity; if anything, it is a way of helping to restore it. Beginning a marriage in a divided fashion is a countersign and gets the union off on the wrong foot. That's why it is pastorally inadvisable, with little or nothing to do with the Mass making others feel "uncomfortable."

As far as how we ought to behave in our churches in the presence of non-Catholics, it goes without saying that any and all Catholic practices need to be observed; after all, guests should always accommodate themselves to the normal procedures of the family they are visiting.

Seeking salvation

Q. I have a friend who is divorced and is now attending the Rite of Christian Initiation of Adults (RCIA) to become a Catholic. She has never been baptized and has no religious background. Her father was Catholic; her mother was not — she believed the children should choose their religion when they got old enough. However, none of them did. Her father is now deceased, and she feels he would have wanted her to become Catholic, so she has chosen this religion. She was told her first night at RCIA that she would not be baptized at Easter inasmuch as she had to get an annulment first, and it would take until after Easter to accomplish this. She is not remarried and doesn't intend to marry at this point. Why would this interfere with her being baptized? Also, is she actually married in the eyes of the Church? As I read the *Catechism of the Catholic Church*, I understand it to say that both parties must be baptized to have a valid marriage. Please let me know why she would have to have an annulment before being baptized.

A. There are many issues here that need to be unraveled.

First, one does not become a Catholic (or anything else, for that matter) simply because a parent might have wished for it. One becomes a Catholic because he has become convinced that the Catholic Church is the one true Church established by Jesus Christ and, as such, has the fullness of the truth and the means of eternal salvation.

Second, if the person in question is not involved in a second union, I see no reason why her baptism is hanging on receiving a decree of nullity (which may or may not be granted). If she were living with someone in an invalid union, this procedure would make sense, but presumably she is not living in an adulterous relationship.

Third, both parties must be baptized — not to have a valid union — but to have a sacramental union.

Mass musings

Q. There is a religious house in our area that celebrates the Tridentine Mass. Our bishop allows this Mass to be celebrated twice a month in his cathedral, even though he has told me that he strongly opposes the Tridentine Mass. I find hostility expressed toward the Tridentine Mass very odd, especially since it is such an elegant, reverent, and beautiful Mass. Being a former Episcopalian, I find it so much more comforting than the Mass celebrated in the vernacular. We have been told, in this diocese, that we should not attend Mass celebrated by this religious community because by going to Mass there we are not fulfilling our Sunday obligation. Is it improper to do so? Doesn't the Pope outrank a local bishop?

A. You raise a number of interesting and confusing points.

First, if your bishop has given the use of his cathedral for this Mass, how can attendance at it not fulfill one's Sunday obligation?

Second, the options are not quite so stark as you seem to indicate. It is not a choice between the new rite in the vernacular and the old rite in Latin; it is also possible to celebrate — with no one's permission required — the new rite in Latin.

Third, the Pope does not "outrank" a local bishop in his own diocese, in the sense that the diocesan bishop is, as the Second Vatican Council taught, Christ in and for the local church. If he is in communion with the Bishop of Rome, there would never be a need for the Pope to reach into the affairs of the diocese; the Pope's jurisdiction is, of course, immediate and universal, but he does not exercise it capriciously. In an ideal world, he would never have to do so.

Life Teen Mass

Q. We were completely dumbfounded by your response in an issue of *The Catholic Answer* magazine to a question concerning the Life Teen Program and Mass. We attended the Life Teen Masses for eleven years at the church that founded the program. Your response suggests that casualness is the focus of an important part of this program. Nothing could be further from the truth. The focus of this program is on the Eucharist. The program reaches the teens on four levels: spiritual, educational, emotional, and social. The founder, Father Dale Fushek, was given the prestigious Pope Paul VI Award for Evangelization for his work. It is estimated that some forty thousand teens are involved on a weekly basis in the Life Teen Program. You also raised a liturgical question about the Life Teen Mass. The liturgical background of Father Fushek includes a graduate degree in liturgy, ten years as vicar of worship for the Diocese of Phoenix, and service as an instructor of classes in liturgy at the Kino Institute in Phoenix. His parish in Mesa, Ariz., has received national recognition for its liturgy. In addition, when Pope John Paul II came to Phoenix in 1987, it was Father Fushek who was asked to coordinate the liturgy for the papal Mass. To suggest he is ignorant in the area of liturgy is completely unfounded. Our greatest concern is that some people will read your response and accordingly will not consider adopting the Life Teen Program. This would be unfortunate because the Church has done little to reach out to our youths.

A. I received an inordinately large volume of mail in response to my statements about the Life Teen Mass. Yours was the only one that challenged my view; in fact, most responding thought I had been too easy on it, and some even sent me videos of one of these Masses, celebrated precisely by Father Fushek. I do not normally get into personality discussions, but since the program is so closely tied to an individual personality, I have no choice.

The video I saw was an abomination — I don't think I've seen anything worse in years, even in the loony decade of the seventies. The pre-Mass "warm-up" was a disgrace; no one could have imagined he was in a church, let alone being prepared for the offering of the Eucharistic Sacrifice. The joking on the part of priest and entertainers (choir, cantors, etc.) was bizarre; the music was rock 'n' roll at its worst. Once the Mass started, formal aberrations began and never stopped: improvised orations, constant commentary, self-communion by many, a carnival atmosphere. I watched it with a group of people who had been in the Archbishop Marcel Lefebvre schism and have returned to the Church; they regarded the video as evidence for why and how the schism began. I couldn't say much to the contrary. I must note, however, that the homily was superb — a clear and direct challenge to be countercultural; the sad part of it all, though, was that it had no context because everything that preceded and followed it was ludicrous.

Regarding someone's liturgical credentials, I only note that it doesn't take a graduate degree in liturgy to read and execute the General Instruction of the Roman Missal; the depressing truth is that all too many with those degrees are among the prime offenders in failing to give to God's people the worship which the Church has fashioned. With more than twenty years of experience in youth work, I can assure you that it is not necessary to be a ringmaster in order to get young people to appreciate the Sacred Liturgy; in reality, it is quite simple, and it involves little more than giving them proper catechesis and a noble, uplifting style of celebration — that is, it ought to be a sacral event.

Whatever the good intentions of the Life Teen Program, it fails miserably with the Mass if what I saw is the paradigm for all of its liturgical celebrations. I stand by and reaffirm my prior evaluation — and warn priests and parents to shy away from the program unless and until dramatic changes are made.

Sharing your concern for good programs to engage our Catholic youths is just what makes me take the position I have; in its present state, this program does not fit the bill.

Nurturing organization

Q. I get bombarded with "begging materials," and all too often don't know whether they are good or bad. The latest literature to come across my desk is from the so-called Nurturing Network. Do you know anything about this group? Are they worthy of support?

A. I have just received some information on them, which I hope you find helpful.

The Nurturing Network was founded in 1985 by Mary Cunningham Agee as an international charitable organization whose mission is to provide practical, life-saving service to all women who face the crisis of an unwanted pregnancy. It has served twelve thousand women through its extensive network of twenty-two thousand volunteers, who offer counseling, medical services, nurturing homes, emergency financial assistance, and specialized educational and employment resources. Simply put, this group gives someone all the aid she needs to nurture her child's life, all the while safeguarding and fostering her own.

To seek help — or to offer help — call the twenty-four-hour toll-free lifeline: 1-800-TNN-4MOM; or write to The Nurturing Network, Franciscan University, 1235 University Blvd., Steubenville, OH 43952.

Headpieces

Q. Most women no longer wear headpieces, which were once worn as a sign of respect for the Blessed Sacrament. Should the use of a veil be reinstated? I have noticed in our parish that more and more women are using headpieces.

A. Frankly, I was never a great devotee of chapel veils, etc. Once hats went out of style (for men and women alike), the use of mantillas and even smaller head coverings came off as extremely artificial — never mind the pinning of hankies and Kleenexes to one's head! In sum, I would have no strong feelings one way or the other. However, if women want to restore such a practice for themselves, it should be clear that this is a private devotion and that in no way does it reflect on the orthodoxy or heterodoxy of those who employ it or refuse to do so.

Sunday Sabbath

Q. A rabbi on television said that all Christians are going to hell for not keeping the Sabbath (Saturday). Where did we get a Sunday Sabbath?

A. I find it strange for a rabbi to be discussing hell since most Jews don't even believe in an afterlife, let alone a place of eternal punishment. I must say I have never heard Jews complaining about this Christian practice; usually, that comes from Seventh-day Adventists.

The early Christian community attended the Sabbath synagogue service and then celebrated their own distinct rite (the Eucharist) in their homes, usually on Saturday night. When the Christians were excommunicated from Judaism after the year A.D. 70 (the Jewish Council of Jamnia), Christians then joined the two services into one, so that we developed a Liturgy of the Word (the Jewish component) and a Liturgy of the Eucharist. Theological reflection also led the Church to consider that commemoration of the Lord's resurrection would be more appropriate than mimicking Jewish practice, along with the desire — in all likelihood — to place some distance between Church and synagogue, given what had just happened.

On the right side

Q. After having read numerous books on the subject, I have to conclude, as Cardinal John Henry Newman did, that "to delve deep into history is to cease to be a Protestant." In my mind, the scriptural and historical evidence is irrefutable — that is, Martin Luther, his benefactors, and all of his modern progeny were and are, quite simply, wrong. However, I have been unable to find any literature on the schism of 1054, and no one I have asked seems to know too much about it. As a cradle Catholic, how am I to know Rome was on the right side of the schism? Can you direct me to any good books on the subject?

A. The quickest answer — and the best — to determine if the Church was right or wrong in the schism is to consider the promise of Christ to be with His Church until the end of time and to preserve her from error through the abiding presence of His Holy Spirit. Of course, history also presents a compelling case — for example, I have never found a secular history book that indicated anything other than the "Catholic line" on the whole sad story. That does not mean that Catholics did not make mistakes — for example, in political judgments — but the basic theological outline can be found by consulting Our Sunday Visitor's *Catholic Encyclopedia* under "Schism, Eastern." A valuable book on the scriptural basis for the primacy of the Bishop of Rome is by Scott Butler, et al., *Jesus, Peter and the Keys: A Scriptural Handbook on the Papacy*, published by Queenship Publishing.

Prayer is not voodoo

Q. My brother is a practicing homosexual. I love him and his friend very much. I have talked with them about the situation. I told them that God didn't make Jack and Bob to be together, but rather Jack and Jill. At times, I feel my brother thinks I feel as if I'm better than he is. He knows I've turned my life around and that God comes first. Maybe he faces the truth when he is around me. I do not condone his lifestyle, and I pray for him and his friend every day. My mother told me to quit praying about him, because I might pray something bad on them. She's afraid that that will happen. I know that if anything would happen to my brother, mom would blame me for praying for him. So, I tell her I don't pray for him anymore. I know I am to love my brother and his friend — and I do — but it is so difficult when it is in my immediate family. Sometimes I just sit and cry about it, and other times I get angry. Other times I feel sorry for them. If I go to his home, they think I'm condoning their lifestyle. But I am not. I can't just shut my brother out of my life, can I? Please direct me.

A. I don't know of a single family that is not touched and indeed torn by dysfunctional situations, whether of adulterous second unions, abandonment of the Faith, or the problem you identify. It seems to me that our first response to any such crisis should be to echo St. Paul's line: "There but for the grace of God go I."

From what you say in your letter, I think you're handling things very well. The one who concerns me most is your mother. Why would she ever imagine that praying for someone will bring that person harm? Christianity is not voodoo. Perhaps if she got her act together a bit better, you might have some additional support to help your brother. See if she is willing to visit a priest or counselor to deal with her spiritual and psychological baggage.

Fashion police

Q. When Jesus rose from the dead and visited His disciples, what was He wearing? I pose this seemingly impertinent question to provoke a discussion of the nature of the Resurrection.

A. While we do not know what Jesus wore after the Resurrection, we do know that He ate and drank (see Lk 24:42f). It would appear that the evangelists did not consult a fashion expert, perhaps supposing that food was more important than clothing. Seriously, though, the clearest reason for the insertion of information about the "bodiliness" of Christ in the post-resurrectional period was apologetical in nature — that is, to prove beyond a shadow of a doubt that He was truly alive and that He had risen in a human body, albeit one that had been glorified and which thus transcended the limits of time and space, as seen in His ability to pop in and out at will (see Jn 20:19, 26).

Mixed meaning

Q. Enclosed is the prayer of the faithful, which our parish used last Sunday. The third item really struck me as bordering on heretical: "For all Catholics, that they recognize that no single group or viewpoint in the Church has a complete monopoly on the truth, we pray." Please let me know if I am reading this correctly or being overly critical.

A. One reading of the above petition can be harmless, if one means that the personal agendas should not be presented as normative for everyone. For example, praying in tongues versus praying the Rosary. If both come under the Catholic tent of spirituality, we ought not to dogmatize one over the other. Another reading could lead one to believe that all contending viewpoints are co-equal, so that what one believes or does not believe about birth control, divorce and remarriage, the ordination of women is a matter of indifference. This is obviously impossible for a Catholic to hold or to teach — since the magisterium has spoken decisively on such matters, thus closing the door to further debate and alternate opinions.

Eucharistic norms

Q. I have been attending a pastoral-ministry workshop that is basically reaching out to the sick and homebound. Throughout the discussion, the topic of giving these people the Eucharist came up. Most of the people in this program are already eucharistic ministers. Several people asked if the wife or husband of the person you were visiting were not Catholic, if he or she could receive the Eucharist if he requested it. It was my understanding that we, as eucharistic ministers, cannot give Communion to someone who is not Catholic even though he may believe in the Real Presence of Christ. I know, through reading the canon laws and *Ceremonies of the Modern Roman Rite*, that priests are allowed to give someone Communion not from our Church, but it never addressed the use of extraordinary ministers being allowed to do that. After much discussion in our group, we decided to ask the priest whether or not we, as eucharistic ministers, could decide to give Communion to a "good person" who wants to receive but is not Catholic. The priest said he would give Communion to someone like that, implying that it was permissible. What is the teaching of the Church on this subject of priests and eucharistic ministers giving Communion to non-Catholics? I feel that the priest did a disservice to the group by causing more confusion about the teachings of the Church.

A. A very good reason for us not to use extraordinary ministers of Holy Communion is that judgment calls such as you describe are not within the competence of the laity. The general theological and canonical principle is simple: Only baptized Catholics in the state of grace are to be admitted to Eucharistic Communion. Exceptions run along these lines: The non-Catholic Christian in question professes the same Eucharistic Faith as we; he has no access to a minister of his own ecclesial community for a prolonged period of time or it is an emergency situation; he makes a spontaneous request for the sacrament. In most parts of this country, one or more of those conditions would be very difficult to be verified. Certainly, my pastoral experience does not bear out the normative nature of such exceptions — if that is not a contradiction in terms.

In sum, I do not think the non-ordained ought to be making judgments on the suitability of others for Eucharistic Communion, and I think the response of your priest was, at best, inadequate.

Cautious approach

Q. One of my sisters and several friends from her parish had started a prayer group, which meets weekly to pray for vocations. They had been using a program from the Marian Movement of Priests, which included an opening prayer, the Rosary, a reading from one of the Blessed Mother's revelations to Father Stefano Gobbi, and a closing prayer. Some disgruntled parishioner contacted the archdiocese and received a response, which he/she anonymously forwarded to each of the participants in the prayer group, which called into question the "suspect" nature of the group, and said that Father Gobbi "has been cautioned by Vatican officials not to present his own words and insights as if they were revelations or inspired messages." Naturally, none of those involved in the prayer group would want to continue in an activity considered to be of a "suspect" nature. Could you please provide a little information on why, if true, the Vatican considers the activities inappropriate?

A. I have not made an in-depth study of the Marian Movement of Priests, but I, too, have heard of Vatican skittishness about some of the "revelations" and that the movement has been asked not to equate Father Gobbi's musings with those of heavenly revelation. To bring people together to pray for priests; to pray the Rosary in common; to learn more about the Faith — these are all good things that I know are part of the movement. Relying on private revelation is something I always shy away from — no matter from whom, just on the fundamental Catholic principle that all such revelations are "suspect" until categorically approved by the Church. A new book on this topic comes from the pen of Kevin Orlin Johnson (whose work has been featured in *The Catholic Answer* magazine), entitled, *Apparitions: Mystic Phenomena and What They Mean,* published by Pangæus Press.

"Pastoral provision"

Q. Several years ago, you wrote about the Vatican's "pastoral provision" that gave permission for "Anglican-use" parishes to continue using elements from the Book of Common Prayer in Catholic liturgies. Is anything in the works for a similar provision for former Lutherans, or converts from other denominations?

A. To the best of my knowledge, no. I think that the almost unique attachment of Anglicans to the Book of Common Prayer and the large numbers of them involved in coming into full communion with the Catholic Church (relatively speaking) made the Holy See more open to the maintenance of some kind of liturgical reality that allowed them to remain connected to their roots — especially since Anglicanism is such a liturgical communion, and since the genius of the Book of Common Prayer was precisely that it could always be interpreted in a Catholic sense.

Not inappropriate

Q. I am wondering if it is proper to underline or use highlighters in my Bible.

A. There are people I know who have such a love and respect for books that they would think it nearly sinful to mark up any book, let alone the Bible. I don't fall into that class of individuals. As far as the Bible is concerned, it needs to be accorded profound respect, but it is not to be worshiped. As such, I believe that noting the fruits of one's reflection and meditation or an insight gained is hardly destructive, let alone sacrilegious. In my opinion, it actually enhances the value of the volume.

Word of caution

Q. I have been dating a man who is twice divorced. He is a baptized Catholic; his first marriage was to a non-Catholic; his second marriage was also to a non-Catholic; and other marriages were by civil ceremony. I am Catholic, and I never married. Can I marry this man in the Catholic Church with a Mass and also receive Communion?

A. My first word would be one of caution. With all these unions, should we not pause to consider the proverb, "Where there's smoke, there's fire"?

I cannot answer your question because I lack an essential piece of information: Was his first marriage one that took place in the Church? If it was, it is presumably valid and, therefore, he is not free to marry. Surely, the subsequent unions were not valid, but the first one holds the real question mark. On your last point, if you are free to marry him in the Church, then there is no question about Mass and Communion.

Games of Chance

Q. A non-Catholic relative, in response to my remark that the Church says gambling is a sin, said many Catholic parishes have offered bingo games on a regular basis for many years and asked why that isn't considered gambling. I can't answer this apparent inconsistency and even wonder if there is any difference between a person playing bingo and, say, someone who goes to Atlantic

City, N.J., for a day of enjoyment, part of which includes spending $10 on slot machines?

A. Gambling is not considered necessarily sinful. The *Catechism of the Catholic Church* is clear on this (see no. 2413). If someone has extra money and enjoys gambling, he is free to participate in that form of entertainment. The problem comes in when people use money destined for necessities (food, shelter, etc.) to gamble or when the activity becomes compulsive. In this sense, gambling is like alcohol consumption; in and of itself, it is neutral, but it can become sinful when abused.

Territoriality

Q. Is there a Church law that states that we, as Catholics, must belong to a particular parish?

A. In Canon 518 it reads: "As a general rule a parish is to be territorial, that is, it embraces all the Christian faithful within a certain territory; whenever it is judged useful, however, personal parishes are to be established based upon rite, language, the nationality of the Christian faithful within some territory, or even upon some other determining factor." So, yes, the Church considers the parish to be the basic cell of ecclesial life and, even if the membership is not rooted in territoriality, it should be a stable and ongoing reality.

Prison not a war

Q. I now have the privilege of volunteering for prison ministry. The first time I went, we gave Communion, and I was appalled to see everyone receiving Communion, except one person. I do not believe they were all Catholics. When I said something about this, I was told that this was considered like wartime and was permitted. I told a Dominican priest about this, and he stated that under no circumstances should I give Communion to a non-Catholic. What are your views on this important subject?

A. Being in prison is hardly comparable to a wartime scenario. Even if it were, the three standard conditions must prevail, to wit: the would-be non-Catholic communicant must have the same Eucharistic Faith as we; he must be deprived of a minister of his own for a prolonged period of time; he must make a spontaneous request for the sacrament. I don't see any of these criteria verified in your case.

Group canonization

Q. Often, the Pope canonizes a group of people. When this happens, is each individual in the group investigated as thoroughly as in a one-person canonization? Are there miracles required through each person, or as a group? When we read about canonizations, sometimes we have never heard of the person(s) before and never hear of them again. Also, sometimes in reading, there will be a beautiful quotation from a more obscure saint. We are inspired to know more about them and their writings. Is there a place to find out more about newly canonized and obscure saints? Catholic bookstores are filled with books about the most famous only.

A. Each person within a potential group canonization must be thoroughly investigated, but only one miracle is needed. For the more recent canonizations, I have found the short biographies that appear in L'Osservatore Romano (the official newspaper of the Vatican) to be both helpful and interesting. Another worthwhile resource would be the respective religious congregations to which newly canonized saints may have belonged. For instance, the Claretian seminarians martyred in the Spanish Civil War are presented in a vivid and edifying manner by a publication done by the Claretian Fathers in Chicago.

Consultative in nature

Q. I am the parish-council president of a military chapel overseas in Puerto Rico. In that role, I am often put in the uncomfortable position of having to question the practices of the assigned priest.

I find this uncomfortable because I was always taught that the parish priest was the final word and authority on all religious matters, and that he would never go against Church law. While I am no longer that naïve, I still have qualms about questioning pastoral practices. Are there any specific guidelines or suggestions for the role of the parish council? I would like to establish a role for our successors to minimize future confusion.

A. It is a sad commentary on the present moment that lay people have to take on the role of watchdog for the parish priest, but, if necessary and if done with respect and charity, a vital role is played.

The *Code of Canon Law* mandates a finance council for every parish; it does not do so in regard to a parish or pastoral council. Individual dioceses may have a particular law that does do that; in some places, the same people may serve on both boards. That having been said, it is critical to know and to accept the fact that all these bodies are consultative, or advisory, and have no deliberative status. In other words, the parish priest is required to consult, but he is not required to follow the advice that is offered. This is the same situation as the relationship between the diocesan bishop and a presbyteral (priests') council. The role of the president or even of the body itself is not spelled out in universal law because it would be impossible to take into consideration the myriad possibilities that could surface from diocese to diocese, let alone from country to country. Particular guidelines are usually given by diocesan officials.

Stages to sainthood

Q. Why are there the three beatification stages of blessed, venerable, and saint? Wouldn't it be simpler just to declare someone definitely in heaven or merely hopeful? Are canonization decisions given the charism of infallibility? Who is the devil's advocate, and what is this office's history?

A. The canonization process actually involves four stages: Servant of God, Venerable, Blessed, and Saint. For a detailed explanation,

I would recommend consulting Our Sunday Visitor's *Catholic Encyclopedia* under "canonization" and "beatification."

In summary form, let me note the following: Preliminary phases of the process entail obtaining information on the candidate's life, studying his writings, and getting testimonies from eyewitnesses (if possible). One miracle is needed for beatification and another for sainthood; miracles are not needed for martyrs. It is common theological opinion that the final act of canonization is truly an exercise of the charism of infallibility.

Wrong signal

Q. Is it permissible to blow military taps, on a trumpet, inside the church, immediately after Mass on Palm Sunday?

A. What would be the point? This is yet another example of attempts to make liturgy into an all-too-literal dramatization of historical events. While the liturgy "re-presents" historical events, it does not "re-enact" them in a slavish way. Furthermore, playing taps might well be appropriate for a military hero (which Jesus surely was not), but our faith is not in a fallen hero but in a Risen Lord; hence, the wrong signal is given at several levels.

Open to the supernatural

Q. I recently told a priest-friend of mine that I wanted to go to Mary's House in Loreto, Italy. He said that Mary was never in Italy and that he thought that it was all a myth. Is this so?

A. The tradition behind the Holy House of Loreto has never asserted that Our Lady ever lived in Italy; it holds that the house in which she lived in the Holy Land was transported to its present site by angels. Obviously, Catholics are free to believe this story or not — as they are with any other supernatural phenomena. For a more detailed account of this pious tradition, consult Our Sunday Visitor's *Catholic Encyclopedia*, under "Loreto, Holy House of."

While I tend toward the skeptical in all such situations, I feel compelled to remind others (and myself) that we cannot rule out the possibility of miraculous events, lest we do violence to so much of Sacred Scripture, which actually takes these as givens. Modern man's discomfort with the miraculous is his problem, not God's, as he has tried consistently to limit God to what man can or cannot do, to what man can or cannot conceive. In effect, then, we forestall and obviate the entrance of the "God of the surprises," Who is just as willing to make appearances in our lives today as He was two thousand and five thousand years ago.

Differing orders

Q. I would appreciate some information on the different orders of religious life and the duties they entail. Frankly, I always thought that priests, friars, monks, and brothers were all ordained and that the only difference between them is that some took a vow of poverty, or lived in religious or cloistered communities.

A. Friars, monks and brothers are all Religious — that is, bound (*religio* in Latin) by vows or promises of poverty, chastity and obedience. Some priests belong to the secular clergy (most of whom are diocesan priests), while others also belong to a religious order or congregation. All Religious likewise live in community, unless special circumstances demand otherwise for a period of time — for example, a sick parent requiring one to live at home outside one's religious family. Secular clergy may or may not live a common life. Some of the better-known male religious communities would be the Jesuits, Dominicans, and Franciscans.

Perpetuating schism

Q. I have a question regarding bishops ordaining bishops without papal approval. This is not just academic, since my brother and part of his family are involved. If the Archbishop Marcel Lefebvre group can never have bishops, when the priests die, will the religion become invalid, since the archbishop cannot ordain new priests? Please explain.

A. Perhaps the first point to make is that the Lefebvre schism is just that — a schism, not a new religion.

Archbishop Lefebvre's ordinations were illicit once he himself was suspended. His episcopal consecrations were not just illicit but also brought with them, by those very facts, an excommunication for him and for those who accepted his consecration, for the very reason that perpetuating a schismatic hierarchy perpetuates schism, which is totally destructive of ecclesial unity. To sum up, the men he ordained as either priests or bishops were indeed validly ordained and thus confect valid sacraments, but they do so in a manner that fosters disunity; hence, the penalty of excommunication. You ought to do your best to dissuade your brother from supporting such efforts.

Illicitness run amok

Q. My question concerns Archbishop Marcel Lefebvre. Recently, a Bishop Williamson administered the Sacrament of Confirmation in a church in Phoenix. His homily included very patronizing remarks about Pope John Paul II. My question is, what is the situation regarding Archbishop Lefebvre? Since this Bishop Williamson is associated in some way with Archbishop Lefebvre, is the sacrament he officiated at valid? What should my reaction be as a practicing Catholic in a case such as this? Fortunately, there was no one I knew of who was participating at this ceremony, but it bothered me when I heard about it and thought I should react — outside of prayer, of course.

A. To all external data and appearances, Archbishop Lefebrve died in a state of excommunication. The four bishops he consecrated, including Bishop Williamson, were all excommunicated with him because they participated in episcopal ordinations that occurred not only without a papal mandate but in defiant disobedience of a direct papal order not to proceed with the ordinations.

Bishop Williamson's confirmations are valid but illicit and, as acts of repudiation of papal authority, sinful and sacrilegious; no good Catholic ought to support his movement in any way. It must be mentioned that weddings witnessed by schismatic priests are not only illicit but invalid, because those priests lack proper jurisdiction and delegation for the Sacrament of Matrimony.

As I have said many times before, while I have a strong empathy for Catholics who have suffered much lunacy at the hands of their clergy over the past three decades, no good Catholic can countenance actions or movements that are set up as parallel ecclesial communities. This is hardly different from the goals of left-wing extremists such as Call to Action and the Women's Ordination Conference. In all these instances, individuals are trying to create their own church to gratify their own desires/needs, independent of the Church that Jesus Christ established on the rock of Peter.

Solemn exposition

Q. While Mass is being said in the church proper, should the monstrance in the chapel be covered, especially if all adorers go into the church for Mass? What if there is someone in the chapel? There is a curtain in the chapel that I speak of, which is drawn before Mass, but because of the round style of the church, it is possible for some (not many) in the congregation to view the monstrance in the chapel.

A. Solemn exposition should never occur without at least one adorer present. If, therefore, the priest foresees that everyone will indeed leave the adoration chapel to attend a service in the main body of the church, the Blessed Sacrament should be reposed in the tabernacle and not just have a veil placed over the monstrance.

Self-denial

Q. My wife is a Methodist. She brought home the bulletin, which had a reflection on Lent, in which the minister wrote: "At the heart of it, the purpose of Lent is not self-denial or self-negation." I have enclosed the piece for you. I have always thought that self-denial is a major part of Lent, contained within the three traditional observances of prayer, fasting, and almsgiving. Your comments, please.

A. Your wife's minister goes on to say: "Lent is a preparation to receive God's most powerful gifts: a transforming grace that forgives us even from the Cross, a Resurrection that overcomes the power of death, and the promise that God is with us always through the abiding Spirit of Jesus Christ." He is absolutely correct, however, we cannot receive those tremendous gifts without preparing ourselves for them — and, as you noted, a major aspect of that preparation requires self-denial. Indeed, one of the reasons we need God's mercy is the very fact that we are usually so self-absorbed. Self-denial seeks to break that hellish cycle, to provide the Lord with an opening for the outpouring of His redeeming love. When we are full of ourselves, there is no room for Him — and that is the fundamental sin. Emptying ourselves of ourselves is an essential step on the road to conversion and new life.

Nuncio duties

Q. Just what is a papal nuncio?

A. The technical name is "apostolic nuncio," who is an archbishop appointed by the Pope to represent him in two venues — to the hierarchy of a particular nation or region and to the civil government (for whom he serves as an ambassador of the Holy See). The most important role his office plays, however, is in the surfacing and selection of candidates for the episcopacy. After hearing the advice of local bishops and receiving input from laity and Religious as well, the nuncio recommends to the Holy See priests to fill diocesan vacancies. Such lists are passed on to the Congregation for Bishops in Rome, which in turn passes on their recommendations to the Pope.

Priestly attire

Q. Enclosed is a newspaper clipping of a local priest saying Mass without a chasuble. This is a common practice in our parish in warm weather. Is this kosher?

A. The picture you enclosed was that of a priest celebrating Mass at a correctional facility. Technically, for just cause, one may wear only an alb and stole for Masses celebrated outside a sacred place. I do not agree with that norm for several reasons, but that is the norm. So, in this particular case, no liturgical law was violated. In a church or other sacred place, however, it is never permissible for the principal celebrant to omit use of the chasuble. If it's so hot, get lighter vestments, or open the window, or turn on the air conditioning — or, offer it up.

Blessing forms

Q. I recently heard a lecture by a priest in which he said that any baptized person can/may bless rosaries, statues, water, etc. When questioned on this statement, he added that a priest "is not needed to bless these religious objects." His firm belief was that lay Catholics should exercise their right and responsibility of baptism. I subsequently checked the *Code of Canon Law* and the *Catechism of the Catholic Church,* and I could find no justification for his position; even deacons are limited to certain blessings.

A. The *Book of Blessings* allows for the laity to bless certain objects when a priest is not available; the form of the blessing is different, and no Sign of the Cross may be made. The possibility for this to be done in limited and extraordinary circumstances has clearly opened up a Pandora's box, and now ecclesiastical officials find themselves scrambling to try to get the proverbial cow back into the barn. The law is unambiguous, but my experience leads me to conclude that in many quarters it is roundly ignored — for the very reasons you heard from the lecturer you quoted. In other words, there is an intense desire on the part of some in the Church to contribute to that process so condemned by Pope John Paul II of "clericalizing the laity and laicizing the clergy."

What we are discussing here, however, should not be construed as an attack on such traditional practices as a parent blessing one's child/children before bed; that blessing generally consists in tracing the Sign of the Cross on the child's forehead, accompanied by a prayer for the child's restful and safe sleep. That is the kind of blessing that fits in perfectly with the idea of the family as the "domestic church," very different in scope and intention from attempts to make priests out of lay people to advance a hostile theological agenda.

Mistranslation likely

Q. I recently read an excerpt from St. Louis de Montfort that has caused me concern. In part, it reads: ". . . among those who claim to worship the Blessed Virgin." I am troubled that a saint would consider worshiping Mary.

A. I would be troubled, too, but I suspect that it's more than likely a problem in translation or in the change in meaning of words over time. Also, we find, at times, in the writings of Marian devotees such as de Montfort, the language of exuberance and love, more than precise theological terminology, is not unlike a man saying to his beloved, "I worship you." Presumably, he really doesn't!

The Church is eminently clear, though, that there are three gradations of *cultus* (another problematic word in English!): *latria* (the worship due God alone); *hyperdulia* (the veneration due Our Lady); *dulia* (the veneration owed the other saints). In no way can we ever cross the line and give the adoration due the Holy Trinity to any created being, including the Blessed Mother. Not only would it be theologically wrong, but it would thereby be most displeasing to the very saints so treated because they want nothing more than for God to shine forth in all His glorious splendor.

Dissident gimmick

Q. For all the wrong reasons, I am an unconfirmed Catholic, married outside the Church twice to two Catholic women who were divorced, whose husbands were alive. I finally got tired of being deprived of the Eucharist for so long when I always had felt it to be so important. To compound the matter, I became convinced the Mormon Church was the only place I could find peace of mind. As a member, I learned more about the Catholic teaching than in all my previous years in the Church. And you must know, the whole foundation of the Mormon Church (and other Protestant Churches, I guess) rests on the belief that the so-called "Great Apostasy" has taken place, invalidating the entire Catholic Church. Since the Bible clearly states the Church (Catholic) Jesus Christ established during His ministry shall prevail until the end of time, what is the right answer to those who claim the apostasy is complete and therefore calls (in the case of the Mormons) for the reestablishment of the Church or as an offshoot of Lutheranism? I would truly welcome your help.

A. You really have two distinct questions: one, personal; the other, theological.

Your personal reconciliation with the Church depends on whether or not you are living with one of the divorced-remarried women. If you are, your ongoing state of objective adultery does not allow you to receive any of the sacraments, unless you are willing to live as brother and sister. Then you may approach the Sacrament of Penance, return to Eucharistic Communion, seek out a priest to take instructions for Confirmation, receive that sacrament, and continue on living a truly Catholic life. If your partner has received a decree of nullity for her previous union, or if her husband has died, then you would be free to marry in the Church and should proceed as I suggested above.

As far as the "Great Apostasy" is concerned, this is a gimmick used from time immemorial by dissidents to justify themselves and their causes. Martin Luther argued in that fashion and, yes, so does the Church of Jesus Christ of Latter-day Saints. You are quite correct, however, in citing Our Lord's promise that He would be with His Church until the end of time — that Church which is built on the rock of Peter (see Mt 16:17-19). Furthermore, any objective historian — religious or secular — will tell you that no existing ecclesial entity can lay claim to such foundation except for the Catholic Church, presided over by the Bishop of Rome. Finally, logic helps, too: Are we to believe that Christ allowed His Church (His Bride) to wallow in ignorance and error for more than a millennium, so that Joseph Smith could come and be her Savior, as though the Lord Himself and His Spirit could not do the job Themselves? To accept such a theory is a sign of either tremendous arrogance or incalculable naïveté.

Anglican-use parish

Q. What in the world is an Anglican-use parish?

A. Two decades ago, large numbers of Episcopalians in this country began to join the Catholic Church as a result of serious problems within their own ecclesial community in areas relating to both faith and morals. In some instances, groups of laity with their priests expressed interest in a kind of communal entrance into full communion with the Catholic Church — probably the first time that had happened since Father Paul Watson of Graymoor entered with his entire religious family in the early part of this century.

The Holy See looked favorably on these requests and has allowed such parishes to be formed, retaining certain elements of their Anglican liturgy and other cultural dimensions, under the direct oversight of the local Catholic bishop. To provide for communication between these Anglican-use communities and the Holy See, and to tend to their happy incorporation and ongoing life in the Catholic Church, Cardinal Bernard Law, former archbishop of Boston, was named the direct representative of the Pope.

This canonical reality is part of a larger picture, properly known as "The Pastoral Provision," which also allows for a married Anglican cleric to petition the Holy See for Catholic ordination, along with a papal dispensation from priestly celibacy.

The entire pastoral provision is, in fact, a concrete sign of the pastoral solicitude of the Holy Father, not to burden unduly people who want to be organically united to Christ's one Church, although unable to fulfill all the normal, but not essential, aspects of Catholic identity. In other words, following the ancient principle, Pope John Paul II has determined that we should take the course of "in essentials, unity; in doubtful matters, liberty; in all things, charity."

Catholic community

Q. I know many priests from area churches, but none personally. My problem is that when I die I really don't have a particular priest to say a Mass. I have made all my arrangements at the funeral home in the chapel, but I don't just want a strange priest, who didn't know me, saying my Mass. I want a Rosary said with a Mass and do not know a priest close enough to ask to do my funeral. I have no children and my brothers and sisters all live out of state and are Baptist. I am a convert since 1988 and attend Mass every day, wherever I am. I feel my home parish priest doesn't like me because all my money does not go to his parish. What shall I do?

A. Let's unravel some of your problems.

First, you ought to be registered in a parish and support that parish financially and otherwise. That does not mean, however, that all your resources must go there, and your pastor has no right to expect such. The parish priest, by the way, may not refuse to bury someone who is a Catholic in good standing.

Second, the Church has a standard ritual for Christian burial, consisting of a service at the funeral home, the Mass itself at the church and prayers at the grave. Personal preferences would be taken into account for choosing from among many Scripture passages that are assigned for funeral Masses and selecting music. Beyond that, there is not much else that calls for personal touches.

Third, you refer to a "strange" priest as undesirable. In a Catholic understanding of things, no priest is ever deemed a "stranger"; indeed, every priest is a father to every member of the community of the Church. We have begun to lose sight of this in recent years, under the influence of clerical personality cults. And so, people ask for particular priests as celebrants for Sunday Mass, and all too often many priests encourage this unfortunate development.

The theological truth is that any validly ordained priest can do God's work of salvation for us, for which we need to be immensely grateful. That does not mean that certain priests are not more attractive than others at any number of levels, but that personal dimension ought never cloud the more fundamental, essential fact of Catholic life.

Shut-in visits

Q. I would like to speak up for me and my fellow lay eucharistic ministers who have been visiting nursing homes each Sunday. We pray and listen to all the residents, and then we distribute Jesus to them. For the most part, they are Catholics, and we must assume they are practicing Catholics. You have implied that lay ministers do not have the competence of making the decision about whether to distribute Holy Communion to people who may or may not be Catholic. You clearly imply the priest or deacon can make the judgment call much better. How wrong you are. We lay people are visiting and praying with these residents each week. Our pastor/deacons visit two times per year. Just because they are ordained, according to you, they are more competent to make the judgment call.

A. Let me start off by indicating that I think it shocking that shut-ins get visited by a priest (or a deacon, who can't even anoint or hear confessions) only twice a year! That phenomenon, however, is not unique to your area. In fact, I have visited the sick, who have told me that they have not seen a priest in a decade; this is indeed scandalous. Ministry to the sick should be a top priority of every priest, something that should never be pawned off onto others, especially on a regular basis.

In truth, lay people fulfilling emergency roles (which is what an "extraordinary" minister should be doing) do not have the competence to make pastoral decisions. Far more distressing, however, is your offensive and haughty tone, which more than suggests your conviction that you are performing these tasks by right, not by delegation and not under abnormal conditions. If that is your concept, either you were terribly trained or you have taken onto yourself quasi-clerical status, which development has been roundly condemned by the Holy Father.

Obligation holds

Q. This statement was in our bulletin under the Pastor's Pen column: "We as Catholics never worried too much about evangelization in the past because parishioners were a captive audience; they had to come to Mass under pain of mortal sin. That is not the attitude so much now. Something to think about." Is it no longer a serious sin to miss Mass on Sundays and holy days without sufficient reason?

A. Although Catholics should want to participate in the Eucharistic Sacrifice each Sunday, we still have the obligation, whether we like it or not, whether we are faithful to it or not. This is not unlike various parental obligations, which may or may not be met. We don't change the nature of the responsibility, but we do distinguish between good parents and bad parents, depending upon how well they fulfill their duties toward their children. The *Catechism of the Catholic Church* (nos. 2180-2183) and the *Code of Canon Law* (Canons 1246-1248), along with Pope John Paul's apostolic letter *Dies Domini* (on keeping the Lord's day holy) — all make the same point: To be a good Catholic demands Sunday Mass attendance. The *Catechism* and the *Code* place the discussion in a positive context by noting that such participation is a "serious" obligation; the negative, or flip side, is that failure to observe a "serious" obligation results in the commission of a "serious," or "mortal," sin.

I would also take exception to your pastor's caricature of the past. I think we were exceedingly concerned with evangelization in the 1950s, for example, which would explain why millions of non-Catholics found their way into the Catholic Church during that decade in this country, which is surely more than we can say about the last two decades.

Seeds of faith

Q. To have a Catholic baptism, both parents must be Catholic — correct?

A. Incorrect. Neither parent must be Catholic if the candidate is an adult. If the candidate is a child, it would make no sense to baptize if at least one parent were not a practicing Catholic, since it is necessary for the seed of faith planted in baptism to grow, and growth requires nurture, and the most important form of Christian nurture is good example.

Baptism normative

Q. If a person has never been baptized into any faith, is he considered Christian? What is the teaching of the Church on entering heaven without receiving that sacrament?

A. Being a Christian means being baptized. No one can be considered a Christian without baptism, which incorporates one into Christ and His Church, granting access to eternal salvation.

The Church has traditionally recognized three forms of baptism: water (the usual); blood (by which an unbaptized person dies for his faith in Christ); and desire (by which someone wants to be baptized but is incapable of receiving the sacrament).

The sacraments in general and baptism in particular are the ordinary means of salvation, but, as St. Thomas Aquinas reminds us, "God is not bound to the sacraments." By this, he means that although God has ordained that salvation should come through the Church's sacramental system, God, as sovereign Lord, can act outside that system for His own reasons. An analogy might be helpful here: God has established the laws of nature, which He generally allows to go on their way. However, as Lord of nature, He is free to suspend those laws according to His Will; such suspensions we refer to as "miracles."

Christian baptism?

Q. I've heard that the Catholic Church recognizes the baptisms of all Protestant churches, and that converts do not need conditional baptism. We attended the baptism of a Methodist baby — and it was anything but valid. It did not even mention the Trinity, but mumbled some reference to God. It was strictly informal, the words were chosen by the young minister, and very watered down in meaning. So perhaps we ought to rethink the possibility that not all such ceremonies are valid. In one Presbyterian church, the children were "dedicated," not baptized, using only a damp finger on the forehead. How can a person entering the Catholic Church be assured that an earlier baptism was truly valid?

A. You are absolutely correct. In many denominations, especially under the influence of feminism, the baptismal formula has been changed from "in the name of the Father, and of the Son, and of the Holy Spirit," to "in the name of the Creator, Redeemer and Sanctifier." This is a substantive change and invalidates the sacrament.

At a doctrinal level, the alteration substitutes functional titles for personal names for the Godhead. In other words, our notion of God deals with what God does for us, instead of who God is within the inner life of the Holy Trinity.

And so, now it behooves a priest receiving a non-Catholic Christian into full communion with the Catholic Church to ascertain the precise rite followed for that person's baptism. If there is cause to doubt that the traditional Trinitarian formula was used, accompanied by the pouring of water, the candidate should be at least conditionally baptized.

Generation gap

Q. I recently read a statement by Pope John Paul where he said, "Unburdened by the ideological agenda of an earlier time, they (the young) are able to speak simply and directly of their desire to experience God." What ideological agenda was the Pope referring to?

A. I suspect the Holy Father was trying to say, with some delicacy, that today's youths do not have the psychological baggage of the preceding generations. All too often we find people of the previous generation exhibiting knee-jerk reactions, especially relating to authority issues. Young people find leftover hippies and flower children to be "weird," and they are not interested in engaging in silly battles, particularly in terms of matters related to faith.

Recently, a priest shared with me an anecdote that might illustrate what I'm talking about. This young priest has beautiful, solemn Masses every weekend in his parish. Not too long ago, a new chaplain was assigned to the nearby military installation; his style was, shall we say, more "casual." A woman of forty approached my friend to inform him that henceforth she and her family would be going to the base Masses because she found them more "meaningful" and "less formal." Last weekend, her two teenage children showed up for Mass at their own parish. When the pastor asked them why they were not going with their mother, they simply said they didn't like the new scene, and thought it "goofy."

The generation gap identified by the previous generation has now come full circle, as young people think their agenda to be very dated and not in keeping with their concerns.

Perpetual virginity

Q. Lately, while watching a television program about Mary, the theme was that Jesus was not the only Son of Mary — that He had brothers. To me, it was very confusing since, as a Catholic for sixty years, I was never told by any priest or read in any book or magazine that Mary also gave birth to other sons — and that one of them, James, was the first Bishop of Rome (I always thought that Peter was the one). Please shed some light on that matter. What is Rome's position on any brothers/sisters that Jesus supposedly had?

A. It is a dogma of faith that Mary was a virgin before, during and after the conception and birth of Jesus. In the early Church, when some began to question this teaching, the adverb "ever" was added to Our Lady's title of "Virgin" — thus "ever-Virgin." The so-called brothers and sisters of the Lord were, in all likelihood, cousins or other close relations who, to this day, in Semitic languages, are referred to as "brothers and sisters." The St. James usually referred to as the Lord's "brother" was the first bishop of Jerusalem, not Rome. The clearest biblical evidence to me that Jesus was an only child comes from St. John's version of the crucifixion, as Our Lady is given into the care of St. John. If there had been any other natural children, why would Our Lord confide His Mother to someone not related to them by blood? And, would any of Mary's children not express outrage at having their mother given away to a stranger?

It is good to know that all the principal Protestant reformers (Martin Luther, John Calvin, and Huldrych Zwingli) believed in Mary's perpetual virginity; it is only modern fundamentalism that has taken to a denial of this doctrine with a vengeance. Zwingli, interestingly, even attempted to prove the perpetual virginity from Scripture by citing Ezekiel 44, which speaks of the messianic gate being shut closed once the Messiah has passed through; Zwingli saw that passage as applicable to the womb of the Blessed Virgin Mary.

Good eating

Q. I would like to know what the legend of "hot-cross buns" is since we only have them during Lent.

A. Many of these old customs are lost or shrouded in history. As best as I can uncover it, in this case it seems to go like this: In medieval England, there seemed to be a practice of baking sweet buns, icing them with a cross and eating them on Good Friday. A rather strange penitential practice, I would hazard! Eventually, they ended up being eaten throughout Lent. My guess is that at the outset, they were designed to be imitations of the unleavened bread of Passover, and then someone "put icing on the cake."

Orthodox standing

Q. Much has been written in recent years regarding the standing of Eastern Orthodox Churches. Recent letters by Pope John Paul II and Curia officials continue to emphasize the legitimacy of their apostolic succession, validity of their sacraments, and the catholicity of their teachings. In short, they are fully "catholic" in all things but recognition of papal primacy. The theological and jurisdictional differences between the Orthodox and Oriental Catholics have, for practical purposes, all but disappeared — even to the point of permitting shared sacraments when appropriate to the good of the Faith. The core of my question is this: What is the theological standing of a Latin-rite Catholic who transfers faith allegiance to an Eastern Orthodox Church? If one has a proclivity to the Eastern spirituality and liturgical worship, is transferring to a sacramental Catholic Church, recognized as based on the apostles, schismatic?

A. Regardless of personal spiritualities and liturgical proclivities, truth is always a foremost consideration in seeking out an ecclesial home. In other words, no matter how beautiful the music or the incense, if the fullness of truth is not present, one cannot — in good conscience — belong to such a body. And the unfortunate truth in this instance is that, despite the theological nearness, Eastern Orthodoxy is still defective in at least one substantive way: It lacks the whole truth about the hierarchical nature of the Church in that it fails to accept the primacy of Peter's successor. Therefore, one could never encourage another or consider for oneself the option of being Eastern Orthodox. What we must do, following the lead of the Pope, is to pray mightily that this critical issue will be so resolved that full ecclesial and Eucharistic Communion can be restored between the Church of Rome and the separated churches of the East.

Twenty-twenty hindsight

Q. I recently met a Jewish convert to Catholicism who claimed that St. Josemaría Escrivá worked with and assisted Francisco Franco in his rise to power in Spain. This is a most distressing accusation because of the many good works I have read of him. I have never doubted the spiritual advice that has come from his books or his organization, Opus Dei. Do you know of any historical evidence that could shed light on his activities?

A. I am often amused at how Monday-morning quarterbacks always have twenty-twenty vision, if you would pardon the mixed metaphor.

The persecution of the Church during the Spanish Civil War was one of the most vicious and violent the Church had ever undergone at any time or in any place in her history. Thousands upon thousands of clergy and Religious were martyred, along with thousands of committed laity. I personally know one priest who endured it all as a twenty-two-year-old seminarian, and his stories are the stuff of the catacombs — and worse. Whatever Franco's faults were, he was certainly not an anti-clericalist, and his ascendancy did mean relief for the Church. Whether or not Escrivá collaborated with him, I do not know. But I do know that in an imperfect world like ours, when the Church has to deal with civil authorities, who are also less than perfect, various arrangements are not necessarily what we would always desire. One thinks of the several concordats worked out between the Holy See and certain governments — for example, post-Risorgimento Italy; pre-World War II Germany. These were judgment calls, which were hard to make in very difficult historical circumstances and not done in the luxury or convenience of arm-chair philosophy or history from the vantage point of half a century. Our own involvement with politicians today on the pro-life cause is another case in point: Do we refuse to talk to any who do not "buy" our approach hook, line, and sinker? Or, do we endeavor to do the best we can — in small increments — to return our society to being a culture of life?

If St. Escrivá did see some merit in Franco's rise to power, I imagine it was in that light. And unless strong evidence to the contrary could be marshaled, both justice and charity would dictate such an assessment.

Sound-byte theology

Q. My boss, a young Catholic woman, is engaged to a young Catholic man. She is planning to run away with him to a tropical island in August and, in a very romantic fashion, get married on a cliff overlooking the sea. She already inquired about the possibility of a priest on this island performing the matrimonial service, but was told that it had to be done in the church. She said that she will resort to getting married even by a justice of the peace, if it means that she can be married on top of the cliff. I've tried several times to urge her to make arrangements to be married by a Catholic priest here, before or after her jaunt to the island, so that her marriage would be valid in the eyes of the Church, but she kept coming back with, "I was told that we would have to undergo five days of pre-Cana, and I just don't want to do that." In an attempt to justify her loose form of Catholicism, she said to me: "Adam and Eve were not married! Where was marriage then, if it is so important?" I said that the Sacrament of Matrimony had not been established at that point. I'm not exactly sure of what my answer should have been. Could you give me some insight on what I could say?

A. It should be clear to anyone that this young woman does not have a strong identification with the Church. Indeed, this is generally so for people who want to be married on beaches, mountaintops or the rim of a volcano, let alone underwater or being dropped from an airplane by parachute! This is frivolous and nonsensical, making a mockery of a sacred act, which, of course, is why the Church doesn't allow such things. For a good Catholic, his or her concrete point of contact with the living Church is the parish church, the site of one's sacraments of initiation, sacramental reconciliation, and at least weekly nourishment through the Holy Eucharist. Not to have one's marriage solemnized in that environment would make no sense at all. If one finds another ambiance more conducive to prayer and the spiritual, it is a sign that one's spirituality is fueled by something other than Catholic gases, and that issue would need to be addressed long before any serious discussion of a Catholic wedding could take place.

On her second assertion about the non-marriage of Adam and Eve, you are absolutely correct, in that sacraments did not emerge until the coming of Christ. However, it is the constant teaching of Judaism and Christianity alike that God's placing of Adam and Eve in the garden was the establishment of marriage as a divinely ordained state and not a privately arranged affair. Certainly, by the time we get to the Decalogue, it is clear that marriage is mandated by God, hence, the prohibition against adultery. Since she seems to revel in sound-byte theology, suggest to her that you would be willing to discuss her approach to things when Almighty God plops her and her fiancé onto that tropical island, without any assistance from airplanes, boats, etc. Then the Adam and Eve analogy might have more applicability.

Grave abuse

Q. I have a non-Catholic cousin who receives Holy Communion during our family Masses. The priest is unaware of this. I have given him the holy chalice though I always feel guilty in doing so. Am I committing a sin?

A. If you are aware of this fact, surely the rest of your family is, too. Where are they? Why have they said nothing, either? This is a grave abuse and should be stopped immediately. If your cousin is invincibly ignorant of the Church's position on this, be very gentle and kind in bringing this to his attention, explaining carefully why the Church holds what she does (as we have done on numerous occasions in *The Catholic Answer* magazine; see any of *The Catholic Answer* books for a detailed presentation of this matter). The priest should be informed as well, and let's hope that he sees the problem for what it is.

Scandalous

Q. At the Memorial Mass for John F. Kennedy Jr., on the night before his so-called burial at sea, I couldn't believe how the priest went outside the church handing out Communion to any and all who stuck their hands out. In the paper there is a picture of a hand holding the Host and a copy of *U.S. News and World Report* magazine. Why do priests allow this to happen?

A. I, too, witnessed that debacle. The laughing, joking, and grabbing for Hosts was scandalous to me and to everyone who has spoken of the episode to me. I can't begin to justify what happened, but, then, some wonder why two-thirds of Mass-going Catholics don't believe in the Real Presence!

Schismatic group

Q. Could you please provide me with some information regarding the Society of Pius X and its official status in the Church. I have teens who are attending Mass with this group, and they have been told the opposite of what I have been saying about the group.

A. This is a community comprising followers of the late Archbishop Marcel Lefevbre, who was in a tenuous ecclesiastical position for many years and was finally excommunicated in 1988 for consecrating four bishops not only without a papal mandate, but in open defiance of a specific order not to do so. The official reason generally given for association with this schismatic group is a desire to have the Mass in Latin — that is a red herring, in plain English.

Mass can always be celebrated in Latin by any Catholic priest at any time, according to the revised rite of the Church. Or, where the local bishop has allowed, the preconciliar rite may be celebrated. Therefore, Mass in Latin is rather generally available. Other issues are much more germane to its existence: an overall rejection of the Second Vatican Council; a specific refusal to accept the conciliar document on religious liberty; and various social and political theories.

Now, I hasten to add that I am often in great sympathy with the average people who frequent these churches, given the lunacy to which they are not infrequently subjected in many main-stream parishes around the country — that is, their attendance is sometimes not occasioned by dismissal of Church teaching or liturgical renewal, but by a desire to find refuge and safety in a par-ticularly bad time or place.

At any rate, the Holy See has been crystal clear in forbidding Catholics from involvement with the group: Those who actually join are subject to the same penalty of excommunication; those who are less formally associated (only through Sunday Mass, for instance) are guilty of the sin of perpetuating schism and disunity in Christ's Church.

Basic civility

Q. My neighbor is a barber; he is also a Lutheran. This past spring, the barber was invited to the ordination of one of his cus-tomers. He knew he would not be able to attend because of his work, but asked me what would be an appropriate gift. I sug-gested money, so that he could buy personal things since all his other needs would be taken care of. He sent the new priest a check; the check was cashed, but the new priest never thanked my neighbor in any way. What can I tell my neighbor about this?

A. There is no excuse for bad manners in anyone, let alone a newly ordained priest. In my experience, I find Catholic people most tol-erant of the foibles of their clergy, but two areas seem to rouse the greatest resentment: unanswered phone calls and failure to send thank-you notes. Pope John Paul II, in *Pastores Dabo Vobis,* his apostolic exhortation on the formation of priests, talks about the importance of candidates for the priesthood having what he calls certain fundamental "human" qualities, long before we endeavor to develop any supernatural dimensions — on the presumption that, in the words of St. Thomas Aquinas, "grace builds on nature." Basic civility is one of those characteristics, in my judgment. The most you can do is apologize to your Lutheran friend for the behavior of the new priest; if you know the priest, you should likewise bring it to his attention in a kindly but firm fashion.

Pushing it a bit?

Q. I would like to have your explanation about the following situation going on in our family. My third son, Charles, has been married for ten years, outside the sanction of the Church, but has the desire to return to Mass and Holy Communion. In the process of talking to our parish priest, the pastor gave Charlie collection envelopes to start supporting the church. That I know is one of the precepts of the Church. The problem is this: I have a niece whose situation is the same as Charlie's (married outside the Church), goes to Mass every Sunday, would like to contribute, but wants her envelopes listed in her married name (civil), but our parish priest agreed only to give her envelopes in her single name. Her grandmother, who is my sister, has been in disagreement about this situation, who thinks our priest is too strict with the young ones, causing them to leave the Faith. Is there really any solution to this matter? My sister thinks the female should be treated just the same as the male. This situation may seem like something trivial, but our Catholic theology must have an answer.

A. While I don't think the ministers of the Church ought ever to appear to countenance an irregular marital union, my hunch is that the priest in question may be pushing the issue a bit too far, with the potential for counterproductive results. Suppose the same couple had children in the parish school. Would he expect the teachers to refer to the mother of these children by her maiden name? The fact that there is an obvious desire to do as much as possible to live a Catholic life, just short of the whole nine yards, is reason to rejoice — not to punish.

Double-dipping

Q. Two years ago, our son and his wife (who is not Catholic) had their daughter baptized, first at his wife's church in the morning and then again at the Catholic church in the afternoon. Was this wrong? This just doesn't seem right to me. I think our granddaughter was baptized by her mother's stepfather, who is a minister. I wonder if the priest knew of the first ceremony. Everything tells me this was wrong. If so, would you explain why?

A. Your Catholic intuition is very strong and very good. To repeat a sacrament that confers an indelible character — for example, baptism — is wrong and sacrilegious; the second ceremony is, in reality, but a simulation of a sacrament. If the priest knew about the earlier rite, he should not have performed the second; in all likelihood, he was kept in the dark.

Intercommunion

Q. I have a son who left the Catholic Church and joined the Anglican Church because, for one thing, he could get a job there. (He's also on his third wife.) He later came home for a visit and mentioned he'd like to go down to my parish church for Mass. I said something about the fact that he couldn't receive Communion, whereupon he gave me a long story about how in the Middle East it is considered quite acceptable to have intercommunion between Catholics and Anglicans (if they couldn't get to their own church). It was news to me, but I didn't want to be more Catholic than the Church, so I said nothing. The pastor went along with it (he had been in Jordan, an Arab country), but I never felt right about it. Then I came across, in a good Catholic magazine, the statement: "The Catholic Church does not allow intercommunion with Anglicans, while the Anglican Communion encourages the practice." It also quoted Pope John Paul II in *Ut Unum Sint* ("That All May Be One"): "For the sake of furthering ecumenism, these norms must be respected." So it looks as if we'd been had. The pastor may have made an honest mistake since he had been in Jordan. But my son has been in Jerusalem for the past thirty years, and he knows there's a Catholic church on every block and an Anglican church on every other one (and all the rest of the denominations, too). Can you give me some appropriate sources that will settle the matter once and for all?

A. The most obvious point to the entire discussion is your comment that just because something is possible in Jordan does not necessarily make it either possible or right in Vermont! It sounds as though your son wants his cake and to eat it, too. This is immature. If he made a deliberate decision to leave the Catholic Church, he shouldn't try to cash in on his Catholic inheritance when convenient and leave it aside when inconvenient.

Every missalette carries the Catholic discipline on this matter in plain English, stating not only the universal law of the Church, but also the specific application to the United States, enacted by our bishops' conference. That should settle it "once and for all," but I suspect it won't!

Funeral attendance

Q. My question is about a relative that I'm very close to. He was baptized and raised in the Catholic Church, but later was divorced. He remarried in the Lutheran Church and is now a member. Should this relative pass away and his funeral be held in the Lutheran Church, as a Catholic can I attend his funeral?

A. Certainly, your attendance at his funeral would not encourage his ongoing membership in the Lutheran Church! Therefore, seriously, I would not hesitate to go and pray for the repose of his soul.

Pure spirits

Q. I was having a discussion with a Baptist about angels. He believes all angels are men. When I hear about angels, I always think more of women, though it could be either a man or a woman. Can you answer this question for me?

A. Angelic beings are pure spirits — that is, beings possessed of intellect and free will, but no bodies. On that very count, then, they are asexual. When they are deputed by Almighty God to represent Him to men, they take on human form and, inasmuch as the three angels whose names we know are masculine, it seems that perceptions of them are along those lines. For a fuller and authoritative discussion of angels, see the *Catechism of the Catholic Church* (nos. 327-336).

Money's worth

Q. I am aware of the so-called evolving teaching of the Church as regards capital punishment. I believe in the necessity of having an ultimate penalty. I am, however, greatly outnumbered on this issue in my department. Does the Catholic Church still uphold the right of the state to execute felons? If not, I need to submit my intellect to the teaching of the Church. Further, if the Church no longer upholds this right of the state, would not that constitute a change in the teaching of the Church? I tell my students that the Church's teaching on abortion is unchanged and will remain so for as long as the Church proclaims the truth. I am confused on this one.

Am I correct when I state to my students that for the individual Catholic, "salvation is not assured"? When Protestants preach about one's assurance of salvation, aren't they really committing the sin of presumption?

I was reading a biblical commentary by a rabbi. One of the interesting comments was: "The Bible is not a book for children." Would you agree? I run into difficulties trying to explain the crucifixion to my four-year-old daughter, along with floods and plagues, et al.

I was reading some back issues of *The Catholic Answer* magazine and was glad to see your response concerning the Eucharist's being the "risen" Body of Our Lord. However, how does that fit with the teaching that the Last Supper was the first Eucharist, there having been no Resurrection yet? My intellect is curious here; I mean no disrespect.

Last, I remember being taught not to chew the Eucharist. I think it looks tacky, almost disrespectful. I want my eldest daughter to be correct, as her time for First Communion is fast approaching.

A. The Church still holds that the state has the right to exact the death penalty. However, the Holy Father has hemmed that in by numerous qualifiers, such that capital punishment would be deemed almost always immoral. For a detailed discussion of this, refer to *Evangelium Vitæ* ("The Gospel of Life") and to the revisions thus necessitated in the *Catechism of the Catholic Church* (found in the supplement).

Salvation is assured for no one, and anyone who claims to have such assurance flies in the face of St. Paul's warning about our need to work out our salvation "with fear and trembling" (Phil 2:12), and — even more to the point — "Let anyone who thinks that he stands take heed lest he fall" (1 Cor 10:12).

The Bible is the kind of work into which one grows. Certain passages are more immediately comprehensible than others. That doesn't mean it's not for children at all, just that one should be judicious in introducing little ones to the sacred text. Concepts of evil, divine retribution and the like are not easily explained, but sooner or later they need to be faced since they are integral to the full message of the Gospel.

The Last Supper, we can say, was Act One of a two-act drama, with the Lord's crucifixion on Calvary as Act Two. You have undoubtedly noticed that Christ's words of eucharistic institution have future verbs: "will" be given up; "will" be poured out. Furthermore, St. John's approach to the Paschal Mystery would have us understand that on Calvary, Jesus' death, resurrection, and communication of the Holy Spirit happened simultaneously, which is entirely in keeping with the notion that God lives outside time and in an eternal present. Therefore, a linear method of interpretation does not do justice to the Johannine presentation of events.

Finally, there is nothing inherently wrong with chewing the Lord's Body, but it should be done gracefully and respectfully.

Health concerns?

Q. In your negativity about Communion under both kinds, you have often alleged that there are "health concerns" that should be considered. Our diocesan worship office says that is a lot of nonsense. Can you back up your statement with some medical facts?

A. First of all, I am not at all negative about Communion under both kinds by intinction. Nor am I doctrinally concerned about Communion from the chalice.

I am pastorally concerned for several reasons, which I have aired frequently. The health risk, however, is not my personal "take" on the situation; it comes from the Centers for Disease Control in Atlanta.

Back in 1985, when the Bishops' Committee on the Liturgy was pushing hard for both species at all times, concerns were raised about the risks involved. Some people had even expressed fear of the spread of AIDS from this method of Communion distribution/reception; that, of course, was unwarranted, given the fact that the disease cannot be transmitted by casual contact.

At any rate, after going through the various levels of risk, Dr. Donald Hopkins of the CDC concluded thus: "In summary, we cannot quantitate [sic] a risk for disease transmission by use of a common Communion cup, nor can we provide an absolute endorsement that the practice is safe." Hardly a rousing statement of "all clear," I'm sure you would agree.

Religious attire

Q. I have heard it stated that clerics must wear clerical garb when in public. Where can I find such statements? Also, where are nuns told to wear their habits?

A. In 1994, the Congregation for the Clergy came out with its *Directory for the Life and Ministry of Priests.* In no. 66, we find the following: "The attire [of a priest], when it is not the cassock, must be different from the manner in which the laity dress.... A cleric's failure to use this proper ecclesiastical attire could manifest a weak sense of his identity as one consecrated to God." This merely reinforces what was already contained in the *Code of Canon Law* (canon 284). This past summer, that same dicastery published a new document on priestly life and ministry, with equally strong statements such as: "It is easy to understand the significance and pastoral role of the discipline concerning clerical garb, to which the priest should *always* conform since it is a public proclamation of his limitless dedication to the brethren and to the faithful in his service to Jesus Christ. The more society is marked by secularization, the greater the need for signs" (IV.3, emphasis added).

As for Religious (male and female alike), the *Code of Canon Law* deals with the matter thus: "Religious are to wear the habit of the institute made according to the norm of proper law as a sign of their consecration and as a testimony of poverty" (canon 669). Numerous other documents from the Congregation for Institutes of Consecrated Life and Societies of Apostolic Life and the Holy Father (including the post-synodal apostolic exhortation *Vita Consecrata* [on the consecrated life and its mission in the Church and in the world], no. 25) have called for the same, apparently to no avail in all too many instances.

Appropriate attire

Q. Enclosed is an article in which Sister Sharon Euart of the National Conference of Catholic Bishops apparently disagrees with you. She said that "the term 'usual attire' leaves room for priests to wear more casual dress when it is appropriate."

A. Sister Sharon Euart does not interpret documents for the Holy See; the Holy See does. I stick by my original remarks because they were quotations from Archbishop Crescenzio Sepe, then-Secretary of the Congregation of the Clergy, who presented the *Directory for the Life and Ministry of Priests* to the press. So, to sum up, aside from athletic events, the Church expects her priests to be identifiable as such, regardless of what some may prefer.

Labyrinth info

Q. Here is a paper I wrote for a theology class on the labyrinth. I hope it will help you explain it to those asking about it.

A. Thank you — and, literally, about seventy-five other readers who sent me information on this topic — far more than I could ever need or want to know about it, in reality.

It seems there are two points of view about the labyrinth. All agree that the most famous example of it is in the Cathedral of Chartres, where it represented the path of prayer, or perhaps just served a decorative function; in many medieval churches, it was also provided as a kind of substitute for people who could not go on pilgrimage to the Holy Land. Many respondents to my inquiry sent me detailed information about labyrinths and their use today, with allegations that they have been dragged into various kinds of New Age projects. Once more, we find that something can be positive, neutral or negative, depending upon the mentality of the person presenting or using it. Therefore, *caveat emptor!*

Habit beginnings

Q. How did the wearing of religious garb or the habit begin? Was it the dress of a widow in mourning? Why did religious orders change? Someone said for health reasons. Most senior seculars do not accept this updating of religious garb. Please respond with a positive answer if possible. Are religious orders being phased out? If so, why?

A. The wearing of distinct garb for either widows or consecrated virgins goes all the way back to the origins of Christian life. We find entire treatises written on the matter by authors such as Tertullian, St. Ambrose, and St. Jerome — long before the existence of religious orders as we have come to know them. The idea was simple: These women had a special role within the Christian community, especially as being dedicated to works of charity and prayer, and the faithful wanted to know who they were, so that they could approach them with their requests, to be edified by their presence, and to express their reverence for them. The veil is a particular sign of the consecrated life, and the Fathers of the Church see it as a symbol parallel to the bridal costume of a woman joined to a man in holy matrimony — that is, this virgin is mystically married to Christ.

Distinctive habits for various religious congregations, of course, did not begin until a variety of such communities were founded. Sometimes the garb was simple, sometimes elaborate. Certainly, there were habits that were not very conducive to proper hygiene or to safety in modern conditions — for example, driving — and, for such reasons, Pope Pius XII urged sisters to update their habits back in the 1950s. We should note, however, he did not tell them to shed habits altogether. Interestingly, few congregations paid any attention to his wise counsel. The Second Vatican Council repeated the Pontiff's advice in exactly the same terms; this time around, many communities took "updating" to be a synonym for "eliminating."

Popes Paul VI and John Paul II both decried the adoption of secular dress by Religious (male and female alike); the *Code of Canon Law* and every other piece of ecclesiastical legislation since the Council has required distinct religious garb. Unfortunately, most religious congregations in the United States and other "developed" countries have roundly ignored this norm, largely to their own destruction, as we have watched with distress the dissolution of these very same communities. Refusal to accept the law of the Church and an equal refusal to correspond to common sense is generally punished by extinction. Not surprisingly, faithful communities are thriving.

By the way, the distaste for Religious in lay clothes is not limited to "seniors"; if anything, I have found even greater nonacceptance of it among the young, who understand and need visible signs of consecration to the Lord and His Church in this terribly secularized world in which we live.

Mortal interpretation

Q. I have heard priests state that, because our Blessed Mother was born without original sin and its effects, she felt no physical pain. It was stated that her delivery of Our Lord was painless, and some believe that is was not even a true physical delivery, that a bright light shone in the stable and Our Lord was transformed from being in her womb to being in her arms. We all know that our Blessed Mother experienced great anguish and suffering over many events in her motherhood, most especially when her Son died for us, so I always thought she also felt physical pain in the same sense that we do. When I delivered my children, I always cherished the thought of sharing in a blessed event with our Blessed Mother. Is there a concrete definition that explains without a doubt what constitutes a "grievous" or "mortal" sin? I am especially concerned with young people and their idea of what is serious in the area of chastity. It seems that most young people believe that if the act of intercourse outside of marriage is not committed, then the sexual sin is only venial. The *Catholic Encyclopedia* has a definition of mortal sin, but it is still vague. When is a sin mortal?

A. Regarding Our Lady's bearing the Christ Child and its effects on her, there is no binding teaching. Many Fathers of the Church argued that since no stain of original sin touched Our Lady, one of the effects normally associated with it (pain in childbirth) would be absent from her experience. If one can (and must) believe that the conception of the Lord was miraculous, surely it would not be preposterous to accept the second notion, on the principle that if God can do the greater (bring about the birth of His Son without the agency of a male), He can do the lesser (preserve the mother from the normal experience of childbirth). I think it is an issue on which good Catholics can have divergent points of view — just as is the case with regard to whether or not Our Lady died or was merely "translated" to heaven at the end of her life.

As far as an understanding of mortal sin goes, allow me to refer you to the *Catechism of the Catholic Church*, which goes to great lengths to explain the distinction between mortal and venial sin (see nos. 1854-1864); this is also treated carefully in Our Sunday Visitor's *Catholic Encyclopedia* under the heading, "Sin, Mortal and Venial."

It is not surprising that young people would be confused by sexual sins and their gravity when they are constantly bombarded by gross immorality wherever they turn. Of course, how can we be surprised that they think that the only sexual sin is actual intercourse when the president of the United States himself attempted to redefine reality in just such terms? As in all manner of sin, the true disciple does not seek merely to avoid mortal sin, or even venial sin, but likewise the very occasions of sin — that is, any thing or any person that could logically lead one to break one's relationship with Almighty God.

Presented in that light, it is easy to see that whatever reduces one's sensibilities to chastity — for example, pornography, immodesty of dress or speech, acts short of full intercourse but clearly designed and intended to arouse sexual passion — ought to be avoided for both theological and psychological reasons — namely, that they lower one's resistance to evil and make serious sin that much more possible.

God forgives

Q. When I was younger, I was coerced into having pornographic pictures taken of me. I love God very much, and the guilt is tremendous. I feel that God is very disappointed in me because I knew better. The priest here says I have done nothing wrong. I don't believe him, I'm sorry to say. Please advise me. This is affecting my relationship with everyone.

A. I don't think we help people deal with guilt by telling them they've done nothing wrong, particularly when the person in question knows otherwise. So, my approach would be this: Yes, you did wrong and need to confess this in the Sacrament of Penance, if you have not already done so. Once confessed, the sin is blotted out in

God's "mind," and should be in yours, too. It is an essential dogma of faith that God, in His mercy and compassion, can and does wipe clean the whole slate when we come to Him in sorrow and with a firm purpose of amendment.

The basic problem for many people is not that God has failed to forgive them, but that they have failed to believe that God has done so or that they find it impossible to forgive themselves. My simple advice is to put this sad episode behind you, trust in God's mercy and get on with living a wholesome Christian life.

Dancing dilemma

Q. My husband and I want to learn how to dance the tango. Is it sinful to learn how to dance? Some say that dancing can lead us away from God. Also, is it correct to say that a person who carries a Bible is holier than a person who does not?

A. Dancing, in and of itself, is not immoral. Certain kinds of dancing can lead one into impure thoughts or actions. When the tango first appeared, many observers asserted that its movements were erotic or quasi-erotic; with the desensitization that has occurred over the past forty years, that evaluation would probably no longer hold. I do believe, however, that caution and prudence are important in judging things like this; after all, even objectively good things can be perverted by our weakened human natures.

As far as carrying around a Bible goes, that is neither here nor there. What's the purpose of it? To look holy? If so, the action is superficial and hypocritical. To have ready access to God's written Word to use during downtime or to have handy for friendly discussions about matters religious? Those are worthy purposes. However, let's also recall that we don't worship a book, any book, even *the* Book — that's bibliolatry! To equate toting a Bible with sanctity is silly, and anyone who holds that view needs to remember Our Lord's words: "Not every one who says to me, 'Lord, Lord,' shall enter the kingdom of heaven" (Mt 7:21).

The Seven Joys

Q. We have received a rosary from someone with seven decades on it. We have never heard of this or seen one like it before. The medal on it has St. Francis on one side and St. Anthony on the other. Is this a special rosary to be said in their honor?

A. What you have is called "the Franciscan crown," a collection of the Seven Joys of Mary: the Annunciation, Visitation, Nativity of Our Lord, Adoration of the Magi, Finding of the Child in the Temple, Resurrection, and, as one meditation, Mary's Assumption and Coronation.

There are many "chaplets" dedicated to various devotions or saints, but the average Catholic is most familiar with the Dominican form.

Maid of honor

Q. I was wondering if it is all right to stand up as the maid of honor in a non-Catholic but Christian church, as long as I don't miss Mass on Sunday?

A. There would be no problem with what you propose, so long as the persons being married are not Catholics violating Church law by going through a non-Catholic ceremony without proper dispensation.

Flag-waving

Q. An issue has developed in our parish over the placement of flags in the sanctuary. The two flags are, of course, the Church flag and the American flag. All here are in agreement that the greater honor, and hence the pre-eminent position, be given to the Church flag. The disagreement stems from determining which is the pre-eminent spot for a flag. The issue is complicated by the floor plan of our church, which, unfortunately, is not the traditional *ad orientem* layout, but rather a semicircle with odd angles and projections and walls. For that reason, I have enclosed a floor plan to aid you in visualizing the placement of the flags. They are represented on the plan by circles with an X in the middle.

A. I must say that I have very little sympathy for having flags (papal or otherwise) anywhere in a church. I should also mention that this practice is, to the best of my knowledge, uniquely American. The historical explanation is simple: As a persecuted minority whose civic loyalty was constantly questioned, Catholics in the United States often tried to assuage doubts about their patriotism by being "super-patriots," and one way to do that was through flag-waving. I find the religious test of American culture very offensive, and never have and never will submit to such a degrading procedure. And I see efforts at proving my patriotism as integral to that traditional anti-Catholic game.

Now, if you still want to go the flag route in your church, there are no official policies about placement, but I would venture a personal opinion: I do not think they belong anywhere in the sanctuary or on the central axis. In churches for which I have been responsible and in which parishioners seemed strongly attached to this practice, I insisted that they find a home either hanging from the choir loft, situated by the back doors (as one exits the church), or in the vestibule of the church. The bottom line, however, is that they should never attract attention to themselves; the American flag is a secular symbol and, therefore, should not have any significant position in a place where worship is conducted, while the symbol for Catholicism is not the papal flag but the Cross of the Savior.

Church adornment

Q. Perhaps it's trivial, but I need some clarification as the tabernacles on the side altars (Joseph and Mary) have been removed from our church since Lent 1999, without any announcement or explanation, leaving many of the parishioners confused and some annoyed since they made financial contributions for these tabernacles when the church was originally built in 1962. We have had a series of pastors since then, but none removed the tabernacles, even temporarily. Also, the baptismal font donated to the church in 1962 by a very pious woman, now deceased, has been removed and replaced with an old one that had been stored in the basement of a church in another county for a long period of time. The parish church is beginning to look more like an empty, big wooden barn.

A. Several neuralgic points coalesce here, making for a very sticky situation.

First, I don't think priests ought to make changes without informing and catechizing their people.

Second, memorializing objects for churches and the like is a time-honored practice, but it also presents problems — namely, that some folks adopt a proprietory attitude toward those things (that is, they think they are theirs, rather than God's or the parish's). This is surely not a healthy posture. At the same time, I don't think pastors should operate insensitively in moving or disposing of things that were given in memory of someone, especially if the donor or family members are still on the scene. I must say, though I have inherited religious artifacts that were, in plain English, god-awful, getting rid of them is never easy.

Third, regarding tabernacles on side altars. The purpose of a tabernacle is to reserve the Blessed Sacrament. Church law is clear that the Blessed Sacrament can be reserved in only one tabernacle in any standard church. From what you indicate, I am presuming that the tabernacle being used for that purpose is in the center; therefore, the others are not performing any real function. Removing them makes sense to me, unless they are integral to the structure of those "side altars." Given the modern nature of the building in question, I am frankly surprised the architects/ builders ever put in side altars to begin with, recalling that the reason for an altar is the offering of sacrifice, and the Eucharistic Sacrifice may not be offered in the same church simultaneously at different altars in a standard church. Granted, your church was constructed in 1962, when those norms were not completely in place.

At any rate, I think what your pastor has done is legitimate and proper — although I think an element of catechesis would have been appropriate.

Sins have occurred

Q. I am writing a question in regard to information received while attending a humanities class in college. While studying the history of music, we were told, by our instructor, of atrocities carried out by the Catholic Church during the Middle Ages. I was shocked, and it greatly upset me. I tried to defend my faith and the Church after class, but evidently did not have enough information to debate what he said. We were told the following: Many boys were castrated to allow soprano singers in the church. If people spoke out against the Church, they were taken out and burned. There was brutalization of people by the Church, which justified itself in the name of God. The entire Church was corrupt. There were many orphans who were slaughtered because the Church did not have the means to care for so many. The instructor stated that Pope John Paul II had made a public apology for these evils of the Church, and I received an article in my Catholic newspaper where the Pope was seeking penance for the sins of the Church. Are these the "sins" he was referring to?

A. I never tire of reminding people that we should not try those of a former age by the lights of ours. What I mean is this: Each era has its specific sensitivities and its unique biases. I am not relativizing morality, but simply taking note of an objective fact of life.

The first two points you raise have some historicity to them. Yes, boys were castrated for musical purposes. Now, this was not done just by the Church; this was normal operational procedure in the world of music, period. Few suspected there was anything wrong with this; rather, it was perceived as allowing a boy with a magnificent voice to continue to have a musical career once he reached and passed puberty.

That heretics were executed is another fact of life. In general, such executions were the work of the state, not the Church. The

Inquisition would judge the teachings and/or writings of theologians and, if found wanting, would invite them to modify their positions, so as to bring them into conformity with Catholic doctrine (an innocent and valid enough demand, I am sure you would agree).

Now, with the union of Church and state, theological dissenters were also regarded as threats to the unity of the state, which would then take recalcitrant heretics and try them for civil crimes, with penalties including imprisonment and death. Technically, then, the Church merely rendered a theological judgment, which the state used as it saw fit. It is likewise important to know that execution of heretics was not limited to the Catholic world; all other Christian bodies did the same (I don't say this to justify the practice, just to put it all in perspective).

On the other two items: That corruption existed (and still exists!) in the Church, no one could or should deny, for the Church is every bit as human as she is divine, and where the human element is present, the potential for corruption is real. That the whole Church was corrupt is patently false; proof to the contrary resides in the simple realization that constant calls for reform came from the Church at every level — from Popes to paupers. That the Church killed infants to spare them from starvation sounds like some kind of nonsense from the anti-Catholic literature of the eighteenth and nineteenth centuries — totally unsupportable from any objective source of historical information.

Yes, the Holy Father called for a historical examination of conscience for the Jubilee Year 2000, but we must be careful about what he said. As a Church, we must acknowledge the sins of our members, past and present, seeking the pardon of those offended, and of Almighty God. The Church herself is the sinless Bride of Christ, incapable of sin, but her members (all of us) fail to live up to the demands of the Gospel in every age, thus sullying her beautiful countenance. So, in this special time of reconciliation and renewal, we should learn from the mistakes of the past and resolve not to repeat those mistakes and sins in the future — and that is the primary goal of the Jubilee celebration.

Limbo land?

Q. For a Catholic baptism, both parents must be Catholic, correct? When having to use proxies, does this also hold true? Does the old rule of choosing a saint's name still hold true today? If a person has never been baptized into any faith and wishes to marry a Catholic, can he have a Catholic wedding while not having a full Mass? If a baby is not baptized, what is the Church's belief if something happens to this child? Is a baby considered baptized if a layperson conducts it without the knowledge or consent of the parents?

Q. My son drifted from the Church, beginning in high school, but has made a return and is now fascinated with the study of apologetics. On a radio program, he heard a priest ask about what happened to limbo. He found the priest's answer to be inconclusive and indefinite as he is old enough to remember the former teaching. Since he has a firm conviction regarding the unchanging nature of Catholic truth, he wonders what this might mean. We note also that limbo is not even mentioned in the *Catechism of the Catholic Church*.

A. To the first inquirer, let me respond briefly: No, neither parent must be Catholic to have a child baptized; parental consent is, naturally, needed or at least to be reasonably presumed. Proxies do not alter the situation. The Church encourages the taking of a saint's name, but allows other names, so long as their meaning does not conflict with Christian life and virtue. A non-baptized person marrying a Catholic can certainly have a Catholic wedding, with or without a Mass (although I would caution strongly against a Mass where non-Catholics are concerned). Athough this would be a valid union, it would not be sacramental, since both parties must be baptized Christians for it to be such.

Regarding the state of infants who die without Baptism, the *Catechism* says we should commend them to the mercy of God (see no. 1261). In an emergency, any person (lay or clerical, Catholic or non-Catholic) can and should baptize, and does so validly. As I suggested above, if one thinks the parents would want a child baptized or would have no objections to it, one should proceed; I am thinking of a nurse in a hospital setting as an example.

As far as limbo goes, it is critical to realize that this was never an official teaching of the Church but a theological opinion, admittedly an opinion that had great currency, but nonetheless no dogmatic commitment. In the paragraph of the *Catechism* I cited above, we read: "As regards *children who have died without Baptism*, the Church can only entrust them to the mercy of God. . . . Jesus' tenderness toward children . . . allow[s] us to hope that there is a way of salvation for children who have died without baptism" (italics in original).

On the more general question of theological opinion and its weight, it must be stressed that preachers and teachers should be very cautious in presenting even commonly accepted theological opinions as though they were doctrinal/dogmatic statements. We can see the damage done and the confusion caused when such opinions fade away after they have been perceived as being more than they ever were.

Sacramental barrier

Q. My only sacrament is baptism. I have been to church very few times but now feel the need to make my confession, but I don't know how. Do all churches have reconciliation rooms, and if they do, is that where you go for a face-to-face confession? I am really scared about this and embarrassed. I am married to a divorced Catholic. Would I be able to have Communion? Am I still in mortal sin because of my marriage? How about confirmation? Can one be confirmed if the only sacrament you can receive is reconciliation? I fear for the loss of my soul.

A. Given your present state, which God judges as objectively an adulterous one (due to the previous presumably valid marriage of your current partner), you cannot approach the Sacrament of Penance or any other sacrament. As I have explained on many occasions, the ongoing and unrepented state of adultery closes the door to sacramental reconciliation since the purpose of amendment is lacking (unless you and your partner are willing to live as "brother and sister"). Ask him to consider applying to a marriage tribunal for a review of his marriage, with a view toward determining its validity or invalidity. If that union is judged invalid, you would then be free to contract a marriage in the Church and receive all the other sacraments. Until that might happen, I would urge you to continue a life of prayer and to attend Sunday Mass (even though incapable of receiving Communion), since these are still Christian obligations you should be meeting and, furthermore, are sources of grace, which could lead you to accept and live the Church's teaching on the indissolubility of marriage.

Gesture's significance?

Q. Can you provide me with the history, origin and meaning of kissing one's thumb after making the Sign of the Cross? My three young children attend a Catholic school in which they are instructed by their teachers to form a cross with their thumb and forefinger and kiss it. This idiosyncratic gesture appears to be more a veneration of one's thumb than a sign of devotion, and I would like some basis for my argument in opposition to my children being instructed to kiss their thumbs.

A. We don't have to suppose that everything children are taught is weird or "New Age." The practice in question, it seems to me, is probably teaching your children to bless themselves in Eastern or Byzantine fashion: Holding the first three fingers together (symbolic of the Blessed Trinity), with the other two fingers free (symbolic of the two natures in Christ). Now, of course, the Eastern method would also be right to left shoulder, instead of left to right. Another possibility is that they are being introduced to an ethnic custom (many Latin countries such as Spain, Italy and those in South America) have this tradition, which is merely a sign of reverence or devotion to the Sign of the Cross. If you have any questions, rather than suspecting the worst, just ask the teacher what the significance of the gesture is.

Two valid approaches

Q. I read a Catholic newsletter that contains people's stories of miraculous cures of medical conditions after praying for the intercession of a particular priest who died in the 1960s. As I get older, and the world becomes more sophisticated, I find that I am adopting a different attitude toward the whole idea of asking God to cure us or relieve our sufferings. It seems to me that people who believe that God will, as a matter of usual course, intervene in the affairs of mankind to the extent that He will cure the illness and physical problems of all who ask Him is to treat Him as some sort of shaman or magician. I have come to see that pain and suffering are a necessary part of the human condition. If we are "rightly ordered" toward God as our heavenly Father, we will understand that there is always order in the universe, even in the seemingly senseless and random acts that result in the debilitation of our physical bodies. To ask God to change the course of nature for our comfort seems to indicate a lack of willingness to accept God's Will. I ask myself if rather than asking to be spared some discomfort and pain, we should be asking for the wisdom to understand God's Will for us, and the strength to carry it out. Am I on the right track?

A. There is nothing wrong with the way you present the case — perfectly fine from a theological view and even psychologically. There is, however, an alternate approach, which is equally valid, and Christ Himself employed it on at least one occasion of which we are aware. In the agony in the garden, He asked the Father three times to spare Him — if it were His Will.

Sickness and death were not a part of God's original plan; they entered our world as a result of original sin, and when Our Lord came among us, He worked signs and wonders, precisely to show that the power of Satan was shattered, thus replacing infirmity with wholeness. Granted, not everyone was cured, but many were, and Jesus never castigated people for seeking such cures (He did condemn sign-seeking for its own sake).

My own reading of this would run along these lines: To accept illness as a cross coming from a loving Lord, Who wishes to unite you to Him, is a great grace. To seek healing, albeit with the understanding that you desire it only if God does and if it will be for your spiritual welfare, is also a good and holy thing. Different spiritualities exist because we all have different personalities; the Creator is not a divine "cookie-cutter" Who insists on sameness among His creatures. The two attitudes you identify are equally compatible with a mind-set that accepts God's Will.

Blessing objects

Q. I am a cradle Catholic, but I still need help with some basics. I am giving a friend a Christmas ornament as a gift. I bought the ornament at a religious-articles store, and later had it blessed along with other items by a Religious brother. I need help explaining to my friend the significance of having an article blessed.

A. Traditionally, a blessing is a prayer that evil spirits would be driven from the object/person and that it be dedicated to a sacred purpose. Contemporary blessings also involve a prayer of thanksgiving for God's creation, from which we receive things that aid us in our life of prayer and devotion; they also contain prayers for the person(s) who will use the blessed objects. It should be noted that while the non-ordained — for example, the brother in your letter — may bless things under certain conditions, the formula and gesture are different from those of an ordained minister. A priest or deacon uses a declarative form ("I bless . . . in the name of the Father, etc."), whereas someone else would ask that the object "be blessed." The former makes the standard Sign of the Cross over the object; the latter signs it with the thumb.

EWTN move

Q. Are things going weird even at EWTN (Eternal Word Television Network)? Lately, I have noticed a young man helping with the distribution of Holy Communion; I think he used to be one of their seminarians. I never thought I would see EWTN using extraordinary ministers of the Eucharist. What's your take on this?

A. I, too, have noticed the phenomenon. When they had Mass down at the main site, where the friars' residence is still located, they had a steady supply of priests and installed acolytes at their disposal. Since the move into the hinterlands, only one priest makes the drive up to the monastery. However, the crowds are also greatly diminished in the new setting; therefore, I find it hard to understand why there is any need for any Communion help at all. The celebrant can just distribute Holy Communion to the nuns and then go to the rail for the lay faithful. Their present practice does not square with a correct interpretation and/or application of the norms.

Voting patterns

Q. Would you tell me if it's permissible for a Catholic to vote for a candidate solely based on the fact that the candidate favors and even promotes abortion? The reason I ask this is because recent polls reveal that sixty percent of Catholic women voted for Bill Clinton. I always thought this triggered automatic excommunication (assuming full knowledge and consent).

A. An enlightened, informed conscience would always hold that a candidate who favors abortion is, *ipso facto,* unfit for public office in a nation that believes in unalienable rights coming from the Creator God. Being pro-abortion, or "pro-choice," is an automatic disqualifier, just as most reasonable citizens would say is the case with one who is a racist. In other words, no matter how noble his positions on a host of other issues, he has proved himself to be seriously flawed in a fundamental or foundational way. Back in 1974, the Holy See spoke out clearly on this issue:

"A Christian can never conform to a law which is in itself immoral, and such is the case of a law which would admit in principle the liceity of abortion. Nor can a Christian take part in a propaganda campaign in favor of such a law or vote for it. . . . On the contrary, it is the task of law to pursue reform of society and conditions of life in all its milieux, starting with the most deprived, so that always and everywhere it may be possible to give every child coming into this world a welcome worthy of a person."

Practically speaking, that means a refusal to support pro-abortion politicians. Is this single-issue voting? Let the distinguished ethicist Germain Grisez reply to that objection: "Single-issue voting is irrational," he wrote. But, he continued, "the proper standards for evaluating candidates for public office are competence and character, [and] any individual seeking public office who supports the legality — much less the public funding — of abortion, manifests a character which makes him or her unfit for public office."

How does a conscientious voter handle the situation? Grisez concluded: "I will vote for such an individual only if the alternative is someone of equally bad character and in some other respect less suited for the office."

The bishops of the United States, in 1998, also issued an excellent and extremely strong statement on this topic.

Telling titles

Q. When reading obituaries, I noticed that sometimes the priest's title is written as "Reverend," "Father," or "Pastor." Which is the most appropriate title when writing a priest's name? What title should be used for a deacon?

A. Much confusion exists on this in the United States, because so many Protestant clergy have assumed some of these titles, but generally incorrectly. "Reverend" is an adjective, not a noun; hence, it should be preceded by the article "the." It would be used in addressing a letter to a priest or in a formal introduction: "The Reverend John Smith"; in this sense, it corresponds to the title of "The Honorable" for civil officials (one would not call one's congressman "Honorable" in direct address, but "Congressman" or "Representative"). In the same way, a priest would not be called "Reverend Smith," for the oral title is "Father." "Pastor" is a job description, not a title.

When we come to deacons, the situation varies from diocese to diocese, and often also depends on whether or not the man in question is a permanent or transitional deacon. Standard practice seems to be that a permanent deacon has as a written title "Reverend Mr." and "Deacon" as an oral title (although I must confess I dislike the latter since it tends to have a Baptist ring to it, inasmuch as we have never used this title in the Catholic Tradition before; it also smacks of a kind of functionalism suggested by "Pastor" as well). In some places, transitional deacons have the same titles; in others, a distinction is made, with "The Reverend. . ." (such as a priest) and "Father" as the oral title.

Comfortability factor

Q. Is it disrespectful and/or sinful to pray (all or part of the Rosary, for example) and/or raise our minds to God while lying in bed just before going to sleep, or upon awaking just before getting out of bed, or when waking up in the middle of the night before falling asleep again? This would be in addition to saying our morning and evening prayers on our knees.

A. Not at all. One should pray in any position in which one feels comfortable; in fact, St. Dominic offered numerous possibilities for such. For myself, I most frequently pray Compline, or Night Prayer, in bed.

Joyful attitude

Q. Forty years ago, a famous Catholic theologian wrote that "divine joy is infallible evidence of the presence of God." Recently, on television, a humble black preacher imparted, "Faith is explosive, and divine joy is the fuse!" My experience confirms that when there is no divine joy, there is no "explosion" of living faith. Divine joy is the fruit of the Holy Spirit that sustains faith, kindles enthusiasm, inspires good works and evangelism, and graces the faithful with charisms that build up the Church. Forgive me, but some of *The Catholic Answer* magazine seems so much on the dismal side, which suppresses divine joy. There seems to be a hidden agenda to motivate by inciting fear. Should not "fear of the Lord" (in Scripture) be correctly understood as "reverence for the Lord"?

A. I fully agree that joy is critical to a full and proper living of the Christian life, but that is in no way opposed to propriety and a healthy fear of the Lord, which is manifested in obedience to His commandments and those of His Church. Let's not forget that Christ said that a fundamental sign of fidelity to Him would be the meticulous observance of even the least of His commands — and the teaching of them to others (see Mt 5:19)!

Dichotomies do not exist for God or for mature Christians; they are the fabrications of small-minded individuals who all too often are looking for an escape hatch from some moral or spiritual obligation. Sometimes one hears a seminarian say, "Do you want me to be holy or a theologian?" Why can't he be both, like St. Thomas Aquinas, for instance? Why can't his study be an integral aspect of his spirituality and thus become prayer? Similarly, why can't a priest be joyful and obedient to rubrics, or why can't a layperson be joyful and observe the Church's teaching on artificial birth control? Could it not be that one can actually come to experience joy by foregoing one's personal desires in favor of the Will of Christ and the good of the Church?

Penitential mode

Q. What do I do about a husband who hasn't been to confession in years and yet presumes to receive Holy Communion? We are, at least he proposes to be, traditional Catholics, and we have heard from the pulpit numerous times the necessity of confession, to say nothing of that being basic Catholic knowledge. Now that we are getting older, I have to wonder what I would do in the event of his death with regard to a funeral. And I wonder now if accompanying him to Mass is in any way a participation in this sacrilege. My speaking to him of it would do no good, and I have always been cautious not to stir his unreasonable anger. Do you have any suggestions other than prayer?

A. I am glad to hear that your priests have been preaching on the importance of sacramental confession, and I regret that your husband seems to have some kind of visceral reaction against it. Perhaps he had some negative experience that has colored his thinking or emotions in this regard; and perhaps you could help him discover or discuss these issues. That having been said, and with the importance of sacramental confession being underscored, are you not jumping to a number of conclusions that may not be warranted? For instance, Church law requires annual confession only if mortal sin has been committed; without that, there is no necessity to use the sacrament, even though it is extremely laudatory and beneficial to do so. Assuming he is fulfilling his Christian duties (as your letter suggests), I still think there must be a psychological hurdle he needs to overcome, rather than a theological one. Providing him with some good articles or books on the value of the Sacrament of Penance might break the ice — for example, Pope John Paul's apostolic exhortation *Penitentia et Reconciliatio* ("Penance and Reconciliation).

Clear lines needed

Q. I was very distressed by the enclosed article, and I wrote the magazine and told them, "If there is no priest, there is no Mass." I wondered if you knew anything about this?

A. For the benefit of readers, the article referred to by our inquirer is about women serving as pastoral ministers. In the course of the interview, the woman in question spoke of the service she conducts as "Mass"; needless to say, what she does is not a Mass, because "if there is no priest, there is no Mass." All too many of these situations have been allowed to get out of hand, and this article confirms that. Until the lines of demarcation are clearly drawn once again between the ministerial priesthood's responsibilities and various legitimate forms of lay collaboration, we will never have sufficient numbers of priestly vocations; we will never have liturgical sanity; we will never have ecclesial peace. Which is why the Holy See has stressed this so much over the past several years, but not many people are listening.

Repository's purpose

Q. Why do we have a repository during Holy Week, and can the repository be the tabernacle?

A. A repository is a tabernacle. When the Blessed Sacrament was reserved exclusively on the high altar, a repository (temporary tabernacle) was set up on a side altar for the reservation of the Eucharist during the Paschal Triduum. In a church where the Blessed Sacrament is regularly reserved on a side altar or in a separate chapel, a special repository for Holy Thursday would not make sense.

Lay activities

Q. Some friends and I have been discussing lay activities, services and vocations within the Church. In the course of this I was reading Pope John Paul's apostolic exhortation "The Lay Members of Christ's Faithful People" (*Christifideles Laici*). The Pope discusses "Criteria of Ecclesiality" for lay groups, which generally seem to be further guidelines for the laity in their involvement in various types of group activities. The criteria that caught my attention were, respectively, "professing the Catholic Faith," "authentic communion in filial relationship to the Pope," and "conformity to and participation in the Church's apostolic goals." My question involves how it would be possible for any lay group, or association, to meet these criteria if the group were ecumenical in membership? For example, in the area in which I live there are established groups of lay people that are in ecumenical communities and ecumenical Bible study groups, etc. But the Pope's criteria would seem to suggest that groups in which laity have membership should be Catholic in identity. Am I misunderstanding something here? If I'm correct, how do the laity involve themselves in authentic ecumenical efforts? Are we to be a part of Catholic groups that then work with non-Catholics toward improved ecumenical relations?

A. What the Holy Father is treating is the establishment and maintenance of various lay movements within the Catholic

Church. Ecumenical groups, on the other hand, are not — by definition — Catholic; therefore, the same criteria could not and should not apply. For information on those criteria, I would suggest consulting the Second Vatican Council's *Unitatis Redintegratio* (decree on ecumenism), and the *Directory for Ecumenical Activities*, published by the Council for Promoting Christian Unity. In that type of action — whether spiritual or social — the goal is to be faithful to one's own faith Tradition; to discuss differences with honesty and in charity; to engage in prayer, study, and joint action, where that is feasible (theologically and otherwise), without compromising the truth and one's own convictions; all the while creating a climate of mutual trust, which would allow for further growth in Christian unity. Collaborating in the running of a soup kitchen or in pro-life efforts come to mind immediately as projects apt for ecumenical outreach; prayer or study in common to advance spiritual ecumenism operates at a different level.

Trivializing matrimony

Q. My wife's sister's step-daughter is getting married, and my wife and I have been invited to the wedding. The bride-to-be is Protestant and the groom-to-be is Jewish. Neither has been married before. The wedding is on a yacht and country club, so I assume that a clergyman will not be performing the ceremony, although I do not know this as fact. As a Catholic, should I have any concerns at all about attending this wedding and celebrating the marriage? Would it be morally right for me to do so?

A. If the parties involved were Catholic, my response would be completely negative, but given the circumstances, you have nothing to worry about — although I do think that ceremonies of this kind (especially the yacht aspect) trivialize the sanctity of matrimony.

An example for us

Q. Why was Jesus baptized? What do the different colors of the vestments represent?

A. The baptism given by St. John the Baptist was a baptism "for repentance," however, we also know that, being divine, Jesus had no sin and thus needed no such baptism. In the encounter between Our Lord and His cousin, as recorded in Sacred Scripture, we find John protesting that he should be baptized by Jesus, not the other way around.

Our Lord's response was simply that John should cooperate, "for it is proper for us in this way to fulfil all righteousness." Throughout His earthly life, Jesus was intent on fulfilling every precept of the Law: He Who had no need to be made a son of the covenant through circumcision was circumcised on the eighth day; He Who had no need to be presented to the Father in the Temple was nonetheless presented on the fortieth day; He Who had no sin of which to repent was baptized by John in the Jordan — all this by way of example for us, thus teaching us the holiness of God's Law and the importance of humble submission and obedience to it.

As far as the colors of vestments are concerned, we should note that the color scheme is more elaborate in the West than in the East. In the East, there is a twofold distinction – bright (white, gold, etc.) for joyous celebrations and dark (red, purple, black) for events of a somber or penitential nature. In the West, the colors are as follows: white (or gold) for solemnities, feasts and memorials of Our Lord, Our Lady and saints who were not martyrs; red for Palm Sunday and Good Friday (for the triumphal, regal aspect of these occasions), commemorations of martyrs (obviously the connection to blood) and Pentecost Sunday (for the fire of the Holy Spirit); green for the time *per annum* (those weeks throughout the year not part of either the Advent/Christmas or Lent/Easter cycle) as a sign of hope and growth in one's divine life; purple, or violet, for seasons of anticipation or penance (Advent and Lent). In Masses for the dead, purple, black or white may be used, at the discretion of the celebrant.

Absolution for abortion?

Q. I read in the *Catechism of the Catholic Church* that the sin of abortion requires excommunication (no. 2272). Absolution for this cannot be granted except by the Pope or bishop (no. 1463). Additionally, the acts of the penitent (nos. 1450-1460) require that one must have: contrition, confession to a priest, and reparation, or satisfaction. Many abortions are being performed in this country. How can we welcome back these lost sheep, given the above? How can reparation occur? Absolution?

A. First of all, let's clear up some terminology. The sin of abortion does not "require" excommunication. Excommunication is automatically leveled against one who procures or helps another to procure an abortion because of the particularly heinous nature of the crime, but the penalty only "kicks in" if the party is aware of the penalty.

Second, while it is true that abortion is what is technically called a "reserved sin" — that is, absolution of it is limited to either the Pope or bishop — because of the unfortunately common nature of the crime in so many countries, faculties to absolve from it have been granted to ordinary priests in most places, including the United States.

Third, as far as fulfillment of requirements for absolution go on the part of the penitent, I would note the following: Most people who go to confession for any sin (but especially this one) tend to be very contrite, and the priest must presume such contrition unless given contrary signals. And if the priest must presume such an attitude, the rest of the Christian community certainly must do so. Now, I admit that at times we have whitewashed all too quickly the condition of women and girls who have had abortions, making each and every one of them out to be victims. While I have found that scenario to be true in most instances, I have also encountered some incredibly hard-hearted, selfish and even cruel women whose personal convenience was the only criterion for determining whether a baby ought to live or die. As a confessor, I have had to confront such would-be penitents with the need for them to undergo a profound conversion experience, demanding a change of mind and a change of heart. By and large, however, that has not been the case.

Sacrificial nature

Q. During the Easter homily, our pastor told of an incident that occurred on Easter Sunday, when someone spray-painted (in reference to God the Father and Jesus the Son) the outside wall of the church with the following, "How could a father kill his own son?" Although the pastor went on to address this question, his explanation (somehow) was lost on me, probably due to my inability to follow along in the abstract. To me, this question is a profound one, and I wonder how you would answer.

A. In reality, of course, the Father did not kill His own Son; sinful human beings did, and, as the Council of Trent reminded us, we continue to do so every time we sin.

There is a very deep theological issue here, nonetheless, related to divine love, and that is this: God the Father loved us so much that He sent His only Son to live and die for us, and the Son desired to make His Father's Will so completely His own and loved us so much, that, in fact, He freely, willingly and lovingly gave His life for the human race. This is the mystery of God's love, not the story of a vindictive God Who would demand a pound of His only Son's flesh. Thus did the Father hope, literally, to "love us" into loving Him. True love, of the sacrificial nature, has a transformative power, and when we are not moved to conversion by it, that is a signal that our hearts are still hardened and far from God. People who have not had this experience of the Father's mercy toward us can only see vengeance and wrath, and they end up misunderstanding the most critical truth of the Christian Faith.

Personal conflict?

Q. I am in need of advice. I am in an institution in California and am an altar server for the church. We have a "female chaplain" who is employed by the state. We also have a retired priest who comes every Sunday. The problem is that our chaplain has told our priest only to come one time a month, even when he wants to come every Sunday. I noticed her personal dislike for our priest at the Easter Vigil. Now we have not had a Mass since Pentecost. I thought I should ask your advice before I write the bishop.

A. Your priest must take really long vacations! I agree with you that something smells "fishy"; write the bishop and find out the story. If she's the cause of the problem, you need to involve the institution, so as to ensure you have regular access to the sacraments — this is your civil right and the institution's obligation.

Novenas

Q. During the first half of the 1940s, I attended evening novenas in honor of various saints — for example, Sts. Ignatius, Francis, Paul of the Cross, Gabriel — at respective churches in Baltimore. These novenas were well-attended on weekday evenings. The novena service usually consisted of hymns to the saint, a brief homily followed by prayers to the saint, and then the congregation would approach the Communion rail to receive the blessing of the relic of that particular saint. The only public novena that I have heard of today is in honor of St. Jude. Why have these novenas seemingly disappeared from the scene?

A. I think a large part of the answer has to do with the advent of television; the other, the advent of pseudo-sophistication.

My experience as a parish priest showed me that although the laity often complain about the unavailability of these devotions, all too often they have become unavailable because the people stopped attending, claiming to be "too busy" or afraid to come out at night. When people lacked ready entertainment — for example, television — they were more disposed to venture forth from their homes to church for various activities.

Second, now that so many Catholics think they are much wiser than their parents and grandparents, they look down on what they consider to be "peasant" forms of spirituality, symbolized by the old novenas. Truth be told, they have frequently been aided in developing this mentality by not a few clergy.

I must say that I think there is a resurgence of interest in such devotions and, where the priest sticks it out for a time, attendance seems to build. All kinds of novenas exist; for an excellent resource check out *(Mention Your Request Here) The Church's Most Powerful Novenas*, by Michael Dubruiel, available from Our Sunday Visitor (800-348-2440).

The saints above us

Q. I am a Catholic convert, converting six years ago. I hear that when people are trying to sell their home, they bury a statue of St. Joseph in their backyard. When the house sells, they give the praise to the saint and not to God. I must admit this does bother me. I feel as though it is walking a thin line of being in violation of the First Commandment. Could you please help clarify prayer to Mary as well as the Communion of Saints so that I will have a better understanding?

A. Burying a statue of St. Joseph is a silly practice and, at times, borders on superstition. And so, I would strongly discourage it. Thanking a saint for his intercession is not a problem, and God is not jealous of the attention given the saint. However, it must be clear that the saint's "effectiveness" comes from Almighty God and not from the individual saint, which leads to the next matter — the communion and intercession of saints.

We can join the question of the place of Mary and that of the saints together because Mary is, after all, a saint — that is, a human being who has "made it." What is said about her applies, to a lesser degree, to the others who have "made it." The Church honors certain men and women with the title of "saint" because their holiness warrants it, but also because the Church on earth can benefit from their example.

Patron saints for various professions or nations are holy people who are offered to believers as models worthy of emulation. Feast days of saints are opportunities to celebrate throughout the year Christ's victory over Satan in the lives of His Chosen People. Such a devotion reminds us that God is glorious in His saints (see 2 Thes 1:10), and that every Christian is called to be a saint, even if never publicly honored by the Church through the process of canonization. The universal call to holiness is celebrated each year on November 1, All Saints' Day, as the Church honors all the holy men and women of every time and place (most of whom are known only to God), who stand before the throne of the Lamb (see Rev 7).

To answer the critical question, then, "Do Catholics worship Mary and the other saints?" No, we accord them special honor because of their lives of faithful witness, and we seek their intercession before the Lord (remember, if we sinners on earth can and should pray for one another, why not the saints in glory?), as all believers in heaven and on earth unite their prayers to the perfect prayer of Christ. This is what St. Augustine was referring to when he spoke about the fact that in the Church the "whole Christ" prays — Head and members together. And that should be an inspiring and consoling thought as I come to realize that I do not pray alone.

Visible priests

Q. When I was growing up, every day when school let out there was a priest in front of the school or on the corner, sometimes more than one. He would greet the children, sometimes joke with us or pass the time of day, talk to the boys about the latest scores. There was always a group of boys and girls waiting outside the sacristy to talk to the priest, share good news and bad. The vocations that came out of that parish were boys who had a relationship with the priests, who were friends, mentors, confidants. Where are the priests today? To most children, they are the figures in vestments on the altar on Sunday, if they go to Mass. If they don't go to

Mass, the priest is the person who hears their confession once a year during CCD or in school. How can a child aspire to be something he knows nothing about? My theory? If the priests were more visible, more accessible, more present in the lives of children today, I think one would see more vocations.

A. I cannot agree with you more. My experience of priests in my boyhood (like yours, also spent in the Garden State) was exactly the same — the omnipresence of priests. Some folks today argue that priests can't be everywhere as they used to be due to the "priest shortage." I don't buy that argument for a number of reasons. First, I think part of the problem of the shortage is due precisely to the non-visibility of priests for almost thirty years — either because they don't dress like priests or because they have chosen to withdraw to other venues to spend their time. Second, back in the 1960s and 1970s, some bright light came up with the idea that Christianity was not "kid stuff" and that we ought to concentrate our efforts on adults. Well, we see the results or, better yet, the "non-results." Third, with the burgeoning bureaucracy that has emerged in the past two decades, priests are asked to spend their time going from one silly, meaningless meeting to another; at the end of the day, they often wonder if they have accomplished anything at all, and rightly so.

In "the old days" (which were by no means perfect), at least the priest had normal human contact in a variety of contexts: Teaching in the school, playing ball with the kids at recess, visiting the sick, taking office calls, greeting people on the streets as he did his own daily chores. Most of that type of spirituality, or theology of "presence," is lacking today (what some have foolishly and sarcastically dubbed the "Bing Crosby" or "Bells of St. Mary's" approach to priestly life and ministry), and we all are the poorer for it — not just the children.

I am happy to say, however, that many young priests are trying to get back to this older and more effective style of ministry, and report high levels of "job satisfaction." That will bring about major changes over the next several years, in my estimation.

Storytime

Q. I am hoping you could end a disagreement I am having with a friend of mine. He is a good Catholic, but he told me a story about a priest walking into the bakery and saying "This is my body" and thereby consecrated all the bread in the bakery. I firmly believe that priests have the power to consecrate, but I do not believe that a consecration would take place under these circumstances. He is basing his opinion on the statements of two priests. I have presented him with much documentation, from the *Catechism of the Catholic Church*, the *Catholic Encyclopedia*, and *The Catholic Answer* magazine, which to me states that it would not, but he is not convinced. Can you please help?

A. The power to consecrate is given to priests for the good of the Church, not for frivolous or magical purposes. Therefore, the case you present demonstrates a lack of proper intention; furthermore, many items in a bakery would not even consist of valid matter and hence are incapable of being consecrated under any circumstances.

Fact or fiction?

Q. Can you tell me if circumcision of Catholics was practiced in Germany prior to the purge of the Jews in the 1930s and early 1940s? The reason why I ask is that some novels and movies about the Hitler era often depict German authorities "proving" that a male was Jewish by whether or not he was circumcised. If German Catholics did practice circumcision at that time, it seems to me that either the writers of these novels and movies were ignorant of actual events, or there probably were many Catholics mistaken for Jews.

A. My understanding of things is that most Catholic countries did not practice circumcision unless particular health concerns called for it.

Good books

Q. In the Book of Genesis, God is quoted as saying, "Let us make man in our image" (1:26). Is He talking to other members of the Trinity . . . or other gods? Who is the "us"? Second, is there one Catholic book that has "official" Catholic doctrine.

A. On the first matter, exegetical opinion is divided. Some would say that benefiting from the *sensus plenior* (the full understanding of Scripture) that comes with time, we can hear a faint voice of Trinitarian theology. Others would maintain that since absolute monotheism was not firmly in place from the beginning of Judaism and only came into focus gradually (like, for example, belief in the resurrection of the dead), this is an echo of residual polytheism.

The *Enchiridion Symbolorum* in Latin contains all doctrines of the Faith; its English counterpart is *The Christian Faith*, edited by J. Neuner, S.J., and J. Dupuis, S.J., and published by Alba House. Another reliable work in this area is Ludwig Ott's *Fundamentals of Catholic Dogma*.

Indulgence gained

Q. I need help with a question regarding the plenary indulgence for a Holy Year. To gain this, must a person attend Mass and receive Holy Communion at one of the designated churches, or may he attend his own church and then go to one of the Jubilee churches to fulfill the rest of the requirements?

A. The requirement for Mass and Communion may be met at any church at all.

Feasts of unbaptized

Q. I am a fourteen-year-old altar boy and happen to be very inquisitive about my religion. I have recently come upon a mystery that I hope you can shed some light on. On the feast of the Holy Innocents, while I was getting ready for morning Mass, my priest asked my brother and me a question: "Why do we celebrate the feast of the Holy Innocents when they weren't even baptized?" Not knowing the answer, I asked him why, and he said that they were baptized by blood because they gave their lives in order that Jesus might escape the wrath of Herod. The next day, I asked him what the requirements were to be declared baptized by blood; he replied that you willingly and knowingly have to give up your life for God. So then I asked him how that could apply to the Holy Innocents, since they couldn't have known what they were dying for. He didn't know the answer and told me to write to you. So?

A. You have a wise pastor! I think he got himself into trouble by his first question — namely, how we could celebrate a feast in honor of the Innocents, even though they were never baptized. The Church liturgically honors many unbaptized people — for example, Sts. Ann and Joachim on July 26. We have no evidence of their baptism, or even of John the Baptist, for that matter. And the Eastern Church has feasts for Moses, the prophets, the Maccabees, etc. — all of whom lived under the Old Dispensation and therefore never received Christian baptism. Righteousness of life is critically important; after all, there are people who have been baptized who, due to a lack of holiness of life, may find themselves in hell, while those not baptized through no fault of their own, but living holy lives, will end up in heaven.

Catholic Doctrine

Reliable source

Q. Is there a reliable source in English that I can consult for the principal teachings of our Faith from the writings of the Popes and the Councils? It seems very difficult to find these documents without having access to a library. Could you please advise me?

A. Josef Neuner, S.J., and Jacques Dupuis, S.J., are the original compilers of the classic compendium of the doctrinal documents of the Catholic Church in English called *The Christian Faith*. Based on the new edition of the *Enchiridion Symbolorum*, first edited by A. Schönmetzer in 1962, this work includes the creeds of the Church from the earliest times, along with major extracts from all the important decrees and declarations of Councils, Popes, and Vatican congregations, touching on matters of faith and Christian living. The sixth revised and enlarged edition has now been fully updated through June 1995.

All these documents have been organized in chronological order under themes, each with a helpful introduction and outline, so that developments in teaching the Faith, as well as the concerns of theology and authority at various periods in the history of the Church, become more fully apparent.

Indices and tables enhance the value of this unique collection for professors and students of Church history and theology, as well as for all those interested in knowing what the Catholic Church teaches. These documents were extensively quoted in the English-language versions of the *Catechism of the Catholic Church*, and provide additional insights into its text, as well.

The work is available from Alba House. The only regret I have is that the editors caved into political pressure and have made some of the texts "inclusive."

Watch the approach

Q. As a Mariologist, could you please comment on the book *In Search of Mary*, by Sally Cunneen? I have found it very disturbing. The author recognizes that Mary is the most celebrated woman in all human history, however, her approach makes me uncomfortable.

A. I share your reaction. The author is a confirmed feminist and uses theology to advance her ideological agenda, which is revisionist. In other words, she frequently uses traditional terminology and concepts, but manipulates them in such a manner that they no longer retain their traditional meaning. The book, however, does contain much interesting information.

Ready to go?

Q. I am only nine years old, but I have a question about the airplane that crashed (TWA flight 800). I am saved; was Jesus there with those two hundred thirty people when they died? I pray for them because I don't think it was their time to go.

A. Your sensitivity is great for one so young. Just because you have been spared and they were not has nothing to do with the presence or absence of Jesus. God is everywhere, first of all. St. Thomas Aquinas teaches us that if God were not, or if He ceased to think about us for but a moment, we would cease to exist. Second, while God does not cause evil or natural disasters, He does permit them and, in ways unknown to us, they fit into His eternal plan. And so, it is not correct to say that you don't "think it was their time to go." Whenever God calls us, it is the "time to go." Or as Pope John XXIII put it, "Any day is a good day to be born, and any day is a good day to die. My bags are packed, and I'm ready to go." We just have to be sure we are ready for the Lord when He does call us.

Mary's earthly end

Q. In a recent newsletter, our diocesan director of divine worship wrote the following: "August 15 is a festival of Mary's death, burial, and resurrection — her passover. Too often we tend to ignore this day's imagery of death and burial, which gives the feast its fullness. In some areas, the vigil is an occasion to enter into this imagery with a wake for Mary." Is it true that the feast of the Assumption is given its fullness by a consideration of Mary's death and burial? Do we know for sure whether or not Mary died? Does the Pope or any of the bishops have a wake for Mary?

A. The Church has carefully steered away from formal declarations about the end of Mary's life. Even Pope Pius XII, in his solemn definition of the dogma of the Assumption, left it an open question. Therefore, he phrased it as follows: "When the course of her earthly life was finished. . . ." This allows for belief that Mary did indeed die (the predominant view in the West), or for her simple "falling asleep," or passing into the next mode of existence (predominant in the East and, hence, the basis for their title for this feast as the "dormition").

The differences are not essential, but they do have doctrinal implications (and roots). If one argues that Mary did not die, it is based on the fact that since she had no stain of original sin, she would not have undergone the penalty of death. If one holds for her true death, one identifies her with the entire human race, including her own Son, Who experienced death.

As far as a "wake" for her is concerned, I see no problems with such a service; in fact, I remember very fondly participating in just such an event in Spain a couple of years ago on August 15. I would say, however, that before planning anything like this, it would be important to ensure that the cultural groups within a parish do not have conflicting viewpoints on this question; if they do, best to leave a "holy ambiguity," as the Church has done both doctrinally and liturgically — that is, in the official texts.

Ghost tales

Q. What, if anything, does the Catholic Church have to say about "ghosts"? Who and what are they? Are they really the disembodied spirits of dead persons? If so, why aren't they in heaven, hell, or purgatory? I used to think that ghosts were not a serious topic and there was no point in exploring it. However, I am convinced that many sincere, credible witnesses have come forth who are seeing *something*, and this issue has to be addressed in some way. What does the Church have to say?

A. I suspect that different people understand ghosts in different ways, but the usual meaning is shadowy forms of dead people who "roam" the earth. Your intuition is correct — namely, that such beings ought to be in heaven, hell, or purgatory. Granted, God can "send" a saint, for example, to communicate something to us on earth. But that is not what most people have in mind; rather, they envision restless spirits, often seeking revenge or some other equally unsavory objective.

Concern about ghosts is probably about as old as the history of mankind, for we certainly have evidence of interest in ghosts and fear of them recorded in all the major civilizations, including Greece, Rome, and biblical Israel. In the last instance, we find the Scriptures taking aim at the practice of divination, that is, the "conjuring up" of the spirits of the dead to gain knowledge of events, especially of the future. The *Catechism of the Catholic Church* condemns all forms of idolatry, divination, and magic (see nos. 2111-2117).

A friendship

Q. I was shocked to find that Cardinal Joseph Ratzinger is connected to the movement "Communion and Liberation." Does this involvement mean that he is no longer opposed to liberation theology?

A. You seem to be confused about the nature of the movement

Communion and Liberation. It is not a group of supporters of the type of liberation theology earlier censured by the Vatican.

Communion and Liberation is many things: a community, a religious movement, an event; but above all, it is a friendship. One does not join Communion and Liberation by making a vow or joining an organization, but by being drawn into a communion of friendship with those who already share it.

What makes this friendship possible is an experience of the reality of God incarnate, of Christ, not as an idea but as a historical and still-living presence. This presence manifests itself through the living faith and renewed humanity it creates.

Communion and Liberation is only one of the movements through which the Holy Spirit awakens the Church to her own reality — a particular mode in which He makes her live. When the Spirit quickens us, He makes us members of Christ's Body. As His members, we make Christ present to one another and to the world.

Pope John Paul II has said: "With this name [Communion and Liberation] you have manifested your awareness of the expectations of modern man. Liberation, which the world longs for, you have reasoned, is Christ; Christ lives in the Church; man's true liberation, therefore, comes about within the ecclesial communion; to build up this communion is, then, the essential contribution that Christians can give for the liberation of all."

For more information on Communion and Liberation, contact their national office at 6728 11th Ave., Brooklyn, NY 11219; phone, 718-745-7052. By the way, they have a very fine and attractive periodical: *Traces*.

To tell the truth

Q. Several times during my priestly ministry I have faced a situation that leaves me at a loss. I am forty years old, have been ordained six years and am just completing my first year as a pastor. I try to teach the true Catholic teachings on all matters to the best of my ability and understanding. What leaves me at a loss is when I present the Catholic teaching on a subject and a parishioner says, "Well, Father John Doe says. . ." and it is the opposite. For example, at a parents' meeting for First Communion, I explained to a mother why she could not receive Holy Communion since she was in an invalid marriage. Then another mother spoke up and said that Father Doe told her she could receive Holy Communion in her invalid marriage because she had done nothing wrong (her husband was awaiting his annulment). I do not wish to be unkind to a brother priest, as I know many times people take what we say out of context; however, it does leave me for a loss as to a charitable response. It makes me angry when brother priests do allow things that are contrary to what the Church teaches; it makes it harder on those of us who try to do the right thing. Your opinion and thoughts on the matter would be greatly appreciated.

A. The problem you cite, Father, is regrettably widespread. Being confronted with the situation constantly in my work, I have come up with the least confrontational and least embarrassing means possible to deal with it. I begin my response by suggesting that the person may have misunderstood the priest, which is, after all, a real possibility. If he insists to the contrary, I simply present the teaching or discipline of the Church as calmly and objectively as possible. When the person invariably asks why the conflict between the two positions, I just say that we are not living in the best of days, from an ecclesial point of view, but that, thank God, we do have a Pope who teaches clearly, and we do have the *Catechism of the Catholic Church*, which is equally forthright. Finally, I suggest that the person spend some time each day praying for fidelity for all in the Church — clergy, Religious, and laity — to Christ's teaching as it comes to us through the divinely appointed teachers of the Church, that is, the bishops in communion with the Holy Father.

Translation problem

Q. I am a permanent deacon, and once every several weeks my wife asks me the same question, which I cannot answer. None of my friends who are educated in theology can give an adequate answer, either. In the Liturgy of the Hours [Week III, Wednesday, Evening Prayer], the last intercession reads: "Be merciful to the faithful departed, keep them from the power of the Evil One." Once one is among the faithful departed — that is, dead — how can the Evil One have any power over that person? Or does that part of the intercession refer to the time of life? I would be very grateful for whatever assistance you could offer in explaining this.

A. Well, once more, we find a problem of translation! The original Latin says the following: "*Misericordiam tuam fratribus nostris concede defunctis, neque in potestatem maligni spiritus tradas eos.*" A correct rendering would go something like this: "Grant your mercy to our departed brothers, and do not allow them to fall into the power of the Evil Spirit."

In other words, we are not praying "for the faithful departed," but for our deceased brothers and sisters, who may or may not fall into the category of "*faithful* departed." So, confusion is understandable: The faithful departed are beyond the clutches of the Evil One, and this is precisely the point made in the *Catechism of the Catholic Church.* We pray for their further purification, yes, but not for their rescue from hell — that has already happened once someone is "sent" to purgatory (see the *Catechism*, nos. 1030-1032).

Apologetics texts

Q. As a high school teacher, I am always on the lookout for new material to use in my religion class. I have discovered a revised high school religion series in three volumes ("Catholicism and Reason," "Catholicism and Life," and "Catholicism and Society") from C.R. Publications. If you are familiar with the publication, could you please advise me of its strengths and weaknesses?

A. Yes, I have seen the books to which you refer, and I am pleased to recommend them. What they are, in essence, are works of apologetics, that very lost but most necessary branch of theology

— especially suited for both Church and society today. The teaching is clear and thoroughly Catholic, and some excellent illustrative stories are offered. I think students in either Catholic high schools or colleges would resonate well to this material. A teacher's manual is also available. The books may be obtained by contacting: C.R. Publications, 345 Prospect Street, Norwood, MA 02062 (fax no.: 617-762-8811).

The devil's reality

Q. I have written to two clergymen — one Catholic and one Protestant — and neither responded to my question. The topic is not delicate, but perhaps highly subjective. It has to do with who the devil is. When I was taught back in the 1950s, the devil was presented in a very real way. He walked among us in human form causing people to turn from God. A more enlightened view seems to be that Satan is a state of mind — more of a mental process than a grotesque figure that we sometimes see depicted in Bible stories. I watch Christian television programs and have seen cases of people who were living a life of sin be freed by turning to God. These people equated this with being freed from demons. When Jesus cast demons from people in the Gospel, was it literal or allegorical? I do know that the Catholic Church did exorcisms; now it is hardly ever talked about. Does the Church still believe in this? While, admittedly, I am confused about this whole question, I do still believe the devil is real.

A. The Church believes the devil is real, too, and you can discover that by looking up references to him in the *Catechism of the Catholic Church*.

Like you, I was taught in grammar school of his existence as a real person, but I was never taught that he necessarily took on human form. On the contrary, it was explained that since he was an angel (albeit a fallen one), he and his demons were spiritual beings who could, on occasion, assume a bodily form. Pope Paul VI and Pope John Paul II have often catechized the faithful on the real existence of a personal devil — not just a vague notion or influence of evil abroad in the world. And, yes, the rite of exorcism still exists in the Church, although it is not performed very often (it was always hemmed in by very careful strictures and utilized as a last resort — in this, the movie, "The Exorcist," was most accurate).

Catholicism does not spend inordinate amounts of time discussing the devil, but does acknowledge the reality of him, even while having an equally sure knowledge that Christ has already conquered him in the most definitive way through the power of His passion, death, and resurrection. Our attitude needs to be cautious in regard to his power, but hopeful with regard to our final victory over him, because the Lord Jesus has communicated His grace for that to us through His Church and her sacraments, most especially baptism and the Holy Eucharist.

Body and Blood

Q. In all of our parish worship books, a parishioner has changed the wording in the Liturgy of the Eucharist from "Ministers of Communion assist the assembly to share the bread and wine," to "Ministers of Communion assist the assembly to share the Body and Blood of Christ." Which is correct, and why?

A. What is originally printed is heretical, because it denies transubstantiation. We receive the Body and Blood of the Lord.

Science, religion

Q. There has been a wide variety of popular books published lately describing advances in cosmology, astrophysics, and quantum mechanics. The authors present rather convincing arguments in support of the belief that the universe was not created by an "interventionist" God, and the Divinity of Christ is "not possible." Understanding that this type of thought has been around since at least the middle of the nineteenth century, I was wondering whether or not there are any official Catholic responses to this recent challenge posed by the scientific community — specifically responses that address and refute the atheistic conclusions these scientists seem to be drawing from the available data?

A. Decades ago, Archbishop Fulton Sheen wrote a book called *Old Heresies with New Labels*, the point of which was to say that there really isn't all that much new under the sun. When would-be scientists made such charges in the nineteenth century, they were essentially rehashing things said in the fifteenth century, and so on, back to the time of the ancient Greeks. Religion and science should not be seen as antagonistic disciplines, a point repeatedly made by Pope John Paul II. A fine book on this topic is by Bishop Mark Hurley, *Religion and Science*, published by the Daughters of St. Paul. A good resource that looks at the subject of heresy is *Dissent from the Creed*, by Father Richard Hogan, published by Our Sunday Visitor.

Eucharistic reception

Q. My sister is Catholic, but married to a non-Catholic. It is the second marriage for both of them, and both received annulments. He has two children from a previous marriage, who visit him every other weekend. For the ten years they have been married, all four of them attend the Catholic Church. In the past year, her husband said he considers himself Catholic and began receiving Communion (he does believe in the Real Presence). Now, his children have also begun receiving Communion. Is this permissible? I thought they should receive some kind of official instruction first. Should I say something to them? And if so, what? I'm sure they will question me, and I need some concrete information. Thanks for your help.

A. You need to encourage your brother-in-law in his interest in the Church, but he does need to be told at the same time (gently, but firmly) that the Church does not permit what he is doing. Participating in Eucharistic Communion presupposes and demands ecclesial communion — that is, one must be a member of the Catholic Church in order to receive the sacraments (except in extraordinary circumstances, such as danger of death). Both the *Catechism of the Catholic Church* (see nos. 1399-1401) and the *Code* *of Canon Law* make this point (see Canons 842, 844, 912). And, yes, you are certainly correct that instruction is required.

Athanasius' words

Q. In a previous edition of *The Catholic Digest* magazine, there was a trivia question about the New Age movement and man becoming God. The *Digest* quoted the *Catechism of the Catholic Church* (no. 460), which cited St. Athanasius: "For the Son of God became man so that we might become God." I don't agree with the new *Catechism* on this point. There is only one God. We can become holy or Godlike, but never God. Would you please explain St. Athanasius' statement?

A. The Eastern Fathers of the Church were fond of speaking of the Christian life as one of "deification," which means our being made divine. Now, that does not mean that we become God — the gap between us and God is a chasm. He is the Creator, we the creatures; He is our Father, we His children by adoption. That having been said, by the mystery of the Incarnation, God's self-emptying in Christ enables us to share in His divine life. It is what the Latin Mass of Christmas identifies as the *admirabile commercium* — the wonderful exchange between God and man, so that God becomes man, precisely so that we can take on His Divinity. Grace, after all, is nothing more or less than the divine life infused into our immortal souls. At the commingling of the water and wine, the priest prays that we might come to share in the Divinity of Him Who humbled Himself to share our humanity. This is a bold prayer, to be sure, but it must be understood properly, lest someone get the impression you seem to have: God is God, and we are not and never will be. The doctrine you have struck out against is classical Mormonism, not Christianity.

Uncharitable analysis

Q. I am sending you a copy of *The Great Sacrilege*, which purports to give all the "inside dirt" on the Mass of Pope Paul VI. Among other things, the author says that it is "a mortal sin" to attend this Mass. I know you may not have time to read the whole thing, but could you at least look at the passages I have highlighted and give your reaction to them. I am extremely upset by this book and don't really know what to do.

A. The book in question has been on the market for a quarter of a century, unfortunately published by Tan Books. It is unscholarly, unhistorical and uncharitable, to say the least; it is filled with errors of all kinds, as well as half-truths and outright lies. It's not worth getting upset over, but, for your sake, I will offer some comments on a few of his statements (please note that all the emphases are in the original).

— "There has not appeared a scholarly treatise, nor any other treatise for that matter, *upholding* the soundness of the Mass changes" (from the publisher's preface). This is a special pleading of the publisher to sell books. In point of fact, a brief computer search would find literally hundreds of books explaining the "new Mass," including at least two of my own.

— "The Decrees of the Council [of Trent] on the Holy Mass have always been understood to be *ex cathedra* definitions" (p. 35). Of course, that is true, but the dogmatic definitions of the Council are one thing, while the liturgical or rubrical prescriptions are another. No Catholic is free to deny the dogma of the Church; no Catholic is bound to like or approve of any and every aspect of liturgical life. Thus, prior to the Council, Catholics were quite capable of being loyal to the Deposit of the Faith even as they suggested ways to improve the Mass. Similarly, today, no one is disloyal for intimating that a particular change was unnecessary or unwise — or that other changes (including "steps backward") could be prudent. In other words, no liturgical form is sacred in itself since none has ever come to us from God, but is always mediated through human instruments. The freedom the author claims to criticize the so-called "Novus

Ordo" Mass is his, but that same freedom allows others to critique the Mass of Pope St. Pius V.

— "Popes are not infallible in the exercise of their legislative power." (p. 43). The author makes this statement to justify his nonacceptance of the Mass of Paul VI — and he is correct. However, that same rationale applies to the Mass of Pius V — for the reasons I offered above.

— "Intrinsic to the very idea of the 'New Mass' is that the *people* are more important than Christ the Savior." (p. 51). Says who? What document? What authority in the Church? No one is entitled to make such outrageous statements without offering proof for the allegation.

— "And those priests who have no other *intention* than that expressed by the 'Novus Ordo' certainly do not effect the transubstantiation of the bread and wine!" (p. 84). The intention of the "Novus Ordo" is precisely the same as that of the old "Ordo" — a point clearly made by Pope Paul VI in his introduction to the revised rite.

The poor priest who wrote the book, about whom I know nothing, totally overstates his case and does it in a manner which is unprofessional, disrespectful, and plainly wrong. One need not be an enthusiastic cheerleader for the new rite of the Mass itself, let alone for abuses of it which have been tolerated for all too long, to know that this work is the result of anger and bitterness and, thus, is evidence of the lack of the presence of the Spirit of Christ.

Face-off

Q. Even though your columns in *The Catholic Answer* magazine are clearly a forum for ultraconservative malcontents to weep and moan about refreshing changes in the Church and about progressive Catholics, you admittedly provide some interesting reading material, even though some of what you offer is truly bad. (I must admit that abuse exists, but I wonder if you stick long pins into your copy of *The Documents of the Second Vatican Council* each night!) Your most preposterous response was entitled "Not demanded," especially when coupled with your response on "Common distribution." Those two responses reek of self-righteousness. You seem to be saying, "I have never received Communion in the hand," implying that the practice is unquestionably bad, and "I know that the decisions to receive Communion in the hand, and for the laity to receive Communion under both species were bad decisions!" Your duty is to accept, obey, and comply, not to fertilize polarization and undermine authority. We can't look at the Eucharist as was practiced in the dark ages of Roman Catholicism to be the norm. We must look at the Eucharist at its inception, a meal or banquet where all present apparently took part. As for your self-righteous comment that "I have never received Communion in the hand in twenty years," Wow! When you are a concelebrating priest, I can just picture you receiving the Host on your tongue, but when you preside, how do you get the Host from the paten to your tongue? I assume that you use your mortal fingers, just as I receive the Host in my fingers. What's the difference? Do you also discourage the sign of peace, the ordination of permanent deacons, and standing during the eucharistic prayers? Please direct your efforts toward joy, warmth, and *koinonia* in the Mass, toward unity, and continuing needed change in the Church, and toward "cleaning up" the priesthood and seminarians. I left the seminary to be married, and I know. You are in my prayers.

A. I see that Christian charity is a strong suit of your brand of Catholicism! The push for "joy, warmth, and *koinonia*" just oozed out of every line of your letter. Obviously, one need not be a right-wing extremist to have the corner on nasty judgmentalism, eh? Letters such as yours rarely find their way into print in any periodical, but every so often I like to give readers a clue as to the type of material that does pass my desk. At any rate, I shall attempt to respond to your many concerns.

I have not an iota of difficulty with any document of the Second Vatican Council — as any reader of *The Catholic Answer* magazine ought to be aware. I have many problems with people who use the Second Vatican Council as a mere "jumping off" point for their own bizarre practices and ideas.

I do indeed think that the decision to permit Communion in the hand was pastorally imprudent, and that it now has begun to have doctrinal fallout one generation later. Your admonition that my "duty is to accept, obey, and comply" sounds like the echo of a nonthinking authoritarian from the "bad old days."

I do not know which period you identify as "the dark ages" of the Church, but to my way of thinking, any age that has more than seventy percent of their weekly communicants confused about the Real Presence must be classified as an incredibly dark age. That time is, as you undoubtedly know, the present. Furthermore, Catholics are not "antiquarians," in that we do not romanticize the practices of the so-called Primitive Church. Our grasp of doctrine increases and, with that, our practice often changes to ensure that what we believe is preserved — even at the symbolic level.

As far as my own reception of Holy Communion, allow me to clarify. When I am the principal celebrant or a concelebrant, I have no choice but to take the Host directly from the paten, but in those very circumstances I am acting in *persona Christi* in a unique manner. I was referring to times when I am simply attending Mass, and then I receive on the tongue. The difference between your "mortal fingers" and mine is that mine were anointed.

Evolution

Q. The Holy Father has recently explained that it is compatible with our Catholic Faith to accept Darwin's theory of man's evolution if we hold that at a given time God infused an immortal soul into a male and a female of a species. Maybe my way of explaining it is not accurate? Could you provide me with a better explanation so that a non-Catholic friend might find it easier to understand? Is there a reference which would be helpful?

A. What Pope John Paul II said got a great deal of coverage from the media, but I don't know why — because it was nothing new whatsoever. In fact, it was exactly what I was taught in grammar school in the 1950s, which in turn was a faithful reflection of what Pope Pius XII had taught in *Humani Generis* (concerning some false opinions threatening to undermine the foundations of Catholic doctrine) in 1950, but not all that different from what even St. Augustine had taught nearly fifteen centuries earlier.

The synopsis of your explanation sounds fine; for something in print, consult my Our Sunday Visitor's *Catholic Encyclopedia*, under the topic of "Evolution," as well as *Humani Generis* for a decent shorthand treatment.

Sacramental signs

Q. Recently, I attended, with a friend, a course on sacramentality at the Kino Institute in Phoenix, Ariz. At the end of the course, my friend said she believed that since we as individuals receive sacraments, we as individuals *are* sacraments. I am having a difficult time understanding her assumption, since we receive grace through the sacraments. Please clarify this for me.

A. The word "sacrament" means "sign." Christ is the primary sacrament, or "sign," of the Father's love for the human race; the Church is a secondary "sign"; the seven sacraments are "signs" in a tertiary manner. To the extent that you and I reflect Jesus and the Father's love, we, too, can function as "sacraments" in an analogous way; and, yes, we can also be means or channels of grace by leading people to Christ and His Church. But one must be very careful not to be sloppy in our terminology. The seven sacraments of the Church are unequivocal, constant signs and means of grace; you and I, regrettably, are not.

The sedevacantists

Q. Among so-called traditionalist groups, there are those — sedevacantists — who believe that the Church since the Second Vatican Council is not Catholic, and that somehow those in authority have personally defected from the Faith, thereby losing their authority. They believe that the present Pope is not legitimate and that the "see is vacant." Their reasoning proceeds: The Church cannot teach error or permit evil, but the Church since the Second Vatican Council has done so; therefore, this Church cannot be the Catholic Church. They quote St. Robert Bellarmine, who said that a heretical Pope would lose his office. Two common examples they give of errors are: (1) Their claim that the Pope personally denied the fifth article of the Apostles' Creed in his January 11, 1989, audience; (2) Their claim that the new *Code of Canon Law* (specifically, Canon 844) by allowing non-Catholics to receive Holy Communion is implicitly heretical since it denies the unitive element of this sacrament. Can you please comment on their arguments, in general and on the specific examples?

A. On the first score, the fifth article of the Creed deals with Christ's descent into hell and resurrection from the dead. The critic of the Pope whose letter you enclose is unsigned, it should be noted. I have read both the Holy Father's address and the critique, which allege the Pope has contravened the teaching of the *Roman Catechism*, or *Catechism of the Council of Trent*; I fail to see that at all. If anything, entire portions of the present Pope's talk seem to be almost verbatims from the Tridentine document. The only thing Pope John Paul II does is expand the notion of "hell," or "hades," to offer a more comprehensive view of what the Jews understood by "sheol," the Hebrew equivalent of those terms. The critic is upset that the Pope excludes the hell of the damned from the purview of this doctrine, but his rebuttal is not a citation from Trent's *Catechism* but his own words.

In regard to the second matter, while Church discipline on intercommunion is extremely important, it is discipline and not doctrine; therefore, someone may feel that contemporary practice in this regard is too loose or imprudent, but he cannot assert that this is heretical.

The sedevacantists, in general, are a bunch of malcontents who often have problems not only with Pope John Paul II but also with Pope Paul VI. Pressed even more, some of them refuse to acknowledge the legitimacy of the pontificate of Pope John XXIII and even that of Pope Pius XII. I have heard yet others maintain that even Pope St. Pius X is suspect because he initiated the entire liturgical reform and approved the first mitigated eucharistic fast. As you can readily see, when individuals set themselves up as the norm, no authority figure is free from their critique. In point of fact, these types are qualitatively no different from Protestants, who hold that their view of theology and ecclesial life are controlling, not some Pope's.

With a more jaundiced eye, one can also see that it is much easier to raise funds for one's personal schism if one can accuse the Pope and his minions of infidelity.

Objective reality

Q. I just bought a book entitled *Paradigms Lost*, by John Casti, and a chapter in it reveals a position taken by many leading physicists of the twentiethth century that I think needs to be answered. In the chapter "How Real is the Real World," Casti presents several views of leading physicists on the implications of quantum theory. It would seem that most of the leading lights of twentieth-century physics believe that there is no real world — that is, that unless a person makes an observation, nothing exists. Casti does present the opposing view of objective reality, a view shared by no less than Albert Einstein. You don't need a Ph.D. in physics to weigh in on this question. I would like to hear the Catholic opinion on this issue.

A. Good philosophy, good theology, and good science all come to the same conclusions, even if from different perspectives. I am in no position to debate physicists, but the question has surely been considered by philosophers and theologian for millennia, with the overwhelming majority of thinkers coming down on the side of objective reality. And I think the preponderance of scientists would hold to the same.

Heresy-speak

Q. Since I'm confused and you are the greatest apologist in this country, I'm asking for your help. Please read the enclosed article by Cardinal Joseph Ratzinger. It seems to me that he speaks out of both ends of his mouth. The last piece by him that I read stated that the all-male priesthood is part of the Deposit of Faith and is taught infallibly by the ordinary, universal magisterium. The case was closed, and those who did not accept this teaching put themselves outside the Church. Now he says that this is not heresy, but only an error. Bull!

A. Let me say that I appreciate your regard for me, but even as you might consider me to be "the greatest apologist in this country," I deem Cardinal Ratzinger to be "the greatest theologian in the world!"

The comments of Cardinal Ratzinger to which you refer were made in a press conference on January 24. *Origins* (February 13, 1997) summarized the cardinal's remarks thus: "The Church generally groups teachings into three categories: first, dogmas contained in revelation; second, definitive doctrines not formally revealed but linked to revelation; third, other teachings requiring an attitude of respect and assent." He indicated the teaching on the all-male priesthood falls into the second category, such that the rejection of it "perhaps should not be put in the category of heresy, but in that of 'alien to and incompatible with the Faith.'" The news summary continued: "The cardinal added that according to Church legal experts, canon law clearly spells out juridical consequences for those who reject Church teachings of the first and third categories, but is not clear about the second category. He described this as a 'gap,' but said it remained apparent that such people were in serious doctrinal error." Given the traditional categories, however, he observed that this "would not be heresy in the strict sense of the word."

Confusion seems to come to surface whenever heresy is discussed because the average Catholic is not aware of the gradations of Church teaching, that is, that there are different "levels" of "certainty" demanding different degrees of assent. This is not a new-fangled notion; it can be found in all the old, preconciliar theology manuals. Ludwig Ott, in his *Fundamentals of Catholic Dogma* (originally published in English in 1955 and reprinted by Tan Books in 1974), lists and explains them. Allow me to quote him extensively and then comment:

"1. The highest degree of certainty appertains to the immediately revealed truths. The belief due to them is based on the authority of God Revealing (*fides divina*), and if the Church, through its teaching, vouches for the fact that a truth is contained in Revelation, one's certainty is then also based on the authority of the Infallible Teaching Authority of the Church (*fides catholica*). If Truths are defined by a solemn judgment of faith (definition) of the Pope or of a General Council, they are '*de fide definita.*'

"2. Catholic truths or Church doctrines, on which the Infallible Teaching Authority of the Church has finally decided, are to be accepted with a faith which is based on the sole authority of the Church (*fides ecclesiastica*). These truths are as infallibly certain as dogmas proper.

"3. A Teaching proximate to Faith (*sententia fidei proxima*) is a doctrine, on which the Teaching Authority of the Church has not yet finally pronounced, but whose truth is guaranteed by its intrinsic connection with the doctrine of revelation [theological conclusions]."

Ott goes on to speak of "Common Teaching," which is open to free opinions and "theological opinions," which are of even lower ranking.

Pope St. Pius X essentially subscribed to this method in producing his *Syllabus of Errors*, citing the relative seriousness of each error condemned. To come under the rubric of "heresy," the teaching in question must belong to either the first or second category listed by Ott. However, simply because something is not a "category-one or -two" teaching does not mean that it is "up for grabs," and Cardinal Ratzinger has consistently warned against a mentality that opts for a minimalistic approach to the reception of Catholic doctrine. In other words, it is just as immature to argue that if something is not infallibly defined that one is free to dissent as it is immature to say that if an action is only a venial sin, there is no problem with committing it.

Whose will be done?

Q. A few weeks ago, talking to my sixteen-year-old son about the omniscience of God, he startled me by saying that God did not or does not know what we are going to do in a given situation and that if He does, there would not be the need to do anything or make any effort because everything would have been predetermined. This view seems to be evidenced by the account of Abraham's readiness to sacrifice his son, Isaac. My counterpoint to his argument was that by removing the foreknowledge of God in human events, it would seem to me that we are denying one of God's attributes, omniscience. I also argued that while God knows the outcome of all events — including who is going to be saved and who is not — He will not interfere with our will. How are these two points of view reconcilable? Please explain.

A. Divine foreknowledge or omniscience is a reality, but that does not necessarily mean direct causality on the part of God. Perhaps an analogy from human experience will be of some value. Say that there are two mountains, and you are standing on top of one and can see the other, which has a train track surrounding it. You observe a train approaching from the east and another from the west on the same track. With as much certitude as is humanly possible, you "know" that a collision will occur. Do you cause it? No. In much the same way, Almighty God knows all things — past, present, and future — but He does not directly cause each and every event. The laws of nature that He set in place govern affairs normally, and His permissive Will allows us to use our free wills to go counter to His. The evil done, then, is not caused by God, nor directly willed by Him.

Error-free

Q. My pastor says that we should ignore what the ecumenical

Councils taught prior to the Council of Trent. He says that only the last three Councils (Council of Trent, the First Vatican Council, and the Second Vatican Council) were free from error, and the others were not. I thought that all ecumenical Councils were prevented from teaching error by the Holy Spirit, but my pastor said that is incorrect. Is he correct?

A. Obviously, your pastor is not "free from error"! The doctrinal and moral positions of all ecumenical Councils are binding on all the faithful — and that is the constant teaching of the Church.

Everlasting choices

Q. The revolt of the angels shows that sin was possible for pure spirits in heaven. After death, will human beings be capable of sin in purgatory? What about in heaven after the particular judgment? After the final judgment? (I am assuming that sin continues in hell.) If the answer is yes, from where will the temptations come, and what would be the nature of them?

A. All testing of human beings ends with physical death. Otherwise, we would be involved in some kind of Judaeo-Christian take on reincarnation. Our earthly existence is definitive, therefore, and we must live in that awareness. That thought can be frightening or consoling, depending on how one lives his life on earth. Our free will enables us to make such definitive choices for or against God, and those choices establish a mind-set, or orientation, from which it becomes difficult to deviate. Because God takes our freedom, intelligence, and dignity seriously, He allows us to choose eternity in time. Thus what we do on earth literally has eternal consequences.

Entrance into heaven is entrance into a state of eternal happiness which, by definition, can never end. Admission to purgatory is embarking upon a period of purification (not testing), such that the time of preparation will conclude in heavenly beatitude; purgatory, then, is likewise a "guarantee" of everlasting bliss. Hell is a state of eternal separation from God, but since further choices are not possible in eternity, I would not speak of the continuation of sin in hell as you do (because that would imply that sinful choices can still be made). Rather, I would say that a sinful attitude or state of mind continues to exist, and from which no one in hell has any intention of diverging.

Boniface's words

Q. I have always been taught that the Pope is infallible in matters of religion and God, and that he basically has the last word on any subject. Recently, I discovered a quote from Pope Boniface VIII, for which I needed clarification, and so I called a canon lawyer in our diocese. The quote states: "The Roman Pontiff judges all men, but is judged by no one. We declare, assert, define, and pronounce: To be subject to the Roman Pontiff is to every human creature altogether necessary for salvation. That which was spoken of Christ, 'Thou hast subdued all things under his feet' may well seem verified in me. I have the authority of the King of Kings. I am all in all, and above all, so that God Himself and I (the Vicar of God), have but one consistory, and I am able to do almost all that God can do. What, therefore, can you make of me but God?" (*Unam Sanctam*, November 18, 1302). The Pope here is declaring that the Popes are God on earth. He was never excommunicated or charged with blasphemy. The canon lawyer at first didn't believe me, but I had him look up the quote. He insists that Pope Boniface was speaking blasphemy and could have been put to death. Is this true? Do the modern Popes hold this dogma? How can the Pope presume to be God? I find this all very distressing, especially since my church bears the name of St. Boniface.

A. Let's start at the back and then move forward. Whether you like or not like what Pope Boniface VIII wrote, you need not worry that your parish is named after him, since he was never canonized; your parochial patron is St. Boniface, the apostle to Germany, in all likelihood.

In interpreting papal or conciliar documents, we must do the same thing as we do in interpreting Sacred Scripture — that is, we must place the text within a context. Pope Boniface lived during a tumultuous time for the Church, when the authority of the Popes was severely challenged by civil authority, and the Popes had taken refuge in Avignon, France. Pope Boniface was attempting to explain how all legitimate authority must be rooted in submission to spiritual authority, which is, of course, a most valid point — although our mode of expression today might be somewhat different. The dogmatic statement of the decree is limited to two points: the necessity of the Church for salvation and the need for all to be subject to the Roman Pontiff. Those teachings must be believed by every Catholic, as they have been proposed and understood within the Church's Tradition; the rest of the document does not have the same weight.

As far as the line asserting that a Pope is God is concerned, a bit of nuance is required. The entire decree goes to great lengths to show the unity between Almighty God and the Sovereign Pontiff, so that they form one entity, just as do Christ and the Church. There is certainly a way to understand this properly; at the same time, however, it can be misinterpreted, so that great caution is needed.

Honest labels?

Q. I have been reading *A Concise History of the Catholic Church*, by Thomas Bokenkotter, in which he asserts that much of the progress achieved at the Second Vatican Council was due to the work of dissenting theologians whose views were labeled as "heresies" before the Council. I am trying to understand why people feel they can dissent from Church teaching and still be good Catholics.

A. First of all, I would note that the book to which you allude is not the most reliable work, since it often engages in a revisionist approach to Church history, and strives mightily to justify a leftward-leaning ecclesiology.

The theologians whom the author probably has in mind would be men such as Henri de Lubac, Père Garrigou-Lagrange, and Yves Congar, who were definitely ahead of their times but in no way outside the Church. They were proposing not new teachings but newer ways (which often enough were actually older but forgotten ways) of presenting the unchanging doctrine of the Church.

The dissenters today do not fit into that camp. When Hans Kueng denies papal infallibility, he is denying a dogma of faith, not helping us to understand something in a deeper way. When Charles Curran says the Church is wrong in her teaching on artificial contraception, he is placing himself in total opposition to the constant moral tradition of the Church, spanning two thousand years.

Honesty demands that we label things for what they are, and dissent is infidelity to the truth of Christ, fractious of the Church's unity, and a source of scandal to those within the Church and without. Therefore, it is a terrible offense against faith, justice, and charity.

Merit badge

Q. If a Catholic commits a mortal sin after many years of his life and sincerely makes a good confession, what happens to all the merit he may have obtained prior to his falling into grievous sin? Are these merits lost forever? Does God take into account the good he did prior to that fall?

A. When we talk about merit, we must be extremely careful, lest we give the impression that somehow or other we achieve our own salvation, independent of the grace of Christ. Of course, we must cooperate with God's grace, and there is "merit" in doing that. When the Church talks about merit, she often falls back on the analogy of a treasury, from which graces are drawn or into which they are "deposited." Like all analogies, this one limps; however, it can be somewhat helpful. For example, the overflowing merits of Our Lady and the other saints constitute a treasury on which we can all draw because of the doctrine of the Communion of Saints, constituting one body as Christ's Church.

If a person in mortal sin receives a sacrament (for which he ought to be free from serious sin), he receives the sacrament if all other conditions are fulfilled, but not the graces; when he returns to the state of grace, the graces of the sacrament — for example, the Sacraments of Matrimony or Holy Orders — then flow into him, the dam being released — as it were — and allowing for the completion of the sacrament. In some way, I would see your concern being dealt with in much the same manner.

Love-giving, life-giving

Q. I understand that the Church teaches that the marital act is meant to be both love-giving and life-giving. From many things I've read and heard, it seems that society in general believes that the Church has traditionally taught that the life-giving aspect is the only important one. I suspect that this has not really been the traditional teaching of the magisterium, but the way it has been taught by many priests in the past. When discussing this with others, I would like to be able to refer to Church documents or Councils in which both aspects were upheld as important. Do any exist? Someone suggested that St. Augustine held such a view, but I don't know where to begin to look. Is there anything between his time and our century?

A. Your suppositions are largely correct. However, we also should note that in this area of theology — as in others — there is growth in understanding with the passage of time. Hence, St. Augustine would not have been very strong on the unitive aspect of marriage (although never denying it); St. Bonaventure, on the other hand, had tremendous insights into this matter. A fine book on this topic was written recently by Sister Paula Jean Miller, entitled *Marriage: The Sacrament of Divine-Human Communion* [*Volume I, A Commentary on St. Bonaventure's* Breviloqium], published by Franciscan Press in Quincy, Ill. By reading Pope John Paul II's writings and addresses on the nature of Christian marriage, you will get a good overview of contemporary Catholic teaching on the subject; indeed, he has certainly broken much new ground in this regard. By paying attention to his footnotes, however, you will see the authors from the past in whom he grounds his developments.

Free will

Q. I recently watched a program on PBS in which a group of religious educators (at least three of whom were from Catholic institutions) were discussing the Book of Genesis and what it related to us about God. The consensus seemed to be that the "fall" was a "set-up" — God knew that man would choose to eat the fruit just as a parent knows that a child is likely to raid the cookie jar. Why did God permit Satan to tempt Eve?

A. The series to which you refer was really quite shallow and unscholarly. No substantive issues were dealt with. It is necessary to distinguish between God's permissive Will and divine predestination, and it is important to appreciate the meaning and dignity of human free will. It is also critical to understand the nature of temptation and to realize that the Son of God Himself was tempted, but never sinned. Cardinal Joseph Ratzinger has written a wonderful commentary on the Genesis texts related to the creation and the fall, published by Wm. B. Eerdmans Publishing Co., titled *'In the Beginning. . .' A Catholic Understanding of the Story of Creation and the Fall.* You will find much more value in what he wrote than in what the would-be scholars contributed.

Exposé

Q. I have been told that it is not proper to have prayers such as the Rosary recited before the Blessed Sacrament exposed. Are the documents that are quoted accurate, or is there a slant to them?

A. We have handled this question before, but it keeps coming up, so let's try it one more time.

First, the decree *Eucharisticum Mysterium* does not forbid the type of prayers to which you allude; the American commentary on it attempts to do so, which is the first "slant," as you put it. The original document (now more than two decades old, by the way) does urge that prayers to Christ be offered during exposition; it does not say "to Christ alone."

Second, as I have remarked before, Christ is not a jealous God Who demands our undivided attention when we come to Him; He is certainly not envious of prayers to His own Blessed Mother or other saints. Why? Because the Scriptures inform us that God is "glorified in his saints" [2 Thes 1:10]. They constitute part of the whole Body of Christ, and they are now members of God's family in a unique and wonderful manner.

Third, in reference to the Rosary specifically, let me make the following point. As Pope Paul VI's *Marialis Cultus* observed, the Rosary is essentially not a *Marian* prayer but a *Christological* prayer, bringing before our minds the mysteries of the redemption wrought by Christ. It is worth mentioning that the same Pope who wrote *Marialis Cultus* was also responsible for *Eucharisticum Mysterium*; presumably, he would not have seen a problem with the recitation of the Rosary before the Blessed Sacrament exposed. Furthermore, using the logic of the people you have been in touch with, one should not be able to pray the Rosary in any church where the Blessed Sacrament is reserved because Christ is just as truly present whether in the tabernacle or on the altar.

That's the truth

Q. A while ago, Ann Landers wrote in her column that Roman Catholicism was founded by Jesus Christ, while all other Christian denominations were founded by ordinary men. She was immediately taken to task by many readers. One of them wrote that "Jesus Himself founded no specific church. He established a faith." How can the faith be separated from the visible body that confesses it?

A. While Ann Landers is hardly a theologian, every so often she does get it right. Of course, the witness of secular history demonstrates clearly that Jesus did indeed establish a Church, which founding is first recorded in the 16th chapter of St. Matthew's Gospel. You are quite correct in asserting that faith cannot "be separated from the visible body that confesses it." The New Testament is replete with passages that indicate Our Lord intended to found a Church, and that His early followers understood that to be His Will.

Christianity is not a philosophy; it is composed of a creed, code, and cult, which have little meaning apart from the body of believers who live according to them. An amorphous Christianity is a contradiction in terms; surely, this is what St. Paul learned on the road to Damascus as the Lord identified Himself, not with a list of theories, but with a body of believers (see Acts 9).

Physical dimension

Q. I would like your take on Msgr. Mannion's explanation of how Christ is "present" in the Eucharist in his Q & A column "Pastoral Answers" in the *Our Sunday Visitor* issue of May 21, 2000. Having viewed and kissed the miracle Host of Santerem, I have a difficult time accepting his explanation.

A. I suppose you take exception to Msgr. Mannion's assertion that Christ is not "materially" present in the Eucharist, which he argues is different from "substantially." I agree with him. The substantial presence of Christ has a physical dimension to it, by all means, but we must remember that the Body we receive is His Risen Body, which has elements in common with His earthly Body, but also differs from it.

In *Mysterium Fidei*, Pope Paul VI explained it in this way: "For there no longer lies under those species what was there before, but something quite different; and that, not only because of the faith of the Church, but in objective reality, since after the change of the substance or nature of the bread and wine into the Body and Blood of Christ, nothing remains of the bread and wine but the appearances, under which Christ, whole and entire, in His physical 'reality' [the Pope uses the quotation marks] is bodily present, although not in the same way as bodies are present in a given place."

Notice how the Pope Paul teaches a physical presence, all the while highlighting the fact that this presence is not like others.

Holy Spirit's I.D.

Q. I am concerned about our pastoral administrator's writing the following in our Sunday bulletin: "The Holy Spirit is alive and well and knows what *she* [emphasis added] is doing." When I expressed my discomfort about this to the author, she responded to my objection with a rambling article, *The Wisdom Literature: The Wisdom Woman*. I feel like the guy who asked a friend what time it was and she built him a watch! I have had sixteen years of Catholic education, graduating college in 1950; however, I feel inadequate to discuss this interpretation with someone who should have more training than I do. I don't feel comfortable with many of these recent changes, and so I turn to you.

A. The piece you enclosed with your question is, I agree, rambling, offering little of value. We know well that Wisdom is personified in the Old Testament as a woman, but Wisdom is not the only part of the Holy Spirit's identity. Can we forget that Our Lady is referred to precisely as "the Spouse of the Holy Spirit," because it is by the Spirit's overshadowing that she bears the Second Person of the Blessed Trinity in her body. And very much to the point is that the recently released norms from the Holy See on "inclusive language" categorically *forbid* the use of either a neuter or feminine pronoun for the Holy Spirit.

Apathetic response

Q. If God came in His glory, He would be thronged by the crowds; yet His presence is just as real in the Eucharist, and Our Lord spends all but a few hours a week alone in the tabernacles of our churches. If we Catholics believe, as the Church teaches, that Jesus is truly present in the Eucharist, why are so many of us so-called believing Catholics so apathetic in our response to this almost incredible reality? It just seems like such a dichotomy to believe in the Real Presence and then to ignore that Presence in our churches outside of Mass?

A. Your instincts are completely on target, and that is one reason why Pope Paul VI, in *Mysterium Fidei* (on the Holy Eucharist), and our present Holy Father, have stressed with such urgency and frequency the importance of Eucharistic Adoration. While Christ is present in many ways in the Church and in the world, as the Second Vatican Council reminds us, His presence in the Holy Eucharist is unique and irreplaceable (see *Sacrosanctum Concilium* [Constitution on the Sacred Liturgy], no. 7). In conjunction with that realization, one must also conclude that not only is it essential to spend time with our Eucharistic Lord, but also to extend to Him under the veiled signs of bread and wine the adoration due the Second Person of the Blessed Trinity: reverential silence, genuflection when passing before the tabernacle, or before receiving Holy Communion, and a central location for the tabernacle — all of which are called for in the Church's liturgical documents, but most of which are roundly ignored in most parishes.

One fundamentalist minister put it quite starkly after visiting several of our churches and observing our behavior: "If I believed about the Eucharist what you Catholics say you believe or are supposed to believe, I would have to come up the center aisle to receive crawling on my belly!" I suspect that man is "not far from the kingdom of God" (Mk 12:34).

Careful study

Q. I have tried to study the Pope's documents for years now, and I'm not a stupid man (sixteen years of Catholic schooling), but he seems so much "in the clouds." For example, I've been reading *Evangelium Vitae* ("The Gospel of Life") for a year now, and it's still a mystery — not the doctrine, but the argumentation. Any suggestions?

A. Pope John Paul II, remember, is a philosopher by trade. Someone has joked that a philosopher never says something in five words when he can do it in five thousand! So, this Pope is not an "easy read," to be sure. What I have found helpful, however, is to read through the entire document first and then to go back and plough through it, inch by inch.

The Knights of Columbus have come up with a good study guide on *Evangelium Vitae*, done by Russell Shaw, a veteran Catholic journalist who is theologically astute and thoroughly orthodox. It may be obtained from the Knights at: 1 Columbus Plaza, New Haven, CT 06510.

Procreative ethics

Q. I have recently read an article that made mention of the Pope Paul VI Institute in Omaha. Just what do they do to help so many well-intentioned but uninformed, or ill-informed, married couples who need to regulate the size of their families?

A. A publication of the institute that is very worthwhile is called *The NaProEthics Forum* — that is, a forum on natural procreative ethics — published six times each year. The editorial, feature articles, and book review of each issue are aimed at promoting the intellectual formation of Catholic educators in the home, school, diocesan, and health care settings. With an accessible and engaging menu, the newsletter discusses the moral principles and specific concerns pertaining to sexual, familial, and marital ethics — issues that are often troubling to discerning Catholics today. Subscribers can keep abreast of very thoughtful analyses of the Catholic perspective on the ethical aspects of human procreation and procreative-related medicine. For more information, write to Pope Paul VI Institute, and send to: Editor, Center for NaProEthics, Omaha, NE 68106-2604.

Eternal musings

Q. Before the first coming of Jesus, where were the souls of the people who had died until that time? The Apostles' Creed says that Jesus "descended into hell." Did He do this to release the dead to heaven, purgatory or hell? If so, did the release of these souls happen immediately, or did everything wait until the moment of the resurrection on the third day? The Creed also says that "He will come again in glory to judge the living and the dead." Does this mean that those who are alive at the time of Jesus' second coming will not experience the particular judgment?

A. The first point that must be understood is that God dwells in eternity, not in time, therefore, many of our questions are entirely too conditioned by the normal human reference points of past, present, and future. That would apply to your concern about whether the releases of the souls "happen[ed] immediately" or "wait[ed] until the moment of the Resurrection on the third day." Since God lives in an ever-present moment, everything happens for Him all at once.

Our Lord's preaching to the souls "in hell" has been traditionally understood as His proclamation of the Gospel to the just who had died before His coming. In other words, these were people who were entitled to heaven by their holy lives but who, by an accident of birth we can say, had not lived to see the salvation wrought by their long-awaited Messiah. Jesus' preaching to them and their acceptance of His message gained them access to the beatific vision.

Regarding the particular judgment for those who are alive at the Lord's second coming, I am unaware of any definitive teaching. I would hazard the following reasoned guess. Since, as I indicated above, God operates in an eternal present, and since the Parousia will usher in eternity for us all, I would suppose that the particular and general judgments would be "merged" — at least in our consciousness. All this having been said, we need to be humble enough to realize that what we know about such events is nothing compared to what we do not know, and that delving into them is often a rather unhealthy sign for spiritual maturity and a creaturely posture.

Love versus doctrine?

Q. A recent article in the newspaper has me confused. The title is "Parents told to support their gay children before doctrine," and is in reference to the pastoral letter of the U.S. bishops. I know that we should love our children, but is it correct to position that love against Church teaching? Has this document been approved by the Vatican? I am sure many other parents are also curious. I hope you can shed some light on this matter.

A. The document in question is *Always Our Children*, produced by the bishops' Committee on Marriage and Family Life.

I have read the letter in great detail several times, precisely because of the furor raised over it. The headline you found is completely without foundation because the letter clearly begins with noting Catholic teaching on homosexuality and homosexual activity; it then moves on to pastoral considerations. Doctrinally, then, the document is sound; we can question the pastoral advisability of it, or certain parts of it, but that is an entirely different matter. Furthermore, it is not a statement of the full body of bishops and thus has no true standing.

My biggest objection to the letter stems from the fact that it was submitted to the administrative committee of the National Conference of Catholic Bishops for their approval, rather than being presented to the entire conference. The timing made no sense, since its submission was only a few weeks before the plenary assembly of the bishops would convene for their annual meeting. Many bishops were annoyed at this procedure, which could give the impression that there was an attempt to conduct an "end-run" around the full body of bishops on a rather sensitive topic.

The content, nonetheless, violates Church teaching in no way.

Looking East

Q. I understand that in November 1996, the U.S. bishops issued guidelines stating that members of the Orthodox Churches, the Assyrian Church of the East, and the Polish National Church may receive Communion at a Catholic Mass. Have the bishops of those Churches given permission to their faithful to receive Communion in Catholic churches? Also, I've never been able to distinguish clearly between the many Eastern Orthodox Churches and the Eastern-rite Catholic Churches; could you list those churches that fall within each category? Finally, in which of those churches may a Roman Catholic receive the Eucharist, and in which may he fulfill his Sunday Mass obligation?

A. In general, the Eastern Orthodox do not permit their faithful to receive Holy Communion from us — except in danger of death or other serious emergency. And this is one reason why many bishops thought that our guidelines would be poorly received by the Orthodox hierarchy, since it could seem as though we were inviting their people to disobey their own law in this regard. The only body with which we certainly have a reciprocal agreement is the Polish National Catholics.

As far as Eastern Churches, Catholic and Orthodox, go, let me note the following. Every Eastern Church in union with the Holy See (except for the Maronites, who proudly point to the fact that they have lived in uninterrupted communion with Rome from the very beginning) has an Orthodox counterpart — for example, Russian, Greek, Ukrainian, etc. See Our Sunday Visitor's *Catholic Encyclopedia* for a detailed presentation on these matters.

As far as our reception of Holy Communion and fulfillment of the Sunday Mass obligation is concerned, since the Orthodox do not welcome us to inter-Communion, we ought to refrain from receiving, out of respect for their theology and discipline. Attending the Eucharistic Sacrifice in any Orthodox Church on an irregular basis (for reasons of information, friendship, etc.) would fulfill one's Sunday obligation.

Christ's representative

Q. I enclose a clipping from a recent parish bulletin: "Beginning today and for the rest of the liturgical year, the eucharistic prayer will be enhanced musically, with chant, response, and instrumental accompaniment. Most often it seems that the eucharistic prayer is the priest's monologue, giving the impression that the priest does the consecration. But actually it is the prayer of thanksgiving of all the church." Does this opinion represent good theology or liturgy? I thought only an ordained priest could validly consecrate the bread and wine at Mass.

A. A practical point first: The eucharistic prayer, while it may certainly be chanted by the celebrant, should not be accompanied by an instrument; beyond that, aside from the *Sanctus*, memorial acclamation, and the Great Amen, I can't imagine to what responses the bulletin is referring.

In regards to the more substantive matter that you correctly highlight, the priest at the altar and everywhere else is not the delegate of the people; he is the representative of Jesus Christ, which is why our theology reminds us that the priest stands *in persona Christi* ("in the person of Christ"). An ordained priest, and only an ordained priest, can confect the Eucharist — that is, perform the consecration. While it is true that the eucharistic prayer is "the prayer of thanksgiving of all the Church," for what are we giving thanks, and how is that to be done? The prayers make it crystal clear that our act of thanksgiving is nothing other than the offering of Christ to His heavenly Father. And so, the concluding doxology says that this work we have just completed has been done "through Him, with Him, and in Him." The human priest offers, in the name of the whole Church, the divine Victim to His Father. All the liturgical documents stress the fact that the place of the priest-celebrant is to be pivotal to make sure that all these connections are easily apprehended at the sign-level.

In short, both the practice and the theology in your parish are off. In reality, this ought not surprise us because, when one is off, it inevitably affects the other.

Our Lady's "commands"?

Q. Why don't you finally admit that the collegial consecration of Russia to the Immaculate Heart of Mary has not been done, as Our Lady has commanded? Furthermore, why can't you see that unless Russia is converted, her errors will continue to spread all over the world, continuing the cycle of violence and bloodshed?

A. Yours was not the only letter I received as a result of my answer on this matter, as it comes through the filter of Father Nicholas Gruner.

To suggest that Our Lady has "commanded" the Pope to do something is nonsense; the authority of Our Lady in the Church is not jurisdictional! The Vicar of Christ is the Pope, not the Blessed Mother. For the sake of argument, however, let's suppose that there is some element of truth here. The notion of a collegial consecration is something brand new to the equation; after all, in 1917, the concept of episcopal collegiality was nearly unknown. If anyone thought that an act had to have universal implications for the Church and/or the world, the idea was that the Pope would do it himself. Therefore, to interject a postconciliar theological development is an anachronism.

Second, when the Holy Father consecrated the entire world to Our Lady's Immaculate Heart, do you think he consciously withheld Russia from his intentionality?

Last, when the Blessed Mother spoke of the spread of Russia's errors, it seems clear to me that she was talking about those of atheistic communism, not those of the Russian Orthodox Church. The Soviet Union has fallen, precisely because the weight of the errors was too great to support the system.

The Orthodox Church is a true Church, with apostolic succession and valid orders and sacraments, albeit, unfortunately, not in full communion with the Bishop of Rome. To suggest that her errors are on a par with those of the former Soviet Union is both absurd and insupportable from theology or history.

Grace now available

Q. I have learned more about my Catholic Faith from *The Catholic Answer* magazine in the past few years than I had for the first thirty years of my life — including years spent in parochial schools. I desperately need you to answer this question. I led a promiscuous lifestyle as a teenager and had an abortion at the age of twenty. I married at twenty-three, started a family, and went to

Mass for five years before I went to confession at the age of twenty-eight. My previous confession was at age nine. I have since tried very hard to be a good Catholic. A priest told me that my sin of abortion, as well as excommunication, was lifted when I confessed. But I have one question — since I not only contracted marriage in a state of mortal sin, but was excommunicated at the time — am I validly married? If not, what should I do? (My husband does not know of my abortion. We hadn't met yet.)

A. First of all, thanks for the kind words about your involvement with *The Catholic Answer* magazine.

Regarding the substantive issues in your question, allow me to make the following points. For an excommunication to have taken effect, you would have had to know that the penalty for abortion was indeed excommunication. So, did you know that (many people do not)? Next, if you were excommunicated, did the priest hearing your confession know you were, and did he have both the intention and the faculty to lift the excommunication?

As to the validity of the marriage, I have checked this rather thoroughly with a number of canonists, and the consensus is that even if you were excommunicated at the time of the wedding, the marriage was valid, so long as you had the proper intention and the priest-officiant had proper delegation. Between the day of your wedding and your confession, you were married but living in a state of serious sin because of previous unconfessed mortal sins and the additional sin of sacrilege (receiving a sacrament outside the state of grace); therefore, the grace of the Sacrament of Matrimony was not available to you until the obstacle of sin was removed. After that, you were able to benefit from the graces of the sacrament.

So, be at peace.

Due respect

Q. We have friends who are of Armenian origin. They are members of the Armenian Apostolic Church, which is a Monophysite Church. Several times over the past seven or eight years, I have had occasion to visit our friends' church. On the altar, there is no tabernacle such as we Catholics are used to. Instead, there is a small monstrance with a piece of Eucharist in it. Clearly, the idea is to reserve the Eucharist on the altar for devotional purposes. I have felt it appropriate to show respect, even some degree of devotion to the reserved Eucharist in the Armenian Church. My question is this: Does the Catholic Church recognize as valid the Eucharist of the Monophysite Churches in the same way that she recognizes as valid the Eucharist of the Eastern Orthodox Churches? If the answer is affirmative, are all of the Monophysite Churches equal in this expect? That is, does the Catholic Church recognize as valid the Eucharist of the Coptic, Ethiopian, Assyrian, and Malabar Christians? The answer to this question is, of course, not just academic. If the Monophysite Eucharist is valid, I will show devotion to it and instruct my family to do the same.

A. In November 1994, a theological agreement was signed by the Holy See and the various Monophysite communities, noting that what appeared to be a heretical expression regarding the nature of Christ, was not, in fact, understood that way by the communities in question. As a result, there are no serious doctrinal concerns — except for papal primacy. Like all the Orthodox, these churches have apostolic succession, hence, valid orders and a valid Eucharist.

Unbloody sacrifice

Q. I am a Protestant, and a subscriber to *The Catholic Answer* magazine, and have found the questions and your answers to them to be very interesting. I also have the *Catholic Encyclopedia* that you edited, and have just ordered *The Catholic Answer Book* and *The Catholic Answer Book 2*. How can the Catholic Church proclaim that the wine used in the Eucharist is the actual blood of Christ, on one hand, then, on the other hand, call the Mass an "unbloody sacrifice?" A related question is how can the Mass be called an "immolation" and a "true and propitiatory sacrifice," on the one hand, then, on the other hand, claim that it is not a different

offering of Christ than that which He offered two thousand years
ago on the Cross? (I am thinking specifically of Heb 9:25-28;
10:12-18; indeed, chapters 7-10).

A. The presence of Christ in the Holy Eucharist is a Real Presence, but sacramental, which is more than physical (although it
includes that dimension).

When the Church gathers in faithfulness to the Lord, remem-
bering Him and His saving action by using His words and invok-
ing His Spirit, that same Spirit overtakes the elements of bread
and wine and transforms them into Christ's Body and Blood. His
presence among us is every bit as real as when He walked the roads
of Galilee, but because He is risen, it is His glorified Person —
unbound by the limitations of space and time — which are present. And so, while His self-oblation on Calvary was bloody, our
sacramental representation of it in the Holy Mass is unbloody
because of the new circumstances by which the Lord exists. Our
present liturgical action is connected to His one, all-sufficient sacrifice, which connection makes it both valid and efficacious.

Sacrament flowing

Q. What is a sacramental marriage? My husband and I were married eleven years ago with a Nuptial Mass. I, a cradle Catholic,
received the Holy Eucharist. He, an unbaptized Christian, did
not. I was never told that we did not receive a sacramental marriage. However, in August 1997, he converted and was baptized,
confirmed and received the Holy Eucharist. Now, if we don't have
a sacramental marriage, what can we do to have one?

A. A sacramental marriage is one contracted between two baptized Christians.

You entered into a valid but non-sacramental marital union.
Upon your husband's conversion and baptism, the grace of the
Sacrament of Matrimony began to flow to you both, which is to
say that the union became "sacramentalized" by his baptism. It
might be a nice idea, however, to renew your vows (as couples

often do on their wedding anniversaries, for example) within the context of a special Mass.

Confused

Q. I am somewhat confused about an answer you gave where you implied in your answer that a priest would have to drink wine that was poisoned because failure to do so would break the seal of confession, since a penitent indicated that he had poisoned the wine. I was under the impression that the seal of confession would be broken if someone else was made aware of the penitent's sins. You refer to the "old manuals of moral theology." Since reception of Holy Communion in those days did not include both species, I think it would not jeopardize the seal of confession for the priest to avoid committing suicide and use untainted wine.

A. The seal of confession is so absolute that a priest may never use any information gained in confession for any purpose outside the sacrament — and that includes saving his own life. In other words, he must act as though he does not know what he has learned under the seal.

Heaven-bound?

Q. Do Catholics believe that when they die they automatically go to heaven?

A. Catholics believe that it is possible for someone to go to heaven immediately upon death for those who die in a state of grace, with no temporal punishment due to sin. Far more likely, however, is that the dead need some degree of purification to meet God worthily — which process we speak of as being completed in purgatory. You may want to check the *Catechism of the Catholic Church* on this, nos. 1030-1032.

"Leaping for joy"

Q. Recently, I heard that two people were born without the stain of original sin: Mary and John the Baptist. I must admit that I had never before heard that about John the Baptist. I can find no evidence for that belief anywhere. Can you clarify that?

A. As you know, the Church teaches in a formal way that Our Lady was not only *born* without original sin but was *conceived* without it. A long-standing theological opinion — but not formal Church teaching — holds for John the Baptist's having been born without original sin, albeit having been conceived in sin. The scriptural basis for such a position rests in the encounter between the Baby Jesus in the womb of Mary and the Baby John in the womb of Elizabeth. The theory goes that John's "leaping for joy" (Lk 1:41) was a sign of his sanctification *in utero*, launching him, as it were, on his critical mission of being the precursor of the Messiah — and doing so in sinlessness.

There is a certain logic to this position, as well as no small degree of charm (which I intend to be taken positively), but it is a matter of freedom for good Catholics to take or leave.

Accurate summary

Q. We should like to have your comment on the following paragraph we vigorously denied to our Protestant friends, but they will not accept our explanation of false statements made in the article. This is what they believe, taken from *Reckless Faith*, by John F. MacArthur (Crossway Books). The author wrote: "While Vatican II issued no new anathemas, it did ratify all the previous ones. The Council also made clear that Catholics are still forbidden to question official Church doctrine: 'In matters of faith and morals, the bishops speak in the name of Christ, and the faithful are to accept their teaching and adhere to it with a religious assent of the soul. This religious submission of will and of mind must be shown in a special way to the teaching authority of the Roman Pontiff, even when he is not speaking *ex cathedra*. That is, it must be shown in such a way that his supreme magisterium is acknowledged with reverence, the judgments made by him sincerely adhered to, according to his manifest mind and Will.'"

A. The author you cite has accurately and completely summarized traditional and, therefore, current Church teaching on the necessity of accepting all that the Church presents for our belief. The quotation given is from *Lumen Gentium* (Dogmatic Constitution on the Church). It is intriguing that very often people outside the Church — and even those not especially well-disposed toward us — can get it straighter than those within the fold.

By the way, what would be your objection to the text offered?

Not prohibited

Q. A priest I know recently allowed a Lutheran minister to use his chalice as an ecumenical gesture when the minister was being installed as the new pastor of a nearby Lutheran church. I have told him that he should not have allowed his chalice to be used in a Protestant ceremony. I have offered to find documentation of a prohibition of using a blessed chalice for anything other than Mass, but have found only one reference in Msgr. Peter Elliot's book stating that "the chalice is a unique, sacred vessel reserved for the Eucharist." Can you help me with more documentation?

A. No, I don't think you'll find any. To the contrary, current discipline and ecumenical guidelines (even from the Holy See) would see your pastor's gesture as Christian hospitality. After all, if we can offer the use of our churches and altars to other Christian bodies, why not a chalice? If the sacred vessel were to be used in a sacrilegious act, that would be a different story.

No limit

Q. Can a penitent be told to limit his sins to two or three during confession?

A. No, for two reasons. First, if mortal sins are present, Church law requires what is called an "integral confession" — that is, the confession of *all* mortal sins, not just some. Second, if a person's conscience is burdened by any sins (mortal or venial), that person has the right to confess any and all of them — and the confessor has the obligation to hear him out, not limiting the penitent to some arbitrary number calculated to speed up the process.

Health care matters

Q. Did you know that most health care plans subsidize abortion?

A. In his encyclical *Evangelium Vitae* ("The Gospel of Life"), Pope John Paul II writes that "health care professionals can be strongly tempted at times to be manipulators of life, or even agents of death" (no. 89). What can be done to promote pro-life and pro-family health care?

First, educate pro-life and pro-family people to demand pro-life/pro-family health insurance from their employers. Union members could have a significant impact since unions pride themselves on giving their members a "choice."

Second, lobby Congress so that pro-life/pro-family people can make a conscious choice when they are purchasing a health care plan. Three things are needed for this: (a) A tax-law change is needed that will allow all people the opportunity to purchase health care with the same tax dollars. (Present tax laws discriminate against families that do not have employer-paid insurance, since they must pay for health care with after-tax dollars; employees with employer-paid insurance pay for health care with pre-tax dollars. This is very unfair and a significant economic disadvantage that forces pro-life families to subsidize abortion). (b) An amendment to the new privatization of Medicare is needed to allow physicians who choose to accept private money for health care to continue receiving federal money from Medicare. Privatization of Medicare will assure pro-life families the opportunity to choose a pro-life physician. (c) The defeat of the Norwood Bill is needed. This bill could eventually put health insurance, except for religious organizations, in control of the insurers that force families to participate in funding abortions.

Third, promote the pro-life/pro-family advantages of Medical Savings Accounts for the self-employed and encourage supporters to shop for health-insurance plans that do not pay for abortion, abortifacients, in-vitro fertilization, genetic, and prenatal testing that prepares mothers for abortion, or that do not pay for couples that are in a homosexual or unmarried heterosexual relationship.

Presumption

Q. This question refers to the *Catholic Encyclopedia* you edited. Under "Holy Spirit, Sins Against the" (p. 504), it lists several sins, including presumption. However, there is no reference to Jesus' declaration that sins against the Holy Spirit are not forgiven in this world "nor in the next." *The Catechism of the Catholic Church*, quoting Scripture, speaks of it as an "eternal sin" (no. 1864). The *encyclopedia* article states, "Ultimately, sins against the Holy Spirit are sins against faith." I do not understand how presumption is a sin against faith. Those who, before sinning, plan to confess it later would seem to be presuming upon God's mercy. Have they committed the unforgivable sin against the Holy Spirit?

A. Those who sin and do so with the intention of confessing the sin after its commission are, in fact, committing two sins — the original act, whatever it is, and the sin of presumption, which assumes or presumes on God's forgiveness. This kind of attitude makes a mockery of the Sacrament of Penance, which is not intended to be used as an insurance policy; looked at from this perspective, we are also involved in the sin of sacrilege (the misuse of a sacred thing).

What the *Catechism* and the Tradition of the Church are talking about when using the expression "sin against the Holy Spirit" is a final act of unrepented sin — either through presumption ("I know that God is too loving to hold me accountable") or despair ("My sin is too great ever to be forgiven").

Christ's DNA

Q. I am concerned about Christ's human nature — that's not to say I doubt it. I firmly believe that Christ had both a divine and a human nature simultaneously. My concern arises in the technicalities of His human nature. I suppose my concern would be satisfactorily addressed by a full explanation of Christ's DNA. When the Holy Spirit overshadowed Mary, was a fertilized egg miraculously implanted in her, or was one of her eggs fertilized? If a fertilized egg was implanted in Mary, that would pose enormous questions regarding one hundred percent of Christ's DNA and make suspect Christ's lineage from David. If the Holy Spirit fertilized one of Mary's eggs, that would answer the question regarding fifty percent of Christ's DNA, but the issue of Christ's lineage from David would then probably be twice as problematic as ever. If Mary didn't supply the egg (and Joseph certainly did not supply the sperm), then where's the link to David? For that matter, where's the link to Adam and Eve? If Mary did supply the egg, does that jeopardize her perpetual virginity — and what sperm was used? Christ was fully human, not a haploid. Did the Holy Spirit take sperm from Joseph to use in Mary? I think there are fundamental theological issues here, and I'd appreciate your addressing them. I also understand there are already rumblings in some Church quarters about Christ being the product of the first artificial insemination, and that the Church's official stance against artificial insemination is on shaky ground because of this logical interpretation. I imagine there are also issues that I haven't thought of, but which you have, and I'd appreciate your dealing with them, too.

A. Remember that the Lord's Davidic lineage was not from Mary but from Joseph, which lineage he enjoyed not by virtue of Joseph's physical paternity but through legal paternity.

That having been said, I think the questions raised — while interesting, to be sure — smack of prurient interest. However, just to raise one more question: Whence came the DNA of Adam? Wherever that was, perhaps we have found the same source for that of the new Adam, Jesus Christ.

While the Catholic Church always encourages rational discourse and intellectual inquiry, she would also subscribe to the dictum, "Fools rush in where angels fear to tread!"

Christ in the Church

Q. I found something strange-sounding in an article from a Catholic magazine. It said: "The Church of Christ is imperfectly embodied in, but is not identical with the Catholic Church."

A. If the quote is accurate, it is wrong.

Lumen Gentium (Dogmatic Constitution on the Church) teaches that "the Church of Christ subsists in the Catholic Church" (no. 8), which is another way of saying that the Catholic Church and the Church of Christ are identical, because the Latin verb *subsistere* is the technical, theological, and philosophical language for the verb "to be." "Imperfect embodiments" of the Church of Christ are found in other churches or ecclesial communities.

Perhaps the author was confused between this matter and another related one — namely, whether or not the Kingdom of God and the Catholic Church are identical or coextensive. Here, we can say that the Kingdom of God is greater than the visible Church on earth for many reasons, not the least being that here, below, reality is conditioned by human imperfection, while the Church in heaven participates fully in the Kingdom of God. Yet again, there are people who will be members of the Church of the eschaton who are either imperfectly related to the Church now or are members by "desire."

Breathe easy

Q. Does the Catholic Church believe that God created Adam as a human out of dust and breathed life into him as the Bible says? Or does the Church have an understanding other than this? How does Pope John Paul II's address to the Pontifical Academy of Sciences on October 22, 1996, relate to the Church's historical stand on the subject of evolution; has there been any change with regard to the validity of the theory of evolution versus Scripture, since 1950, or before 1950?

A. I think we've been around the track on this one a few times, but let's stake out the territory ever so briefly again.

From the very beginning (with direct, written evidence going back at least as far as St. Augustine), we do not find the Church committed to a literal interpretation of the creation accounts in Genesis. So, this is no capitulation to modernity. Pope Pius XII simply restated the basic principles, applying them to the new scientific questions.

Catholics are free to accept (or to reject) the various theories of evolution. The doctrines that must be safeguarded in assuming any particular scientific explanation of human origins, however, are the following: (a) The entire creative process began with Almighty God. (b) At a certain point in evolution, God took what He considered to be "apt" matter and "breathed life" (metaphorical language) into that being, thus endowing it with an immortal soul. (c) God sustains all creation until the end of time. (d) God is directly, personally involved in the creation of every single human being since our first parents (by giving each and every one an immortal soul). If any scientific theory casts doubt on any of these teachings, such a theory cannot be held by a Catholic; otherwise, one is free to make a personal determination about the matter, based not on theology but on the convincing nature of the scientific data.

Documentation

Q. Where can one purchase the document, *Some Questions Regarding Collaboration of the Non-ordained Faithful in the Sacred Ministry of Priests*?

A. I presume that, in due course, the Daughters of St. Paul will make this available in pamphlet form. In the meantime, one could obtain this wonderful text from Origins, the documentary service of the U.S. Catholic Conference in Washington, D.C.; call 202-659-6742.

Freeing souls

Q. Does the Catholic Church still believe that Masses celebrated on All Souls' Day result in an increased number of souls being released from Purgatory?

A. Yes, she does, which only makes sense because the very purpose of the commemoration is to aid the poor souls in a special way by the heightened consciousness of the whole Church on their behalf on that day.

Eternal Life

Q. How do you believe that a person receives eternal life from God?

A. I am not quite sure of what you are asking, but let me hazard a few guesses.

Perhaps you mean: What must a man do to be saved? If that is it, then we have several answers in the New Testament. Jesus tells the rich, young man to keep the commandments and to pursue perfection by selling all that he has and follow the Lord (see Mt 19:21). In the Acts of the Apostles, we find potential converts told to reform their lives, believe in the Lord Jesus and be baptized (see Acts 16:30-34).

On the other hand, are you wondering how Almighty God can and does communicate His divine and eternal life to mortals? That is a great mystery, but it is all part of the unfathomable condescension of the Triune God, Who loves us so much that He desires to share Himself with us at the deepest level possible, by offering us a share in His beatitude for all eternity.

Or, is your question: How can you believe that such an eventuality is possible? If that's it, my answer is that I believe on the authority of God Who, as we say in the Act of Faith, "can neither deceive nor be deceived."

For an excellent treatment of all of these facets of the doctrines of the resurrection of the dead and everlasting life, read nos. 988-1060 in the *Catechism of the Catholic Church*.

Spirit-filled moment

Q. When does the person being baptized receive the Holy Spirit? Is it during the "pouring of the water" or when anointed with chrism, or both?

A. Whenever a sacrament is administered, the entire Trinity is present because where one has one Person, the whole Triune God is there. So, if your question is at what point in the ceremony is the baptism effected — that is, when has the sacrament "taken" — we would have to say that the pouring of the water is "the moment," for the simple reason that that action, along with the baptismal formula, constitute the matter and form of the Sacrament of Baptism. For example, in an emergency, only the pouring and the formula are required and make for a completely valid administration of baptism.

Free will working

Q. How could Peter deny Christ? How could anyone present at the Transfiguration deny Him? I am having trouble with faith and understanding this.

A. I suspect the question is really tied into the problem of free will. After all, we can ask how Lucifer and the other rebellious angels could have done what they did when they were living in the presence of Almighty God. And to defend my patron, let me say that I think his sin of denial was not so much a premeditated, conscious act of the will against the Lord as it was an act of cowardice — surely not to be applauded, but just as surely a bit easier to understand, and to forgive.

Unfulfilled unity

Q. I am a Lutheran. When will Catholics comply with the Second Vatican Council and start sharing Holy Communion with *all* baptized Christians to fully effect Christ's sacrament of unity to be one with Him as He is with the Father?

A. I am sorry to disappoint you, but you will search in vain for a single line from the Second Vatican Council to support your point of view. In fact, just the opposite is the case. The Council Fathers, in several places, bewail the lack of full unity among Christians and, therefore, that eucharistic sharing is not possible under normal circumstances. I would refer you to passages such as the following: in the Decree on Ecumenism (*Unitatis Redintegratio*), such indiscriminate intercommunion is explicitly enjoined (see no. 8); in the Decree on Eastern-rite Catholic Churches (*Orientalium Ecclesiarum*), the ban is repeated as a general principle, admitting of exceptions for the Eastern Orthodox (see nos. 26-29).

As I have noted many times before, the Catholic (and Eastern Orthodox) stance on the matter runs like this: Eucharistic Communion is a sign of the ecclesial communion that already exists; therefore, it would be a countersign if we "jumped the gun" by anticipating such ecclesial unity by receiving Holy Communion from one another. Furthermore, many of the denominations that did decide to engage in intercommunion at the turn of the century are no closer together, organically speaking, than they were ninety years ago, and I would maintain that the reason is that they lulled themselves into a false sense of unity by intercommunion and then got sloppy about dealing with the delicate theological issues that ought to have been resolved first.

Love and life

Q. I have three questions to ask you. First, as a child in Catholic school, I was taught that sex within marriage was for the purpose of procreation only. Does this mean infertile couples should not have marital relations? Second, I have been given the diagnosis of infertility, along with that of endometriosis, a painful condition that attacks the woman's reproductive organs. I have been told by most doctors that I have almost no chance of achieving pregnancy without in vitro fertilization and, since this procedure is not allowed by the Church, I refused to consider it. So the doctors have recommended a hysterectomy to rid myself of the pain and suffering. I must also add that I did achieve pregnancy two times — once in 1991 with a son born with severe mental handicaps and then in 1996 with a daughter I lost in my sixth month. Is a hysterectomy for medical purposes in a woman of child-bearing age considered a sin? Is it interfering with God's plan (like artificial birth control)? Third, since my husband is a fundamentalist, he has read me the Scripture passage, "The sins of the fathers descend to their children." He believes that God is punishing him with our son's mental condition because he married a Catholic. He also believes that I lost our daughter because I intended to have her baptized (she did receive emergency baptism from my doctor who is a member of my parish) and to raise her in the Catholic Church, but God wanted to save her from this so He took her. How do I respond to my husband's accusations?

A. The use of the sexual faculties within marriage is intended for what we might call a dual primary purpose: procreation and expression of love. Every act of intercourse must be a communication of love and must never directly obstruct the possibility of procreation. Sexual relations between the sterile or the old is not violative of God's Law because they have not placed the obstacle in the way of procreation.

Second, a hysterectomy for medical reasons is not sinful, either, because one's intention is not contraceptive but medicinal. Not being capable of conceiving is an unintended side effect of the procedure.

Third, it sounds as though you did not know your husband too well before you got married. His rabid anti-Catholicism is sick and distinctly un-Christian. I am glad that as Catholics we do not worship the same Lord he apparently does — that is, one who is so hateful and vindictive. Pray for his genuine conversion to Christianity.

No inferiority claim

Q. Pope John Paul II has "closed" the discussion on the ordination of women to the priesthood, apparently because men make better "leaders," are less emotional and can keep the seal of the confessional more easily. However, Sacred Scripture shows that St. Paul sends greetings to Phoebe, deaconess at Cenchreae (near Athens). Women already carry out most functions of a deacon, such as parish administration, teaching religion, distribution of Holy Communion, reading the Scriptures at Mass, etc. Why can't women become deaconesses?

A. I must begin by dissenting from your declaration that the Church refuses to ordain women because they are naturally inferior to men. Neither *Inter Insigniores* nor *Ordinatio Sacerdotalis,* the women's ordination documents of Popes Paul VI and John Paul II, respectively, use any such logic. Indeed, the papal magisterium has actually gone out of its way to say the very opposite.

The matter of deaconesses is different from that of priestesses, but admittedly, related. What or who deaconesses were or did in the New Testament Church is a subject of much study and discussion. For the generations following the apostolic Church, we have a better idea. We know, for example, that they were never commissioned by the laying on of hands and that their primary purpose seems to have been to assist in the baptism of adult women (since full immersion was still the usual method). By the time theological terminology was refined, we never hear of the female diaconate being referred to as part of the Sacrament of Order. And so, if some people want to revive a female diaconate today, it would have to be along the lines of its historical existence, that is, non-sacramental.

Just defense

Q. In the post-Vietnam era, I was abandoned and ridiculed by my Church leaders in my search to understand God's Will toward killing to protect the innocent. Why have you abandoned me? At age sixteen, with tears in my eyes, I fell to my knees and begged my God to help me. I prayed, "Heavenly Father, if it be Your Will, I will freely stand by idly with my weapon at my side while my own mother is raped, beaten and her body torn to pieces." Or,

"Heavenly Father, if it be Your Will, I will travel ten thousand miles and fight to my death to defend a stranger's mother from persecution. But please, Father, with all my heart I beg of You — What is Your Will?" What do you say God's answer is?

A. I'm going to assume your fundamental question has to do with fighting in a war. For the first few centuries, Christians refused to fight in wars, largely due to the fact that soldiers in the Roman Empire were required to engage in pagan worship as part of their duties to the state. With the legalization of Christianity and then the making of Christianity into the imperial religion, the situation changed dramatically.

St. Augustine evolved a political, philosophical, and theological position known as the "just-war theory." A shorthand description of it would go like this: The military action envisioned must be proportionate to the real or potential harm; all other means must be exhausted; greater evils should not follow; the military action must be called by legitimate authority; civilian populations must never be targeted (see *Catechism of the Catholic Church*, no. 2309).

War is always to be avoided, and is always to be regretted when it occurs. In the Old Testament, the ancient Hebrews made this clear by offering Temple sacrifices to atone for wartime killings, even when they would have been considered moral acts. Of course, someone who has a serious personal difficulty with combat is entitled to classify himself as a "conscientious objector," and that holds up both politically and theologically.

As you should see by now, the Church has not abandoned you, but has a very detailed theology on this topic worked out over a several-century period.

Mutual choosing

Q. Today, I heard a homilist (a deacon) state that we do not choose Christ, but that Christ chooses us. This did not sound right. (It sounded to me as if the ideas of Calvin and others who taught predestination.) On the way home, I talked to my children about it, telling them that salvation is for all mankind, that we all have free will, and that we are saved by faith and good works. I then looked in the *Catechism of the Catholic Church*, hoping to find an explanation, but had no luck. I read the section on predestination in your *Catholic Encyclopedia*, but I still have questions, especially after reading what St. Augustine wrote. My understanding of free will was that God wants all people to be saved, however, He does not prevent us from exercising our free will. The last sentence in your entry on predestination seems to say just that. Was St. Augustine wrong in writing that God chose those whom He Willed to be saved? Does the Church teach that salvation is for all?

A. In discussing this very complicated matter, we must balance a number of variables, keeping them in a creative tension: the sovereignty of God; His universal salvific Will; human freedom.

God is totally and absolutely free, but He is not capricious. He is "bound," we can say, by His own law of love and by His unfailing justice. Next, in the New Testament, we read that "God desires all men to be saved and to come to the knowledge of the truth" (1 Tm 2:4), which teaching is commonly known as God's universal salvific Will. In other words, it is not — and never has been — in God's intention or plan to damn anyone, which is where human freedom enters the equation. God endowed man with freedom because He first of all endowed him with dignity. Therefore, we are not marionettes, compelled to do God's Will.

Putting all three pieces of the puzzle together, we come up with something like this: God can do whatever He wants, but He must be faithful to Himself in the process, demanding that all His actions be both loving and just. God desires the salvation of each and every human being but, given our freedom, we can choose to move away from God's offer of eternal salvation.

The bottom line, then, is that the Triune God does choose us, but our free will demands that we choose the Triune God in return. Without the proper human response to the divine call, God's plan is thwarted, revealing both the mystery of human freedom and the mystery of divine love.

Christ, the victor

Q. I have my doubts that the devil has already been conquered by Jesus Christ, simply because the prayer to St. Michael speaks of "casting the devil into hell." It is speaking in present terms, not past tense. Please correct me if I am wrong here. I firmly believe that the devil is loose on this earth. Otherwise, why would there be so much evil in this world of ours? I know that the devil is a spirit, an angel — a powerful angel, so powerful that we need our Lord Jesus Christ, the Holy Spirit, the Virgin Mary, and the angels on our side to do battle with him.

A. Through the Lord's Paschal Mystery — that is, through His efficacious passion, death, and resurrection — Christ has achieved the definitive victory over the devil. In other words, the war has been fought and won. Various battles and skirmishes are yet to be fought and won — and that is our work, to be done in cooperation with the grace of Almighty God. So, yes, the devil is "on the loose," as you say, but he is not omnipotent. Only God is — and when we respond to God's grace, we have the potential for being victorious in the little battles and in our final hour of temptation. As St. Augustine reminded his listeners fifteen centuries ago: "If in Christ we have been tempted, in Him we have overcome the devil. Do you think only of Christ's temptations and fail to think of His victory? See yourself as tempted in Him, and see yourself as victorious in Him."

Saving grace

Q. Some friends of mine feel that no matter what they do in this life, their salvation is assured, since they were redeemed by Jesus accepting their sins and the sins of the world, being placed on the Cross and giving His own life for their freedom from sin. I cannot believe that we are not bound to live according to the commandments in order to be worthy of the Lord's sacrifice. Otherwise, one could live a sinful life and still go to heaven, even without confession.

A. One need only look at the *Catechism of the Catholic Church* to discover that Catholic teaching makes absolutely clear the necessity of living "a moral life." Indeed, nearly two hundred pages of the *Catechism* deal with this topic. If there were no need to lead a particular style of life, why would Our Lord proclaim His Sermon on the Mount and why, in that very context, would He warn His listeners that following a "way" other than His would "lead to destruction" (Mt 7:13)?

The layout of the *Catechism* also helps elucidate the pattern for a believer: What we believe (Part I) is celebrated in worship, wherein we receive the grace or life of Christ (Part II), precisely in order to live according to His "way" (Part III). In other words, it is not possible to claim to believe in His saving death and resurrection without living according to that pattern of existence. Dozens of New Testament texts remind us that because Christ died and rose, we have to live accordingly. For example, St. Paul reminds the Colossians: "Seek the things that are above, where Christ is, seated at the right hand of God" (3:1).

Christ's death can never be used as the excuse for profligacy; in fact, it would be a great blasphemy if that were to occur.

Blurred distinctions

Q. At the end of the Litany of Saints, the names of the parishioners who had died during the year were added to the list, followed by the customary "Pray for us." Now, I can see where it would be of consolation to the living to imagine that their loved ones are already in heaven, but I couldn't help but think that if, by some chance, any of the deceased happened to be in purgatory, isn't it we who should be praying for them instead of vice versa?

A. This is more of the confusing stuff that is foisted on people by priests and liturgists who feel compelled to be clever, instead of just doing what the Church's liturgy stipulates. Listing deceased parishioners in a "Book of the Dead" is a nice idea, and reading out their names on All Souls' Day is equally worthwhile, for instance, during the prayer of the faithful. Treating them like saints, however, is not a good idea for many reasons, not the least of which is that it deprives them (if they are still in purgatory) of the benefit of our prayers for their purification.

What has happened in recent years on the part of some is a collapse of heaven and purgatory into one reality, which is why all too often we hear funeral homilies that sound like decrees of canonization. While it is possible for the souls in purgatory to pray for us, inclusion of them into the Litany of Saints is an inadmissable mixture of two spheres of the Communion of Saints — the blurring of a distinction important for Catholic doctrine and practice.

Apostasy a problem

Q. Here's a scenario: A child is raised in the Catholic Faith. As an adult, he leaves the Catholic Church because he does not like the Catholic teachings. He joins a different religion. Will that individual be saved?

A. The first question we have to determine is just what you mean by "a different religion." Many people use that expression with some degree of imprecision. Often, they mean that Johnny has abandoned Catholicism for Lutheranism or fundamentalism, for instance. While either scenario would be regrettable, neither constitutes "joining a different religion." Why? Because both bodies are still Christian. Apostasy, the technical name for your term, means giving up the Christian Faith completely, either to embrace another religion — for example, Islam, Judaism, or Buddhism — or to live as an atheist or agnostic.

Next, one does not join or leave a religion because one likes or dislikes a religion's teachings; that decision is made because a religion's teachings are either true or false. Therefore, the question about our young would-be apostate is whether he clearly knew and understood the doctrines of the Catholic Faith and then consciously rejected them; or, whether he never really had an intelligent grasp of them and, therefore, left in ignorance. If it is the first case, the Fathers of the Second Vatican Council have some pretty strong language for that kind of action: "Hence they could not be saved who, knowing that the Catholic Church was founded as necessary by God through Christ, would refuse either to enter it, or to remain in it" (*Lumen Gentium*, [Dogmatic Constitution on the Church], no. 14).

Erudite, Orthodox

Q. Just when I thought I was on the right track recognizing the people who have influenced the radical and un-Catholic teachings and liturgy in the Church today, you throw me a real curve! In the "Short Reviews" section of an issue of *The Catholic Answer* magazine, you reviewed a book by Father Avery Dulles, S.J., published by Paulist Press. You highly recommended this book as must reading for every priest and seminarian. I thought Father Dulles was one of the Jesuits who helped to give and promote some of the extreme liberal interpretations of the documents of the Second Vatican Council. Isn't he a follower of the Teilhard de Chardin/Karl Rahner school of thought? I have been following recommendations through EWTN and Franciscan University at Steubenville in my study of the teachings and history of the Church. I found these two entities are truly following Rome. It was through EWTN that I found your publication and have enjoyed it immensely. Now, however, I do not know what to think. Am I wrong about Father Dulles?

A. Like many theologians of the immediate postconciliar period (including Cardinal Ratzinger in many ways), I suspect that Father Dulles was a bit starry-eyed about the prospects of reform and the Church's potential to engage in the secular dialogue. As time has gone on, such theologians (who were never even bordering on heretical views) have come to see the complete picture much more clearly and have adjusted their thinking and writing accordingly. At times, too, these men produced works which were not problematic in themselves but which were used by others in very problematic ways; I think this applies very strongly to Father Dulles' situation. For the past several years, however, Father Dulles could not be any stronger and more forcefully "on the side of the angels." Several of his lectures, including the book I reviewed (which is a collection of lectures on the priesthood), have been masterpieces of erudition and orthodoxy.

Purgatory, hell

Q. For the past fifteen years or so, I have never heard about the subject of hell or purgatory mentioned by a priest or by the prayer books at Mass. Does our Church still recognize hell or purgatory?

A. Yes, the Church does still teach and believe in the existence of both realities. I agree that the two doctrines have received short shrift in both preaching and catechesis in the past three decades, prompting Cardinal Ratzinger to assert that the greatest post-conciliar theological crisis is one of eschatology. His point is simple: If we do not have a perspective on life grounded in eternity, nothing makes any sense.

The liturgy does, however, continue to witness to these teachings. For example, All Souls' Day (if its meaning is not subverted by deficient preaching) is the most forceful statement possible on the existence of purgatory, and every eucharistic prayer has a prayer for the dead, that they might be admitted to eternal bliss — which is a recognition of their need for release from purgatory. On hell, the most obvious liturgical testimony comes from the Roman Canon (Eucharistic Prayer I), which says: "Save us from final damnation."

Our Sunday Visitor has published a book, simply titled "Purgatory," by Father Michael Taylor, S.J., in which we are reminded that this is "a critical and important doctrine of Faith."

Capital punishment

Q. My question concerns the debate on capital punishment. Where in the Bible does Christ defend capital punishment, if at all? Does He make any mention or inference to the validity of this kind of punishment? If not, where do we receive the permission to impose capital punishment?

A. From time immemorial, the Church (following Old Testament teachings and even New Testament passages on the rightful duties and responsibilities of civil government) has acknowledged the right of the state to exact the death penalty — all the while expressing less-than-enthusiastic support for it.

In recent times, Church teaching has become even more uncomfortable with this practice, so much so that we read Pope John Paul II's very strong and nuanced position presented in *Evangelium Vitæ* ("The Gospel of Life," no. 56). That teaching was subsequently incorporated as a revision to the *Catechism of the Catholic Church*: "The traditional teaching of the Church does not exclude recourse to the death penalty, if this is the only possible way of effectively defending human lives against the unjust aggressor. If, however, non-lethal means are sufficient to defend and protect people's safety from the aggressor, authority will limit itself to such means, as these are more in keeping with the concrete conditions of the common good and more in conformity with the dignity of the human person. . . . The cases in which the execution of the offender is an absolute necessity 'are very rare, if not practically non-existent'" (no. 2267).

What the Church is saying, then, may be summarized thus: Although the state has the right to demand the death penalty in certain situations, it ought to be used rarely, if ever, since alternate forms of punishment exist to guarantee the welfare of society as a whole. Its use contributes to a climate of disregard for the sanctity of human life (and even a convicted criminal's life is still sacred in God's eyes). There is no evidence that it serves as a deterrent (except for the one executed); and gross inequities are found in its application, largely based on access to political power and money for top-notch lawyers. Last, but not least, it is not easy to reconcile with the Lord's injunction to "turn the other cheek." Society has both the right and the responsibility to protect its members from hardened criminals, but the Church is asking us to consider if capital punishment is the most moral and effective way to achieve that very legitimate and necessary goal.

God's Mother

Q. How can Mary be the Mother of God? I am concerned mainly with this syllogism: Mary gave birth to Jesus (true); Jesus is God (true); therefore, Mary is the Mother of God (wrong). This conclusion does not make sense to me. God cannot have a mother. A mother must be older than her child. Since there is only one God, He pre-existed Mary. In fact, He created Mary. The hypostatic union does not mean a thing to me. Mary gave birth to Jesus, a human being. The fact that Jesus may also have been God does not give logic to the above syllogism.

A. Your framing of the question is perfect and thus gives me the perfect opportunity to show exactly why the Church has historically insisted on the title "Mother of God." You say: "Mary gave birth to Jesus, a human being." That is false. Jesus was/is not "a human being." Jesus is the Second Person of the Blessed Trinity, Son of God and Incarnate Word. As such, He existed as a Person from all eternity — even before His conception and birth. In the mystery of the Incarnation, the Eternal Son (a Person — and a divine One) took upon Himself a human nature. Now, natures do not exist independent of persons; so, His human nature was joined to His divine Person and nature (which, as we already noted, He possessed from all eternity). Therefore, Our Lady gave birth to the Second Person of the Blessed Trinity in the flesh. Which fact makes her not only "Mother of Jesus" but, likewise, "Mother of God Incarnate," or "Mother of God."

This discussion took place in the early Church and was settled at the Council of Ephesus, which, in opposition to the heretic Nestorius, proclaimed Mary to be *Theotokos* (in Latin, *Deipara*) — that is, "God-bearer." The purpose of the title was not to aggrandize Mary but to safeguard the Divinity of Christ from Nestorius and his minions, who failed to accept, in their fullness and creative tension, the Lord's true Divinity and true humanity. And, to this day, people who refuse to accord to Mary the title of "Mother of God" end up falling into the very same Christological trap. Mariology, then, protects Christology — a point strongly underscored by Cardinal John Henry Newman a century ago in his attempt to show how Catholic Marian doctrine and devotion did not detract from the uniqueness of Christ; rather, it preserved it and pointed to it.

Seasonal directives

Q. Our parish has a newsletter, which was recently mailed to all parishioners. The reference source for an article excerpt was from a book by William J. Bausch, *A New Look at the Sacraments*. This book was also used two years ago by the pastor in a class on the sacraments, which he taught most specifically for those trying to be certified as religious-education teachers. I questioned the contents of the book at the time also, but never followed up on the author. What do you know about the orthodoxy of William J. Bausch and the above-mentioned book? Also, in his book, he stated that, during the season of Lent, there can be no baptisms or weddings since this is a penitential season. He also stated that there can be no confessions or funerals from Holy Thursday to the Easter Vigil. Is this Church teaching?

A. Most of Father Bausch's books are uniformly unreliable, mixing a jaundiced view of Church history and defective theological principles into the soup. On the specific points you highlight, please note the following: Lent is a "privileged season," which means that "ordinarily" weddings ought not to be celebrated; I would interpret that rather strictly, but it takes a lot of catechesis to get us back to the spot where we were before the Second Vatican Council, given the disregard of it all for the past thirty years. There is no ban on the celebration of baptism at any time. Funeral Masses cannot be held during the Paschal Triduum, but confessions are actually encouraged during that time, as evidenced by the personal example of the Pope himself by his hearing of confessions each year on Good Friday in St. Peter's Basilica.

Disunifying sin

Q. You have made reference to "a sin against unity" in several answers to questions that were printed in *The Catholic Answer* magazine. I read the *Catechism of the Catholic Church* (nos. 820-822) and, frankly, it wasn't real helpful. What is a sin against unity? How is it committed? Can you offer a few examples?

A. The unity of the Church was the Lord's dying wish — the very focus of His high priestly prayer offered to the Father on Holy Thursday night and recorded in St. John's Gospel. Christ envisioned for His Church a unity of doctrine and a unity of charity. When people reject the teaching of the Church; when people fail to observe the Church's norms for the liturgy; when people engage in divisive behavior; it is then that the unity of the Church is attacked — and this saddens Christ.

Sound doctrine

Q. I recently read in another Catholic publication that a doctrine exists within the Church, "the teaching that others may share with Christ in the mediation of God's grace, whether that mediation takes the form of intercessory prayers of the saints, the instrumentality of Mary as 'co-redemptrix' or 'mediatrix,' or 'offering up' one's own earthly suffering in 'reparation' for the sins of others." It is on this basis, the author asserts, that asking for the prayers of others is really a way of involving us all in the role of co-redeemer. I would like to know if this is sound doctrine, especially the part about offering one's own sufferings to mitigate the sins of others.

A. Properly understood, everything in your citation is orthodox Catholic doctrine. Indeed, the very heart of the doctrine of the Communion of Saints is precisely the belief that we who make up the Body of Christ, the Church, are members of one another and have a responsibility to be involved in one anothers' salvation. So, yes, our prayers and sufferings can truly benefit the other members of the Church, whether those still on earth or the souls in purgatory.

Problematic books

Q. Recently, I started reading a book by the late Anthony DeMello, and have heard several people mention that there is some controversy with his writing. What is the problem?

A. Father DeMello was an Indian Jesuit, known for his attempts to harmonize Eastern and Christian thought — not a bad goal in itself. During the course of his career, his efforts became more and more problematic, especially as he seemed to veer off course in downplaying or even denying the necessity of Christ for salvation. His books, even posthumously, have been translated into dozens of languages, causing the Congregation for the Doctrine of the Faith to express concern about the errors that may be propagated by his work. Therefore, last year, the Congregation for the Doctrine of the Faith asked that his books be taken from circulation in Catholic bookstores and that Catholic publishing houses not promote them.

Nuanced statements

Q. Have you read Hans Urs Von Balthasar's *Dare We Hope . . . That All Will Be Saved*? I've tried reading it, but it's too tedious for me. The premise seems to me that we need not fear damnation, for the mercy of God won't allow it (correct me if I'm wrong). I have serious problems squaring that with all I've been taught in my sixteen years of Catholic schooling. Yet my pastor claims to have read it and totally agrees with it. Another parish priest has not read it, but said that Von Balthasar is Pope John Paul's favorite theologian and, based on that, he can't be wrong. Help!

A. First off, Von Balthasar is not easy sledding for anyone and, on that score alone, can be prime turf for misunderstanding his generally carefully nuanced statements. So, second, I think you go beyond what he actually says. Having read the book a number of years ago, I did not come to your final judgment of his position; I think he stops just short of saying what you say. However, I am extremely uncomfortable with the work and believe it does indeed open itself up to your "take" on it. I am afraid to say that Von Balthasar himself did not help the situation, because when confronted with a simple question like, "Can any human being ever go to hell?" he was always less than forthcoming, giving credibility to those who assert that he does not believe in the possibility. That aside, he was a wonderfully faithful theologian, and I do not doubt that he would be among the Holy Father's favorites — surely one reason the Pope had named him a cardinal (although he died the day before the ceremony).

Of course, we must also remember that just because a theologian is normally "safe" does not mean that he is universally so; even St. Thomas Aquinas held positions that the magisterium would not endorse today. The only sure guide to the Faith is the magisterium.

Timeless truth

Q. The Spirit is not bound by physical time. It is clear that the Spirit of Christ flows out from His death and resurrection to all present, future, and past of physical time. At the Last Supper, before Christ's death on the Cross, He offered up the Eucharist: "This is my Body" and "This is my blood." We can be assured there is the Real Presence of Christ in the eucharistic feast at the Last Supper. My question: Is there not the Real Presence of Christ in the peace offerings of Old Testament times? Many times Christ identifies Himself as the sacrificial Lamb. When a son of Aaron and Moses offers up a sacrificial-lamb peace offering, it forgives people of their sins. Only Christ can forgive sins through His death and resurrection. I am sure that the spiritual, eternal, omnipresent Eucharist of Christ flows out from His death and resurrection to not only the future Church but also to the Church of past time. Christ's sacrificial peace offering upon the Cross spiritually flows out into the past to the Last Supper and beyond to the beginning of time. How do you see the Eucharist?

A. I agree with you. If it is true that God created everything in and for Christ and with Christ in view, all reality has its meaning tied up in His Sacred Person. In terms of sacrificial offerings, I think it fair to say that any offering ever made — whether Jewish or pagan — if done "in spirit and in truth," would have been received by the Father in virtue of Christ's self-immolation, whether preceding that event in human history or following it.

Scripture

⁓

A relative good

Q. The citations in Scripture about abstinence from sex between validly married parties confuse me. Why did Moses abstain from sex with his wife? And why did people practice the same abstinence for three days before the revelation of God on Mount Sinai? God made sex; isn't it all right to practice it? Or is it considered dirty or sinful?

A. Abstaining from something does not necessarily mean it is evil — rather that a higher good is being sought. Fasting from food (which is an objective good) recognizes the need to moderate or control our appetites, either for a period of time (for example, Lent or diet) or permanently (due to a chronic condition such as diabetes). Abstaining from marital relations is based on the notion that the love of God is the highest good possible and that all other loves should be subordinated to it. The Scriptures tell us that after Moses' experience of Almighty God on Mount Sinai, he had to veil his face since it had become so radiant from his contact with Divinity. Similarly, the rabbinic literature talks about Moses' sexual abstinence after his Sinai encounter because he now saw reality from a totally otherworldly perspective.

This concept is, of course, an important part of the Church's discipline of priestly celibacy. In this context, it should be noted that, until recently, rites of the Church that permitted married priests required them to abstain from marital relations the evening before celebrating the Eucharist; some Catholic cultures had the same norm even for lay people who wished to receive Holy Communion — in essence, an extension of the Communion fast.

The long and the short of all this is not that sex is evil, but that it should be seen in relation to other goods. In that light, we recognize the fact that it is not an absolute good, but a relative good — like many others.

The wood

Q. In a Rosary meditation for a sorrowful mystery, the following quotation is included: "For if men use the green wood like this, what will happen when it is dry?" Could you please explain what this is supposed to mean?

A. The citation comes from the Gospel according to St. Luke (see 23:31); its context is the exchange between Jesus and the women of Jerusalem seeking to comfort Him on the Way of the Cross. Our Lord responds to their efforts by focusing their attention on the end times, when, He says, the present difficulties will look mild by comparison. Using the image of green and dry wood, He teaches — in essence — that if men behave so badly now (the green wood), what can we expect later (the dry wood)?

Excellent

Q. *The Eerdmans Bible Dictionary* has received some very high praise. Could you advise me whether or not it is a good reference for Catholic Scripture study?

A. I think it is excellent.

Bible Text

Q. There is a difficulty in finding Bible texts that have not been infected with the disease of inclusive language. *The New Revised Standard*, which lacks being truly Catholic, is found in almost every religious store. Is it still possible to get copies of the 1970 St. Joseph's Edition of the *New American Bible*? Can we expect a new *Lectionary* text complete with inclusive language by the year 2000?

A. I doubt that the 1970 edition is available, but I must say that I do not find the 1990 edition of the *New American Bible* to be problematic; the later edition, which has an "inclusive" Psalter, is another story.

I see no possibility for any prostitution of the biblical or liturgical texts on the horizon, particularly with the appointment of the new pro-prefect for divine worship in Rome.

ICEL background

Q. Who appoints the people who function on the International Committee for English in the Liturgy (ICEL)? Are they all Catholics? To whom are they accountable? Are they above the magisterium? Possessing a little knowledge of Latin, I am often confused by their work and wonder if you could help me understand the workings of ICEL a bit better.

A. As a twenty-year-old seminarian, I was invited to be part of the work of ICEL. Because I believed the work ought to be one of translation, rather than paraphrase, I found myself disinvited in short order.

As the structure is set up, a bishop from each English-speaking episcopal conference in the world sits on the board; they in turn recommend individuals who are supposed to have talent in Latin, English, theology, and liturgy. These individuals work under an executive director who stakes out the various tasks; they are assisted by lower ranks of collaborators as well (which is where I fell in the ICEL hierarchy back in the early 1970s). These translators are to submit their work to the episcopal board for review and comment; each bishop is to return to his own episcopal conference to obtain feedback. The finalized texts are then presented to the Holy See for ultimate confirmation.

Personally, I feel that this process is flawed throughout, because the basic translation principles are wrong and because the procedure is so cumbersome and the amount of the work so massive that individual bishops find themselves unable to provide the oversight that the seriousness of the task demands.

Not official

Q. What is the status of the booklet *Morning and Evening*, published by the Liturgy Training Publications of the Archdiocese of Chicago? It seems to have unapproved texts.

A. The rendering of the psalms that is offered in this work are not approved, and they never should have been incorporated into a booklet that is intended for official public worship, which is what the Liturgy of the Hours is — whether that is celebrated in a parish church, a convent, a seminary, or any other place. I note with interest that there is no imprimatur given for the text, which means that it cannot be used in a liturgical setting. In short, we have a most dishonest attempt to *look* official without *being* official — indeed, to deceive users into thinking that this is all "kosher" when the Holy See has said exactly the opposite.

Nomenclature

Q. There often seems a very free exchange of the words "disciples" and "apostles" in the Gospels. For example, "the disciples recognized Him in the breaking of the bread." Were these disciples present at the Last Supper or was the act so important that God revealed Himself at that time to highlight the importance? I find the interchanging of the terms makes it difficult to understand the Scriptures sometimes. Please comment.

A. St. John's Gospel never uses the word "apostle"; the Synoptic Gospels often make a division between "apostles" and "disciples," such that the larger, wider group of followers of Jesus are called "disciples" while the "core" group of "The Twelve" are referred to as "apostles" — but this is not universally so. We can say that all apostles were disciples, but not all disciples were apostles. In terms of the Last Supper, we find that St. Luke alone indicates that the participants were "apostles," as opposed to "disciples" (the broader grouping).

Admonish with love

Q. What are the biblical and historical sources of both the spiritual and corporal works of mercy? Is there a conflict between the teaching to admonish sinners and the teaching not to judge others? It seems that a judgment of another's actions is a prerequisite to admonishing him.

A. The corporal works of mercy have their origin in Our Lord's description of the final judgment, as that is presented in the Gospel of St. Matthew (see 12:36-42). The spiritual works of mercy are culled from a variety of New Testament texts that encourage us to be actively involved on behalf of the spiritual welfare of our neighbor.

Jesus does not actually tell us not to judge others; He says that we should not judge, unless we are prepared to be judged ourselves. In other words, we should not be hypocritical in holding others up to a standard that is higher than that by which we are willing to live. Admonishing a sinner is surely a good and holy thing to do, as long as it is done with love and compassion, motivated by a sincere desire for that person's eternal beatitude.

Proto-Gospel

Q. My husband insists on watching the television program "Mysteries of the Bible." They often seem to quote from the "Gospel of St. James." It sounds like malarkey to me! What is this "Gospel of St. James"? And which St. James are we talking about?

A. The "Proto-Gospel of St. James" is not a canonical work and thus has no standing in the Church for purposes of revelation, doctrine, etc. It is technically known as an "apocryphal" book and was attributed to St. James the Apostle, in order to gain for it a greater and more respectful hearing. Interestingly enough, it has provided much fodder for Catholic and Eastern Orthodox devotional life, especially in purporting to give otherwise unknown details about the infancy of Our Lady and the "hidden life" of

Christ. Where it does not conflict with revealed truths, there is no difficulty in using it.

Careful interpretation

Q. What significance does "666" or the "mark of the beast" hold in Catholic theology? I was taught that these phrases originated in Jewish or Hebrew numerology hundreds of years ago, and that they were symbolic to the people of the time, but not today. I hear many lay Catholics interpreting the Apocalypse in literal terms, exactly as Protestants do. I thought that approach was a fundamentalist one. Can you enlighten me?

A. Nearly all ancient cultures attached significance to numbers. The Hebrews, as you undoubtedly know, saw the number "seven" as symbolizing perfection, while "six" stood for incompleteness or imperfection. The Romans assigned certain numerical values to certain letters of the alphabet — for example, I = 1; V = 5; X = 10.

The author of the Book of Revelation sought to provide a guide for Christian living to those undergoing persecution; therefore, he used "code" language to keep his message secret from Roman authorities. Hence we find animals, numbers and colors signifying certain things that the initiated would understand, but which would remain mysterious to those outside the community. The Antichrist, or "beast," was one such figure, with the number 666 on his forehead. That number is the sum total of the letters of the name of the Emperor Nero in Latin — the enemy or Antichrist, *par excellence*, for those Christians living during his reign.

Apocalyptic literature must be read very carefully, using the tutelage of acknowledged experts and the teaching authority of the Church. To be sure, the Book of Revelation has valuable insights for us. But, given its literary form (which is poetic and symbolic), it needs to be interpreted accordingly, which is to say that in general it ought not to be done in a literal fashion. Father Alfred McBride, O.Praem., has produced a very fine guide to this important but difficult book of the Bible, published by Our Sunday Visitor.

Scripture study

Q. There seems to be such a dearth of good, basic material for Scripture study. I am a newly ordained priest and intend to start a Bible study group in my new assignment; I shall also be teaching in our local Catholic high school in the fall. Do you have any suggestions for texts for either or both groups?

A. First, welcome to the priesthood! May you always keep this initial zeal you currently demonstrate.

At the risk of coming off as self-serving, allow me to recommend my own book, *The Catholic Church and the Bible*, just published in a revised edition by Ignatius Press, taking into account the *Catechism of the Catholic Church*. The book offers an introduction to biblical study, contains study/discussion questions, as well as a detailed resource guide for books, magazines, and other aids. There also is a Bible-study set that looks at the four Gospels, Acts of the Apostles, and the Book of Revelation, by Father Alfred McBride, O.Praem., published by Our Sunday Visitor (800-348-2440).

Human and divine

Q. St. Luke's Gospel reads, "And Mary wrapped her child in swaddling clothes and laid Him in a manger" (2:7). What is the fascination of artists (both ancient and modern) and their rationale for depicting the many crèche scenes with the child naked, even though snow and ice were outside the heart of the scene? Is there some spiritual significance?

A. Artists have always been given — and gladly taken — "poetic license" in many ways. For instance, how many portraits of St. Paul's conversion have you seen that depict him falling off a horse. If you look at the scriptural accounts, however, no horse is ever mentioned. Showing the Child Jesus naked may have some additional significance. First, it helps us appreciate the poverty of the Holy Family, the lowliness of His birth and, therefore, the depth of the divine act of loving condescension. Second, with so many early heresies that questioned the reality of the humanity of Christ, this artistic attempt reinforces the correct teaching regarding His possession of a true human nature, along with His divine nature, united in His one divine Person.

Old Testament retribution

Q. I'm in search of a book or a series on the Old Testament that can help me to understand how the unusual amount of bloodshed in the Old Testament can be reconciled with our loving and merciful God. It seems that God frequently used mass slaughter to drive home the point that He was in charge. It would be helpful if this book or series also gave some insight into the psalms. As you can tell, I'm not very well read in Old Testament commentaries. I would be most grateful for any suggestions you could make.

A. The question of violence and seemingly divinely mandated retribution in the Old Testament has been a vexing problem for millennia. One of the best treatments I have seen on this topic is the work of Father Michael Duggan in *The Consuming Fire: A Christian Introduction to the Old Testament*, published by Ignatius Press. Undoubtedly, you are referring to the so-called cursing psalms, which have also troubled Christians for centuries. C.S. Lewis handles this well in his *Reflections on the Psalms*.

Loving God

Q. In Mark 12:28-34, Matthew 22:34-40 and Luke 10:25-28, the subject of the "Great Commandment" is addressed. Jesus responds that we must first love God, and then love our neighbor. These readings appear several times in the *Lectionary* cycle. I have heard several priests follow up these reading, with a homily saying, "Love of God and love of neighbor are the same thing." The rest of the homily then goes on to deal with love of neighbor, never the love of God. Does this mean that the Persons of the Blessed Trinity and my neighbor are the same? Why do we no longer hear homilies on the love of God? Have we become a religion dedicated to "love of neighbor," as opposed to the "love of God"? It seems to me that we are bordering on heresy.

A. It was not an accident that the Son of God taught us that the love of God must come first — in every sense of the word. All we need do is look at the sad witness of the confused 1960s, when thousands of priests and Religious hied themselves off to the inner city to express their "love of neighbor," which, presumably, was inspired by the love of God — which so many forgot about entirely in very short order. Such folks left religious life in droves, and a good percentage of them left the Church as well.

No, love of God is fundamental to any other love. No less an apostle of "love of neighbor" than Mother Teresa understood this clearly, which is why she required her sisters to devote the first hours of their day to prayer and the Holy Sacrifice of the Mass. Her angle was quite simple: Love of God gave her the motivation to express her love for her neighbor, and the ability to recognize Christ in the Holy Eucharist enabled her to recognize Christ in the broken bodies she tended later in the day.

The two "loves" are indeed related, but the priority order must be maintained. We all know dozens of "good" people who are very kind and compassionate (they "love" their neighbors), but they have no relationship with Almighty God — and have no desire for one. In other words, love of neighbor is no assurance that one will eventually end up loving God. On the other hand, true love of God always and necessarily demands a movement toward one's neighbor in love.

Bible references

Q. Sometimes when I am reading the Scriptures, I come across unfamiliar terms that are not found in the dictionary, or seem to have a different understanding of a known term. Is there some handy reference that could help ease my confusion and enhance my understanding?

A. For modern readers often confused or put off by unfamiliar ancient terms and phrases, the *Illustrated Dictionary of Bible Life and Times* is a comprehensive reference and an invaluable guide. More than one thousand five hundred household items, occupations, trades, laws, customs, religious rites, festivals, and pastimes common in the days of the Old and New Testaments are clearly explained in easy-to-grasp language, complimented by more than five hundred full-color photographs, artifacts, maps, charts, and specifically commissioned paintings. It is published by Reader's Digest Books.

The Collegeville Bible Handbook is also an informative and easy guide to reading and understanding the Bible. The brief commentary on each book of the Old and New Testaments and the time lines, maps and illustrations that pertain to the biblical lands and peoples are a help to those who are beginning Bible study as well as to those who are continuing such study. The handbook attempts to kindle in readers a desire to know the Bible, the times in which the different books were written, what the Bible said to the people for whom they were written, and what the Bible says to us about the work of God in our midst. It is available from Liturgical Press.

Scripture Version

Q. At a baptism recently, we all recited the Lord's Prayer, including the doxology ("For thine is the kingdom. . ."). Is this the way the Church officially recognizes and prays the Lord's Prayer now? It makes me uneasy to know that we are now saying the prayer that Jesus gave us the way Protestants say it and not the way it has been given to us in Scripture. If the Church has not endorsed saying this prayer like the Protestants, would it be out of place for me to speak out against this practice when I hear fellow Catholics saying the prayer in this manner?

A. As I have pointed out on several previous occasions, the version of the Lord's Prayer you cite is not, strictly speaking, Protestant in origin, but Eastern. You are correct, however, that it is not the prayer as given to us in Sacred Scripture, which is why the Catholic Church — even in the Eastern rites — uses the doxology differently, either by separating it from the main body of the prayer with another (as in the Roman rite's "*Libera nos*" insertion) or in other rites having the congregation pray the Lord's Prayer proper, with the priest concluding with the doxology. The only Catholic rite that does otherwise is the so-called "Anglican Use" which, because of its adherents' roots in Protestantism, have been permitted to retain certain elements of their spiritual and liturgical patrimony.

Language roots

Q. Latin is the official language of the Church. As Jesus was never in Rome and didn't speak Latin, but rather used Aramaic to address the multitudes, why isn't Aramaic the Church's official language?

A. Aside from Hebrew and Aramaic, we don't know what languages Our Lord did or did not know. Given the ambiance in which He lived, it would not have been inconceivable for Him to have been conversant in Greek — and Latin likewise could have been possible. The Church's reliance on Latin had nothing to do with imitating Jesus' speech patterns; it had to do with the very practical question of using the *lingua franca* of the Roman Empire. As Rome faded, Latin still held sway since it was the basis for the then-developing Romance languages of Western Europe. As time went on, even with multiple languages brought into the family of the Church, Latin then took on the role of an instrument of unity, especially for the Sacred Liturgy, and as the language of theology, philosophy, and canon law. Even within secular society — well into the nineteenth century — any educated person could communicate with any other through the medium of Latin.

Regrettably, today, we find an abysmal ignorance of Latin, even among supposedly intelligent and well-educated people. The near demise of Latin in the Church has aided the secularization process (especially on the liturgical front) and fragmented our efforts in many ways, particularly as that affects a unified approach to the sacred sciences.

Human approach

Q. The Bible has it that you must be "born again." To me, being born again is to receive Jesus Christ in your heart — to become a new person. You've got to give up gambling, drinking, and pick up your cross and follow the Lord. Catholics gamble and drink. Priests and nuns must live for the Lord. When you become a born-again Christian, you can backslide if you live for the worldly things. We live in this world, but we don't need to live for the world. I'm not saying that only Catholics drink and gamble. How can you get to heaven if you don't live for the Lord?

A. Search the New Testament all you want and you'll never find a condemnation of either gambling or drinking. Granted, abuses are possible but, as the old Latin adage reminds us, *abusus non tollit usum* ("abuse doesn't take away use"). If someone enjoys gambling — in moderation —and is faithful to his various obligations, there is no sin involved in innocent games of cards or bingo intended for entertainment. Similarly, with alcohol, social drinking, again in moderation, is not problematic for a believer; after all, Our Lord Himself worked His first miracle by changing water into wine, precisely to keep that wedding feast going longer. The big mistake made by folks like the Puritans was that they saw the potential for difficulties in certain kinds of behavior and, instead of advising caution and prudence, they declared whole classes of activity to be off-limits. This is not surprising for many Protestants, however, because without a well-developed concept of how to live a life of virtue (the Protestant stress is much more on avoiding sin) and without the Sacrament of Penance, what else can you do to ensure — as much as possible —that people won't "backslide"?

The Catholic approach is much more human, less mechanical and more open to genuine growth and psychological well-being, achieved by aiming for personal responsibility and maturity.

Bible references

Q. How or what do you tell a granddaughter who has "shacked up" with a man still going to college? I've hunted the Bible over and don't find an answer.

A. The Bible is replete with references which condemn, in the clearest of terms, the sin of fornication, which is what "shacking up" is properly called. See, for example, the following texts: Lv 21:9; Mt 15:19; Mk 7:21; 1 Cor 6:9,18; 2 Cor 12:21; Eph 5:5; Col 3:5; 1 Tm 1:10; Heb 12:16, 13:4; Rev 2:14, 9:21, 17:2, 18:3, 18:9, 21:8, 22:15.

Scripture's role

Q. My Protestant neighbor constantly argues in favor of *sola Scriptura* and says that her position is that of the Bible, which is why the reformers espoused it. Can you help me with her?

A. There is nothing in Scripture, logic, or Church history to recommend, let alone require, belief in the theory that Scripture alone is the norm for Christian doctrine and morality. In fact, the Scriptures teach exactly the opposite. Interestingly enough, not even the reformers held to this principle as tenaciously as most contemporary fundamentalists. For an excellent treatment of this important subject, get hold of a new work on this topic, edited by Robert Sungenis, titled *Not by Scripture Alone* (Queenship Publishing Co.). It is an exhaustive study of the matter from every conceivable angle. I was delighted to be a contributor to the volume, along with others known to *The Catholic Answer* magazine readers, such as Mark Shea and Patrick Madrid.

A fine companion is *Not by Faith Alone*, also by Sungenis.

According to "Q"

Q. I would like you to speak to the issue of the Gospel according to "Q", a concept that some say is proven by the deciphering of the Dead Sea Scrolls. As I'm sure you are aware, some scholars hold that numerous doctrines of our Faith were added by later generations and not taught by Christ Himself, including Jesus' awareness that He was the Son of God, the Resurrection, etc. Is it possible to hold to the "Q" source and still have a Catholic approach to Scripture?

A. For the benefit of the uninitiated, "Q" is shorthand for the German word "Quelle," which means "source" — as in the literary source for the Synoptic Gospels. As this theory goes (and we should recall, it is no more than a theory), the sayings of Jesus were collected into a single document, from which the authors of the first three Gospels drew their material. In and of itself, this theory has no doctrinal implications, pro or con. Of course, it must also be admitted, from a scholarly perspective, that no one has ever proven that such a source ever existed, let alone having found it. So, to sum up, a Catholic is free to accept or reject this hypothesis.

Menu items

Q. Was Jesus a vegetarian? The Bible says "Do not eat meat" many times.

A. We know for a fact that Our Lord was not a vegetarian because He ate the Passover supper with His disciples, and that menu includes lamb. Furthermore, we know that He multiplied loaves and fishes and cooked fish for His disciples after the Resurrection; presumably, He would not make available to others what He Himself was adverse to eating.

Suspicious

Q. I was a lector for the Third Sunday in Lent and, as part of my reading, I was to give the enclosed overview to the Exodus reading. I have been frustrated on several occasions with misleading comments and statements that seem totally unfounded in the Catholic Faith. The highlighted line states, "Biblical scholars tell us [the Ten Commandments] may have come about over a much longer time, a collaboration of wise minds." Are we to believe that the biblical account of Moses receiving the Ten Commandments didn't happen, or worse, that the Bible is a storybook and not the Word of God? My priest responds to my questions in various ways but never in a clear, definitive way. He also believes Mary was married and had other children; perhaps he gets all this from the same source.

A. All too many so-called biblical scholars operate from a "hermeneutic of suspicion." Simply put, that means that, in knee-jerk fashion, they conclude that whatever the Bible says must never have happened. It is the exact opposite of a fundamentalistic, literalistic approach, which would hold that every single word of the biblical text means just what it appears to say. The Catholic method of scriptural interpretation is much more nuanced — and has been for nearly twenty centuries.

Beginning with the Fathers of the Church and continuing right on up through this century, we have read Sacred Scripture with reverence and respect, starting with the presumption that it contains the truth. At what level is that truth — that is, historical, theological, spiritual — is the question that needs to be answered. We situate the passage within the whole book from which it comes, and that book — in turn — within the entire Bible. Beyond that, we try to determine the literary form of the particular passage — that is, is it poetry, a parable, a straightforward teaching? All of these determinations influence how we interpret that portion of God's Word. A fine guide to this process was published in 1993 by the Pontifical Biblical Commission, titled *The Interpretation of the Bible in the Church*.

As far as the source of the commandments is concerned, direct divine composition is not absolutely necessary to posit, any more than it would be to require one to hold that God literally and personally wrote every word of the Bible. God can and does use human instruments to make known His Will and Law; this process is called divine inspiration, and the end product is inerrant.

Regarding Our Lady, of course she was married, but perhaps you mean married to someone after St. Joseph. Mary's perpetual virginity is a dogma of the Catholic Faith, requiring us to believe that Jesus was the only child she ever bore. Holding or teaching something contrary to that is heresy.

Miraculous moment

Q. Is it consistent with authoritatively promulgated teachings of the magisterium of the Church to publish claims that Jesus' birth was not of a miraculous nature?

A. No, it is not, because the Gospels clearly teach that Jesus' conception occurred through divine intervention — that is, without the seed of a man. In fact, we know that fundamentalist theology, which has very little interest in things Marian, upholds the doctrine of the virginal conception of Our Lord precisely because it is so absolutely taught in Sacred Scripture. Furthermore, they see this doctrine as a strong testimony to the miraculous.

"Amen, Amen"

Q. Jesus always said, "Amen, amen, I say to you." Can you tell me what that meant in his day, and what would be a term used in this day and age.

A. At the time, it signified something like, "I solemnly assure you" (which is the translation used in the New American Bible) — that is, an attestation of the truthfulness of the statement which follows. I, however, would prefer to retain the original form because it is so Semitic; we can always then explain its meaning, as I just did.

A challenge to us

Q. For the past two years, on the feast of the Holy Family, in the second reading (Col 3:13-17), verses 18-21 were omitted, even though they are printed in the missalette. It may be politically correct to omit: "Wives, be subject to your husbands, as is fitting in the Lord. Husbands, love your wives, and do not be harsh with them. Children, obey your parents in everything, for this pleases the Lord. Fathers, do not provoke your children, lest they become discouraged." It is frightening that we are beginning to pick and choose that which we want to hear, while that which makes us uncomfortable is thrown out. Would you please comment?

A. Unfortunately, a few years ago the bishops' conference gave permission for the elimination of the verses you cite. I think that was a very unwise decision, for the very reasons you offer. The irony in all this is that the "problematic" verses actually give the key to interpreting the whole passage in a way which is extremely profound — and not in the least "sexist"! If we continue to rid ourselves of passages that certain people find offensive, we'll end up deleting texts dealing with murder, adultery, robbery, homosexual activity, etc. In truth, we would end up with a very small Bible, with the result that we would be challenging God's Word, instead of allowing God's Word to challenge us, our attitudes, our behavior.

Revealed religion

Q. On the Eighteenth Sunday of Ordinary Time, our parish priest read the Gospel of John regarding the multiplication of the loaves and fishes. In his homily, he said the multiplication of the food was actually a story of the sharing of food by the five thousand men, women, and children. I wrote to him and said that this is not the teaching of the Church, and that he should tell his parishioners that his homily was his opinion. He wrote me back defending his position of choosing to offer another way to interpret what had happened, which, he states, is perfectly legitimate and within his right. Can you help me to answer my priest who, I should note, has written to me in the past declaring, "We must rid ourselves of this present Pope."

A. The last line of your letter gives us all the information we need to evaluate the entire sad picture.

The issue is not the interpretation of one particular passage of the Gospels; it deals with an obvious discomfort with the miraculous. The spin given the passage by your parish priest is not new; indeed, it is rather dated, harking back to the silly 1960s.

The problem for so many supposedly "modern" men is that they have decided that what they cannot do, God cannot do, either. Or, as Voltaire put it, "God made man in His own image and likeness, and man has never ceased to return the compliment."

If we can believe in the miracle of creation (and I hope all believers can, otherwise, what do we believe in?), why can't we accept other miracles of an infinitely lesser scope? Acceptance of the miraculous is connected to critical issues such as: the existence of God; His omnipotence; Divine Providence. These are hardly peripheral matters. To question these teachings strikes at the heart of biblical, revealed religion.

No right

Q. What do you think of a pastor who lets his lectors change the words of Holy Scripture during the Mass? They meet on Monday nights to prepare for this.

A. As we say repeatedly and, I am sure, our readers tire of hearing: No one has the right to change a word of the Sacred Liturgy, let alone the Sacred Scriptures. Your priest and lectors would spend their Monday nights better by gathering for a holy hour to meditate on the Word of God, asking for the grace to proclaim it with fidelity and conviction.

Interpretation

Q. I love the Lord Jesus with all my heart and enjoy reading the Bible and meditating on God's Word, but I am perplexed by some passages of God's written Word. Could you be so kind to explain these to me? In 2 Corinthians 12:1-4, the apostle Paul refers to a revelation during which he was caught into paradise to the third heaven and heard unspeakable words. Was he praying in the Spirit?

A. I think standard interpretations of this text, from time immemorial, hold that St. Paul was reflecting upon an ecstatic experience that he had. Since he gives rather sparse detail to it, we would be hard-pressed to hazard too many guesses, but it surely seems clear that it was some kind of supernatural, mystical phenomenon.

Reading the Scriptures is a wonderful and important thing to do, but many passages are *not* self-explanatory, as you have discovered. This was also the insight of the Ethiopian eunuch whom St. Philip met; wisely, he observes that he cannot understand the sacred texts completely, "unless someone guides me" (Acts 8:31). Many fundamentalists deny the truth of this verse of Scripture by declaring that anyone who is "in the Spirit" will be able to interpret the Bible with no difficulty, and apprehend the true meaning the Lord God intends.

Needless to say, this does not square with Christian history or personal experience: If God's Word is so plain, how come there are so many different "spins" put on it? And why do we have more than fifty-five thousand Protestant denominations, all alleging to be Spirit-filled bodies teaching the full truth of the biblical Word?

No, the old eunuch got it right, to begin with, and the Church has seen the necessity of offering both scholarly and magisterial help to aid the comprehension of her members. Don't get frustrated by troublesome or confusing passages; just seek out the appropriate assistance.

Bible battle

Q. Is the *Catholic Living Bible*, with an imprimatur by Bishop Leo A. Pursley of Fort Wayne-South Bend, dated January 9, 1976, approved by the Catholic Church? It is published by Tyndale House Publishers. I know what the *imprimatur* means, but this book is a paraphrase, not a translation when I compare some verses. The first chapter of St. John's Gospel is one I question. My brother-in-law has left the Catholic Church and joined a small Baptist, anti-Catholic group, and his statement, based on this Bible, is that the Catholic Church changed the Word of God. He uses the *King James Bible*. I responded with the other Bibles approved by the Catholic Church, as well as the *King James* text. I am hoping your answer will clear up this question.

A. A paraphrase is not a real Bible and cannot be used for catechetical or liturgical purposes. The imprimatur attached to it merely states that nothing in the work is opposed to Catholic faith and doctrine.

I hope your brother-in-law does not imagine that the *King James Version* was handed down by God Himself! In point of fact, it is laden with thousands of errors — and acknowledged as such by Protestants, which is why many of them have begun to distance themselves from that version.

The Church holds that the only definitive texts of Holy Writ are the texts in the original languages; translations are mere second-bests. That having been said, I would proceed to ask your brother-in-law how we have supposedly "changed" the Word of God. Lacking that information, I could not venture an intelligent response.

Fine exegesis

Q. I came across *The International Student Bible,* and since it was easy to understand I thought it would be good for teenagers. It has the *nihil obstat* and *imprimatur* for the articles on Pages 1-126 and the sidebar annotations. I need your advice about the translation itself and the advisability of giving it to my grandchildren.

A. For those who missed my review of this work in a recent issue of *The Catholic Answer* magazine, let me repeat that the general editor is a fine Catholic scholar with impeccable credentials.

Everything I have looked at in the volume squares with standard principles of Catholic exegesis.

Apostolic title

Q. How do you distinguish between an Apostle and a disciple? Is Paul an apostle, even if he is not a member of the original Twelve?

A. The lines of demarcation are not all that clear — for example, the Gospel according to St. John never uses the word "apostle" at all. In the Synoptics, a distinction is made, so that all the followers of the Lord are "disciples," while the term "apostle" is restricted to the inner circle of the Twelve — indicating greater intimacy with Christ and greater authority to act in His Name. The criteria for "apostleship" were set forth at the time of the election of Matthias; St. Paul appears to have used them for himself, except that he was not among the apostolic band during the Lord's earthly life and ministry. Nevertheless, he maintained, the direct call from the Risen Christ and the experience of Him on the road to Damascus superceded other demands. Paul was certainly clear in his own mind on his genuine possession of the apostolic character, and challenged others to show convincing evidence to the contrary. Consider, for example, the following passages in this regard: Romans 1:1; Romans 11:13; 1 Corinthians 1:1; 1 Corinthians 9:1; 2 Corinthians 1:1; Galatians 1:1; Ephesians 1:1; Colossians 1:1; 1 Timothy 1:1; 2 Timothy 1:1; Titus 1:1. Don't miss how he always sets the tone, precisely by setting forth his identity. With a touch of humility, however, we do find him referring to himself as "the least of the apostles" in 1 Corinthians 15:9!

Not "Sola Scriptura"

Q. I am taking a college class called "Pastoral Care." Technically, it is a class on Christian counseling, and is being given by a Baptist minister. Everything being taught is Scripture-based. I am the only Catholic taking the class, and I don't agree with some of the things being taught. I need to know where in Scripture masturbation and artificial contraception are condemned. The textbook that we are using, *Christian Counseling*, by Gary Collins, teaches that neither of these behaviors is sinful. I have looked these up in the *Catechism of the Catholic Church*, and there is reference to *Humanæ Vitæ*, but not to Scripture. I hope you can lead me to a convincing Bible-based argument.

A. I suppose the first point to make is that the Catholic Church does not accept the idea that she can and must teach only what is explicitly taught in Scripture, for the Church receives enlightenment from the Holy Spirit regarding faith and morals. That having been said, the classic text cited historically on both topics is the condemnation of Onan for having spilled his seed, found in the Book of Genesis (chapter 38).

The Church understands sexual intercourse as comprising two elements — the procreative and the unitive — neither one of which can ever be directly thwarted. Masturbation has neither element; contraceptive intercourse blocks the procreative in a direct and deliberate manner. This rationale, of course, also explains the Church's negative judgment on homosexual acts; in other words, such actions are also and perforce contraceptive.

It is important to underscore the fact that prior to 1930, every Christian body condemned in the most absolute terms contraceptive intercourse. The first to break ranks in that regard was the Anglican Communion at its Lambeth Conference in 1930; their declaration was responded to within a matter of months by Pope Pius XI in *Casti Connubii* (on Christian marriage) — the first in a long and unbroken line of such magisterial denunciations for the rest of this century, including Pope Pius XII, the Second Vatican Council, Pope Paul VI and Pope John Paul II. For an excellent treatment of this question by an evangelical Christian, see *The Bible and Birth Control*, by Charles Provan (Zimmer Printing).

No reincarnation

Q. How can I respond to my friends who claim reincarnation is in the Bible? They say that, in four places, Elijah is mentioned as being reincarnated as John the Baptist — in Matthew 11:10-14, Matthew 17:10-13, Mark 6:14-16, and Mark 9:11-13. They are non-Catholics, sincerely seeking the truth. Is there a book or article that I might recommend to them?

A. Those passages do not speak of Elijah being reincarnated but simply of his coming back to earth. According to Jewish apocalyptic and messianic expectations, Elijah would return and, depending on the school of thought, either be the Messiah or usher in the days of the Messiah.

Reincarnation, on the other hand, talks about a being coming back as another type of life form — for example, a human returning as a cow, or a chicken as a man. Human life, in the biblical view of things, is irrepeatable. Whatever good or evil we do has eternal consequences — an incredibly important aspect of human dignity. We don't come back in greater or lesser forms to correspond to those acts; rather, our eternal destiny is conditioned by them. *The Catechism of the Catholic Church* makes this clear: "Death is the end of man's earthly pilgrimage, of the time of grace and mercy which God offers him so as to work out his earthly life in keeping with the divine plan, and to decide his ultimate destiny. When 'the single course of our earthly life' is completed, we shall not return to other earthly lives: 'It is appointed for men to die once.' There is no 'reincarnation' after death" (no. 1013).

On the moon

Q. One question pops up about the image of Our Lady of Guadalupe: Why is the Blessed Mother (miraculously appearing on Juan Diego's *tilma*) shown to be above a black crescent moon?

A. This traditional Marian depiction has scriptural origins: "And a great portent appeared in heaven, a woman clothed with the sun, with the moon under her feet" (Rev 12:1). The moon figures in the Miraculous Medal image as well.

Parousia meaning?

Q. What exactly does the term "parousia" mean, and what is the Catholic argument in supporting it? Also, what exactly do Protestants mean by "rapture" or "rapture of the saints"?

A. The parousia is the Lord's second coming, which is clearly taught in Scripture and in the Church's creedal documents — for example, "He will come again in glory."

The Rapture is discussed in the New Testament in several places — for example, 1 Thessalonians 4:16-17 — but not very clearly and with enough divergencies as to be unhelpful in coming up with a unified view as to what is really involved. Not surprisingly, many evangelicals are very divided among themselves as to the exact nature of the matter. In shorthand form, the Rapture refers to that time when Christ will come in glory and take His "saints" with Him (the saved). Questions start to swirl around when more detail is sought. For instance, does this occur before or after the so-called thousand-year reign of Christ? What about the "time of tribulation"?

The Catholic Church has never been incredibly exercised about these issues, merely taking seriously Our Lord's counsel to be prepared for His coming, whenever it happens. Pope John XXIII exhibited this kind of "Catholic intuition" when, being asked what people should do if told that the parousia was about to occur today, he replied: "Look busy!"

Why, oh why?

Q. In John 1:47-51, why was Nathanael amazed that Our Lord saw him under a fig tree? What's so unusual about seeing someone under a tree? Also, why is the English Mass translation at the consecration, "Take this, all of you"? The Latin consecration says, "Take you all of this" (*"ex hoc omnes"* and *"ex eo omnes"*).

A. The presumption in the passage you cite is that the crowd was vast, and Jesus would have had no objective reason to take note of

Nathanael, who intuited from all this that Our Lord had certain divine powers.

The consecratory formula in Latin says: *"Accipite et manducate ex hoc omnes: Hoc est enim Corpus meum."* That means, "Take and eat of this, all of you: For this is my Body." *"Omnes"* is the vocative plural, a direct address to the apostles. If your translation were correct, it would have to say something like *"omnem"* in the accusative case as a direct object.

Translation issue

Q. What is happening to our Bibles of late? It seems that many changes have been made, especially in the removal of words, phrases, and even whole verses. One example is Luke 1:28; "Blessed art thou among women" is missing from the New American Bible starting in 1991. The 1989 version has it. This verse is the one that the Church used to justify the first part of the Hail Mary, and now it is no longer there after more than a thousand years. Does the *Imprimatur* really mean anything anymore? I have the Catholic Answers Logos package on CD-ROM and its Bible has this line in the Vulgate, yet it is missing in the Greek. I have a difficult time believing St. Jerome added this verse to the Vulgate on his own initiative. Are modernist liberal theologians forcing these changes?

A. Biblical-translation work is not an easy task for many reasons, not least of which being that alternate texts exist, depending on the manuscript used as the original. The verse you mention is a case in point. The Greek lacks the line that concerns you; the Vulgate of St. Jerome has it; the neo-Vulgate (made to conform more closely to the Greek) lacks it. How to resolve the apparent conflict?

If St. Luke refers to Our Lady as *"kecharitomene"* (in Greek, "highly favored"), doesn't that mean "blessed among women"? In all likelihood, this was the thinking of St. Jerome.

A similar but much less neuralgic example comes from the Lord's Prayer. In the Vulgate, we read, *"ne nos inducas in tentationem*" ("lead us not into temptation"); it is not a good translation but, hallowed by centuries of use, it's too late to change, and all we do is explain that what it says is not really what it means.

At times, contemporary translators have a theological agenda at odds with Tradition, and manipulate the translation process to solidify their positions, but I don't think that is the situation here.

"Middle voice"

Q. I am somewhat annoyed with recent translations of the Gospel that state, in English, that "Jesus has been raised," rather than say that "Jesus has risen." What really concerns me more is that the most recent Latin translation of the Scriptures is now saying, "*Jesus suscitatus est*," rather than "*resurrexit*."

A. The difficulty cited here is an ancient one and of grammatical origin. The Greek language has what is called a "middle voice" — that is, a voice for verbs between active and passive. Neither Latin, nor any of the Romance languages, nor English has this. The active voice has the subject performing the action ("John stole a fish."); the passive has the subject as the recipient of the action of the verb ("The fish was stolen by John."). The middle voice has the subject acting on himself, somewhat akin to a reflexive verb in some modern languages (for example, *me llamo* — literally, "I call myself" — that is, "My name is. . ."). The Greek verb "to raise" is often used in the middle voice in reference to the Lord's resurrection (something like, "I raise myself"); in English, we are confronted with two choices, active (I rise) or passive (I am raised). Both have theological truth in them: Jesus, as the Second Person of the Blessed Trinity, rises by His own power; as Son of the Father, His self-oblation is accepted by the Father and the definitive sign of that is the Father's acting on Christ's sacred humanity by raising it to glory. Good catechesis and incisive homilies should make those points, so that no element of the mystery of the Resurrection is lost or downplayed.

Trespasses accurate

Q. Why does the "Roman Catholic Lord's Prayer" use the word "trespasses" while all of the Bible translations I have read of use the words "sins, wrongs or debts." I have looked in the *New American Bible, King James Version, Douay-Rheims, Revised Standard Version* and many more translations.

A. The English translation of the Lord's Prayer predates all the currently available English versions of Scripture. "Trespasses" was the standard word for "sins" or "offenses" ten centuries ago or more.

Morality

⁕

Sex curriculum

Q. It seems that everyone has a different understanding of what should or should not be done in Catholic schools regarding sex education. The dilemma does not only confront parents; it affects teachers and school administrators as well. Could you recommend any program that would both fulfill diocesan requirements for sex education and be faithful to Church teaching on sexuality?

A. Two programs have recently come to my attention, and I have had the opportunity to review both of them in-depth.

First came "The New Corinthians Curriculum," a kindergarten through eighth-grade supplement for religious education that assists parents and educators in teaching the virtues. It is published by the Foundation for the Family, a Cincinnati-based, nonprofit organization dedicated to strengthening family values and chastity education.

"The New Corinthians Curriculum" consists of a three hundred twenty-eight-page manual for parents and teachers, and a fifty-two-page booklet, *Parent-to-Child Instruction on Human Sexuality*.

The purpose of the curriculum is to enable the learner to develop a relationship with God, so that decisions are made on the basis of sound scriptural and catechetical understanding following the 1995 guidelines of the Pontifical Council for the Family's *Truth and Meaning of Human Sexuality*. That document urged that education for chastity not be separated from education in all the virtues, nor descend into mere lessons in biology or "safe sex."

The second is a project by Our Sunday Visitor, called "The Catholic Vision of Love: A Curriculum for Christian Education in Sexuality and the Family," designed for grades five through eight. It was developed over the last eight years in response to requests for such programs by recent Popes and the Second Vatican Council, and has been reviewed favorably by two departments of the Holy See: the Pontifical Council for the Family and the Congregation for the Clergy (concerned with catechesis). All the material is in keeping with Catholic teaching on sexual morality and human personality. Each grade level consists of twelve units of lessons for students, a compilation of teachers' notes, and a parent's guide to the program. Each grade's materials cost $39.95. For further information, call 800-348-2440.

It should be emphasized that the Vatican document cited earlier does not forbid these types of programs in human sexuality from inclusion in Catholic schools; the proviso is that whatever is done must be done in collaboration with parents, who are the primary educators of their children in all matters, but especially so in regard to such intimate matters as human development and sexuality.

Theologically correct

Q. Is a new controversy to arise on the subject of artificial contraception since at least one theologian has taught that birth control is licit for the mentally handicapped? An article that appeared in a national Catholic newspaper seems to contradict itself. Would you please comment on the article (of which I enclose a copy)?

A. The theologian in question is a very reputable scholar who teaches at a pontifical institution in Rome. What he said was this: "Providing the mentally handicapped with contraceptives where the risk of sexual assault is high is morally permissible." He went on to caution, however, that abortifacient contraceptives could not be used. I see no contradiction here. Nor is there any violation of traditional moral principles; here we are talking about no more than warding off an unjust aggressor and the undesirable effects of that act of aggression. Surely, we cannot see in this an opening for contraceptive activity within the context of consensual sex, whether within the framework of marriage, fornication, or adultery.

Book Review

Q. I have seen some reviews of Peter Korn's *Lovejoy: A Year in the Life of an Abortion Clinic*; it has gotten very mixed reviews, but not completely predictable. Have you read it? If so, what do you think of it?

A. In the last three years, the number of American hospitals willing to provide abortions has fallen forty-eight percent. As abortion facilities close, obstetricians get out of what they now consider a dangerous business, and the federal government then forces medical schools to teach the abortion procedure, and the role of clinics that stay in business has become increasingly important.

With extraordinary access to both sides of the front lines of the abortion controversy, this new book profiles one such facility, using one remarkably successful clinic in Portland, Ore., as a microcosm for the overall issue that is tearing America apart. Through candid conversations with Lovejoy's counselors, doctors, and administrators, observations of the clinic's daily dramas and interviews with the right-to-life advocates who "threaten" Lovejoy's existence on its very doorstep, Korn paints a complete picture of abortion as a business, a cause, an option, and a last resort.

The book is perhaps most valuable because it is not written by a pro-lifer (although the author is rather objective). I cannot imagine any abortionist or pro-abortionist being happy with the publication of this work, which certainly shows the seamy, callous, and businesslike nature of the abortion industry. On the other hand, no pro-lifer is going to be ecstatic at such an "evenhanded" approach to *the* moral issue of the last half of this century — not only in the United States, but throughout the world.

Scrupulosity

Q. I have several questions concerning the Sacrament of Penance: (a) Sometimes, I am not able to go to confession when I want to. I've heard of "spiritual communion" and "baptism by desire." Is it possible to have "spiritual confession" or receive "absolution by desire"? (b) Several years ago, I confessed a mortal sin. The priest told me he would not forgive me because he thought I was sick and needed to see a psychiatrist. I recognize that I am neurotic, but I feel that my neuroses stem from anxiety over my sins and not being "right" with God. I have never agreed with people who have physical ailments, but refuse to see a physician because they have faith that God will cure them. Will I also be presumptuous of God's mercy if I don't see a psychiatrist? Also, since the priest did not forgive me, have I been living in a state of mortal sin all these years? I am too ashamed to confess it again. (c) My "method" for confessing is to list two or three specific sins and then conclude by saying, "For these sins and all my sins, I ask forgiveness." Is this acceptable? Do I have to confess all my sins in order for all to be forgiven? Sometimes my sins are too numerous — and too grievous — to mention.

A. Reception of the Sacrament of Penance by auricular confession is the normal means established by Christ for the forgiveness of sins. Both the Catechism of the Catholic Church and the Code of Canon Law make provision for one's reception of Holy Communion without sacramental confession when a genuine emergency exists and when the firm intention exists to confess any mortal sins as soon as the opportunity presents itself.

I don't know why the priest denied you absolution, but from your very brief letter I do tend to agree with his judgment on your emotional state, which seems to be excessively scrupulous, and that is a psychological disorder. Therefore, I would agree with the confessor's advice that you see a psychiatrist — a good, practicing Catholic who is willing to work with you and a sensitive priest to put this problem to rest once and for all. Refusal to deal with the matter in this manner is like someone's decision to rid himself of a headache by burning his hand to distract from the original pain;

it is foolish at best, and potentially most damaging spiritually and otherwise at worst.

States of sin

Q. Fornication is defined as sexual intercourse outside marriage. Civil marriage is obviously a form of marriage. How, then, does one reach the conclusion that civil marriage "constitutes . . . a state of fornication"? Also, how can fornication be a "state"? I have always regarded it as an act. Is a "state" of fornication worse than an "act" of fornication? Finally, do you really think that St. Paul had civil marriage in mind when he condemned fornication?

A. Civil marriage is not a real marriage in the eyes of God; in reality, it is no marriage at all. Therefore, if a man and woman (who are free to enter a valid marriage) commit themselves to a civil union, the act has no effect and thus they are guilty of the sin of fornication each and every time they have sexual relations. If that same couple had been bound by a previous valid union, the acts in question would be the sin of adultery. Although fornication and adultery can be isolated acts, living together with an ongoing and unrepentant intention to engage in such acts changes the nature of the situation, so that one can properly speak of the "state" of fornication or adultery — and, that is, in fact, more grievous than the isolated acts, for which there can be mitigating circumstances, and from which it is easier to repent.

The ecclesiastical form of marriage did not exist in St. Paul's time, at least not as we know it today; furthermore, the Church had no way of enforcing her notion of marriage in a pagan environment. What constituted marriage "in Christ" at that time would have been the submission of the union to the Church and the positive intention of the spouses.

Credible study

Q. There has been so much attention given to sex-abuse scandals involving the clergy that I cringe every time new information is released. However, we cannot pretend that these incidents have not happened. Would you please comment on the book by Philip Jenkins, *Pedophiles and Priests: Anatomy of a Contemporary Crisis*.

A. This book is a welcome contribution to the sad field of clerical pedophilia, welcome because it is so honest and so restrained in its declarations. The author carefully situates the entire crisis within Church and society and informs us of how the media and others got hold of it all, exploiting an admittedly shameful chapter in Church history to advance personal agendas. The credibility of the study is increased by its having been published by Oxford University Press.

Complex matters

Q. Why does the magisterium not stress the immorality of the drug trade more forcefully than it does? If the bishop of Lincoln, Neb., can excommunicate people for wanting women priests and married priests, I think the Church should excommunicate any person who has anything to do with the growing and shipment of drugs. Why does the magisterium not oppose gun control more strongly, when you think about the violence and killings that take place because of these weapons? Furthermore, why doesn't the magisterium encourage agrarian reform in countries such as Haiti, El Salvador, Columbia, the Philippines, and many other Catholic countries where the wealthy people own as much as ninety-five percent of the land and wealth, while most of the people live in squalor? We will always have the poor with us, according to the Bible, but do they have to be so very, very poor?

A. First of all, I think you mean to say that the Church should "support" gun control, not "oppose" it, no?

At any rate, excommunication is a remedial and prudential process, by which I mean that the Church threatens excommunication (or actually does it) as a way of warning people of the gravity of their actions, hoping that the threat or the imposition of excommunication will either keep a person from the act or bring the person to repentance and reconciliation, if the act has already occurred.

If, in the prudent judgment of a bishop, excommunication would be an effective (and not counterproductive) tool to prevent serious evils from being committed, he would be free to impose such sanctions. With several of the issues you highlight, however, given the complexity of the matters, it is not apparent to me and many others that there is a single way to bring about the desired good. Is gun control the answer, for example? Perhaps. But what kinds of guns, under what circumstances, for whom, etc.? The variety of solutions to social problems generally admits of many possibilities, unlike more discreet actions, and that is why the Church restricts automatic excommunications to a handful of very objective acts (such as abortion, desecration of the Blessed Sacrament, violating the seal of the confessional, etc.).

That does not mean that the Church does not consider other acts morally wrong, but she does not believe that all sins should be deemed excommunicable offenses; if she did, none of us would be left in the Church.

Worthy of Respect

Q. I'm concerned about an upcoming mandatory diversity-training session to take place where I am employed. "Diverse" behavior nowadays includes cohabitation, fornication, and homosexual behavior. I work with many types of individuals, but I should not be told to accept people whose behavior is contrary to Christian teaching. Are all people worthy of respect? I'm somewhat confused about what the position of an orthodox Christian should be in such situations. Would you please offer some clarification?

A. People are worthy of respect at all times and in all circumstances — even when they are wrong in their opinions or sinful in their actions. While the adage is correct which asserts that "error has no rights," erring people do have rights. That said, we must also be careful that programs such as the one that causes you some concern can be politically driven, designed to create a social climate in which aberrant behavior is placed on a par with lifestyles that are wholesome, good, and beneficial to society and culture. While we must always be compassionate to sinners, we can never appear to approve acts that are ultimately detrimental to them and destructive of the fabric of society.

No double standard

Q. We all know that it takes two people to commit the sin of adultery. Why is it that only women seem to be described as "adulterous"?

A. Christianity, starting with Jesus Himself, never subscribed to a "double standard" in this regard. Hence, we hear Jesus warn males to refrain from evil, lustful looks, lest they commit adultery in their hearts (see Mt 5:28). Popular culture may utilize a double standard for adultery, but the Church never has. It is just a little bit ironic, I think, that Catholic moral theology has consistently warned people about activities called "near occasions of sin," which were often seen as "puritanical," but now have been taken up into the conventional wisdom of "political correctness," so that actions or speech that are perceived as lewd constitute "sexual harassment."

Love comes through

Q. Have you ever heard of the organization Pflag (Parents and Friends of Lesbians and Gays)? If so, is it a good organization to turn to if you have a son who is a homosexual? Our son doesn't call or come home because he says we don't accept him for what he is. I want to hug him so badly and love him, but he doesn't want to see us. What can we do?

A. I have never heard of the organization in question; my instincts generally move me away from any "special interest" type of group because I've seldom seen much concrete good emanating from such, with most people ending up in "sharing sessions" of self-pity.

Your love for your son comes through most genuinely in your letter. If you haven't done so, write him a letter, from the heart, and call him from time to time — even if he doesn't respond all that positively. It seems to me that if you have exhibited the same kind of affection for him as your note to me suggests, his real problem is not with you but with himself. Perhaps he needs time to assimilate more of who he is and what he expects from life and relationships. The most important thing you can do is to keep communication open from your side, to pray for him unceasingly, and to let him know that you are doing so.

Very little changed

Q. In the recent battle over domestic partnerships in San Francisco, it seems that any compromise actually sells out Catholic principles. Would you please comment?

A. The more aggressive that the secular drive becomes in this country, the more difficult it is going to be for the Church to maintain her presence in a variety of apostolates — for example, schools, hospitals, etc. — which is obviously the goal of the secularists. The situation in San Francisco is merely that situation writ large, but dioceses all over the country are finding themselves in similar circumstances.

San Francisco passed a city ordinance that requires organizations doing business with the city to provide spousal benefits to gay employees seeking those same benefits for their "domestic partners."

Catholic Charities of San Francisco has about $5 million in annual contracts with the city and county of San Francisco, which includes a variety of services such as health care for the poor and homeless of all faiths.

As far as the compromise itself goes, it is clear the archdiocese was put into a nearly impossible position, and the solution of Archbishop William Levada was, in my judgment, almost Solomonic. Now, people of goodwill can disagree about such prudential judgments, but I don't think any fundamental Catholic principles were truly compromised. For proof of that assertion, one need only review the reactions of various gay activists who were almost uniformly angered by the resolution because, in point of fact, it did not establish the principle they were seeking. One such advocate, Fernando Tafoya, bluntly wrote that "same-sex couples are left back where they started." Why? Because, he says, opponents of the ordinance "do not have to recognize same-sex couples."

Truth be told, future developments along these lines across the country will require a united front among committed Catholics, especially with the lay faithful taking the lead, which is exactly what so many of the documents of the Second Vatican Council had in mind when they spoke of the laity serving as the leaven in secular society. Bishops and priests can and should take the lead in terms of preaching and teaching, but it is the responsibility of the laity to put those teachings into a viable context — and it is at that level that American Catholics have always been the poorest, even when they had very strong clerical guidance.

One more soul

Q. I have recently received literature from a group called One More Soul. Can you provide any information about them?

A. One More Soul is a nonprofit organization that seeks to spread the truth about the harms of contraception and the beauty of children. It operates as a sort of clearinghouse of information and resources. At present they are compiling a directory of natural-family-planning-only physicians. These are doctors who do not prescribe contraceptives, do not perform or refer for abortions, and do not perform sterilizations. The hope is that the directory will serve as a resource for families in search of moral medical care. They rely on prayers and donations to continue their good work.

The organization may be contacted at 616 Five Oaks Ave.; Dayton, OH 45406; or call 513-274-2273.

NFP practitioner

Q. I am a married woman of childbearing age and practice natural family planning. My husband doesn't adhere to the teachings of the Church, although he does go to Mass on Sundays. In regard to our conjugal life, during the times of abstinence (required by natural family planning) he wants me to masturbate him. Am I right in thinking this is against Church teaching? Please pray for us.

A. Masturbation is not morally justifiable under any circumstances. In the situation you describe, how can your husband think that asking you to provide him with an orgasm fits into the definition of "abstinence"? Continue to offer him your own example of loving fidelity to him — and to the truth of the Gospel. You both have my prayers.

Defeatist?

Q. Please explain the enclosed article, which appeared in Our Sunday Visitor. How can Catholics with access to the teachings of the Church on artificial contraception readily available be considered in "invincible ignorance," as opposed to "vincible ignorance" or just plain disobedience? Does the Pontifical Council for the Family really believe priests should not instruct, but should allow Catholics who are using artificial contraception to remain in ignorance, so that they will not "formally" sin? Can this principle of "not instructing the ignorant" be extrapolated to other moral issues: adultery, abortion, etc.? What are the implications for catechists? Should they stop teaching about artificial contraception in classes for teenagers and adults since "people will do it anyway" and thereby formally sin? The whole mentality seems defeatist to me. What do you think?

A. The document to which our reader is referring is the so-called *vade mecum*, or pastoral guide for confessors, released by the Pontifical Council for the Family. The document is superb, but has been grossly misinterpreted in certain quarters — both on the right and on the left, to use the political jargon. In truth, the most controversial element is the one highlighted by our inquirer. Allow me to explain what the Council is really saying.

First of all, it is a standard principle of moral theology and traditional guidance for confessors (going back centuries) not to disturb the consciences of those who are "invincibly ignorant," especially if prospects for remediation do not look promising. The point to underscore here is that these are confessional or internal forum procedures, not norms for preaching or teaching (in the external forum). The entire document presupposes that priests and catechists will certainly present the teaching of the Church accurately and persuasively in every circumstance; the confessional situation calls for a different tack, however. In as unequivocal an encyclical as *Humanae Vitae* ("Of Human Life"), Pope Paul VI did not hesitate to direct confessors to be most compassionate in their handling of contracepting couples who submitted themselves to the Sacrament of Penance. In other words, the confessional is not the place to "bully" people. Indeed, if our preaching and teaching on openness to life were better, there would be neither "invincible ignorance" in Catholic consciences nor the desire or perceived need to use the sacrament as a catechetical tool.

Second, you ask how we can imagine invincible ignorance on this question. Given the massive dissent from this teaching for more than thirty years now — coming from theologians, clergy, Religious, and laity alike — we should not be too amazed to find couples who really do think that "following their conscience" means a green light for artificial contraception. Needless to say, those who have been the source of the dissent and confusion will have much to answer for on Judgment Day.

Third, another aspect of the problem is that a priest may never probe in hearing a confession. That is, if a penitent does not raise an issue, the confessor may not ask the penitent if he has committed a particular sin. Now, if the priest suspects that the person has not offered an integral confession, he may say something like: "Are there any other sins you want to confess?" or, "May I help you examine your conscience?" and then proceed to go down the commandments, explaining the implication of each.

Having used the above principles for more than twenty years now, I can assure you that I have never waffled on artificial contraception; nor have I ever disturbed the conscience of anyone I considered to be in invincible ignorance. However, it is also accurate to say that the topic generally does not come up, because those who are ignorant don't confess the sin, and since I am not permitted to ask them, they are in no position to be enlightened — at least in that context. All of which goes back to the critical importance of presenting the authentic teaching of the Church on love and life in every place available to us: in marriage-preparation programs; in Catholic high schools; in pre-Cana programs; in adult education and RCIA; and in homilies. If all that were done, then we could honestly say that no one in the Catholic community could be legitimately described as living in "invincible ignorance" on this sin.

Delicate question

Q. I have a very delicate and embarrassing question. My husband and I have been married for more than forty years. Recently, he had surgery, which has left him partially impotent. Just what are we allowed to do sexually? We have gotten every answer imaginable from priests — from "anything goes" to "nothing goes."

A. Your situation is not uncommon — on both fronts actually — that is, in the problems with sexual activity or in getting a straight answer from some clerics.

I do not like to answer questions like yours in the column, not just because of the matter of "delicacy" (as you phrase it) but also because each case is truly unique and, with so many variables involved, it is well-nigh impossible to handle the matter in such a way that your specific question is fully addressed. A very abbreviated answer, however, would be that sexual acts between spouses are legitimate that are not repulsive to either and if they end in a natural act of intercourse. Even a partial penetration on the part of your husband suffices.

I should take this opportunity to recommend an excellent guide that has just appeared. Germain Grisez, a most reliable lay moral theologian, has come out with the third volume in his textbook series: *The Way of the Lord Jesus: Difficult Moral Questions*, published by Franciscan Press in Quincy, Ill. The first two volumes deal with fundamental principles of morality, while the third handles two hundred questions on specific and hard-to-answer moral difficulties of every kind. No priest or seminarian should be without this excellent and completely faithful pastoral manual.

Helpful leads

Q. I'm writing in regard to a question about the PFLAG (Parents and Friends of Lesbians and Gays) organization. This is definitely not the group one wants to contact for help. It counsels for the pro-homosexual agenda; however, there are several very good organizations that truly do help with this struggle. They include: Exodus International, in California, 405-454-1017; Homosexuals Anonymous, in Pennsylvania, 610-376-1146; Pure Life Ministries, in Kentucky, 606-824-4444; Hope Ministry, in Pennsylvania, 215-735-4673; Thomas Aquinas Clinic, in California, 818-789-4440; Courage, in New York, 212-421-0426; New Creations Ministry, in California, 209-227-1066; and Regeneration, in Maryland, 410-661-0284. Some of these are just headquarters' phone numbers, so one could call to see if and what they have in a specific area.

A. Thank you for the helpful leads.

Thought through

Q. Since the Catholic Church does not recognize divorce, the individuals — while civilly divorced — are still married. It seems to me that the logical conclusion is that they may still have sex with one another as often as they want, even if they choose to marry someone else. I don't know what their new partners would think, but the Catholic Church would approve of it. Guess those unmarried men who make the rules never thought of that.

A. Your silly sarcasm aside, let's sort out some of the issues.

You are correct that folks who are divorced from one another can licitly have sexual relations. However, when you speak of "their new partners," you have launched into a new minefield. "Their new partners," first of all, have no "rights" (inasmuch as they are really not married in God's eyes), but if they are having relations with those "new partners," such actions are serious sins because they are sins of adultery. As you can see, "those unmarried men who make the rules" apparently have thought of that.

Dead consciences

Q. I have tried to conduct my life within the acceptable boundaries given during my formation in the so-called preconciliar Church. Now I find myself in a quandary regarding guilt. When I stray beyond the parameters of moral conduct, I feel that I have committed a grievous sin. Yet others, doing the very same thing with impunity, feel they are doing no wrong. Am I guilty because by acting as I might I feel I am? Are these others who feel that they have done nothing wrong therefore not guilty? If this is the case, one has to question the benefits derived from being reared as I was.

A. It is not at all clear to me what types of prescriptions you have in mind. For instance, do you refer to women wearing head coverings in the preconciliar Church and the elimination of that custom now? Or the midnight eucharistic fast versus the mitigated fast of one hour now? Or are you talking about moral laws? The first two may well be pious practices you wish to continue in your private spiritual life, but failure to observe them should not cause you moral upset. If, however, you have in mind the last category, please realize that the Church's moral law has not changed one iota since the Second Vatican Council (nor could it in the future);

therefore, if people are not adhering to these moral precepts, they are sinning every bit as much today as they would have fifty years ago. The only difference for some seems to be that they now operate with a "clear" conscience, only because they have either uninformed or even dead consciences.

Overscrupulous

Q. I understand that when a person has stolen something, he must make restitution to the person it was taken from. I have been told that when this is impossible, the Church allows restitution to be made by giving to a charity. My question is how you define "impossible." For example, when I was in high school, I found a calculator. Instead of putting it in the "lost and found," I just considered myself lucky and kept it. I have since realized my error. I have given money to charity to make up for this, but now I am wondering if I should try somehow to find out to whom the calculator belonged. This has been more than fifteen years now. When I think about it, I get overwhelmed and discouraged. Should I try to contact everyone who was in the high school at that time? Unfortunately, I have a few other similar situations to deal with. Can you give me some sort of guideline to follow, or tell me where I can get help?

A. The principle you learned is correct. We have the obligation to discover an object's rightful owner to the extent that it is possible, meaning feasible. In other words, if it would cost you more money to put an advertisement in a newspaper than the object itself is worth, that makes no sense because there is no principle of proportionality present. To try to find an owner fifteen years after the fact is like looking for a needle in a haystack.

From the tenor of your letter, I get the impression that you border on the scrupulous, and I would counsel your visit to a priest to discuss the matter. When we have done our best to rectify a situation, have confessed any wrongdoing, and have received absolution, we should rest secure in the forgiveness of our loving and merciful Father — and then forget about it.

Nature of guilt

Q. Can a "wet dream" lead to masturbation, and, if so, what is the nature of guilt?

A. What one does in a semi-conscious state or unconscious is not sinful because, remember, full consent of the will is required. If one woke up during a nocturnal emission and then fully consented to an act of masturbation in order to continue the process, that act would be sinful.

Critic's corner

Q. Many films that have an "R" rating have scenes of nudity. Is it a mortal sin to view such films?

A. Nudity, in and of itself, is not sinful. Our sex-saturated society, however, has turned everything into a prurient, perverted, and cheap experience of sexuality, which is becoming less and less human, and more and more animalistic. When nudity is a normal, natural part of a film's plot, it is generally not problematic; the film industry today, however, seems to think that such a caveat fits the bill every time.

Viewing films with gratuitous sex is sinful for several reasons: First, producing such works assaults the dignity of those involved at every level; second, the availability of such films continues the downward spiral of our culture into one of unbridled hedonism, which then finds expression in adultery, fornication, rape, and sexual abuse of children; third, being a willing observer contributes toward one's own personal dehumanization and desensitization. How gravely sinful the act is depends on the content of the film itself, the degree of scandal caused by one's participation, and the susceptibility of the individual to fall into sin as a result of the viewing.

Scandalous cooperator?

Q. How should pastors handle cases of engaged couples living together before marriage when they refuse to move to separate addresses before the wedding? As a priest, I have long been bothered by the normally large Saturday weddings allowed them, even if without a Mass, feeling I am something of a moral cooperator in scandal. Is that too scrupulous? After all, the big wedding does make it seem that the Church is going along with the trend of the times. My diocese has no policy to deal with these situations, leaving each case to the "pastoral discretion" of the priest. My "pastoral discretion" would be allowing only a small ceremony in the daily Mass chapel. Our judicial vicar told me that I am within my canonical rights as pastor to set such policy, but a howl would go up from many quarters, including from most of my fellow clergy, who disagree with my approach. Am I being too rigid? What is your opinion, please? Remember, with the policy of only allowing a small ceremony in the daily Mass chapel, many couples would go to another parish or even to a Protestant church.

A. This question is emerging with great regularity of late, which means that priests are finally getting tired of the abuse of the Sacrament of Matrimony and the Mass.

I have come to a posture similar to yours, namely that cohabiting couples — since they implicitly declare that they are already married or are at least living like husband and wife — should be treated in exactly the same way as couples who have been civilly married and require a convalidation in church of their civil union. What do we do in those cases? We tell the couple to come to the church for an extremely low-key ceremony, at which are present the priest, two witnesses, and a handful of close friends.

No doubt

Q. Please advise my daughter and her boyfriend, who is considering Catholicism, about the Church law regarding birth control. A recent Catholic article I read encourages sinning by convincing oneself that practicing birth control is permissible as long as one has exercised reflection, faith, and prayer.

A. First, a clarification in terminology. The prohibition against artificial contraception is not a matter of Church law, but of theology and doctrine. Reducing the discussion to a question of law makes it all seem quite arbitrary — like a traffic light on the corner today, which may or may not be there tomorrow.

The Church teaches that artificial birth control is always and under all conditions, objectively speaking, a serious sin. For two thousand years, the Church has taught the same thing, which means that she can never teach something else.

In this century, with the advent of more sophisticated methods of contraception, the magisterium has been extraordinarily emphatic on the immorality of such acts. Clearest of all have been Pope Paul VI in *Humanae Vitae* ("Of Human Life") and Pope John Paul II throughout his pontificate. In an address June 5, 1987, the present Holy Father said this: "The Church's teaching on contraception does not belong to the category of matter open to free discussion among theologians. Teaching the contrary amounts to leading the moral consciences of spouses into error."

I don't think that leaves any room for doubt or confusion.

Crystal clear

Q. If two men or two women make a commitment to each other — that is, a lifelong relationship — why can't they express their love in a physical way? If God is so against the physical expression between two people of the same sex, then why would He have created homosexuals in the first place? I can't help but feel that the Church has not taken its thinking a step further on the subject.

A. We don't really know whether or not God "creates" homosexuals — that is, if a homosexual orientation comes about through nature or nurture, or a little bit of both. In many ways, however, that is not relevant. Being "created" with a certain orientation — for example, a weakness in metabolizing alcohol — does not excuse one from living virtuously and exercising prudence.

With reference to homosexual activity, the Scriptures are crystal clear on the immorality of any and all such acts, as is the constant Tradition of the Church. For all these reasons, the Church does not have the power to "think a step further on the subject."

Undignified

Q. My question concerns the Catholic homosexual group Dignity. First, are the Masses they hold legitimate? Are the Masses licit? I attend weekly Mass in my neighborhood parish, and I also regularly attend Mass at Dignity. Does the Church have a position on this practice? Dignity has fostered positions on inclusive language, gay (but celibate) priests, married and/or female priests, local election of pastors and bishops. I don't personally agree with some of these. What does the Church say? I live in Philadelphia. Are there any dioceses in which the bishop permits his priests to minister openly to homosexual Catholics in a forum like Dignity?

A. Dignity is a most problematic organization, for any number of reasons.

First of all, the vast majority of their chapters refuse to accept Church teaching on homosexual activity — namely, that any and all sexual expression in a homosexual relationship is, objectively speaking, grave matter.

Second, many former (and even some current) members acknowledge that many of the Dignity activities devolve into little more than "dating games."

Third, at a psychological level, I am opposed to bringing people together of a like background simply to make them "feel good" about themselves; this ends up in the formation of a subculture, which does little good for the individuals or for the broader community. And, yes, to anticipate questions, I am generally ill-disposed to various twelve-step programs for this very reason.

Fourth, gathering men and women together to conduct a "gripe" session about the Church's teaching and/or perceived insensitivity is a most counterproductive method of developing a normal and healthy ecclesial life. Wouldn't we think it weird if all the married couples who either oppose or find difficult Church teaching on birth control were to establish a support group?

Wouldn't we think it strange that they had reduced their entire Catholic experience to a battle over one particular issue?

Fifth, as you have correctly observed, Dignity does not dissent from authentic magisterial positions only on homosexual activity, but on a host of other teachings as well. Of course, this should not surprise us because dissent always breeds further dissent. For instance, Catholics for a Free Choice may have started out rejecting the Church's stance on abortion, but they have quickly moved into the dissenting mode on the entire range of "hot-button" topics.

Last, from videos I have seen and from reports of eyewitnesses, I know that Dignity liturgies are usually hotbeds of liturgical aberrations. Again, no amazement need be registered, given the overall direction of the organization: If you're not willing to accept matters related to faith and morals, why abide by man-made regulations for worship?

I think your intuition is correct in that the Church needs to be doing more to counsel her members who have a homosexual orientation. The group Courage is one such effort, and many dioceses have their own programs. Contact your parish priest or chancery for possibilities within your own area. The bottom line, however, is not whether or not a bishop will allow one of his priests to "minister openly to homosexual Catholics," but the manner in which that ministry is exercised. A forum like Dignity is not what the doctor ordered — theologically, philosophically, psychologically, or sociologically. That conviction comes from more than twenty years of providing some fruitful pastoral ministry to the very kinds of Catholics about whom you have expressed concern. Indeed, on all too many occasions, I have found myself having to do a major mop-up operation for people whose lives were thrown into chaos by Dignity's militancy and rebellion against legitimate Church authority and true teaching.

Family hour

Q. Could learned theologians address for families this important moral question, which remains unanswered in the encyclicals and the *Catechism of the Catholic Church*: Is there a moral duty to answer the telephone? In our family, we never answer the phone in evening hours because this is our family hour — devoted to meal, conversation, and prayer. We have voice mail to capture these messages.

A. There is absolutely no necessity to answer the phone, particularly when other important activities are taking place. And I think the activities you cite are all most important.

"Wisdom of God"

Q. I have a question to which I have been unable to get a reply (a canon lawyer evaded me for twenty minutes on this one). Suppose two people participate in a sacramental marriage of certain validity, but afterward divorce and "remarry" outside the Church. As far as I understand biblical and Church teaching, this "second marriage" is basically an ongoing adulterous relationship, regardless of the circumstances, provided the original marriage was indeed valid (no grounds for annulment) and both are still living. Now, suppose these two people come to realize the nature of this second relationship and want to become reconciled with God. One may confess past sins, but to continue living in this state does not seem consistent with the desire to amend one's ways. Is it necessary to terminate the second marriage, even though it might be a very happy relationship, perhaps with children, etc.? This sounds awfully harsh! Or, must the second marriage become celibate (which seems both harsh and unlikely to succeed)?

A. This question comes up repeatedly and the answer must always be the same. You have correctly "staked out" the moral terrain — that is, reception of the Sacrament of Penance requires a firm purpose of amendment from all sins — not just ones confessed — and the second union does constitute an ongoing state of adultery. Therefore, the options by which the sacraments can be received again are the two you note: separation or living as "brother and sister." While one might see this as harsh, there are also other ways to look upon it — for example, as safeguarding the integrity of marriage and family life for the good of society, the Church; as protecting the dignity of human love, which demands an absolute, unswerving commitment; as carrying one's cross in union with Christ and thus as a means for mutual sanctification.

Admittedly, in our world of immediate gratification of all needs/wants, this kind of response seems absurd, but St. Paul looked that demon straight in the eye in his own day and declared the contrary absurd when he said: "But we preach Christ crucified, a stumbling block to Jews and folly to Gentiles, but to those who are called, both Jews and Greeks, Christ the power of God and the wisdom of God. For the foolishness of God is wiser than men, and the weakness of God is stronger than men" (1 Cor 1:23-25).

Liturgy

Illicit, invalid?

Q. In a recent edition of a popular Catholic magazine, someone asked about leavened bread being used at Mass, worrying about crumbs falling on the floor during Communion. The editor replied that, strictly speaking, if the bread was leavened, it was not consecrated because (in the Roman rite) anything beyond wheat flour and water would make it invalid matter; therefore, no consecration would occur. I have never heard this before. Would you please explain?

A. Leavened bread for the Roman rite is illicit, not invalid. How could something be valid for several rites of the Church (most of the East) but invalid for one? Perhaps what the author in question meant was the addition of other elements besides yeast (such as honey, etc.) had an invalidating effect — and that is true and has been so stated by the Vatican.

Communion query

Q. Regarding intinction, how does the communicant indicate to you he wants Holy Communion by intinction versus the Host alone on the tongue? What response should be made to someone who says, "Christ said, 'Take and drink,' not 'take and dip' "?

A. If the celebrant determines to distribute Holy Communion by intinction, the communicant does not have an option, strictly speaking. If, however, the communicant cannot receive under the form of wine (for a medical reason, for example), all he need do is quietly inform the priest of the fact before the priest dips the

Host into the chalice, saying something like, "Only the Host please, Father."

As far as the attempt at a quick-witted retort goes, I hope it wasn't said at Communion time, but two responses are in order. First, liturgy is not an act of aping or mimicking. That is why we don't break the Host when we say that Jesus took the bread and "broke" it; that act takes place in a different context, later in the Mass. Second, it is not at all unlikely that the apostles were indeed fed by Our Lord directly into their mouths, as is still the custom in many countries of the Middle East today, whereby the host of the dinner dips a particle of bread or other food into a sauce or wine and places it into the mouths of his guests — an act of hospitality.

Remembering

Q. My question concerns having a Mass said for someone who has died. Doesn't the priest have to mention the name of the individual specifically during the eucharistic prayer? Our priest mentions the name at the start of Mass and during the prayer of the faithful. I remember when I was young having heard "Remember [so-and-so], whom you have called from this life. In baptism he died with Christ, may he also share His resurrection." If this is not said, how is God supposed to know whom the Mass is for? Also, can Mass be said for more than one soul at a time? Sometimes, there are up to three souls being remembered at the same Mass in our parish.

A. The question of Mass intentions surfaces with some regularity, so it must not be too well-explained. Regarding your specific concerns, we should observe the following: (1) The priest need mention no name at any time before, during, or after the Mass. After all, God being omniscient, knows the intention of the Mass. The insertion of the name into the eucharistic prayer should not be done on a daily basis, only for funerals or anniversaries. (2) One Mass may be offered for multiple intentions — that is, several different people all giving individual stipends — on condition that all parties are aware of this arrangement and agree to it. All appearance of trafficking in stipends, however, must be studiously avoided.

Illicit

Q. I live in a clergy-retirement home, and some of the old "gents" are somewhat careless about the Mass. One recent development has me greatly upset — having the concelebrants receive Holy Communion from the reserved Sacrament. Is this valid? Licit?

A. I have seen this happen myself, and I find it difficult to explain. First of all, even the lay faithful ought to be communicated from bread consecrated at that particular liturgical celebration, unless unforeseen circumstances obviate it. Concelebrating priests, however, are surely expected to do so. Thus, in the *Guidelines for the Concelebration of the Eucharist*, published by the National Conference of Catholic Bishops on September 23, 1987, we find the following: "It is never permitted, however, to distribute Communion to the concelebrants from the Sacrament consecrated at another Mass and reserved in the tabernacle" (no. 36). Why? Because an intimate connection exists between the confection of the Eucharist and the confector[s].

What you describe is certainly valid, but highly illicit and should be stopped.

Reception of the Eucharist

Q. You're always on a tirade against things like Communion in the hand; don't you have anything better to do with your time? People are starving; do you think Jesus cares how the bread is given out — as long as it is given out?

A. I am surely concerned about the poor and the hungry, but there is no dichotomy, so that I am forced to choose whether to be exercised about one but not the other. In point of fact, Our Lord made it clear during His temptation by Satan that "man shall not live by bread alone, but by every word that proceeds from the mouth of God" (Mt 4:4). In other words, spiritual food is more important than physical food.

Second, your own language betrays the problem. What we distribute in Holy Communion is *not* bread, but the Body of the Lord — and if we are not concerned about how that is done, then our priorities are totally out of whack.

My disapproval of the practice you cite is rooted in many realities: First, Communion on the tongue effectively replaced the other procedure before the close of the first millennium, due to a deeper understanding of both the Divinity of Christ and the mystery of the Eucharist. Second, it was specifically adopted by many Protestant reformers, precisely to call into question both the distinct nature of the ministerial priesthood and the doctrine of transubstantiation. Third, in the modern era, it was reintroduced in flagrant violation of Church law and despite numerous admonitions by Pope Paul VI to the contrary.

It is interesting that the original liturgical changes during the English Reformation did not call for placing the Sacred Host directly in the hands of the communicant, but retained the traditional practice. Martin Bucer, a radical reformer, critiqued the Book of Common Prayer in his *Censura*; therein he called for the abolition of Communion on the tongue as a necessary move to eliminate what he called "the superstition" of belief in Christ's Real Presence. Communion in the hand, conversely, would convince recipients that it is only a symbolic presence. You may read this for yourself in a work by E.C. Whitaker, titled *Martin Bucer and the Book of Common Prayer*, published by Mayhew-McCrimmon of Great Wakering (see esp. pp. 34-37).

If the current state of Catholic Eucharistic Faith is not exactly what Bucer predicted, I don't know what is — and I can't think of something that has aided that process more than Communion in the hand.

The Body of Our Lord

Q. What is the proper procedure in caring for the sacred vessels and altar linens after each Mass? I was told that the minuscule particles of the Host, which might be on the corporal are no longer significant; therefore, the corporal can be used more than once. Is this true? How should the altar linens be laundered? Also, if a Host falls to the floor, what should be done?

A. The question of "minuscule particles" should be examined first because it genuinely involves a doctrinal issue. Any particle that can be perceived to the naked eye as a crumb of bread retains its identity as the Body of the Lord and, therefore, must be treated with the same adoration as an entire Host. At the same time, I don't see what that has to do with multiple uses of a corporal; even in "the old days" a corporal was used for days on end. What the celebrant must do, however, is to ensure that all the particles of the Sacred Host are removed (usually with the paten) at the time of the ablutions.

Unfortunately, directives on care of the linens are not as clear as they might be; however, the following can be said, based on no. 239 of the *General Instruction of the Roman Missal*: "If any of the Precious Blood spills, the area should be washed and the water poured into the sacrarium." At a practical level, following the line of Msgr. Peter Elliot in his *Ceremonies of the Modern Roman Rite* (nos. 848-855), I would suggest that linens that come into direct contact with the Sacred Species should be washed first in the sacrarium and then laundered in the usual manner thereafter. If a Host falls to the floor, the priest should pick it up immediately, putting it to one side in order to be consumed later; unless particles have broken off, I don't think any further attention is required. Although the option exists for vessels to be purified after Mass, for a variety of practical and theological reasons, I think it best (whenever possible) to perform the task immediately after the distribution of Holy Communion. This approach guarantees that the job is done, and done so properly; furthermore, it reminds all in a visible way that the Holy Eucharist (even after reception) remains the presence of the Lord and deserves the same loving adoration.

Dangers

Q. In our area, two churches made national headlines because the priests had to post guards due to the stealing of Hosts for use in satanic rituals. Wouldn't it just be easier to stop Communion in the hand?

A. Most priests will tell you that where Communion in the hand is practiced, abuses follow in its wake: Hosts found in missalettes, holy-water founts, and confessionals. Your solution reflects a great amount of common sense, but, as one wag put it many years ago, "The only problem with common sense is that it's not all that common!"

Rite order

Q. Is it permissible for the celebrant of the Mass to pour the wine and water together and also do the washing of his hands prior to the start of Mass, before the entrance antiphon, greeting, penitential rite, and Gospel?

A. No, it is not — that is, if he is celebrating the Roman rite. What you describe could be either the Byzantine rite or the old Dominican rite.

A united body

Q. Is there any justification for saying the Rosary during the Mass?

A. I cannot think of any. Our liturgical worship is to be engaged as a united body — one mind, one heart. That is why when people tinker with the liturgy they commit such an awful offense — because they deny the faithful their baptismal right to worship according to the mind of the Church, thus causing division within the very act of worship to the limit.

Attending Mass multiple times

Q. How many times can a Catholic in grace receive the Eucharist in one day if he attends Mass more than once a day? Is there any Church ruling regarding the maximum number of times a Catholic may receive Holy Communion at Mass, and should he be required to observe the eucharistic fast of one hour between the Masses?

A. One may receive Holy Communion no more than twice in one day, provided the second reception occurs in the context of a Mass — the only exception being viaticum. And, yes, the normal eucharistic fast ought to be observed between such receptions that is intended to show our unity and lead us into a yet stronger unity.

Consuming the Host

Q. Can you open your mouth to receive the Blood of Christ if you have not swallowed the Host?

A. Why would one not have swallowed the Host? Presumably, one could receive as you suggest, but it makes no sense since it doesn't take forever to consume the consecrated Host.

Directly defiant

Q. My brother recently joined a nearby parish. He frequently comes home from church angry because the pastor deletes a word from the Nicene Creed. The line "for us men and for our salvation, He came down from heaven" becomes "for us and for our salvation." None of the other priests at the parish do this. I have attended Mass there recently and noticed the same thing. My brother and I have frequent conversations on the subject. I have asked him why he doesn't ask the priest to clarify the deletion of the word "men." (The seemingly obvious answer is the recent "need" to make women feel included in the Mass.) My brother doesn't want to ask the priest his reasons for the change in the Creed because he feels that it is not his place to question an ordained minister of Christ. I am not as certain of my place, so I would like to know if the deletion of the word "men" from the Creed is current with Church doctrine? Second, does the priest have a legitimate moral right to change the wording of the Creed to make others feel included in the Church? Shouldn't he explain this to the parishioners? The thing that I remember from high school theology (I attended a Marist high school, two of my brothers went to a Jesuit high school, and two more, including the brother in question, attended a Benedictine high school) is that it is the job of the priest to teach the message of Jesus' love to the world, and to guard and nourish the faith where it already exists. Although I have no doubt of my brother's faith — sometimes I envy its strength — I do feel that this priest robs my brother of the joy, solace, and peace that the Sunday Mass is intended to bring to the faithful. My brother's anger after attending Mass makes me upset at the decision this priest makes every Sunday. I hope your clarification on this matter will ease my brother's ire and help me in my quest for a stronger faith in Christ and the Church.

A. I have reprinted your very long letter, exactly, for a number of reasons — because of its sense of the Catholic Faith, its devotion, its sensitivity. I hope that any priests who might be tempted to tinker with the liturgy would be given food for thought in your recounting of the anxiety inflicted on your brother.

On the discreet point, I would observe that several years ago the American hierarchy asked the Holy See for permission to drop the word "men" from the Creed and was denied for reasons connected to the doctrine of the Faith — that is, that deleting that word left in doubt just who was the object of Christ's saving work. Lest anyone say that the situation has changed in the ensuing years, I would agree, but go on to indicate that the Holy See's position now is even more adamantly against such manipulation than ever, as witnessed by denials of approvals and withdrawals of approvals from a host of so-called inclusive-language texts over the past two years.

To sum it all up: The priest in question is in direct defiance of the Holy See and is in direct violation of the rights of the faithful to have the liturgy celebrated as the Church hands it down. He should not hide behind his collar to cow the laity into submission to his liturgical games. I would certainly side with you — and not your brother — on this score. He is capitalizing on his priestly identity to silence those he thinks will obey just on account of his being a priest. This is a bully's tactic and unworthy of a priest.

Liturgical language

Q. I am at a loss to understand why the Catholic Church finds it necessary to have so many ethnic groups, such as African-American, Spanish, Polish, Vietnamese, Puerto Rican, etc. We now have all kinds of Masses here. Why don't they attend the English Mass? We have a Spanish Mass at our church twice a month; however, they never attend the English Masses in between. I thought the Catholic Church was one. Am I missing something? We can't even get a Latin Mass said here. Please explain the Pope's teaching on this.

A. I suppose the first statement to be made is that this is not the type of topic on which the Pope teaches in any significant sense because it is largely a pastoral, or prudential, matter. Allow me to offer some suggestions from my own personal experience.

For seven years, I served as the parish priest for a Lithuanian community, or one that served the Lithuanian community for a good part of the century. By the 1960s, the Lithuanians started to move out of the area and were largely replaced by Portuguese. By the time I arrived on the scene in the 1980s, there was little left of a viable Lithuanian community, but the parish was still canonically identified as serving Lithuanians, and at least one Mass each weekend was celebrated in Lithuanian. The Lithuanian Mass made little sense because every parishioner, either having lived in the United States for thirty-five to forty years or having been born here, spoke English, many using it as their primary language. At the same time, the Portuguese were coming as new immigrants, many of whom were not familiar with English and certainly not with Lithuanian! Add to the mix a sprinkling of immigrants from Italy and various Hispanic countries. All of my neighboring parishes had the same basic situation, but we all came up with different solutions. Mine was rather simple: We kept the principal Sunday Mass as officially Lithuanian, but added healthy doses of English and Latin. For devotions, we threw in Portuguese as well. For Holy Week and other "high holy days," we included all the languages of our parish, with Latin as a unifier for the Ordinary of the Mass. Other priests found themselves having multiple celebrations for the various language groups they served; I did not like the potential for divisiveness in that approach, and I believe that (after a bit of initial resistance) our solution worked best.

I think language is a most important element of someone's life and culture, and the Church needs to be sensitive to this in several ways: (1) When immigrants arrive, they need to be welcomed to the Catholic community in their own tongue and in a manner that lets them know that their cultural heritage is appreciated. In other words, the first task of the Church is not to "Americanize." (2) As people live here for a while and begin to raise families, the Church does them a major service by introducing them to the English language and the mainstream culture. That is often best accomplished through the parish school. All this involves a delicate balancing act if all aspects of the question are to be handled to the advantage of all. It also means that a parish will be serving several different constituencies simultaneously, which calls for a lot of common sense and even more charity. If the parish priest understands the basic issues and exercises genuine pastoral leadership, a harmonious entity should emerge. Otherwise, disaster will ensue. We must remember our primary responsibility, however, is for the spiritual welfare of our parishioners. When that is in focus, everything else should be able to be treated rationally and effectively.

Serious Problems

Q. I am a special minister of the Eucharist, a lector, and a catechist. However, we were assigned a new priest. The first time I
attended a Mass at which he presided when it was time for the
priest's Communion, I noticed that he gave Communion to the
special minister who was substituting for the deacon's station. I did
not, however, see him communicate himself. He then proceeded
to give Communion to the congregation, and as Communion
time came to a close, he finished at his station and got in line to
receive from two of my fellow special ministers of the Eucharist:
first, the Body and then the Precious Blood. This distressed me
greatly, and I decided to do some research in the *Catholic Encyclopedia*. The following week I went to this priest and asked him why
he had done this (since I found the following statement in the
encyclopedia: "They who offer the Holy Sacrifice shall not receive
the Body of the Lord from the hands of those who have no such
power of offering." This is according to the Council of Nicea in
325.) The priest's rationale was that he was carrying out the
admonition of the bishop who ordained him to be at the service
of the people, and by his performance of this act he was mani-
festing that service. He also stated that although the rubrics clearly
state that he should not do this, it was for him a matter of conscience, and that he felt as though it was the correct thing for him
to do. I later discovered that he also does not perform ablutions at
the preparation of the gifts. When asked why, he stated that he
bathed daily and washed his hands regularly during the day, and
therefore had no need of this task. He also omits and changes the
formula for the Creed at Sunday Mass. How much latitude does
he have in these areas? Also, the crowning jewel in this priest's reformation of our parish liturgy was at the Good Friday service.
Father decided not to read the part of the Gospel of John reserved
to the priest, but instead chose to read the part of the narrator and
assigned the part of Christ to one of the lectors, a female, no less.
Didn't the Pope just write a strong encyclical against just such
abuses, or is it just me? What can I do?

A. The poor priest has serious problems, and if charitable conversation doesn't do the job, you need to contact the bishop for a redress of these egregious abuses. If his "conscience" doesn't allow him to celebrate the Mass as the Church directs, then he needs spiritual direction and perhaps a long retreat to discover or rediscover what it means to be an ordained minister of the Church. Ironically, he talks about being at the service of the people, yet he is consistently pleasing himself and denying to the people their right to a Catholic liturgy offered according to the mind of the Church.

Now, a few corrections of your terminology, if you don't mind. First, the non-ordained who distribute Holy Communion are not "special" ministers but "extraordinary." Second, an ablution is the washing of vessels after Communion; you seem to be referring to the washing of the priest's hands at the offertory. Third, the present Holy Father has never written an encyclical on the liturgy; he has written many documents of lesser authority on this topic, most notably, *Inaestimabile Donum* (instruction concerning worship of the eucharistic mystery), and the apostolic letter *Dominicae Cenae* (on the mystery and worship of the Eucharist).

Hear our prayer

Q. Please explain the rules governing the prayer of the faithful (general intercessions) at Mass. It is my understanding that the celebrant prays the general intentions of the Church. Then the members of the congregation may add their specific petitions, phrased to include all the faith community in that category. Your clarification would be much appreciated.

A. Let us take a look at the structure of the prayer first and then who does what.

The general intercessions are a very ancient part of the Mass, essentially lost in the Roman rite for centuries and recaptured after the Second Vatican Council. We see the full-blown version of them in the Good Friday liturgy. These petitions are intended to cover the needs of the Church and the world, in that order, going from the general to the more specific or local.

Therefore, the pecking order might look like this: needs of the universal Church; diocesan or parochial concerns; matters relating to justice and peace; the sick; the deceased. At all costs, the introduction of divisive or political items must be scrupulously avoided, so that the unity of the Church is not harmed, which does not mean failure to mention things that could be construed as having a political dimension (for example, the elimination of abortion-on-demand). Furthermore, these petitions ought not to be mini-homilies.

The *General Instruction of the Roman Missal* indicates that the prayer is to be introduced and concluded by the celebrant; the invocations are to be done by a deacon, cantor, or lector. There is no provision for extemporaneous prayers to be offered by the congregation-at-large. Indeed, this should not occur for several reasons, not the least being that we have no way of knowing what anyone might offer as a prayer, expecting the rest to say, "Lord, hear our prayer." A friend of mine had the shocking experience of having a woman pray for the death of her abusive husband, while another asked that her husband would be given the grace to abandon his adulterous ways.

Rights and wrongs

Q. Enclosed is a letter from our bishop that was reproduced in our parish bulletin. The contents of the letter upset me. Would you please address the issues he mentions: (a) "the time has come for every parish to respect the '*right* [emphasis in original] and duty' of girls and women to serve at the altar along with men and boys"; (b) insistence on congregational singing; (c) mentioning that the Sign of the Cross should not be made during the conclusion of the penitential rite; (d) Communion under both species; and (e) that some accretions, such as the multiplicity of collects and the prayers for the conversion of Russia, remain suppressed. Is he on target?

A. In some areas he is right, but he is wrong in others.

(a) On the altar-girl front, he mistakes permission for mandate. No parish, indeed no priest, can be forced to utilize this option. Just as a bishop cannot tell a priest which eucharistic prayer to choose among the approved texts, nor can he demand this. I would say this is even more the case if the pastor knows that the mind of the parish is against this possibility.

(b) Congregational singing is important; it is not "added to" the celebration, it is integral to it. Now, admittedly, some people just do not like to sing, and a few don't even like music. For that reason, I think it pastorally advisable to have an early Sunday Mass with little or no music — to be pastorally sensitive.

(c) The Sign of the Cross does not belong to the penitential rite. Your bishop is correct in saying that the former rite of the Mass had an additional prayer, to which that gesture was attached. I have made the very same point before.

(d) The procedures he outlines for Communion are proper — although he is mistaken about a non-concelebrating bishop's reception of Holy Communion: He does *not* remain in his place and have Communion brought to him — he is supposed to go to the altar to receive. What your bishop suggests is an older practice, now made obsolete by the *Ceremonial of Bishops*.

(e) Whatever was suppressed remains suppressed and should not be reintroduced.

Forbidden method

Q. For several years, I have received the Host in my hand, and then, dip it in the wine. I have done this in numerous states with no complaint. Recently, a eucharistic minister grabbed my hand and said, "I'll take that." I simply said no and continued. I tried to talk to the priest, but he said that I had a month to change my ways. Instead, I changed parishes with no problem. I do this because I do not want to drink from the chalice after someone might have spit back some of the wine. What does the Church have to say about this?

A. Once again, let's purify our language: One does not receive "wine" in Holy Communion — it is the Precious Blood.

The extraordinary minister in question was absolutely right in asserting that what you were doing is impermissible. I do not think he should have grabbed your hand, but in the confusion of the moment, we can allow for such lapses of courtesy.

While I am surely favorably disposed toward your health concerns (which I have repeatedly expressed in this column to explain my opposition to both species from the chalice), what you are doing is wrong since it amounts to self-communication, which is categorically forbidden. At a logical level, however, your practice makes little sense: If you are afraid of germs, don't you think they will be transmitted almost as readily when you dip the Host into the chalice? Why not just bypass the chalice altogether?

Even major proponents of this practice have to come to grips with statements of the Centers for Disease Control and Prevention, as recently as June 1996, which say things like: "There is a theoretical risk of transmission of some agents that are present in oral secretions, particularly the respiratory viruses, such as those that cause the common cold. In contrast, the theoretical risk of transmitting hepatitis B, tuberculosis, or human immunodeficiency virus (HIV) by this means is exceedingly low." While noting that they are unaware "of any specific episodes or outbreaks of illness that have been associated with the use of the common communion cup," they go on to say that "such an occurrence would be difficult to detect and to distinguish from respiratory or other forms of person-to-person contact."

Because of all these considerations, I always recommend both species by intinction. That is, the communicant stands before the priest, who then dips the Host into the chalice and directly communicates the individual. This is a legitimate option that has the value of both species preserved, but without the health hazards.

Liturgical query

Q. We are longtime members of our parish. Having returned after three months away from the area, we have seen some drastic changes in the way Mass is celebrated by our newly appointed

332		The CATHOLIC ANSWER BOOK 4

parish priest. After consulting with many other concerned parishioners about this matter, we feel compelled to ask you for an interpretation of the Church's teaching regarding the following: (1) If the entrance antiphon is not sung it is omitted — that is, it cannot be recited. (2) For the same reason, the communion antiphon has been eliminated. (3) He refuses to give Communion to those who kneel. (4) He uses the New Revised Standard Version of the *Lectionary*. (5) He refuses to distribute the Precious Blood after his reception of Communion with any of the extraordinary ministers at the altar. Taken separately, these issues may seem trivial to some, but they are significant to those of us attending daily Mass. I have met with the priest and shared these concerns. He replied that he was taught this way and so closed the issue. He will not concede that he may be wrong. We want to be open to new rulings on the celebration of the liturgy, only if they are approved by the Vatican and the bishops. Will you please help us in our search for the truth?

A. On four of the five items you mention, your parish priest is in the wrong; on the fifth, I am confused as to exactly what you mean.

The *General Instruction of the Roman Missal* indicates plainly that if either the entrance or communion antiphon is not chanted, each is to be recited by either a lector, the celebrant, or the entire congregation. Refusing Holy Communion to those who exercise their legitimate option to kneel is in total violation of Church law; only notorious public sinners are ever to be denied Communion. The NRSV *Lectionary* has not been approved by the Holy See — and, therefore, cannot be used.

Regarding the difficulty at Communion time, I am in a quandary as to what you are trying to say, so let me stake out a few possibilities. If you mean that your priest does not allow the extraordinary ministers to communicate from the chalice, he is perfectly within his rights. Does he simply distribute Communion under only one form to the entire congregation — that is, not both species? Again, that is left to his own discretion. Why would extraordinary ministers be standing at the altar, anyway? They surely should not be communicating themselves from the chalice. Without more specifics, I really can't come up with an appropriate response.

On your knees

Q. In a recent letter to the editor in our diocesan paper, the question was put forth about when the congregation should kneel during Mass. The diocesan director of worship replied (in the paper) that the *General Instruction of the Roman Missal* stated: "They should kneel at the consecration unless prevented by the lack of space, the number of people present, or some other good reason." He goes on to suggest that a "good reason" could be theological or in the spirit of the liturgical movement. Two of the eucharistic prayers mention the people praying as "standing." Could you please offer your thoughts on his understanding of the prescription in the *General Instruction of the Roman Missal*?

A. This topic has been beaten to death. Please, then, let this be the absolute last question on standing for the eucharistic prayer. Simply put, in the United States, it is *forbidden* for the congregation to do so. Any priest who says otherwise is intellectually dishonest.

Funeral liturgy

Q. Does the Church have any regulations as to who might be buried from the Church with a funeral Mass. Is it permissible that someone who had been baptized a Catholic, but had been an avowed atheist for the last twenty years, be buried from the Church after a sudden death?

A. What was the man's attitude at the end of his life? Did he see a priest? Did he deliberately reject a visit from a priest? Or was he unconscious in his final days/hours? Without that kind of data, it is difficult to formulate a pastoral judgment. However, I would state as a general norm that I would be most hesitant about denying Christian burial to anyone whose family (presumably, practicing

Catholics) requested it. After all, sixteen centuries ago, St. Augustine reminded us that the funeral liturgy is as much for the survivors as for the deceased. Furthermore, who would need the prayers of the Church and the Eucharistic Sacrifice more than one such as you have described? Ecclesiastical penalties make sense for the living (who can be brought to conversion by their imposition), but not for the dead — unless the individual's wishes and/or lifestyle were so completely abhorrent to Christian convictions.

Language forms

Q. Plans were made in my parish to celebrate a bilingual (Latin/English) "Novus Ordo" Mass for a special occasion. The pastor did not think that special permission was necessary, but decided to write after concerns were raised by someone on the liturgy committee. The proposal was for the introit, gradual and communion antiphon to be sung in Gregorian by the choir; ordinary chants from the *Missa de Angelis* to be done by the choir and congregation; and all proper prayers and readings were to be in English, including the eucharistic prayer, except for the words of institution and the memorial acclamation. The reply from the bishop indicated that special permission is not required for the chants to be sung in Latin, therefore, permission was granted for all of the sung parts requested. He continued, however, to say that he could not give permission for the words of institution to be said in Latin. I did not think that the use of Latin required permission from the bishop, as long as one was using the current rite. Am I mistaken? In what circumstances may permission be granted to have the words of institution in Latin? Could you please clarify the situation for me?

A. No permission of any kind is ever needed for the use of Latin in any or all parts of the Mass, if celebrated according to the Roman Missal of Pope Paul VI. The *Code of Canon Law* states: "The eucharistic celebration is to be carried out either in the Latin language or in another language, provided the liturgical texts have been lawfully approved" (no. 928). In other words, no permission is ever required for Latin, but permission is required for the vernacular — that is, if one is using a language other than Latin, the texts must conform to an approved vernacular edition.

Although I have no aesthetic, pastoral, or theological problem with the notion of a Latin/English celebration, I would not be too pleased to have the eucharistic prayer divided as you describe. My own preference would be to have all in the same language — either completely Latin or completely English, in order to convey the unity of the prayer; but that is a personal preference, not a liturgical norm.

In sum, the only form of the Mass demanding episcopal approval is the Latin Mass according to the Missal of Pope St. Pius V.

Grave abuse

Q. I have recently discovered a response in another Catholic periodical touching on the question of taking liberties with the *Lectionary*. Besides introducing the question of other practices that were not at all a part of the question, such as a family member saying a few words after Communion at a funeral Mass, the answer seemed off-base to me. Could you please comment on the phenomenon of lectors changing the words within the readings? Sometimes it's just one word — for example, "men" changed into "people" — however, other times the whole reading is changed. I thought that the *Lectionary* was to be read as the entry was printed. Who can decide to change the *Lectionary* texts — and using what criteria?

A. The Second Vatican Council was adamant that no one, not even a priest, it says, can change a word of the Sacred Liturgy (see *Sacrosanctum Concilium,* Constitution on the Sacred Liturgy, no. 22). The *Lectionary* is indeed a liturgical text, from which one may not deviate (unless, of course, one replaces weekday readings for a saint's feast, or the like).

Psalm Variations

Q. When it comes to the responsorial psalm, some of the words, and even whole sentences, are exchanged for "similar" words or phrases (however, very often the meaning is not the same), so as to "adapt" the text to the music. Should it not be the reverse? Shouldn't the Bible as the Word of God control the music, and not the other way around? When I spoke to the choir director about it, he indicated that he had the permission of the pastor for this (which really puzzles me). Unfortunately, I had nothing in writing to respond. Am I wrong to feel as I do?

A. As long as the substance of the original text (biblical or liturgical) is intact, the Church permits the type of variation you describe for musical purposes. Granted, this can be a kind of slippery slope in many places; given your description of your pastor, however, I would not be too concerned.

Wedding bells

Q. Our pastor has begun to celebrate weddings on Saturday at the anticipated Sunday Mass. He uses the readings of the Sunday. I always thought that the wedding Mass was to be separate, and not to fulfill a Sunday obligation as well. Is this just a very odd, but permissible, practice?

A. There is no sacramental or canonical reason why a wedding cannot be celebrated as you suggest. I do wonder, however, how people feel about the practice — in both directions: Do spouses want such a celebration? Do parishioners want to witness marriages every other weekend? In some ways, it reminds me of the practice started in some parishes back in the early 1970s of having baptisms every Sunday morning — it wore thin after a while, for all concerned.

Although acknowledging that baptisms, weddings and funerals are all, by their nature, public or communal events, I do think we need to give some margin to the American mentality, which is just a bit more private about these things than in some other parts of the world.

Lack of training

Q. I have recently read your book *The Bible and the Mass* and am very interested in getting answers to several questions that have been prompted by this reading. In your chapter on "Communion and Concluding Rites," you refer to a statement by Pope John Paul II concerning the use of extraordinary ministers on a regular or normal basis as being a "reprehensible" practice. Further, you quoted Cardinal Joseph Ratzinger as saying that the offering of both species "should never be the pretext for using extraordinary ministers of Holy Communion." Recently, our bishop has mandated that every parish in the diocese offer Holy Communion under both species and that each parish priest must make sure that there are enough extraordinary ministers to accomplish this. I have been appalled that it is possible to mandate such a thing in the first place, but also because there seems to be no universal standard for training and initiation of these extraordinary ministers. It seems that the only requirement is that an extraordinary minister is a confirmed Catholic, and at least seventeen years of age. In fact, when an extraordinary minister fails to show up at Mass, we often find parishioners or older altar servers performing these duties. Please comment on both the mandate and the lack of training. Also, should someone faithful to the Church's teaching in this matter accept the duty of an extraordinary minister of the Eucharist when asked by his pastor? It seems to be fostering abuses, such as a lack of respect around the altar, improper purification of the vessels, people chosen on the spur of the moment for the duty, etc.

A. Options cannot be mandated. For example, the Church allows a priest to choose among four eucharistic prayers for most occasions. A bishop would be out of line to insist, for instance, that every priest had to use the third prayer, or could never use the fourth. The decision is left to the individual celebrant for a variety of reasons, one of the most important being that he is supposed to know his people best and can thus make the most informed pastoral judgment about what should or should not be done either in general in his parish or under certain specific conditions.

The training and preparation of extraordinary ministers of Holy Communion is almost universally horrendous at both a theological and liturgical level. I advise people to shy away from this role, first of all because they are almost never genuinely needed, but also because it continues to foster an unhealthy notion of what constitutes the lay apostolate, and contributes mightily to the ongoing secularization of both the Eucharist and the priesthood.

Homily protocol

Q. Would you please clarify the situation of lay people and nuns giving the homily at Mass. I recently attended Mass in a different diocese where this happened. I wrote to the pastor; he replied, citing the *Guidelines for Lay Preaching* issued by the bishop of that diocese. He did not seem to appreciate my concern.

A. No bishop has the authority to tinker with universal liturgical law — and who can preach is one such law. Only an ordained minister (deacon, priest, or bishop) may preach a homily in the context of Mass. On certain occasions (pro-life, family life, etc.), a non-ordained person may be invited to offer a reflection on a discreet topic for which that person has a particular expertise. However, it may not supplant the homily — that is, if the person speaks after the Gospel (as opposed to after Communion), the priest must read the Gospel, give at least a brief (one- or two-minute) homily, and then introduce the speaker, ensuring that everyone (speaker included) realizes that this is an extraordinary situation and that what is being delivered is not a homily (that is, exegesis of scriptural texts).

Dangerous Hymns

Q. A hymn titled "The Supper of the Lord" is appearing in several missalettes and hymnals, including the *Breaking Bread* hymnal. The opening verse is "Precious body, precious blood, here in bread and wine; Here the Lord prepares His feast divine." Am I being overly critical, or is this hymn heretical? It sounds to me as if it is in conformity with the Lutheran doctrine of consubstantiation rather than the Catholic doctrine of transubstantiation?

A. You are not being hypercritical; songs such as this have done irreparable damage to the Eucharistic Faith of millions of practicing Catholics. A maxim of theology informs us: "*Lex orandi, lex credendi,*" which means two things. First, the prayers we recite in the liturgy are a reflection of our faith and doctrinal commitments; second, our faith is influenced by the words we use in the liturgy. No *imprimatur* should be given to any missalette that contains words such as these. Sadly, as comprehensive and attractive a work as "Worship II" or "Worship III" is, each also has heretical statements used for the Holy Eucharist, as when the Sacred Species are referred to as "bread" about to be distributed as Holy Communion.

Forget this song

Q. Our small choir spent many hours learning "The Supper of the Lord" in preparation for its use as a Communion song, and you ripped it apart. At no time did anyone in our group voice concern about the words not reflecting the truths of the transubstantiation. Is it not the faith of the communicant that finalizes the mystery of bread and wine being changed into the Body and Blood of Christ? As practicing Catholics, individually and as a whole, we declare that we have suffered no "irreparable damage" to our Eucharistic Faith by using this hymn.

A. Your own "rebuttal" is the clearest argument that could ever be offered against the song in question.

First, that no one would express concern about the lyrics is telling, in and of itself.

Second, your personal understanding of "how" the Eucharist is confected is heretical (transfinalization). An individual's faith has absolutely nothing to do with whether or not the bread and wine are transformed into the Body and Blood of the Lord (transubstantiation).

Third, if no "irreparable damage" was done to your Eucharistic Faith, it is because your Eucharistic faith is not "in sync" with that of the Catholic Church.

Fourth, my personal pastoral counsel is to give up on "The Supper of the Lord" and to spend your choir rehearsal time more profitably by learning "*Panis Angelicus*" or "Gift of Finest Wheat."

Hand holding

Q. I am an extraordinary minister of the Eucharist, and we have just recently begun gathering around the altar and holding hands for the Our Father. I didn't think it was correct, so when I saw your answer in an edition of *The Catholic Answer* magazine, I showed it to one of the nuns in my parish. She said that your answer was incorrect and encouraged me to write you and ask from what sources you got the answer. Would you please help me respond to her?

A. Kindly remind the nun that rubrics are positive, not negative, in scope — that is, they tell us what we *should* do, not what we should *not* do. In point of fact, she needs to be able to demonstrate to you a liturgical directive which says you folks ought to be holding hands around the altar. Of course, there is no such document, which is why you shouldn't do it.

Illicit

Q. I have attended (and served) a number of Masses where the priest did not pour water along with the wine into the chalice at the offertory, and appeared to skip the prayer completely. Does this action make the matter of the wine invalid? If so, does this affect the validity of the whole Mass?

A. To omit the commingling is highly illicit, but in and of itself, it would not invalidate the Eucharist.

Sing a song

Q. Our pastor is singing the consecration at the Sunday Masses. Is this in line with the magisterium of the Church? It does not seem appropriate to me if we consider Christ on Calvary giving up His life?

A. The magisterium is not directly involved with liturgy, but with doctrine; therefore, technically, the expression you use is incorrect and so it is better to ask if the Church or liturgical law permits the practice you mention.

The answer is "yes" — and it is actually encouraged. It is important to remember that at Mass we do not simply imitate what Christ did, either at the Last Supper or at Calvary — we ritualize those acts of His, and singing is an important and even essential part of such prayer. Inasmuch as the Last Supper was a ritual meal, we know that Jesus and His apostles sang before, during, and after — as is still done at Passover celebrations today.

Communion guidelines

Q. What is your reaction on the new Communion guidelines passed by the bishops' conference several years ago? I find the statement about Communion without confession to be outrageous.

A. For the benefit of those who have not read the document, the norm in question reads thus: "A person who is conscious of grave sin is not to receive the Body and Blood of the Lord without prior sacramental confession except for a grave reason where there is no opportunity for confession. . . ."

The sentence is theologically and canonically correct; the only problem is that it doesn't belong in guidelines to be included in a missalette. Why? Because the presumption is that such norms included in such booklets would apply to cases of attendance at Mass. What do I mean? Yes, it is true that one may receive Holy Communion without sacramental confession in emergency situations — for example, danger of death with no priest available — but what could ever constitute "a grave reason" for doing so at a regularly scheduled Mass? Surely, human respect is not a valid reason.

This statement is pastorally imprudent because it will encourage people to hold themselves excused from legitimate Church law, leading them to laxity in receiving Holy Communion unworthily and in refraining from receiving the Sacrament of Penance under the pretext of "necessity."

Forever and ever

Q. At what point after the consecration does the Body and Blood of Christ revert to ordinary bread and wine? What is the proper way of disposing of it?

A. The consecrated Species never return to ordinary bread and wine, and the proper method of "disposing" of the Sacred Species (presuming they cannot be reserved in the tabernacle — and the Precious Blood can never be reserved) is to consume them.

Revised Missal

Q. I make a point of never calling the present edition of the *Missale Romanum* the "Novus Ordo" because I've read that Rome never called it that; rather, it was a "traditionalist" expression designed to "prove" that the present edition of the missal is Masonic. Would you please comment?

A. You are absolutely correct. In Pope Paul VI's promulgation decree for the new missal, he could not be any clearer in asserting that this is not a new Mass, but a revision. And the truth of that assertion can be tested by simply looking at the preconciliar version and the 1969 text. The two major changes come down to the replacement of the former "Prayers at the Foot of the Altar" with the penitential rite (for which there are three options, and if rite A is taken, it is essentially the same as the older form) and the substitution of newly created prayers for the older offertory rite. Three new eucharistic prayers were also added, with two of them being based on texts dating to before the close of the first millennium.

The Masonic connection is over-played and really quite silly. If the Masons had wanted to destroy the Church, I think they could have chosen something a bit more dramatic than this. A related charge is often made that six Protestant ministers made up the new missal and Pope Paul VI accepted it as a goodwill gesture toward Christian unity; that, too, is bizarre. The clergy referred to were official observers to the Second Vatican Council. Finally, whatever one thinks about the advisability of some or all of the changes made in the 1969 rite, or about the manner in which the rite was introduced and the former rite suppressed, no one can say that it is either heretical or invalid and remain a Catholic in good standing.

And, oh yes, one more consideration: An acceptance or even an enthusiastic endorsement of the Missal of Pope Paul VI in no way should be construed as an endorsement of subsequent changes that had no basis in either the expressed will of the Council Fathers or any genuine linkage to the reform found in that missal.

Off your feet

Q. An issue of *The Catholic Answer* magazine carried an article regarding posture during Mass. Your answers seem to be at odds with what our bishop has recently pointed out in our diocesan paper, relying on the *Instruction on the Worship of the Eucharistic Mystery* and the *General Instruction of the Roman Missal*. Might I hope to see a correction published in a future edition of *The Catholic Answer* magazine?

A. No, you may not, because your bishop has clearly gone beyond what those documents say — and he has no right to do so. Even while acknowledging that the American missal, approved by our entire episcopate and the Holy See, mandates kneeling from the end of the *Sanctus* to the end of the eucharistic prayer, he then goes on to say that he will permit pastors to do otherwise. A change of this kind was heatedly discussed within the National Conference of Catholic Bishops — which alone can propose such a change, then submit it to the Holy See for approval — and was defeated. Therefore, the required posture for our entire country remains exactly what it has been for more than thirty years now.

Liturgy-speak

Q. At a recent liturgy meeting, we were told to use the term "presider" instead of "celebrant" for the priest at Mass. I don't understand why this is so important. If they stressed belief in the Real Presence even half as much, it would be a blessing! I thought a priest was another Christ and not just a minister of an assembly.

A. I agree with your assessment. In and of itself, the term "presider" is not problematic, but the mentality that insists upon it often is. Let me explain, from two different perspectives.

First, some folks shy away from the word "celebrant" for the priest because, they say, it suggests that he is the only one who truly "celebrates" the liturgy. This is not the meaning of the term, nor has the Church ever construed it in that manner. It does indicate, however, that the priest is the celebrant of the liturgy in a way in which no one else is. The *Orate Fratres* of the Mass, in its Latin original, has the priest ask the people to pray that "*ac meum ac vestrum sacrificium*" ("my sacrifice and yours") would be acceptable to God our Father. The inaccurate English translation has collapsed that into "our sacrifice," thus blurring the distinction between the ministerial priesthood and the priesthood of the faithful. To be sure, all believers offer the Eucharistic Sacrifice together, but their relationship to it differs, as the Second Vatican Council reminded us, not simply in degree, but in essence.

What is meant by that? A priest relates to the Eucharist *in persona Christi*, since priestly ordination has configured him to Christ the Priest at the very core of his being; this is not the case for the non-ordained. A simple illustration might be helpful: If a thousand lay faithful show up for a Sunday Mass and no priest appears, there can be no Mass; conversely, if the priest appears and no people do, a Mass can take place (admittedly, the Church does not want priests to celebrate Mass without laity present, unless there is a genuine need). That example highlights the essential difference between the two forms of priesthood in the Church and explains why the priest is the liturgical celebrant in a unique fashion. With all the confusion surrounding various roles within the Church today, maintenance of a word like "celebrant" for the priest seems very prudent.

Now, on to "presider." My first objection to it is that it is not a pleasant-sounding word; it smacks of being a neologism. In Latin or other languages, one does not find it as a noun but in its verbal form ("the one who presides"). Second, "presider" in English is devoid of a sacral grounding. Third, it is generally used by those who want to start making room for "presiders" other than the ordained, especially females.

And so, I would sum up my reaction thus: (1) "Celebrant" is a perfectly good word, with a long history that serves us well, especially at this moment in our liturgical life. (2) "Presider" comes off as a type of "new-speak" and is usually laden with a heavy agenda toward what Pope John Paul II has dubbed as "the laicization of the clergy and the clericalization of the laity."

Surprise announcement

Q. I was taken by surprise when our pastor announced that there would be an Easter Vigil and Mass at 8 p.m., the Saturday before Easter, and that there would be no Mass on Easter Sunday. I am under the impression that an Easter Vigil Mass on Saturday evening does not fulfill our Easter Sunday obligation. Would you please clarify?

A. We should note at the outset that the Easter Vigil should not be seen as somehow separate from the Mass; they constitute one, whole, indivisible worship service. Furthermore, the Easter Vigil liturgy is *the* worship service of the entire Church year. For all these reasons, it fulfills our "obligation" to the nth degree.

I am surprised, though, that your pastor would not schedule a Mass on Easter morning as well — unless yours is a mission church, and he has pastoral responsibilities for other parochial communities.

Money, money

Q. Is it customary to put the collection basket on the altar? I've been having a difficult time concentrating on the Eucharist during Mass because of the basket of money on the altar. I'm a person who believes that money is really the root of all evil. I believe that just as we sold our eternal life for a forbidden fruit, so, too, many lives are destroyed over the almighty dollar. It seems to me that the only one who brought money to the Last Supper was Judas. I realize the Church needs money, but why not put that gift in a collection box at the entrance of the church?

A. If the collection basket is actually *on* the altar, you are correct in being upset; if it is merely in front of the altar, there is nothing wrong with that. Your allusion to money as the root of all evil is not entirely accurate as a scriptural quote; the text says, rather, that the "love" of money is the root of all evil (see 1 Tm 6:10). There is an enormous difference between the two. People do not get into heaven just because they are poor, nor are the rich excluded simply because they have money. It is our attitude toward money which is critical, and what we do with it. An ancient Jewish prayer wisely asks, "Lord, do not make me so rich that I forget you, or so poor that I curse you."

As far as bringing up the collection at Mass is concerned, I consider it a wonderful way to show how we are attempting to unite our monetary gifts to the self-oblation of Christ. This makes it truly a "sacrifice," for the Latin roots of this word mean specifically "to make something holy." This can have the additional effect of helping to change our overall attitude toward money and material possessions.

Posture pickle

Q. I need your help in understanding some information that has just recently appeared in our parish bulletin about the "proper posture for the assembly during and after Communion." The pastor informed us that "he would be talking about this in future weeks," and he just wanted us "to be informed prior to these discussions." The so-called discussions will not include parish meetings; rather, it will be a one-way "discussion" from the pulpit with the aim of further desacralizing our Mass. For the past nine years, our family has sat in the front pew — and knelt during the consecration. Now, if we obey the *General Instruction of the Roman Missal*, we will be openly and visibly disobeying the parish priest. What should we do?

A. As I read your pastor's directive, it has nothing to do with the consecration or eucharistic prayer. Kneeling throughout the eucharistic prayer is mandatory for the United States. The posture for the time frame he mentions is another matter; personally, I don't think it advisable to tinker with such matters, but given the silence of the *General Instruction of the Roman Missal* on that period, what your parish priest has called for is not forbidden by universal liturgical law, nor by the particular law for this country.

Unsuitable

Q. I attended a funeral this week and got very uncomfortable when the song "How Great Thou Art" was sung at the time of the memorial acclamation. Granted, the first line was altered to say something about Jesus' death and resurrection, but this still rubbed me the wrong way. Am I wrong in thinking that this was not correct?

A. There is a certain latitude permitted when texts are sung, but the version of the memorial acclamation you heard was not suitable; in fact, there is no reference to the Resurrection whatsoever — only the passion and death of the Lord.

Extended arms

Q. What exactly is a blessing? Is there a difference in terms of worth, efficacy, or "substance" between the blessing a priest and a layperson can bestow? Our parish priest sometimes has the congregation at Mass share with him in giving someone a blessing. We each extend one arm toward the person while the priest recites the blessing. Is there anything wrong with this?

A. The blessing of a priest is more in the realm of a declarative statement, while that of a layman is a prayer for God's blessing to be bestowed. The difference is signified by the Sign of the Cross being used by a cleric, but not by one of the laity. Lay people are not to give blessings normally — only in the absence of an ordained minister — and the "Book of Blessings" makes that clear.

The situation you describe is a horse of an entirely different color. Your pastor is creating much confusion by his procedure as people are led to believe — at the sign level — that clergy and laity can confer a kind of concelebrated blessing, which is not true. Repeatedly, Pope John Paul II has decried any activity that does not maintain clear lines of demarcation between the clergy and the laity. As the Second Vatican Council reminded us, the ministerial priesthood and the priesthood of the faithful differ not only in degree but in essence (see *Lumen Gentium* [Dogmatic Constitution on the Church], no. 10) — and this needs to be apparent in our symbol system.

Public scandal

Q. I have a really sticky situation to deal with. A good friend of mine is not married in the Church, but receives Communion often. In fact, she is even an extraordinary minister of the Eucharist! Two priests have told me that it is none of my business, and they advised that I not disturb my friend's conscience. The situation is that her former spouse died, but the man she has married now is divorced. I have said nothing up to this point, but I really think I should. My friend is ignorant, not evil. What is my obligation as a true friend?

A. This is related to an earlier question, but incomparably different at the same time. In the first instance, we discussed not disturbing the invincible ignorance of spouses in regard to artificial birth control. The present case, however, involves a matter that is not a private affair, but public in several ways: First, marriage — by its very nature — is a communal concern; second, the reception of Holy Communion is likewise a public matter; third, distributing Holy Communion is even more public because it involves engaging in a ministerial role. Very tactfully, your friend needs to be told the facts; in reality, I find it difficult to believe that she is unaware of the truth. The priests who cautioned you to keep out of it gave very poor pastoral advice. If the woman does not cease receiving and distributing Holy Communion and her pastor does nothing about it, your bishop needs to be informed in order to bring to a halt both the sacrilege and the scandal.

Ecumenical Eucharist

Q. On Ascension Day, my parish hosted the neighborhood Episcopal and Lutheran parishes for an ecumenical Eucharist. My pastor celebrated alone, but the other "clergy" served as *truly* extraordinary ministers of the Eucharist, and it seemed that everyone present went forward to receive Communion. I discussed my confusion with the pastor when this event was first announced. Not being satisfied with the answers I received, I wrote to the bishop; he replied and sent me a copy of the ecumenical guidelines for the diocese. In my opinion, the circumstances deserving of pastoral consideration in the document are not clearly delineated, and its references do not appear to be authoritative. Under what circumstances is such a service licit in the Catholic Church? I fear that such an ecumenical eucharistic celebration might be a compromise of the Faith.

A. Scheduling services such as the one you describe seems to me, at least, to be setting up circumstances for frustration and failure. Why would anyone want to celebrate the Eucharist together when, under normal circumstances, intercommunion is not possible. In a similar situation, I would have planned an ecumenical Vespers service, especially since all three of the communities involved have a venerable tradition of praying the Liturgy of the Hours — and with great solemnity.

To have Protestant clergy distribute Holy Communion during a Catholic Mass is off-base, if for no other reason than the fact that our own *Code of Canon Law* indicates that an extraordinary minister of the Eucharist must be a Catholic in good standing. I have read the diocesan guidelines you enclosed and do not see how the celebration you attended fulfilled either the letter or the spirit of those norms, nor those of the *Code of Canon Law* and of the Holy See's directives on eucharistic sharing, to which your bishop refers in his letter. I don't think anyone could argue that a "grave and pressing need" existed.

I am most committed to the work of Christian unity and think I am rather well-respected by non-Catholic clergy, but I firmly believe that precipitous recourse to eucharistic sharing is counterproductive in the long run. The history of this century alone shows us that various denominations that embarked upon intercommunion with one another other at its outset are not an iota closer to full, organic unity at the century's close. Why? Because casual or regular intercommunion is sloppy ecumenism, putting the cart before the horse and making us lazy to do the praying, studying, and working we need to do if full ecclesial unity is to become a reality which, I trust, is the goal of all who are involved in ecumenical dialogue.

Advent color

Q. I always thought Advent was a penitential time, and so the purple vestments were used. However our pastor said that it is a joyful time, and that for this reason it is preferable to wear a deep indigo blue. He did just that; the candles on our Advent wreath were a brighter blue. Is there any special significance to blue vestments? What's Advent all about?

A. Advent is one of my favorite seasons, but liturgical shenanigans always put a pall over everything, as some self-appointed experts try to improve on the Church's liturgical tradition and law.

Advent is, according to the documents, both joyful and penitential. How can it be both? Very simply. The prayers of the season remind us, for example, that we must "remove whatever hinders us from receiving Christ with joy." In other words, our expectation of the Lord's threefold coming (historically, sacramentally, and eschatologically) is cause for joy or, as we say in the Mass, "we wait in joyful hope." Our sins, however, impede a proper reception of Him, hence the Church's reliance on John the Baptist as her primary voice during Advent.

Now, as far as the colors go, blue is not a color of the Roman rite, except by long-standing indult in Spain for feasts of Our Lady. Your pastor is correct that there should be a distinction in colors between Advent and Lent, but he (like many others) has the color scheme backwards. Because of the joyful nature of Advent, the hue ought to be *lighter* than what is used for Lent. A standard rule of thumb is that Lent's shade is purple (dark), while Advent's is more like the magenta (bright) of a bishop's cassock.

Some liturgists argue that the Sarum rite in England used blue vestments for Advent — and that is true, but what's the point? The Sarum rite has been out of general use for nearly ten centuries! And do we want to revive the whole Sarum rite now — or just engage in more of the now-commonplace picking and choosing?

Translation Woes

Q. Here in England the words "that *our* sacrifice may be acceptable to God the almighty Father" are used at the offertory. Yet in the papal document "The Holy Eucharist" (February 24, 1980, section 9, paragraph 5) the Holy Father, reflecting on the presentation of the gifts, used the following words: ". . .that my sacrifice and yours may be acceptable. . ." He actually has this phrase in quotation marks. He goes on to say in the next sentence, "These words are binding since they express the character of the entire Eucharistic Liturgy and the fullness of its divine and ecclesial content." The dictionary says that "binding" means to be obeyed, or carried out. Has the Church shifted its position regarding these words?

A. The Holy Father, of course, published this document in Latin, and was therefore using the original Latin text of the Mass as his source for the citation. The Latin speaks of "*ac meum ac vestrum sacrificium*" ("my sacrifice and yours"). The official English translation has conflated that to "our sacrifice." This is but one of the hundreds of inaccuracies with which the English version of the Mass is riddled; and it is why it is so important for the revision, currently underway, to be carried out with total attention given to fidelity to a real translation — and not a mere paraphrase. Several times in the *Catechism of the Catholic Church*, you will also find that the editors (in order to make a theological point using the liturgy) had to circumvent the approved English text and provide a more literal translation; this should not have to happen, especially because of our principle of *lex orandi, lex credendi* (the law of prayer establishes the law of belief).

The St. Gregory Foundation for Latin Liturgy has been involved in the retranslation process for almost a decade now, and has produced its own translation of the Mass as a contribution toward the effort to obtain a more faithful rendering of the *Missale Romanum*. The bottom-line answer to your query, however, is that while inadequate and inaccurate, the official English translation is not heretical.

Reasonable cause

Q. In an issue of *The Catholic Answer* magazine, you noted in one answer that "the Church does not want priests to celebrate Mass without laity present, unless there is a genuine need." I need some advice on translating this principle into a practical situation.

I was recently appointed as the administrator of a small mission in a county that is one percent Catholic. There were no weekday Masses here when I arrived. I have encouraged the parishioners to consider participation in daily Mass, but have not yet had much positive response. In the *Directory for the Life and Ministry of Priests*, it states: "It is necessary to recall the irreplaceable value that the daily celebration of the Holy Mass has for the priest, be it in the presence of other faithful or not" (no. 49).

Would you agree that this "irreplaceable value" to the life and ministry of the priest fulfills "legitimate and reasonable cause" or, in your words, a "genuine need" for a celebration of a weekday Mass without a congregation or server? This does not even begin to touch on the benefits of the Mass for the Church, the faithful departed and the whole world.

A. I fully agree with your analysis, Father, and think you are to be commended for attempting to introduce your people to the inestimable benefits of daily Mass. I am sure that, under the influence of your example, devotion, and zeal, many will soon be joining you at the Lord's altar.

Veiled chalice

Q. I thought the veil should cover the chalice used at Mass to call attention to the beautiful and the sacred. Our priest does not use the veil. Has this become an option?

A. With the use of the missal of 2000, its use is now referred to as "praiseworthy" (see no. 118).

Clear rubrics

Q. In my former parish, the people always stood during the reading of the Passion, with the exception of those who were either too old or those who had some infirmity. However, in my new parish we are told to sit before the reading of the Passion begins and to remain seated throughout. Should we ever really sit during the proclamation of the Gospel? Does the pastor have the authority to make this decision?

A. The rubrics instruct us to stand for the Passion. Obviously, the infirm should not be held to the impossible, but relaxing norms for the sake of convenience is never appropriate, let alone on the day when we read about Christ's sufferings and death for our salvation!

No, the pastor has no authority to tell the congregation to remain seated.

Facing the people

Q. I have just come across a pamphlet by Michael Davies titled *A Critique: Mass Facing the People*, published by Neumann Press in Long Prairie, Minn. What do you know about either the author or the publishing house? Is this critique (which is devastating) reliable?

A. I know nothing about the publishing house. The author is a bright, articulate layman, known for his opposition to the liturgical nonsense of the postconciliar period. My only personal objection to his work is that it tends toward extremism, throwing out baby and bathwater together, so that he has come to the basic posture that although the new rite of the Mass is valid, it is an unrelenting disaster and the very cause for all our problems, liturgical and otherwise. In other words, he has taken the abuses as normative and dismissed the entire project.

The essay is rather well-done, historically accurate and largely dependent upon and a summary of the very scholarly work of Msgr. Klaus Gamber on this topic (which book in the original German carried a preface by none other than Cardinal Joseph Ratzinger). Critical to stress is the fact that no document of the Second Vatican Council ever even remotely suggested the "turning around" of altars, and no postconciliar document has ever mandated such.

My biggest personal objection to "Mass facing the people" is not at root theological, but psychological and sociological, and that is that by turning around the altars, the liturgy itself has been turned into a very clericalistic, personal show featuring the priest — ironically, quite the opposite of what genuine liturgical renewal should have hoped for.

We must emphasize, however, that celebrating Mass in either direction is not, in itself, a doctrinal matter, and that history shows both options, usually co-existing. What I think requires evaluation is how this option has worked for the past three decades, and the empirical evidence seems to be strongly negative.

"Inspired 'development' "

Q. Recently, an article appeared in our paper about the commissioning of lay people to serve as extraordinary ministers of the Eucharist. The priest-author recalled that thirty-five years ago no one would have thought about a layperson being able to distribute Holy Communion. He credits these people with enabling many to receive the Eucharist on a regular basis and being able "to bring dying people back to the Faith in their last days," because these sick people had been away from the Church and were not intimidated by the extraordinary minister of the Eucharist. While it doesn't say exactly what happened, shouldn't the extraordinary minister have made arrangements for the priest to come and hear the person's confession before giving him Communion? I'm also not sure that it is a good thing to have these extraordinary ministers conducting eucharistic services in the absence of a priest. He concludes that these extraordinary ministers of the Eucharist are an "inspired 'development' " and should ease our anxiety over the shortage of vocations. What do you think?

A. The Holy See has released an instruction on "the collaboration of the non-ordained faithful in the sacred ministry of the priest."

Article 8 of this document is devoted entirely to our present concern. Among other things, we read that "the habitual use of extraordinary ministers" is to be "eliminated." In other words, their use is to be exactly what their name suggests — "extraordinary." Furthermore, we are told that they are to receive Holy Communion along with the rest of the lay faithful, lest they appear "as though concelebrants." They are to be called "extraordinary" and nothing else, precisely to underscore the "supplementary" and unusual circumstances in which they might function.

Article 9 deals with "the apostolate to the sick," and pointedly indicates that the primary lay role in this sphere is exercised "by being with [the sick] in difficult moments, encouraging them to receive the Sacraments of Penance and Anointing of the Sick, by helping them to have the disposition to make a good individual confession, as well as to prepare them to receive the Anointing of the Sick." It is clearly stated that in no way should the non-ordained (or deacons, either) supplant the ministry of priests in this regard or engage in actions that mimic priestly actions (blessings, anointings, etc.).

Liturgical day

Q. I am puzzled, and here is why. We Catholics are obligated to attend Mass on Sundays and holy days of obligation. The Church has adopted the Jewish way of telling time —that is, that the next day begins at sundown (not midnight). Therefore, those who attend the evening Mass on Saturday fulfill their obligation to attend Mass on Sunday (this is also true for holy days). Now, here's what puzzles me. My parish church has a Mass on Saturday night, at 5:30 p.m., and then several on Sunday morning, plus an additional Mass at 5:30 p.m. Sunday afternoon. Since the 5:30 p.m. Mass on Saturday fulfills one's obligation for Sunday, then it seems logical to say the 5:30 p.m. Mass on Sunday is actually the first Mass on Monday. The poor guy in attendance thinking that he is at Sunday Mass is wrong because it is already Monday. Do I make sense?

A. Sorry, but you've missed an important piece in the calculation puzzle: Sunday is the longest liturgical day of the week, beginning at sundown on Saturday (as you stated), but not ending until midnight on Sunday. So, "the poor guy in attendance thinking that he is at Sunday Mass" really is at a Sunday Mass.

Ordinary minister

Q. Is it correct for a pastor, in whose church a deacon is a parishioner, to conduct the Rite of Benediction when both the pastor and I (another priest) are present with him?

A. A deacon is an ordinary minister of Holy Communion, which means that he can conduct Benediction on a par with a priest. I would add, however, that an appreciation for hierarchy — and a spirit of humility —would recommend that he defer to the pastor, just as the pastor would presumably defer to the local bishop, were he present.

Holy days' folly

Q. Once again, another holy day of obligation has been deleted: All Saints' Day. Is this a common practice in dioceses outside the Northwest? I've posed this question to several clerics in our area, but their answers varied. One area vicar explained that the dispensation would mean that no people would miss their obligation, and thus nobody would be guilty of mortal sin. Another deacon informed me that he thinks eventually the U.S. Catholic Church will celebrate only two or three holy days of obligation, anyway.

A. As I have expressed before, I think the decision to transfer holy days or to remove the obligation was a pastorally and psychologically bad decision. It cannot but hurt our observance of all the holy days and, eventually, of the Sundays. It seems to me that this awareness prompted the presbyteral council of the Archdiocese of New York to petition the cardinal to eliminate these dispensations in the future; the cardinal acquiesced. I think this request of the priests is significant because they are, literally, the "men in the trenches" and they have seen the disastrous effects of this practice. I hope that the reversal that began in New York will take off and spread throughout the country — just as the reverse did a decade ago.

Eucharistic fast

Q. Could you comment on the Church's official requirements in regard to the Eucharistic fast for the elderly who are in retirement homes and the hospital?

A. This is treated in the new Code of Canon Law, no. 919, para. 3: "The elderly, the infirm, and those who care for them can receive the Most Holy Eucharist even if they have eaten something within the preceding hour." This is a change from the old practice of a fast of a quarter of an hour being required of the infirmed.

Latin hymns

Q. Where can I find some Latin hymns (especially psalms, antiphons, and canticles)?

Q. Not long ago, I received a booklet from Mother Angelica written by Pope Paul VI, entitled *Jubilate Deo*. I presented it to our pastor and others on the worship/spirituality committee, and was essentially told that it has been rendered obsolete by other more recent documents. Could you speak to this issue?

A. The St. Gregory Foundation for Latin Liturgy has many resources to promote the celebration of the Sacred Liturgy in Latin — according to the mind and legislation of the Second Vatican Council. Pope Paul did not write the work in question, but he did promulgate it, which means he ordered it published, so alarmed was he that Latin was being lost to the Western Church. As recently as January 1998, Pope John Paul II called for a renewed appreciation of Latin in the life of the Church. If your "worship/spirituality" group asserts that subsequent, more up-to-date documents oppose *Jubilate Deo*, ask them to bring forth those documents. May I tell you that they will not be able to do so?

Ecumenical spirit

Q. On a recent Sunday, in a spirit of ecumenism, our priest delivered a homily at the Baptist church while that minister gave the homily at our church. His homily was on the Trinity. Is this allowed?

A. A priest may preach in any setting, assuming he has the permission of the minister, rabbi, etc. For a non-Catholic minister to preach at a Mass, permission of the Catholic bishop is required. If that was granted, then the action was legitimate.

Alterations

Q. Please give me your opinion regarding the following scenarios. Our new pastor only wears the alb and stole when he celebrates daily Mass. Our deacon claims the *Sacramentary* states that wearing the chasuble for daily Mass is an option. He also claims that Father goes by the book. Other priests who celebrate Mass at our parish always wear the proper vestments. This new priest never purifies the chalice after Communion and fails to recite the Gloria on Sundays. Also, when he recites the eucharistic prayers, he has a tendency to start with Eucharistic Prayer II, and after the consecration continues with III. Plus, when he recites the formula for the consecration over the wine, he adds the words "and then He said" before reciting the words "do this in memory of Me." I like to follow the Mass with my missal, but he makes it such a chore. Our deacon said that after Mass he tells Father when he messes up. One more irritating thing he does is before the lector reads, Father will give an explanation of the readings. Why do we have to have two homilies? Why can't he explain the readings within the context of the regular homily?

A. If your parish priest does everything "by the book," according to your deacon, then why does the same deacon tell him "that he messed up"?

In reality, nearly everything you listed is a violation of the Church's clear liturgical discipline: The chasuble is not optional at any time; the Gloria must be recited on all Sundays (except during Advent and Lent) and on all solemnities; we cannot switch eucharistic prayers in midstream; we cannot add words. One is free to purify the sacred vessels, either directly after Communion or immediately after Mass. While I don't like the wordiness of prepping the congregation for the readings, it is permissible.

"Mass" names

Q. I am a Byzantine-rite Catholic, and I am confused about an article in our diocesan newspaper that read that we should never use the term "Mass" because it is a term that is not in our Tradition. What is the difference between the terms "Mass" and "Divine Liturgy"?

A. The article in question attempts to explain the development of names for the Eucharistic Sacrifice in the early Church, asserting that Eastern-rite Catholics should not use the term "Mass" because it is a "nickname" derived from the dismissal of the Latin rite ("*Ite, missa est*"). The article's treatment of the terms "*Misse*" [sic] and "liturgy" is not totally accurate; a thorough treatment of the terms can be found in the *Catechism of the Catholic Church*.

The *Catechism* explains that Mass (*Missa*) refers to the liturgy concluding "with the sending forth (*missio*) of the faithful, so that they may fulfill God's will in their daily lives" (no. 1332). In other words, the conclusion of the Latin-rite liturgy is not so much a simple dismissal as it is a commission to live the mystery of salvation throughout all the moments of our lives, not just the moments when we are in church. The *Catechism* clarifies this point further by a cross-reference to no. 849, which is on the missionary mandate of the Church.

The *Catechism* explains the term "liturgy" as a "public work" or "service in the name of/on behalf of the people." The word was used in the New Testament to mean divine worship, preaching the Gospel, and active charity (see nos. 1069-1070). Currently, the Eastern rites apply the term "liturgy" only to the Eucharistic Sacrifice, which is called the "Divine Liturgy." In the Latin rite, the term "liturgy" is applied to the Mass (which includes two liturgies — the Liturgy of the Word and the Liturgy of the Eucharist) and the sacraments (see nos. 1097, 1113); the Liturgy of the Hours (nos. 1174-1178); and other celebrations known as sacramentals (such as some blessings, religious professions, exorcisms, etc.) (nos. 1667-1679).

The *Catechism* presents a general treatment of the liturgical diversity among the rites of the Catholic Church in nos. 1200-1209.

Although the term "Mass" derives from a language that is not part of the liturgical tradition of the Eastern rites, its reference to the missionary mandate of the universal Church should make it acceptable as an informal term for the Eucharistic Sacrifice in the Eastern rites.

The author speaks about the "unfortunate" development in the West of the faithful not having access to frequent reception of Holy Communion for centuries. While that is true, that fact had nothing to do with the Eucharistic Sacrifice being called "the Mass." Furthermore, abstinence from Holy Communion was not unique to the West; in truth, that phenomenon was nearly universal and is still very much a part of the landscape of many Eastern-rite communities. Interestingly enough, more frequent reception of Holy Communion among Eastern Catholics is often the result of contact with Latin-rite Catholics!

The bottom line in all this is that, especially within the one family of the Catholic Church, different rites and/or particular churches ought not present their special slant, or bent, as superior to the others; that is surely one lesson we can all take from the Second Vatican Council, which encouraged mutual love and respect among all who claim to be Catholic. A codicil to that is that folks ought to be sure they have the historical facts lined up before they begin to expound on the alleged "history" of a development or phenomenon.

Follow the norms

Q. I understand that the bishops have agreed that in the United States the congregation should kneel throughout the entire eucharistic prayer. If a priest (whether my pastor or a priest in a parish I am visiting) tells us to stand (not giving us an option) during this time (for whatever reason he states), do I have the option to kneel regardless, or should I submit to his directive in a spirit of humility, obedience, or unity?

A. The Church gives us liturgical norms that are to be obeyed by all members of the Church. Any priest who counsels (let alone demands) disobedience is committing a sin, and we know that sinful directives are to be disobeyed. At a logical level, how can a priest expect his people to accept his authority (legitimate or other) when he has rejected the authority of the Church, from whom he receives his authority? Martin Luther discovered this principle in the midst of the Peasant Revolt — to his shock and dismay — and every would-be revolutionary has had to come to grips with it very sadly ever since. As the French say, "The sons of the Revolution are the first to get the guillotine."

St. Vincents

Q. There are three St. Vincents listed in the calendar of saints: St. Vincent de Paul (1660), July 19; St. Vincent Ferrer (1419), April 5; and St. Vincent Pallotti (1850), January 22. Neither in the *Litany of Saints for Ordinations* nor for the *Liturgy of Holy Saturday* do we find mention of a St. Vincent. Can you explain this omission?

A. First off, your Vincent in January is the wrong one: St. Vincent, deacon and martyr, is commemorated on January 22; Vincent Pallotti is not honored in the universal calendar. Second, St. Vincent de Paul is indeed mentioned in the *Litany for Holy Saturday*.

Nonetheless, I do not think that is really the substance of your question. The revised *Litany of Saints* is a pared-down version of other such litanies in history, and clearly envisions the addition of names not formally noted. In other words, the list given is a bare-bones text, to which additional names may be joined, especially if such saints have particular significance for individuals involved in the liturgy or the community celebrating it.

Age limitations?

Q. Our parish has grade-school children acting as eucharistic ministers at Sunday Mass. Can you please advise what the minimum-age requirement for this ministry is, if any, and where I would find that authority?

A. The silliness and lunacy seem to go unabated in certain quarters!

Most dioceses insist that extraordinary ministers of the Eucharist be at least eighteen years of age or are confirmed. There are no universal norms on this matter — although one would expect common sense to prevail.

Tolling the bells

Q. There are two pastors in my town with differing opinions about ringing bells during the consecration at Mass during Lent. One pastor says that bells should not be rung during the consecration at Mass, and does not use bells at his church. The other pastor says bells can be rung during Lent except for Holy Thursday, when a clapper is used. I train the altar servers in one of the parishes, and it is difficult to tell them to do things one way with our pastor and another way with a visiting pastor. What is the correct use of bells during the consecration at Mass?

A. The use of bells at Mass is optional — that is, if the priest is sure that the people will attend to the epiclesis and elevations without them. My pastoral experience leads me to conclude that people do indeed need wake-up calls. However, strictly speaking, it is the decision of the priest-celebrant. The one pastor is correct in saying, however, that bells are not rung from the Gloria of Holy Thursday to the Gloria of Holy Saturday; although the clapper is no longer mentioned in the rubrics, immemorial custom would seem to recommend it.

Adoration

Q. What is the purpose of the elevations of the Host and the chalice at the consecration during Mass?

A. The priest shows the consecrated Elements to the congregation for their adoration, which act he performs immediately thereafter as he genuflects to the Sacred Species.

Distribution rites

Q. My parish has six priests, and I was wondering why the other priests who are not celebrating Mass do not distribute Holy Communion anymore?

A. All available priests are to distribute Holy Communion; that is the clear statement found in *Immensae Caritatis* (Pope Paul VI's document allowing for extraordinary ministers), the *Code of Canon Law*, and the document from the Holy See on lay collaboration in priestly ministry, which is equal in authority to the *Code*.

I suggest you ask your priests the reason for their failure to do what should be the greatest joy of any priest's life.

Justified conditions

Q. I am a priest more than eighty-one years of age but in good health, and I say Mass in a church virtually every day. Traveling by car, the church is not far away, but when there is snow and ice the distance is more difficult. Under what conditions am I allowed to say Mass in my own home, where I live alone?

A. The conditions you identify certainly qualify as justifying causes for private celebrations of Holy Mass.

Life Teen Mass

Q. My question has to do with the Life Teen program in our area. I understand that this program attracts a large number of participants (which would be a positive thing), but I find the LifeTeen Mass very difficult to attend. The teenagers are invited to stand around the altar during the Liturgy of the Eucharist. There is no kneeling, and they stand arms over shoulders as a group. Kids in all manner of dress serve as the extraordinary ministers of the Eucharist. I wonder if they have been through any training program. I make an effort to avoid this Mass, but circumstances sometimes preclude that. Why should a Catholic have to avoid any Mass?

A. While the motivations are, in the main, good behind such events, they are misguided liturgical leftovers from the 1960s, when we thought that "casualness" occasioned intimacy, commitment, and involvement. That experiment was an abysmal failure, so why attempt to resurrect it thirty years later?

Aside from the fact that such Masses reflect an inadequate theological grounding and a poor understanding of adolescent psychology, they are also not permitted by liturgical law. Which goes to the heart of your second question: Why should any Catholic have to endure abuses? The answer is simple: He shouldn't.

Altar servers

Q. I cannot ask this question to my parish priest or bishop because they are liberal. My daughter will be entering fifth grade next fall. She wants to be an altar person. I have heard that the Pope did not actually state that girls could be altar servers. Is this true?

A. No one quite knows what the Pope said or did not say relative to female servers at the altar — at a juridical level. All we know is that a document authorizing the practice was penned by the former prefect for the Congregation for Divine Worship and the Discipline of the Sacraments and that the document never contained explicit notice of papal approval, nor has it been entered into the *Acta Apostolicae Sedis* (Acts of the Apostolic See, in which Vatican legislation is published), which gives all such documents the force of law.

It is important to recall that just because something is permitted does not necessarily say that it is good in general or useful for certain individuals. If you do not want your daughter to serve at the altar, I would never couch that decision in terms of the Pope's personal likes or dislikes; in many ways, that fact (even if we could learn the precise story) is rather immaterial.

When in Rome

Q. In *The Catholic Answer* magazine, your answer to "Illicit, invalid?" invites me to ask for a clarification. You stated: "Leavened bread for the Roman rite is illicit, not invalid." Did you not mean to say "the Latin rite," or has there been a name change of which I am unaware?

A. Historically, there have been differences between the Roman rite and the Latin rite, the former being a particular of the more general latter. Let me explain.

For centuries, the Latin, or Western, Church was united by the use of the Latin language, but great diversity existed in terms of the several ways in which the Mass could be offered — depending on diocese, country, or religious order. Thus we had the Mozarabic and Ambrosian rites (tied to Toledo and Milan, respectively), the Gallican or Sarum rites (used in France and England, respectively), and particular forms used by the Dominicans, or Carthusians, for example.

While many differences existed among these various ways of celebrating the Sacred Liturgy in the Western Church, they all held the use of Latin in common. With the decrees of the Council of Trent, such diversity was greatly circumscribed, due to a concern about the need to restore doctrinal integrity through the liturgy, in the face of the Protestant Reformation. As a result, the

Council Fathers standardized the worship of the Western Church (while allowing for exceptions for those rites that had a heritage extending back two hundred years or more) by making normative the Roman rite — that is, the offering of Holy Mass as done in Rome by the Pope. In essence, then, since that time, to speak of the Roman rite was to use a synonym for the Latin rite.

Since the Second Vatican Council and the admission of the possibility of vernacular celebrations, what should unite the Western Church is Latin as the base for all vernacular translations, Latin for the more common parts of the Mass, and the liturgical form as used in the Diocese of Rome. Hence we find a conflation between Latin and Roman once again.

One final aside. To some degree, we are witnessing a revival of rites within the Western Church, as the Mozarabic rite has been reintroduced into the Diocese of Toledo and the Ambrosian rite has been renewed for Milan. Finally, former Anglican communities that have come into the Catholic Church as a body are entitled to a so-called Anglican use, which is a combination of elements from the Book of Common Prayer, the old Anglican Missal and the contemporary Roman rite.

Power hungry

Q. Your opposition to Communion in the hand goes unabated. Doesn't it dawn on you that you are all alone in such opposition? Wake up and realize that a new Church has dawned in which the "lowly laity" have grown up and no longer need to be fed by the "daddy-figure" some still need to call "Father."

A. Your letter is the best witness I can offer for sustaining my position. You completely construe this issue as one of "maturity" and power. I have repeatedly said that such matters should not even get a blip on the radar screen. We all — clergy and laity alike — are children who need to be fed; that is why, coincidentally, I have noted that in the Tradition not even priests receive Communion in the hand when they are not the celebrants of the Eucharist. We all come before the Lord as beggars — and if that concept is not in place, our reception of Holy Communion loses perspective as it becomes a right rather than a privilege, something I do, more than what God does for me, and to me.

I have not had a fear of being a lone voice on any topic, so long as I am convinced that the position is correct — that is, consonant with Catholic life and practice down through the ages. In addition, warning signals have gone off from several sectors on Communion in the hand: in Pope John Paul II's *Dominicae Cenae* (on the mystery and worship of the Eucharist, 1980); in the pastoral letter of Bishop William Weigand of Sacramento, which we reprinted in *The Catholic Answer* magazine (May/June 1998); in the recently issued pastoral of Bishop Thomas Doran of Rockford, Ill. Add to that the ongoing testimony of all too many priests and laity who continue to see the negative effects flowing from this practice.

Shining forth

Q. For our parish's Easter Vigil, we did not have any candles. I mean the people didn't get candles to start off the Easter Vigil. Is that permissible or not?

A. I suppose your pastor was afraid that the congregation would drip wax all over the church! Ideally, everyone ought to receive a candle, for only in that way does the symbolism truly shine forth (pun intended) — that is, the light of Christ from the paschal candle is diffused throughout the nave of the church, just as it is supposed to happen in the world.

Perhaps next year you could suggest that your priest charge a "dripping fee" to cover the expense of clean-up from careless candleholders.

Indult, not a right

Q. Bishop Pierre DuMaine's recent refusal to allow the traditional Latin Mass to San Jose, Calif., Catholics (article enclosed) has left me extremely agitated. If I could afford to, I would purchase a full-page advertisement exposing his deceit to the Catholics of San Jose. So, I am asking you to address this issue as to the truth of the status of the traditional Latin Mass.

A. I am no fan of the so-called Tridentine Mass indult. According to the decree of Pope John Paul II (Ecclesia Dei), bishops are empowered to permit the former rite of the Mass to be used — according to their own pastoral discretion. There is no papal mandate for this, nor do the faithful have any kind of "right" to this option.

As I have indicated before, an indult (canonically speaking) is what we might call "grudging permission." In practical terms, that means that the Pope is saying that he doesn't really think this is a good idea but, to avoid a greater problem, he will allow this. If the Holy Father were really gung-ho on the Tridentine Mass, he would have simply said that any priest could celebrate it at any time for any group for any reason — which he clearly could have done, but which also he clearly did not do. Therefore, the inescapable conclusion is that this is but a fatherly concession on his part, providing local bishops with the capacity to respond to requests (not demands) as they deem pastorally appropriate.

Now, I am going to get myself into the mode for receiving dozens of nasty letters from both ends of the spectrum when I say the following, but I'll do it anyway, because it's the truth. If devotees of the former liturgical forms want to comprehend the nature of an indult, the best example I can give is Communion in the hand, which is also granted by way of indult. Pope Paul VI tolerated this abuse and conceded to it by an indult, having said that it is a very bad idea, but one which he would countenance, lest greater evils occur. No one has a right to this — it is totally at the discretion of the diocesan bishop — just as is the case with the Tridentine Mass.

Communion in the hand

Q. I have read *The Catholic Answer* magazine for several years and have come to understand your position against receiving Holy

Communion in the hand. I realized that this practice started without papal permission, although the Holy Father finally agreed to allow this practice. (I am reminded of the two-year-old child who has a tantrum because he doesn't get what he wants and, finally, the father gives in to have the screaming and kicking stopped. The practice, as every two-year-old knows, is very effective.) I was in total agreement with you until I took the words of Jesus literally, "Take and eat. . . ." My life has not been the same since. I became aware that I was holding Jesus, my God, in my hands. I was holding Him, Who holds the stars, the sun, and moon in His hands. I became aware that God has made me a very special person because of this realization. He humbled Himself even further to allow me, a sinner, to hold Him in my hands and receive Him in my heart. I think that everyone who receives Him worthily is very special. I wish they realized it. Comments?

A. The first point to realize is that liturgy is not mimicry — that is, there are many instances in the Mass when the words do not coincide precisely with the actions, or vice versa. For example, in the consecratory formula for the bread, the priest says that Jesus took the bread, "broke it and gave it to His disciples." One is not supposed to break the Host at that time; that action is delayed until the *Agnus Dei*, for important liturgical and theological reasons.

Second, Jesus' words at the Last Supper were directed to His apostles, the first priests. Even at that, however, it is doubtful that they "communicated" by hand, since an ancient Middle Eastern tradition (still extant) calls for the host of a dinner to place the first morsel of food directly into the mouths of his guests.

Third, as I have said repeatedly, that while the practice of Communion in the hand is not heretical, it certainly undermines the doctrine of the Real Presence and that of the ordained priesthood. On that score, it is an unwise and pastorally naive practice. Liturgical gestures are not designed to make us feel good, important, or happy; they are intended to reinforce doctrine. Anyone who is properly catechized ought to know that he is known and loved by God, independent of the mode of Communion reception.

"Stick to the book"

Q. I would like you to comment on the following. On Palm Sunday, the long Gospel was read by three lay people and one priest, with each taking a part — that is, narrator, crowd, Peter, and the priest reading the words of Jesus. This was done while the congregation was standing. Holy Thursday centered more on the washing of the feet than on the Eucharist. Not only was there the washing of the feet on the altar, but then the priest and deacon proceeded down the center aisle washing a few more. Then the entire congregation proceeded to the four corners of the church and washed one anothers' hands. In my early years, it was all about the First Communion at the Last Supper — times change. The Liturgy of the Word was done by two lay readers. Each took turns after reading a couple of paragraphs. They started with the first reading, continued onto the Gospel and finished with the second reading. There was no delineation between readings, just one long narrative that we listened to while seated. We could not stand for the Gospel since it was not announced, and the priest just sat there listening. Upon entering the church that evening, I was under the impression that I was entering a high school assembly hall before the bell had rung. The chatter was deafening, and people were flitting about visiting with one another. It is nice to get to church a little early and quietly contemplate. Usually, one's train of thought is broken by someone stopping by to say hello — this sometimes includes members of the clergy.

A. Your description of the reading of the Passion on Palm Sunday sounds correct. Everything else was off-base in one way or another. Once again, I find myself returning to a theme that will undoubtedly earn me the nickname of "one-note Pete," but it's the most important theme possible: "Stick to the book, Father."

"Stick to the book, Father," because the liturgy is not your own; it is the possession of the whole Church, and you have no right to rob the people of their liturgical inheritance or to impose your idiosyncrasies on them.

372   The CATHOLIC ANSWER BOOK 4

"Stick to the book, Father," because to do otherwise is to engage in a particularly subtle but equally reprehensible brand of clericalism.

"Stick to the book, Father," because that's what you're paid to do!

Perfectly all right

Q. When receiving the Host, I have always stepped aside, turned back to the altar, and blessed myself prior to returning to my seat. While attending Mass at a Catholic church I was visiting, at the end of the Mass the priest made a general comment about blessing yourself after receiving the Host — namely, "It should not be done." Have I been wrong all of these years?

A. There is no requirement one way or the other about making the Sign of the Cross after the reception of Holy Communion. I find it rather odd that, in recent years, we encounter some priests and "liturgists" who get so exercised over various devotional practices which, as you indicated, have existed for decades or even centuries. Let's get our priorities straight: first, making sure that the folks in the sanctuary are doing everything correctly, and second, ensuring that the folks in the pews understand and accept the doctrine of Christ's Real Presence in the Eucharist. Then, we might be in some kind of position to worry about lesser matters.

Liturgical directives

Q. I'm a fairly recent convert (Protestant background), and do a lot of reading to learn more about the Catholic Church. I'm friendly with a woman from my church, who recently attended a liturgy workshop. She mentioned three points brought out by a priest who conducted part of the workshop. These were: (1) The reserved consecrated Hosts are no longer supposed to be kept in a tabernacle, and that churches should no longer have a tabernacle. The Hosts are to be kept in the sacristy. (2) Churches are not supposed to have statues any longer, stating that these and items like Advent wreaths are distractions. (3) Churches should not have side altars any longer, just the main altar. Could you please comment on these and give references to official Church documents that apply?

A. On the first two points, the speaker was incorrect. The *Code of Canon* Law indicates that the Blessed Sacrament is to be reserved in a tabernacle located in a spot that is "prominent, conspicuous, beautifully decorated, and suitable for prayer" (Canon 938.2). The Second Vatican Council's Constitution on the Sacred Liturgy (*Sacrosanctum Concilium*) highlights the importance of statues and images in churches: "The practice of placing sacred images in churches so that they be venerated by the faithful is to be maintained" (no. 125). On the matter of side altars, there is no document calling for their abolition if they are already in place, however, new constructions ought to have only one altar to ensure a proper focus and to bring out the unity of the Mass, symbolized by the one altar.

If that speaker ever returns, your friend ought to offer him a scholarship to the liturgy program at San Anselmo in Rome.

Rubrics

Q. This is what our pastor thought of your answer on kneeling: "What a wonderfully wrong answer based on the answerer's own prejudices! He violates the very principle he refers to — namely, liturgical norms. The GIRM (*General instruction of the Roman Missal*), no. 21, states: 'For the sake of uniformity in movement and posture the people should follow the directions given during the celebration by the deacon, the priest, or another minister. . . .' Another incorrect point of the answer is to say that liturgical norms (rubrics) must be followed under the pain of sin. Priests of my vintage learned in moral theology that rubrics have no moral content, so that there is objectively no sin in ignoring, omitting, changing, etc., a rubric nor is there any virtue in meticulously observing them — and this was in the 'old' Church (before the Second Vatican Council)! Disregarding all the rubrics, it was said, might be a sin because then one would no longer have the liturgy of the Church but a personal cult. On the other hand, giving rubrics the weight of the Ten Commandments, we were warned, could lead to Phariseeism [sic], and the Gospels were quite clear on what the Lord thought about that."

A. Poor monsignor needs a refresher course in moral theology. Deliberately to disobey the Church is a sin — venial or mortal — and to argue that in the "old days" this was not the case is to fail seriously in memory or to be disingenuous. Indeed, whole sections of the old manuals of moral theology dealt with the moral status of violating rubrics. Furthermore, he hits the nail on the head when he speaks of disobedience to rubrics being connected to a "personal cult."

Tridentine action

Q. I still use my old St. Joseph's Daily Missal, in which we are told to kneel, starting at the Holy, Holy, Holy, until the reception of Holy Communion and until the chalice is cleansed and put away. This also includes the Lamb of God. I feel that it is most reverent to kneel specifically then. But now we don't kneel until after this is said. Is it wrong to kneel then during this prayer, as my old missalette allows?

A. If you are not attending a Tridentine Mass, I don't know why you would be using a Tridentine missal. While the differences between the so-called Tridentine Mass and that of Pope Paul VI are not very substantial (contrary to what some on both extremes hold), the changes are enough to warrant investing in a new missal since there is an official English translation of the Mass (although rather poor) and an expanded *Lectionary*. Furthermore, liturgical actions correspond to the prayers they accompany; if those prayers are no longer there, trying to use old actions makes no sense. Beyond that, what many people do not realize is that the Tridentine rite really had no rubrics for the posture of the lay faithful; postures grew up out of custom. Finally, since the Sacred Liturgy is an action of the whole Church, and not of isolated individuals, it is important for the faithful to follow the directives of the universal Church in this regard. Otherwise, we end up attracting attention to our idiosyncrasies, rather than participating in a unified act of worship.

Word of the Lord?

Q. Why do we say, "Word of the Lord" (we've dropped the definite article "The," I've noticed) at the end of each reading, when clearly it was one of the prophets or St. Paul who happens to be quoted? Would it not make better sense to simply say, "End of the reading"?

A. You seem to have two questions here.

The first is simple to handle. We now say, "The Word of the Lord" ("the" is still in there), instead of "This is the Word of the Lord," because it is a better, more accurate translation of the Latin original, *"Verbum Domini."*

The second phase of your question almost sounds like a denial of the biblical doctrine of divine inspiration and inerrancy. The Church teaches that the ultimate author of every biblical work is God Himself, Who deigned to use human instruments. In using weak and fallible persons, however, God safeguarded the process of revelation by preserving them from error as they communicated His message of salvation. Therefore, the Word they spoke/wrote was not theirs, but God's. Hence, "The Word of the Lord."

Practically applied

Q. A priest was giving a talk about traditions of our faith and how some are not heavenly inspired (my words). As an example, he used the practice of adding water to wine at the consecration at Mass. He said the reason this tradition started was because the wine (supposedly, in the early days of the Church) was so bad, so bitter, that the water was added to make the wine more palatable. Is this a fact? I have never heard this explanation. I thought the water was added because as the Bible states, when the soldier pierced the side of Our Lord on the Cross, "blood and water" issued forth. What's the Catholic answer?

A. First, a correction. Water is added to wine not at the consecration of the Mass, but at the preparation of the gifts.

Not every ritual act of the Sacred Liturgy is "heavenly inspired." Some have very practical purposes, while others have both a practical and mystical significance. Your priest is essentially correct in saying that in ancient times water was added to wine to dilute it. That very natural and common practice then took on added meaning in one of two ways. As you suggest, it was seen as a "harking back" to Calvary when blood and water flowed from the side of the Redeemer. It has more often been interpreted as a sign of the mixture of the two natures in Christ and our entrance into Divinity through the Holy Eucharist. This is certainly the preferred understanding, since the prayer that accompanies the action alludes to this truth: "May we come to share in the Divinity of Christ, Who humbled Himself to share in our humanity."

No tinkering

Q. Our parish had a newly ordained priest assigned, and when he would say Mass he would not perform the hand-washing ceremony (he would send the altar servers back to the table with the water and the towel). Is this allowed, or do we need to advise someone about this practice? Also another young priest, at the consecration, instead of saying "from East to West" said, "from the rising of the sun to its setting." Is that permissible?

A. The washing of hands is not optional.

The prayer to which you allude is not the consecration, but is part of Eucharistic Prayer III. While your young priest's version is a more accurate rendering of the original Latin text, it is not permissible to tinker with the official texts — even when they are not that great! Let's hope and pray we shall see better translations on the horizon.

It is so

Q. Your definition of an indult in *The Catholic Answer* magazine both surprised and amused me. I had never heard that there were "grudging permission" aspects to the meaning. Would you comment, then, on the indult given American bishops concerning kneeling during the Communion prayer, from the Holy, Holy, Holy to the Great Amen? As I understand it, Catholics in the rest of the world stand during this time, except during the consecration. If it was grudging permission, why was it requested? Or, more importantly, perhaps, why was it granted?

A. First off, you mean "eucharistic prayer," not "Communion prayer."

That noted, let me say that I believe the Holy See would have preferred if the American bishops had accepted the posture of the universal Church. At that time, as I have mentioned before, many liturgists wanted the people to stand for the entire eucharistic prayer, with no kneeling at any point. The Holy See would not agree to that. Those same liturgists did not want to have the people kneel only for the epiclesis and consecration since, in their estimation, that drew too much attention to those parts of the Mass (which, of course, is the very reason why the universal rubrics call for that posture). They convinced the bishops to petition for an indult from universal practice — which was granted.

So, yes, that indult was also "grudging permission."

Moment of disrespect

Q. I'm writing this letter with a heavy heart after being snubbed by a parish priest. I have been reading your magazine for years now and have heard you say that it is compulsory to kneel during the consecration. Most of the churches in and around Seattle have been told to stand. However, several of us never do. I decided to confront the priest after seeing in the bulletin the article entitled, "Standing During the Eucharistic Prayer." I showed him your question-and-answer book and pointed to the page about this subject. He quickly handed it back and refused to read it because it had no imprimatur on it. He then walked away rudely. I am seventy years old and have never been so rudely treated by a priest. What shall I do? Shall I inform the archbishop of Seattle about this?

A. Your priest ought to know that magazines do not get an imprimatur; rather, they are published "with ecclesiastical permission," which is the case with *The Catholic Answer* magazine, which is published by Our Sunday Visitor. What is amusing in a bizarre sort of way is that he tried to find a loophole to evade the truth of my assertion — just as he has tried to find loopholes in liturgical law to justify his own aberrant practice.

I would confront him respectfully and charitably about his unauthorized liturgical norms and about his rudeness. Receiving anything less than a respectful hearing in return and a change in practice, I would enlist the aid of the archbishop.

Meditation

Q. I would like to offer considerations about two questions appearing in an issue of *The Catholic Answer* magazine. The first concerns the failure of an Illinois parish to use candles during the Easter Vigil. This similar issue arose in many churches in our area a few years ago because fire officials expressed safety concerns and noted that it is illegal to have "open" flames in buildings used for public assembly. The second question concerned praying the Rosary at Mass. Being not too talented on extemporaneous prayer, I frequently recite part of the Rosary during the time of meditation after Communion. I offer the prayers said in sorrow, as penance, and in thanksgiving for the gifts received. I find praying the Rosary at that time helps keep me focused. On the lighter side, the late Cardinal Richard Cushing, archbishop of Boston, told a story about his mother noticing that he was picking his nose in church when he was a boy. She told him that that was not the thing to do, and told him to pray the Rosary. Then he went to seminary. When he was found saying the Rosary after Communion, he was told that that was not the thing to do. He should use a missal. Then came the Second Vatican Council, after which some people were told not to use missals at Mass (of course, in complete contradiction of that Council's teachings). "So," said the cardinal, "I am back to picking my nose!"

A. Thanks for all three of your insights!

Changed Gospel

Q. On Sunday, September 27, 1998, at the Mass, the Gospel was about a rich man and beggar. The priest, our pastor, decided to make it a rich "woman" and the beggar, and had a woman read "the rich man's" comments and a man read "Abraham's" comments. Is such a thing allowed? I always thought that the Gospel can only be read by a priest or deacon. Listening to this got me so angry that I whispered to my wife that "this guy, our priest, is an idiot," and being in that state of mind I could not receive Communion. Am I being too critical? By the way, I have had problems with this priest before, with his "liberal politically correct" homilies, method of delivery and his union "no scab newspaper" signs in front of the parish rectory and on rectory doors.

A. The only time (aside from children's Masses) when a "dramatic" rendering of the Gospel is possible is on Palm Sunday and Good Friday. So, what your priest did was indeed wrong. That having been said, try not to get yourself into such a state that you also sin through anger or resentment.

Elemental norms

Q. Please assist with advice as to how to proceed in stopping the diocesan-condoned use of Welch's white grape juice for the Mass! Please advise as to whether or not anyone could have permission to use this (I know it is not wine, or *mustum*); if not, with one of the three required elements missing, aren't the Mass and Communion invalid? Wouldn't those attending such a "service" (not Mass) be idol-worshiping, once advised that only bread and wine were present after the consecration? The remainder of unconsecrated Hosts being placed into the tabernacle would thereby "bread-contaminate" the rest. After contacting the rectory by phone and letter, and receiving no response, I contacted the diocesan office of catechesis and worship, which assured me that there has been permission granted, but cannot suggest where that permission's validity was grounded.

A. In 1995, a response came from Cardinal Joseph Ratzinger's dicastery (his offices at the Vatican), which I reproduce in its entirety; please note that it also includes material on valid matter for the eucharistic bread as well (since we get many inquiries on that topic, too).

"After careful study, conducted in collaboration with a number of concerned Episcopal Conferences, this Congregation and its ordinary session of June 22,1994, has approved the following norms, which I am pleased to communicate:

"I. Concerning permission to use low-gluten altar breads:

"A. This may be granted by Ordinaries to priests and laypersons affected by celiac disease, after presentation of a medical certificate.

"B. Conditions for the validity of the matter:
1) 'Special Hosts *quibus glutinum ablatum est* [from which gluten has been removed] are valid matter for the celebration of the Eucharist;
2) 'Low-gluten Hosts are valid matter, provided that there is no addition of foreign materials, and that the procedure for making such Hosts is not such as to alter the nature of the substance of the bread.'

"II. Concerning permission to use *mustum* [for the priest-celebrant]:

"A. The preferred solution continues to be *Communion per intinctionem*, or in concelebration under the species of bread alone.

"B. Nevertheless, the permission to use *mustum* can be granted by Ordinaries to priests affected by alcoholism or other conditions which prevent the ingestion of even the smallest quantity of alcohol, after presentation of a medical certificate.

"C. By *mustum* is understood fresh juice from grapes, or juice preserved by suspending its fermentation (by means of freezing or other methods which do not alter its nature).

"D. In general, those who have received permission to use *mustum* are prohibited from presiding at concelebrated Masses. There may be some exceptions however: in the case of a bishop or superior general; or, with prior approval of the bishop, at the celebration of the anniversary of priestly ordination or other similar occasions. In these cases, the one who presides is to communicate under both species of bread and that of *mustum*, while for the other concelebrants a chalice shall be provided in which normal wine is to be consecrated.

"E. In the very rare instances of laypersons requesting this permission, recourse must be made to the Holy See.

"III. Common Norms:

"A. The Ordinary must ascertain that the matter used conforms to the above requirements.

"B. Permission is to be given only for as long as the situation continues which motivated the request.

"C. Scandal is to be avoided.

"D. Given the centrality of the celebration of the Eucharist in the life of the priest, candidates for the priesthood who are affected by celiac disease or suffer from alcoholism or similar conditions may not be admitted to Holy Orders.

"E. Since the doctrinal questions have now been decided, disciplinary competence is entrusted to the Congregation for Divine Worship and the Discipline of the Sacraments.

"F. Concerned Episcopal Conferences shall report to the Congregation for Divine Worship and the Discipline of the Sacraments every two years regarding the application of these norms."

Use of invalid matter makes for an invalid sacrament. People attending such a service do not really participate in a Mass, but God can surely communicate to them the graces they would have received had they been present at a valid Eucharist — since this situation has occurred through no fault of their own. And, for the same reason, one could not say they were engaged in "idol worship." What you describe needs to be brought to the attention of the bishop himself; if he takes no action, the nuncio should be contacted in Washington or the Congregation for Divine Worship and the Discipline of the Sacraments in Rome.

Communion Service

Q. Somewhere along the line I read an authoritative quote from Canon Law that weekly Communion services were not to be held in a parish that had at least one regular weekly Mass available. Our parish has five daily and four weekend Masses, yet persists in having a Communion service each Tuesday morning (when Mass is at 5:30 in the afternoon). Is this not a no-no?

A. The controlling document from the Holy See is "Directory for Sunday Celebrations in the Absence of a Priest," issued in 1988. Since then, these supposedly exceptional celebrations have proliferated to an unbelievable degree, so much so that even bishops well-disposed toward them have begun to raise serious concerns. Regarding these ceremonies on Sundays, we note this prohibition: "Therefore a gathering or assembly of this kind can never be held on a Sunday in places where Mass has already been celebrated or is to be celebrated or was celebrated on the preceding Saturday evening, even if the Mass is celebrated in a different language. Nor is it right to have more than one assembly of this kind on any given Sunday." What about weekdays? The controlling document here is "The Worship and Reception of Holy Communion outside of Mass," and although the matter of such services on weekdays in churches where Mass is offered daily is not directly addressed, we can make a logical application of the Sunday document to give a negative judgment. If the Church will not allow such a service on a Sunday because the Eucharist has already been celebrated (or will be) and there is a necessity for such, how can one justify such a service when no necessity exists? A task force of bishops has been appointed to deal with abuses.

Clearly defined

Q. I cannot understand why at the injunction in the Creed where we recall the Incarnation, that none of our celebrants bows his head, genuflects, or just even makes the Sign of the Cross. Since I usually sit in the front row, do you think I should genuflect so that others might follow? I hate to call attention to myself, so I haven't been. What do you think?

A. The rubrics are quite clear as to what is to be done by all — priest and people — at the line of the Creed recalling the Incarnation: All are to "bow," we read, except on March 25 (the Annunciation) and Dec. 25 (Christmas), when all are to "genuflect."

Whether or not your priests do this, you should, but you shouldn't be doing something other than what is called for — for example, the Sign of the Cross.

The Answer Is . . .

Q. At our mission parish in California, we have many visiting priests and each is unique. Please comment on which of the following variations of blessing the wine and water is (are) correct? (1) The priest blesses both before accepting them from the gift bearers. (2) The priest blesses only the wine before taking it from the server. (3) The priest blesses only the water before taking it from the server. (4) The priest appears to bless both before taking the wine and then the water from the server. (5) The priest does not bless either.

A. The rubrics call for no blessing of either water or wine; therefore, none is to be done.

More bad news

Q. Please evaluate two practices performed at LifeTeen Masses. (1) Singing a Creed which leaves out: "conceived by the Holy Spirit," "Virgin" (referring to the Virgin Mary), "Pontius Pilate," and "He shall come to judge the living and the dead." The excuse given is that there is musical license, and so the Nicene Creed does not have to be sung word for word. (2) Teens and others are called to stand all around the altar at the time of consecration. This disobedience to our bishops led to two teenage girls breaking the Body of Christ, instead of the priest.

A. Another letter from another dissatisfied customer. Of course, everything you speak of is categorically forbidden.

Cup optional

Q. We have had a change of priests this past summer. He is changing everything. He recruits in our bulletin for greeters and Precious Blood ministers for every Mass. He stated, "If we pass by the cup of the Covenant, we have to ask ourselves: 'Do I really believe?'" I am seventy years old and not keen about drinking from this common cup. Will you please comment?

A. How can what is an option become a mandate, let alone an acid test of one's belief in the Holy Eucharist? Is your priest equally upset with people who fail to make the proper reverence before receiving Holy Communion? If not, he ought to get his priorities in order; after all, the first instance involves, as I said, an option; the second, a clear mandate. Feel free to follow your instincts on the matter at hand; no pressure should be exerted on you in any way in this regard.

Vigil after sunset

Q. One of the parishes in this area had Masses this past Holy Saturday at 3 p.m. and 4:30 p.m. When the pastor was questioned on this, he said he had talked to the local bishop and it was all right because it was a "pastoral necessity," since it would be impossible for some people to get to Mass otherwise. He also has the Risen Christ on the processional Cross, saying this is the way it was done in early Christianity. Would you please comment on these two things?

A. More than ten years ago, the Holy See issued a circular letter on the rites of Holy Week and clearly indicated that the Easter Vigil cannot take place before sunset, which usually occurs around 8 p.m. in most places. Furthermore, the Bishops' Committee on the Liturgy in Washington sends out an annual reminder about this point, as do most diocesan liturgical commissions. The local bishop has no authority to dispense from this requirement — allowing a daytime celebration of the Easter Vigil does tremendous violence to the meaning and integrity of the service.

The image of the Risen Christ can be used on a Cross, but I think it inadvisable from a number of angles, including both theology and psychology. To argue for a practice simply on the basis of its having been done in the early Church is an example of the "antiquarianism," condemned by Pope Pius XII in *Mediator Dei* (on the Sacred Liturgy). In other words, the value of something is not necessarily determined by its age: Bad things were done in the "old" days, and good things can be done nowadays. Furthermore, when people tell me that they want to do something because it was done in the early Church, I always ask them if they would like to return to the whole "package" from the early Church — like the Sacrament of Penance once in a lifetime; public confession and lifelong penance; etc. In shorthand form, what I'm trying to say is that, of course, we always pick and choose, but it is just a bit silly and/or dishonest to say that I am choosing something only because it was done in the early Church. Intelligent Catholics have more substantial criteria than that — or should.

Last blessing

Q. Is it liturgically correct and permissible for the priest to directly leave the altar, at the end of Mass, after cleaning the altar, and not provide or give the solemn or last blessing?

A. The only time that a dismissal and blessing do not end the Mass is when another service follows immediately — for example, if the Blessed Sacrament is being exposed for adoration. Otherwise, the blessing has an integral place in every Mass. I must say that I have never heard of that aberration before!

Corporal's use

Q. As I prepared to substitute for the sacristan of my local parish while she was out of town, she was showing me how to check the corporal and she found two particles of the Host that had been left from a funeral Mass that morning. I was upset that Our Lord had been left on the altar all that time, and she said it rarely happened. I asked if she would mention it to the priest, and she said it is something that a priest doesn't notice, but that I was welcome to tell him. Two mornings later, I found another. So I left a little note, folded up, for the pastor, asking him to please check the corporal after Mass. The next day I saw the parochial vicar after Mass and spoke to him. He told me that in theology class he learned that if a eucharistic particle is not recognizable as a piece of bread, Christ is not fully present; then, however, he appeared to deny that by saying that the corporal was there to catch any tiny pieces of Host that fell. If Christ is not present in tiny particles, then why is there a corporal at all? He also said that in charity I should not have left the note for the pastor, as he is reverent toward the Blessed Sacrament and, in effect, knows what he is doing. Father, could you address the vicar's assertion of the presence of Christ being only in "recognizable" bread? And was I right in leaving a note for the pastor? Is there anything further I should do?

A. The first point to make is that a corporal is not supposed to be left spread out on the altar. The *General Instruction of the Roman Missal* makes it clear that the altar is to be prepared at the preparation of the gifts; part of that process involves opening the corporal. Similarly, the post-Communion rite for ablution of the sacred vessels indicates that the corporal should be folded up and put aside with the chalice when that rite is completed. Therefore, the question of loose particles ought not even to occur.

Your parochial vicar's point is correct that particles need to be recognizable, but if they are recognizable as particles, it is obviously as bread particles and, therefore, as the Holy Eucharist. After all, what else could they be? Do we make pizzas or croissants during Mass? Hardly. His response, then, begs the question. And, yes, I think you were right in bringing the matter to your pastor's attention. You didn't say if any change has occurred.

An "honest" Church

Q. Can non-Catholic children serve as altar servers? This is happening in my parish, and I was told by the diocesan office to confront the parish priest. So I did, and he said that we had to be an open Church, and that there was no position, except ordained positions, that a non-Catholic person could not fill.

A. Liturgical roles are not open to non-Catholics, except by explicit permission of the local bishop. Various liturgical ministries can be exercised by the non-ordained, but the law of the Church makes clear that these are available to "the faithful" — one who is not a Catholic in good standing is not one of "the faithful." And so, if the person in question is not a Catholic at all, or is impeded from the reception of the sacraments for some reason — for example, divorce and remarriage — that person cannot function liturgically. This has nothing to do with being an "open" or "closed" Church; it has to do with being an "honest" Church, in which reality is taken seriously.

Communion distribution

Q. Enclosed please find an article by a Jesuit that appeared in *Liturgy 90* (January 1999), "Should Father Come over from the Rectory to Give Communion?" He seems to say the exact opposite of what you say and, also, the opposite of what I think the Holy See is saying about the use of extraordinary ministers of the Eucharist. Would you comment?

A. Since I never get a copy of the magazine in question because of so many problematic approaches it takes, I did not see the article you sent until then. This is what happens when you tie yourself too closely to a particular age — something about which Archbishop Fulton Sheen warned us decades ago.

Now, to your specific question. The author plays very loose with history, canon law, liturgical norms, etc. He also has that unhappy faculty of constructing a straw man or a caricature and then, with everything reduced to the level of the ridiculous, going on to recreate his own reality. For instance, he makes fun of situations in "the old days," whereby priests followed the course of the Mass on speakers in the rectory, so that they could come over in time to assist with the distribution of Holy Communion. Is he happier now that the priests are not in the least bit involved or interested in doing what they were ordained to do and in having contact with their people at the peak moment of Catholic life each week? Is he aware of the absurdity of priests vying for the earliest Masses, so that they can disappear for the rest of the day? Does it make sense to him that in all too many parishes, while priests are not assigned (or even permitted) to assist with Holy Communion, they are assigned to church exits to greet the people as they leave?

He notes, correctly, that the *General Instruction* forbids priests from joining in a concelebration if they are late. From that, he argues that priests should not come into a Mass in progress simply to distribute Holy Communion. Where does that norm come from? All the documents that treat the topic of the use of extraordinary ministers — (*Immensæ Caritatis* [on facilitating reception of Communion in certain circumstances], *Inaestimabile Donum* [instruction concerning worship of the eucharistic mystery], and the 1997 interdicasterial document on lay collaboration in priestly ministry, etc.) — all of them presume that every ordained minister who is morally available will be "doing his job." Morally available means that if he has the means to fulfill his ministry, he will do it; no document stipulates or even hints at the fact that a priest or deacon must be present for an entire liturgical celebration in order to fulfill his ministry in a fitting way. In fact, in *Christifideles Laici* (on the role of the lay faithful), Pope John Paul II speaks specifically of the importance of better pastoral planning as a way of ensuring that priests can be engaged to do what they should, rather than reliance on laity to perform priestly roles.

The author expresses displeasure with the idea that someone who would distribute the Eucharist would not likewise receive the Host at that same celebration. Why? If he has already done so, there is certainly no need to do it again — apparently just for show. Furthermore, the thinking behind this objection is very muddled — theologically — as it seems to forget that there is really only one Eucharist, in which we all share in different times and places.

The bottom line, which the author never cites and which he and anyone else who thinks like him must come to grips with, is the stark statement in the 1997 document of the Holy See on lay collaboration. It says simply that the regular use of the non-ordained for the distribution of Holy Communion at Mass is to be "eliminated." It is not a highly nuanced statement and thus fairly easy for anyone to interpret — that is, if that person is truly open to what the Church says she wants done.

Extended hands

Q. Are concelebrants obliged to extend their hands at the consecration? Is the Mass valid if they do not do so?

A. The norms indicate that a concelebrant should extend his hands in the same gesture as the principal celebrant for the epiclesis (the invocation of the Holy Spirit on the gifts of bread and wine), a single hand in the same gesture during the consecration of each element, raised hands (like the principal celebrant, again) for the anamnesis, or prayer of remembrance, following the consecration. These actions are not always possible, especially if the priest needs to rely on a booklet for the text of the eucharistic prayer. Ideally, they should be performed, but failure to perform them would never invalidate one's Mass. I should mention, however, that recitation of the consecratory formula is certainly required.

Church divisions

Q. The divisions in the Church just seem to get worse by the day. Even Our Sunday Visitor looks like a "house divided." I am referring to the fact that you (writing for *The Catholic Answer* magazine) and Msgr. M. Francis Mannion (writing for Our Sunday Visitor) give conflicting answers to questions that should have black and white answers. Case in point: Recently, someone asked Msgr. Mannion what she should do in her parish when the priest instructs the congregation to remain standing during the eucharistic prayer. His response? Don't be different; stand, even though you shouldn't be! You, of course, have been saying the exact opposite for years. What's up here?

A. Let's set the stage a bit, especially for the benefit of those walking in on this discussion.

Yes, we both write for the same parent corporation — Our Sunday Visitor. And, on matters of substance, we are in agreement. Indeed, in the present case, Msgr. Mannion noted clearly that liturgical law requires the faithful to kneel from the ends of the *Sanctus* to the conclusion of the eucharistic prayer. He and I part company on his application of that law, and I disagree with him very strongly on this point. The rest of my answer will endeavor to explain why.

A priest is the servant of the liturgy and of the people. He has no right to impose his idiosyncrasies on either. Furthermore, at ordination, he was deputed to celebrate the Sacred Liturgy according to the rites approved by the Church; in fact, one of his ordination promises deals specifically with this matter. Therefore, when a priest "does his own thing," liturgically, he is — let's say it up-front — committing sin: the sin of disobedience and the sin of reneging on his solemn word given in the midst of the Church on the day of his ordination. Sinning is bad enough on one's own, but to cajole others into cooperation and even to browbeat them into it is even worse, which is exactly what a priest does when he pressures a congregation to ignore or defy liturgical law.

Yet another sin is involved, and that is one against the unity of the Church. The unity of the Church should never be more apparent or visible than during the celebration of the Sacred Liturgy. When a priest consciously leads people into disunity, he fails in a distressingly mighty way to be the shepherd of unity for Christ's flock. For him to disobey legitimate ecclesiastical authority and then to demand the local community to obey him is perverse.

Finally, nearly every liturgical aberration has begun in just this manner. Liturgical law clearly said one thing; individual priests did otherwise; they were corrected repeatedly; they continued on their own way; little by little, Church authority got tired of the fight and said little or nothing anymore; eventually, the dissenters pressured Church authority into "canonizing" their disobedience.

As I hope you can see by now, the fundamental issue here has many ramifications and cannot be reduced to a simplistic question of standing versus kneeling or of not making oneself different from the rest of the liturgical assembly. And I suspect Msgr. Mannion would concur in my judgment, when everything is placed in that larger context.

Good Friday service

Q. I am a recent convert to Catholicism, so perhaps you'll understand my confusion. On Good Friday this year, just before the liturgy began, the priest announced to the congregation that "this is the one day of the year when the Sacrifice of the Mass is not celebrated." Yet we had a Liturgy of the Word, followed by Holy Communion. Was this not a Mass, albeit with the additional rite of venerating the Cross?

A. No, it was not a Mass. A Mass consists of the Liturgy of the Word and the Liturgy of the Eucharist, with the latter containing three parts (presentation of the gifts, eucharistic prayer, Communion rite). The Good Friday service is comprised of four parts: Liturgy of the Word; General Intercessions; Veneration of the Cross; Communion rite. The missing element to make it a Mass is the eucharistic prayer, during which the bread and wine are consecrated. Traditionally, the Eucharistic Sacrifice has never been offered on Good Friday and, until recently, Communion was not even received (which is still the case in most of the Eastern rites of the Church).

Your legitimate confusion is compounded by two other factors. First, the old name for this service was "the Mass of the Pre-sanctified," referring to the fact that the Hosts distributed on Good Friday were consecrated the night before during the Holy Thursday Mass of the Lord's Supper (actually, in the Byzantine rite, on the Wednesdays and Fridays of Lent, the Liturgy of the Pre-sanctified is celebrated, which is Vespers and Communion). Second, the priest who presides at the Good Friday liturgy wears a chasuble (the vestment proper to Mass) since the liturgical reform; prior to that, the priest wore a cope, thus giving a clear signal that the service was definitely not a Mass.

Positive rubrics

Q. At a recent meeting of liturgical ministers, we were informed that we would now assist in the fractioning of the Precious Body and Blood of Our Lord. I own *The Catholic Answer* Books and could not find real information to substantiate my argument against fractioning by eucharistic ministers.

A. It is important to remember that rubrics are positive directives, not negative. In other words, they tell us what to do— not what not to do. The General Instruction (no. 1503) tells us that the priest is to perform this action; since no one else is mentioned (except for concelebrating priests), no one else should do it. There is more than a rubrical issue here. If one recalls that the words of institution/consecration say that Jesus "took the bread, blessed it, broke it and gave it to His disciples," we realize that this action is, in reality, a part of the consecratory formula, which is postponed. Therefore, it is a genuine priestly act, which should not be mimicked by the non-ordained.

Facing East

Q. In an issue of *The Catholic Answer* magazine, regarding the position of Church altars, it is stated: "Critical to stress is the fact that no document of the Second Vatican Council remotely suggested the 'turning around' of altars, and no postconciliar document has ever mandated such." Would you please elaborate on this? If this is so, then why does the Pope offer Mass publicly (World Youth Day, St. Louis, and other places) on an altar that is turned around? If anyone would know about Church documents and put them into practice, it would be the Pope. We have some priests in our diocese (newly ordained) who offer the Mass with their backs to the people. Would you flesh this out please?

A. I did not say that Mass facing the people was forbidden; I simply noted that there is no mandate to celebrate in that manner. Hence, any priest is free to celebrate in either direction at any time. By the way, I don't like the expression "back to the people," because it is inaccurate and poisons the well, so that rational discourse becomes more difficult. Priest and people facing the same direction or facing liturgical east would be more descriptive. As time goes on, I become more and more supportive of the option of facing east, especially since it diminishes in a significant manner the personality cult of the priest. A more theological reason is that, from time immemorial, priest and people celebrated the Eucharistic Sacrifice facing east, in expectation of the Lord's coming again.

As far as reintroducing the practice, my only caveat is the necessity of properly catechizing people, lest today's junior clergy do what their elder brothers did in the 1960s by instituting changes precipitously and without preparation.

Illicit, not invalid

Q. Here's a scenario for you: It has to do with the "liberalism" of the priest we have as a pastor, although the priest who gave a wonderful lecture on the passion and death of Jesus last night at a neighboring parish using mostly St. Thomas Aquinas' *Summa Theologiae*, called it "modernism." Problem one: The recipe for the bread used at our Masses contains ingredients which make it leavened. Some members of our parish have officially brought this to the pastor's attention. His reply is that there is nothing wrong with the recipe. Therefore, the bishop has been contacted concerning the issue. If he doesn't reply by early this week, the St. Joseph's Foundation is going to file directly with Rome on our behalf. Problem two: The other priest cited above, during the question-and-answer session after his lecture, specifically stated that this makes all liturgies involving this bread not Masses, or invalid Masses, with no Eucharist. He cited several things upon which he based this statement, including a letter from Rome in 1972 that dealt specifically with this leavened-bread issue, which stated, in part, that any stipend received at such liturgies should be returned to the people because no Mass occurred and thus no stipend was warranted. Dilemma: All of us present from our parish went into shock. Invalid Mass for the last five to seven years! What do we do about this? Find another church or pursue this issue in our church until it is corrected? What do I do as a eucharistic minister? A lector? A cantor? Is the priest correct? Are all the liturgies invalid? If so, is there some way we can get an official authoritative notice to our pastor to go back to using proper unleavened bread? What are our courses of action if he refuses even with such an official letter?

A. Use of leavened bread in the Latin rite is illicit, but not an invalidating factor. That means it is highly irregular, a serious abuse that needs to be corrected. If additives such as honey or sugar were included in the wheat, that would make for invalid matter.

You were right to contact your bishop. Should no change be effected, you should contact the apostolic nuncio in Washington.

Vestment norms

Q. Is it permissible for a priest to wear a hooded alb, with a stole in the color for the day, without a chasuble for daily Mass?

A. No. A chasuble is always required for the principal celebrant of the Mass, and actually normative even for concelebrants. The only exceptions are the following: If Mass is celebrated outside a sacred place, the principal celebrant may wear only an alb and stole. If sufficient chasubles are not available for all concelebrants, they may likewise wear only an alb and stole. In more and more dioceses, the trend is toward the purchase of matching chasubles for all priests of the diocese, so that concelebrations can take place with the proper dignity and decorum and in an atmosphere of priestly unity, brought out by the unity of vesture.

Eucharistic prayers

Q. When may the eucharistic prayers for Various Needs and Occasions be used? For example, may they be used on the Sundays of Lent, on Easter, on the Sundays of the Easter season? As a retired priest often concelebrating with others, I am confused because the pastor of the parish where I help out uses them constantly.

A. The introduction to this insert into the Missal states clearly that these are "not intended for use on Sunday or other days when ritual Masses are prohibited, as noted in no. 330 of the *General Instruction*."

Washing hands

Q. Recently, at my parish, at the time of the washing of hands before the consecration, the priest, instead of having the water poured from the cruet, dipped his hands into a water bowl for the washing. Is this proper?

A. In "the old days" this was not uncommon. However, the new rite states that the water is to be "poured" over the priest's hands. And note, by the way, it is to be done over his hands, not just his fingers. The reason for this is to make the sign a bit more obvious, rather than a formalistic or ritualistic gesture.

Clericalist attitude

Q. Our pastor of two-and-a-half years brought with him much change. He instituted self-communication of Our Lord's Precious Blood on the altar by the "ministers of the cup" (as he calls them). They take their chalice from the altar, drink and then proceed to communicate the Precious Blood to the faithful. We now have so many extraordinary ministers that we are overflowing. He also lets seminarians give homilies at weekday and Sunday Masses, saying we are "breaking him in." I have spoken with the worship office in our diocese, sent a letter as directed, but have not received a reply. I have spoken with our pastor, and he defends his position by saying he is the pastor and knows what the people need. Believe me, there is also a lot more going on; where do we go when the diocese will not help?

A. These matters have been addressed in these pages many times over. To wit, no form of self-communication is ever permissible; no non-ordained person — including a seminarian — may ever preach the homily. If you don't hear from the Office of Worship in a reasonable period of time, send a letter directly to the bishop, having marked it "personal and confidential." Finally, I find your pastor's attitude to be highly clericalistic and condescending. In truth, "what the people need" is what the Church says they need, not what he thinks or hopes they need.

Knees should bend

Q. In an edition of *Adoremus*, Helen Hull Hitchcock, the editor, headlined her lead article about the uncertainty among some regarding the proper posture to assume at Mass with, "Every Knee Should Bow — But When?" I corresponded with her as to why she would use this illogical phraseology. Her response was to cite two Bibles, the Douay and the Revised Standard Version (Catholic Edition), both of which used "bow" rather than "bend" in Philippians 2:10. However, "bend" is used in the New American Bible and the New Revised Standard Version, the two sources of the readings in the *Workbook for Lectors and Gospel Readers, 1999* (North American Edition). "Bend" is also used in the New Saint Joseph Sunday Missal and in the Daily Roman Missal. How did this happen? Historically, "bend" has been used. Is this another of ICEL's creative translations? I can understand that non-Catholic Bibles might prefer "bow," but I cannot understand why a Catholic Bible would do so. With your permission, I will use your reply in further correspondence with Helen Hitchcock.

A. I find "bow" awkward usage, but I don't think ideology is operative here. After all, we can hardly accuse the Douay version of being tainted by "ICELism"! My guess is that the translators attempted to be uniform in their rendering of the same Greek word into the same English word each time, which is not a bad principle, but one which cannot be followed slavishly. In this instance, the Greek word can be accurately translated as either "bend" or "bow," but the context here would argue for "bend" since knees bend, rather than bow.

I should note, too, that the New Revised Standard Version is not an approved translation for liturgical use.

Profession of faith

Q. At our Sunday Mass this week, instead of praying the Nicene Creed, a different profession of faith was substituted, which is on the pamphlet I enclosed. Is this version authorized? Our parish priest thought it was all right.

A. No, it was not all right. The only possible substitution for the Nicene Creed is the Apostles' Creed — and that only under certain circumstances.

The "creed" you enclosed is trite, silly, and trendy, but also theologically problematic. For example, in speaking of Christ's coming among us, it does not mention His taking on flesh (a form of neo-Docetism), and it fails to speak of Mary as a virgin. It also omits reference to the apostolic origins of the Church and the Fatherhood of God. This is all grossly defective.

Eucharistic norms

Q. I have a few questions. I always thought that the Creed was supposed to be said at all Masses; is it omitted only on certain days? At a Mass I attended recently, when the gifts were presented to the priest, they had a pitcher of what looked like wine that was placed on the altar along with the Hosts. At the consecration, Father used a chalice and wine and water that were poured as in all Masses. Was this pitcher of wine also consecrated as all the Hosts when only the large Host is elevated and as the chalice is elevated? As the priest shook hands with the people, the lay eucharistic ministers took the Body and Blood of Our Lord and divided it among themselves and prepared to distribute It. Is this correct? There were several people who dipped the Body of Our Lord into the chalice. I'm sure that I have been taught that only the priest can do this.

A. The Creed is to be recited on every Sunday and solemnity.

Regarding your eucharistic questions: (1) When Holy Communion is administered from the chalice, sometimes a large flagon is used and, at the *Agnus Dei*, the consecrated wine is poured into chalices. This is done to avoid crowding the altar with several chalices. (2) The consecration of the elements has nothing to do with their elevation; the Lord's words of eucharistic institution are the consecratory formula and they effect the change of whatever is on the corporal — that is, whatever is "consecratable" and whatever the priest intends to consecrate. (3) The priest is not supposed to leave the sanctuary to share the sign of peace. (4) The extraordinary ministers of the Eucharist are to receive from the priest, not from themselves or one another. (5) The lay faithful are not to dip the Sacred Host into the chalice; that is self-communication. If intinction is used — and it is always a valid option — the Host may be dipped into the chalice only by the proper minister, and then placed directly into the mouth of the communicant.

Feeding the flock?

Q. After reading in an issue of *The Catholic Answer* magazine that the Pope declared in 1997 the use of non-ordained persons distributing the Eucharist is to be eliminated, should those of us who have been involved in what was humbly perceived to be a ministry/service to our extremely large parish, discontinue? Our parish has four priests, one deacon and another deacon in training. Our pastor is very diligent in greeting the people at the end of all Masses, yet he does not assist in the Eucharist unless he presides.

A. Clearly, what you describe is a grave abuse. While greeting the faithful is both a joy and an obligation of a priest, far surpassing it is feeding the flock of Christ with heavenly Food. How someone can absent himself from an activity for which he was ordained and yet perform a praiseworthy but nonessential action is beyond me. Furthermore, with the plethora of clergy you have, it is unthinkable to me that any non-ordained person could ever be justifiably used to distribute Holy Communion.

Prayer option

Q. Is it permissible to use eucharistic prayer IV on the Sundays of "ordinary time"?

A. Yes, it is. As long as no proper preface is required for a particular day (Sunday or weekday), Eucharistic Prayer IV is a viable option.

Not in the norms

Q. You have said that the non-ordained may not assist in the fraction rite, however, my pastor has shown me a 1984 document from the Bishops' Committee on the Liturgy, entitled *This Holy and Living Sacrifice*, which says that the presiding priest or bishop is assisted in the "breaking of the Bread" by other priests or deacons "and acolytes or extraordinary ministers of Communion, if the former are not available." Is this correct or not?

A. That directive is not in keeping with the norms of the *General Instruction of the Roman Missal*. Local guidelines can never contradict universal law. Furthermore, the new edition of the *General Instruction* makes a point of specifically forbidding this action, as well as having the non-ordained perform the post-Communion ablutions.

Facing East II

Q. In a previous question entitled "Facing East," your response was (in part): "Hence, any priest is free to celebrate in either direction at any time." In light of the recent "particular law" of Bishop David Foley of Birmingham, Ala., which forbids priests from celebrating Mass *ad orientem*, I wonder if we have reached the point of having a separate and distinct U.S. Catholic Church, as opposed to the Roman Catholic Church?

A. I repeat my original answer, which any canonist will verify: "Any priest is free to celebrate in either direction at any time."

Beyond that, I do not think we should blow things out of proportion by talking about a schism; indeed, if the direction for liturgical celebration is so much left to a priest's discretion, it ought never to be a Church-dividing issue, correct?

Mass purpose

Q. I'm lost, and I don't know where to turn for help. I've just returned home from my parish church after attending Mass there. The carnival atmosphere there made me crazy. To start off with, I got to church a few minutes early so I could say a couple of prayers. It was virtually impossible to tune out the roar of the crowd who was there socializing, with the parish priest circulating the room like the host of a large party. The first order of business was to introduce yourself to all the people sitting around you. Is Mass supposed to be a social event? Before the Gospel, the priest instigated clapping; is this appropriate?

A. The purpose of any worship service, but most especially the Holy Sacrifice of the Mass is fourfold: To offer to God our adoration, contrition, supplication, and thanksgiving. This is found in every single document of the Church since the Second Vatican Council; nowhere will you find an iota of support for the idea that we are there to "celebrate ourselves" or to "create community." This is man-centered worship, which is an abomination to God and equally destructive of the person engaged in the process. Only when we allow ourselves, humbly and devoutly, to be lifted up by God, can we hope to experience the greatness to which He has called us in baptism and in which we grow through each celebration of the Church's sacraments. Silly, self-centered and narcissistic liturgy actually lowers one's capacity to experience true joy, which is a far cry from superficial hilarity and outdated 1960s concepts of self-affirmation.

Communion action

Q. Why are communicants being forced to answer "Amen" at

Communion time before the priest will give Communion? What happened to the options in receiving Holy Communion? I know of parishes where eucharistic ministers are forced to receive in the hand. Some persons have been refused Communion because they would not take Communion in the hand. Some consider it unhygienic and disrespectful to receive in the hand, but their option is ignored. The persons do not wish to take legal action against these priests, but are thinking it might be the only way to stop the use of force on them and their families.

A. You're mixing apples and oranges.

Answering "Amen" before receiving Holy Communion is not an option — it is a clear directive of the Roman Missal as it constitutes a profession of faith in the Lord's Real Presence under the forms of bread and wine. The current formula for distribution and reception of Holy Communion goes all the way back to St. Augustine; so, it's hardly some novelty about which to be suspicious.

Regarding your second point, no one can be forced to receive in the hand. And, yes, if a priest refuses to place the Sacred Host in someone's mouth, and has been personally approached by the communicant about the matter and is adamant, he needs to be reported to the bishop.

Major "faux pas"

Q. Is it permissible to consistently take the eucharistic prayer from the children's liturgy for the daily Mass for adult women Religious?

A. No, and the *Directory for Masses with Children* makes that clear. I've heard some priests say, "But we're all children in God's sight," in order to legitimize their use across the board, but that's just plain dishonesty.

Liturgical law

Q. I strongly disagree with your saying that the priest was wrong to do a "dramatic" reading of the Gospel. Our beloved priest allowed three "dramatic" readings for the last three Sundays in Lent, done by lectors and him. He portrayed Christ. We all enjoyed it. It made the Gospel come alive.

A. Whether or not your priest is beloved, or whether or not the dramatic renditions "made the Gospel come alive," is totally beside the point, which is very simple: Liturgical law does not permit this practice, except for Palm Sunday and Good Friday. My opinion, yours, and your priest's have absolutely nothing to do with the issue.

Index

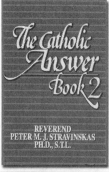
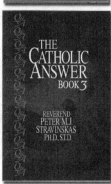

ana & andrew

Martin's Dream

by Christine Platt
illustrated by Anuki López

Calico Kid
An Imprint of Magic Wagon
abdobooks.com

About the Author

Christine A. Platt is an author and scholar of African and African-American history. A beloved storyteller of the African diaspora, Christine enjoys writing historical fiction and non-fiction for people of all ages. You can learn more about her and her work at christineaplatt.com.

For every child, parent, caregiver and educator. Thank you for reading Ana & Andrew! —CP

To my parents, for supporting me from the beginning. —AL

abdobooks.com

Published by Magic Wagon, a division of ABDO, PO Box 398166, Minneapolis, Minnesota 55439. Copyright © 2021 by Abdo Consulting Group, Inc. International copyrights reserved in all countries. No part of this book may be reproduced in any form without written permission from the publisher. Calico Kid™ is a trademark and logo of Magic Wagon.

Printed in the United States of America, North Mankato, Minnesota.
102020
012021

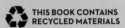

THIS BOOK CONTAINS RECYCLED MATERIALS

Written by Christine Platt
Illustrated by Anuki López
Edited by Tyler Gieseke
Art Directed by Candice Keimig

Library of Congress Control Number: 2020941611

Publisher's Cataloging-in-Publication Data

Names: Platt, Christine, author. | López, Anuki, illustrator.
Title: Martin's dream / by Christine Platt ; illustrated by Anuki López.
Description: Minneapolis, Minnesota : Magic Wagon, 2021. | Series: Ana & Andrew
Summary: For Black History Month, Ana & Andrew visit the Community Center and are tasked with researching Martin Luther King Jr. Later, Papa surprises them with a field trip, during which they get to make one of Martin's famous dreams come true.
Identifiers: ISBN 9781532139697 (lib. bdg.) | ISBN 9781644945230 (pbk.) | ISBN 9781532139970 (ebook) | ISBN 9781098230111 (Read-to-Me ebook)
Subjects: LCSH: African American families--Juvenile fiction. | Travel—Juvenile fiction. | African American History Month--Juvenile fiction. | King, Martin Luther, Jr., 1929-1968--Juvenile fiction. | Dreams--Juvenile fiction.
Classification: DDC [E]--dc23

Table of Contents

Chapter #1
Black History Month

One Friday morning, Andrew looked at the family calendar. He drew a big, red *X* on the last day in January. "Guess what starts tomorrow?" Andrew said excitedly.

"What?" Ana asked. "I want to know. And Sissy wants to know too." She hugged her favorite dolly.

"I'll give you a hint," Papa said.
"Tomorrow is the first day of
February."

"Oh, I know!" Ana twirled Sissy in the air. "It's Black History Month!"

"That's right," Papa replied.

"I love celebrating Black History Month," Mama said.

"Me too!" Andrew did a wiggle dance.

Their baby brother, Aaron, clapped his hands, and everyone laughed.

Every February, people around the world celebrate the history and achievements of African Americans. At school, Ana and Andrew's teachers always had fun activities to do. Also, the Community Center would assign children historical figures to research. At the end of the month, there was a big pizza party.

The year before, Ana and Andrew learned about Mae Jemison, one of the first African American women to become an astronaut.

"I wonder who we'll learn about this year," Andrew said.

"I can't wait to find out," Ana replied.

"You won't have to wait long," Mama reminded them. "We'll find out tomorrow afternoon at the Community Center."

Ana and Andrew were very excited.

Chapter #2
A Civil Rights Leader

Saturday afternoon, Ana and Andrew went to the Community Center with their parents. Many of their friends were there. Andrew sat next to Carter, one of his best friends.

"Is there a special person you want to learn about for Black History Month?" Andrew asked him.

"Well, I'd really love to learn about an African American artist," Carter said. "Someone who liked to draw cartoons just like me."

Ms. Brown overheard Carter and smiled. "I know just the person for you. Carter, I am going to assign you the historical figure Morrie Turner. He created a comic strip called *Wee Pals* that celebrated people's differences."

"Cool!" Carter wrote down the name in his notebook.

"Now, it's time for me to assign everyone else their historical figures." Ms. Brown went to the front of the room.

Ana and Andrew waited patiently for Ms. Brown to call their names. Finally, she said, "Ana and Andrew, your historical figure is Martin Luther King Jr., a civil rights leader."

"He's a great person!" Ana said enthusiastically.

"Yes," Andrew agreed. "Plus, I already know a lot about Martin Luther King Jr."

"Me too," Ana said. "He wrote a famous speech called 'I Have a Dream.'"

"That's true," Ms. Brown said. "But there's much more to Martin's life. You are going to discover many interesting things about him."

Ana and Andrew couldn't wait to get home to start their research.

Chapter #3
All About Martin

Ana and Andrew sat at their computer. They found a lot of incredible facts about Martin Luther King Jr.

"How is the research coming along?" Mama asked.

"Great," Ana said. "Do you want to hear what we've learned so far?"

"Of course," Mama said. They went to the kitchen table and met Papa and Aaron there.

"First, we learned that Martin Luther King Jr. was born on January 15, 1929, in Atlanta, Georgia," Ana said.

"And when Martin was born, America was segregated," Andrew added. "That means that black people and white people did almost everything separately."

"Segregation was very bad and unfair," Ana said sadly.

Ana and Andrew thought about how different their lives would be if they couldn't play with whomever they wanted.

"We also learned that Martin had two siblings," Andrew continued. "An older sister, Christine, and a younger brother, nicknamed A. D."

Ana leaned over and kissed Aaron on the cheek. "He had a baby brother just like us."

"When Martin grew older, he wanted to end segregation," Andrew said. "And he worked very hard to make that happen."

Ana and Andrew told their parents about the Montgomery bus boycott, which ended segregation on buses where Martin lived. They also told Mama and Papa about the civil rights organizations and other leaders he worked with. He'd even won a Nobel Peace Prize! Throughout his life, Martin had done many amazing things.

"You both did such a wonderful job with your research," Mama said. "I am so proud of you."

"Thank you." Ana and Andrew smiled.

"Tomorrow, I am going to take you somewhere really special," Papa said, "to see something that was built in honor of Martin Luther King Jr."

"What is it?" Ana asked. "Is it here in Washington, DC?"

"Yes," Papa said. "But you'll have to wait until tomorrow to find out exactly what it is."

Chapter 4

Dream Come True

The next day, Ana and Andrew continued to research Martin Luther King Jr. They also listened to his "I Have a Dream" speech. One of their favorite parts was:

In the afternoon, Mama and Papa took them downtown for the special surprise. Ana and Andrew couldn't wait to find out where they were going.

"We're almost there," Papa said. "Close your eyes until I tell you to open them."

Ana and Andrew giggled as they closed their eyes. Mama and Papa held their hands to help guide them as they walked.

"OK, open your eyes!" Papa said excitedly.

Ana and Andrew opened their eyes.

"Whoa!" Andrew said.

"Wow!" Ana hugged Sissy.

They were standing right in front of a large statue of Martin Luther King Jr.

"This is the Martin Luther King, Jr. Memorial," Papa explained. "It was built to honor his many great achievements."

Other families were visiting the memorial too. Ana saw other children standing nearby. "Hi," Ana said. "Can we hold your hands?"

"Please?" Andrew asked. "In honor of Martin Luther King Jr.?"

"Yes!" the children agreed. Soon, there were several children holding hands in front of Martin Luther King Jr.'s statue. Everyone smiled as their parents took pictures.

"We've helped Martin's dream come true!" the children said happily.

"This is so special," Mama whispered.

"Yes, it really is," Papa agreed. "This is Martin's dream."